Kim Lindros

PC Basics

with Windows® 7 and Office 2010

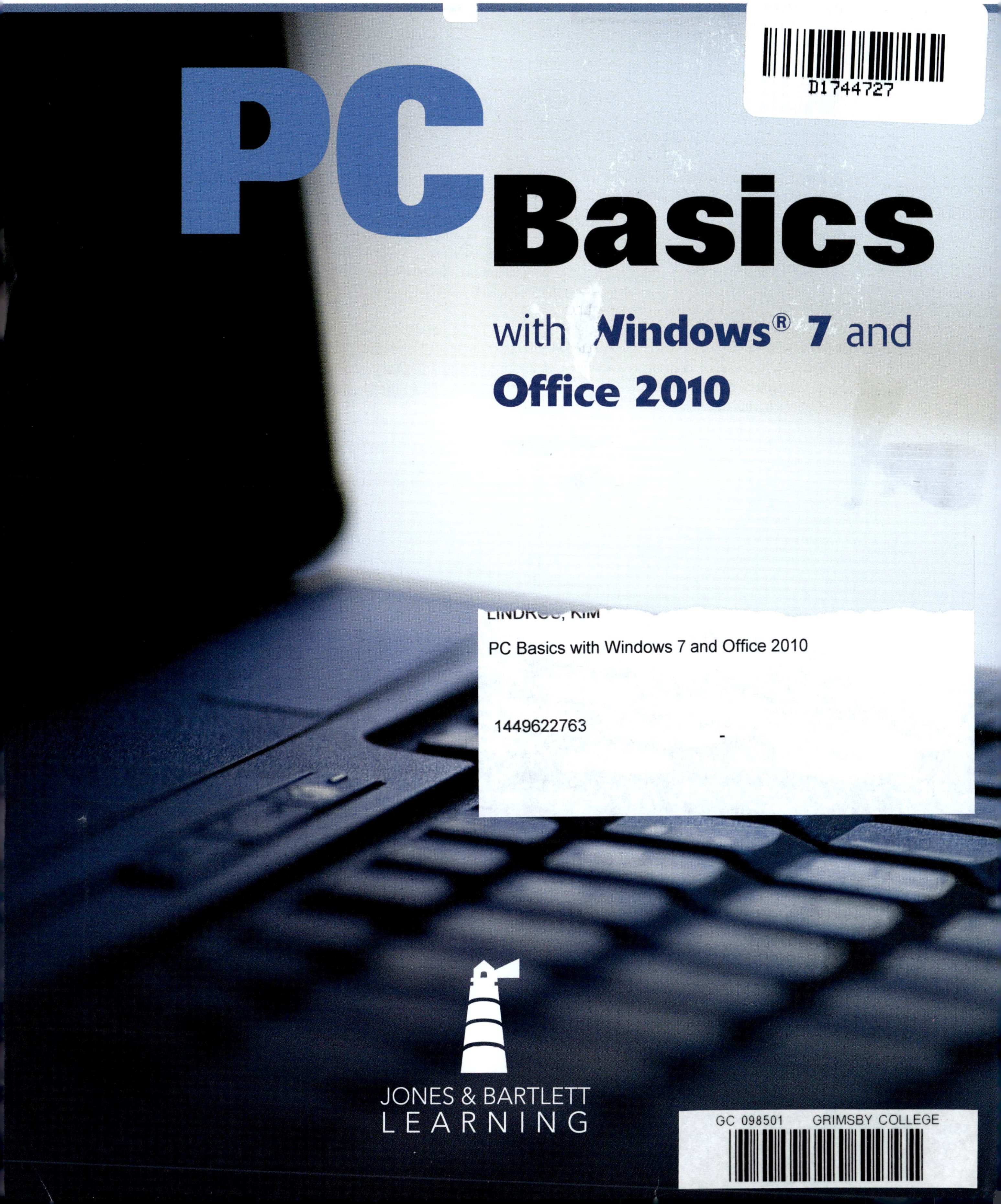

JONES & BARTLETT
LEARNING

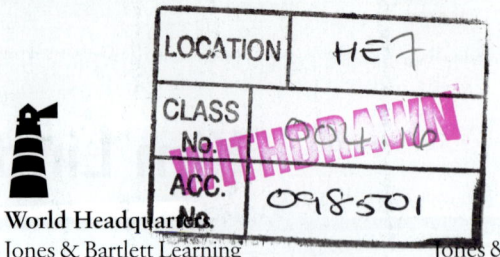

World Headquarters
Jones & Bartlett Learning
40 Tall Pine Drive
Sudbury, MA 01776
978-443-5000
info@jblearning.com
www.jblearning.com

Jones & Bartlett Learning
Canada
6339 Ormindale Way
Mississauga, Ontario L5V 1J2
Canada

Jones & Bartlett Learning
International
Barb House, Barb Mews
London W6 7PA
United Kingdom

Jones & Bartlett Learning books and products are available through most bookstores and online booksellers. To contact Jones & Bartlett Learning directly, call 800-832-0034, fax 978-443-8000, or visit our website, www.jblearning.com.

Substantial discounts on bulk quantities of Jones & Bartlett Learning publications are available to corporations, professional associations, and other qualified organizations. For details and specific discount information, contact the special sales department at Jones & Bartlett Learning via the above contact information or send an email to specialsales@jblearning.com.

Production Credits
Chief Executive Officer: Ty Field
President: James Homer
SVP, Chief Operating Officer: Don Jones, Jr.
SVP, Chief Technology Officer: Dean Fossella
SVP, Chief Marketing Officer: Alison M. Pendergast
SVP, Chief Financial Officer: Ruth Siporin
SVP, Business Development: Christopher Will
VP, Design and Production: Anne Spencer
VP, Manufacturing and Inventory Control: Therese Connell
Editorial Management: High Stakes Writing, LLC, Editor and Publisher: Lawrence J. Goodrich
Editor and Proofreader: Katherine Dillin and Ruth Walker
Reprints and Special Projects Manager: Susan Schultz
Text Design: Anne Spencer
Cover Design: Kristin E. Parker
Composition: John Henry Garland
Cover Image: © Portokalis/Dreamstime.com
Printing and Binding: Courier Companies
Cover Printing: Courier Companies

ISBN: 978-1-4496-2276-3

Library of Congress Cataloging-in-Publication Data
Unavailable at time of printing

6048
Printed in the United States of America
14 13 12 11 10 10 9 8 7 6 5 4 3 2 1

Brief Contents

Acknowledgments xiii
Introduction xv

PART I Essential Computer Knowledge 1

CHAPTER 1 Getting Started 3

CHAPTER 2 Computer Hardware In Depth 25

PART II Applications 43

CHAPTER 3 The Internet 45

PART III The Operating System 71

CHAPTER 4 Windows 7 Basics 73

CHAPTER 5 Windows 7 Files and Folders 93

CHAPTER 6 Windows 7 Programs 117

PART IV Essentials of Word Processing 149

CHAPTER 7 Microsoft Word 2010 Basics 151

CHAPTER 8 Microsoft Word 2010 Formatting, Tables, and More... 175

PART V Essentials of Spreadsheets 205

CHAPTER 9 Excel 2010 Basics 207

CHAPTER 10 Excel 2010 Formulas, Functions, and Charts 229

PART VI Essentials of PowerPoint Presentations 251

CHAPTER 11 Microsoft PowerPoint 2010 253

Glossary 279
Answer Key 291
Index 299
Credits 318

Contents

Acknowledgments xiii
Introduction xv

PART I Essential Computer Knowledge 1

CHAPTER 1 **Getting Started** 3

What Is a Computer? 4
- Desktops and Towers 4
- Laptops 5
- Netbooks 5
- Understanding PCs and Macs 5

What Is an Operating System? 5
Tips for Buying a Computer 6
Communications Devices and Connections 7
- Modems 7
- DSL and Cable Modems 7
- Satellite Broadband 7
- Wireless Routers for Wi-Fi 8
- Mobile Broadband 9
- Bluetooth 9

Common Peripherals: Monitors, Mice, and Keyboards 9
- Monitors 9
- Mouse and Touchpad 10
- Keyboard 10

Speakers 11
Printers, Scanners, and All-in-One Units 11
- Printers 11
- Wired or Cabled Printers 12
- Wireless Printers 12
- Scanners 13
- Flatbed Scanners 13
- Sheet-fed Scanners 13

Handheld Scanners 13
All-in-One Units 14
Digital Cameras 14
Storage Formats 15
CDs/DVDs, Flash Drives, and External USB Drives 15
CDs and DVDs 16
Flash Drives 17
External USB Drives 18
The Fun Stuff 18
Music Players 18
iPads 19
E-readers 19
Smartphones 19
A Quick-Start Guide to the Internet and E-mail 19
Composing a New E-mail Message with Hotmail 21
Test Yourself 22
End-of-Chapter Project 24

CHAPTER 2 Computer Hardware In Depth 25
Introducing the System Unit and Internal Components 26
Power Supply 27
Motherboard 28
Central Processing Unit (CPU) 29
The Chip Set 29
Basic Input/Output System (BIOS) 30
Random Access Memory (RAM) 30
2.1 Exercise: How Much RAM Does a Computer Have? 31
Memory Banks 31
Computer Ports 32
USB Ports 34
Controllers 34
Integrated Drive Electronics (IDE) 35
Serial Advanced Technology Attachment (SATA) 35
Small Computer System Interface (SCSI) 35
FireWire 35
Video or Graphics Card 35
The Sound Card and Speakers 36
The Basic Functions of a Sound Card 36
How the Sound Card Connects to Speakers 36
The Hard Disk Drive 37
How a Hard Drive Works 37
Formatting a Disk 38
How Much Disk Space Do You Need? 39
2.2 Exercise: Checking Your Hard Disk Space 39
Test Yourself 40
End-of-Chapter Project 41

PART II Applications 43

CHAPTER 3 The Internet 45
What Is the Internet? 46
History of the Internet 46

The World Wide Web (WWW) 47
How the Internet Works 47
Internet Protocol (IP) Addresses 48
Uniform Resource Locators (URLs) and Domains 49
Connecting to the Internet 49
Connections 50
Equipment 50
ISP Account 50
Browser 50
Other Popular Browsers 52
Websites 52
Search Engines 53
Downloading 55
Uploading 55
Websites of Interest to Students 56
Web 2.0 and Social Media 57
Social Media Sites and Services 58
E-mail 60
Using Hotmail 60
Using Microsoft Outlook 2010 62
Chatting 65
Blogs 66
Music 67
WAV and MP3 Files 67
Entertainment 67
The "Down" Side of the Internet: Security Issues 68
Test Yourself 68
End-of-Chapter Project 70

PART III The Operating System 71

CHAPTER 4 Windows 7 Basics 73
What Is Windows 7? 74
4.1 Exercise: Interacting with an Icon 75
Using the Taskbar 75
4.2 Exercise: Exploring the Taskbar 76
Using the Start Menu 77
4.3 Exercise: Exploring the Start Menu 78
Sizing and Arranging Windows 78
4.4 Exercise: Sizing and Arranging Windows 80
Running and Switching Between Programs 80
4.5 Exercise: Running and Switching Programs 81
Working with Program Windows 81
Learning Your Way Around Windows Explorer 82
Working with Dialog Boxes 83
4.6 Exercise: Using a Dialog Box 84
Personalizing Windows 84
4.7 Exercise: Changing the Desktop Background and Icon Size 85
Changing the Date and Time 86
4.8 Exercise: Changing Your Time Zone 87
Getting Help and Support 87
4.9 Exercise: Getting Help 88

Turning the Computer Off 88
Test Yourself 89
End-of-Chapter Project 90

CHAPTER 5 Windows 7 Files and Folders 93
Files and Folders 94
Navigating in Windows Explorer 95
Double-Clicking Through Folders 96
Using the Navigation Pane 97
Using the Address Bar 99
5.1 Exercise: Navigating Windows Explorer 100
Customizing Windows Explorer 100
Creating Folders 102
5.2 Exercise: Creating Folders 103
Managing Files and Folders 104
Selecting Files and Folders 105
Renaming Files and Folders 106
Copying Files and Folders 107
Moving Files and Folders 109
5.3 Exercise: Moving a Folder with Cut and Paste 111
Deleting Files and Restoring Files from the Recycle Bin 111
Searching for Files and Folders 112
5.4 Exercise: Searching for an Item Using Windows Explorer 113
5.5 Exercise: Searching for an Item Using the Windows Start Menu 113
Test Yourself 114
End-of-Chapter Project 115

CHAPTER 6 Windows 7 Programs 117
Opening a Program 118
6.1 Exercise: Opening WordPad 120
Navigating Program Windows 120
Understanding Dialog Box Options 121
Creating, Saving, and Printing Files 123
6.2 Exercise: Creating a New WordPad File 123
Saving a File 123
6.3 Exercise: Saving a WordPad File 124
Closing a File or Program 125
6.4 Exercise: Closing a WordPad File 126
Opening a File 126
6.5 Exercise: Opening a WordPad File 127
Printing a File 127
6.6 Exercise: Printing a File 128
Basic Word Processing in WordPad 129
Adding and Editing Text 130
Selecting Text 130
Changing the Font 130
Aligning Text, Indenting Text, and Changing the Spacing 130
6.7 Exercise: Working with WordPad 132
Using Paint 132
Rotating and Resizing Images 134
Selecting and Editing Objects 135
6.8 Exercise: Working with Paint 135

Copying, Moving, and Embedding Text and Objects 136
6.9 Exercise: Embedding a Paint Object into a WordPad File 137
Capturing Screen Shots 138
6.10 Exercise: Capturing and Saving a Screen Shot 139
The Fun Stuff: Using Windows Media Player 139
Listening to Music 139
Watching Videos 141
Looking at Photos 141
The Serious Stuff: Backing Up Files 142
Setting Up an Automatic Backup 142
Performing a Manual Backup 143
Restoring a Backup 145
Installing New Programs 145
Test Yourself 146
End-of-Chapter Project 147
Challenge Project 148

PART IV Essentials of Word Processing 149

CHAPTER 7 Microsoft Word 2010 Basics 151
What's New? 152
Opening Word 2010 152
The Ribbon 154
Tabs 155
Quick Access Toolbar 156
The Mini Toolbar 156
Creating and Formatting a Document 157
Creating a New Document 158
Applying Fonts 158
Using Bold, Italic, and Underline 158
Changing Font Color and Adding Text Highlight Color 159
Aligning Text 159
Indenting 160
Inserting the Date 160
Adding a Picture 160
Saving a File 161
7.1 Exercise: Exploring Microsoft Word Basics 162
Previewing Fonts 163
Using Bullets and Numbering 164
7.2 Exercise: Creating a Bulleted List and a Numbered List 164
Setting Margins 165
Setting Tab Stops 166
Changing Tab Settings 166
7.3 Exercise: Setting Tab Stops 167
Spell Checking 169
Using Find and Replace 170
Printing a Document 172
Test Yourself 172
End-of-Chapter Project 174

CHAPTER 8 Microsoft Word 2010 Formatting, Tables, and More... 175
Document Views 176

Splitting a Document 176
View Side by Side 176
Working with Headers and Footers 177
Headers 178
Footers 179
Adding Page Numbers 179
Creating Title Pages 180
8.1 Exercise: Creating a Report with a Title Page 180
Working with Images and Drawings 183
Clip Art 184
WordArt 185
Shapes 185
Pictures 186
Screen Shots 186
Inserting and Formatting Text Boxes 186
8.2 Exercise: Creating and Formatting a Text Box 188
8.3 Exercise: Creating a Flyer 190
Creating Tables 195
8.4 Exercise: Creating a Table 196
Adding Columns 197
8.5 Exercise: Using Columns 198
Inserting Symbols 198
Creating Equations with Microsoft Equation 199
8.6 Exercise: Using Microsoft Equation 200
Test Yourself 201
End-of-Chapter Project 203

PART V Essentials of Spreadsheets 205

CHAPTER 9 Excel 2010 Basics 207
Getting Started with Excel 208
9.1 Exercise: Comparing the Word and Excel Ribbons 208
Moving Around a Worksheet 210
Entering and Editing Data 210
Editing Data 210
Clearing Cell Contents 211
Saving and Opening Excel Files 212
9.2 Exercise: Creating a Basic Worksheet 212
Selecting Cell Ranges 213
Inserting and Deleting Rows, Columns, or Cells 214
9.3 Exercise: Selecting Ranges and Inserting a Column 215
Changing Column Width and Row Height 216
9.4 Exercise: Resizing Columns 217
Moving Cells 218
Copying and Filling Cells 218
9.5 Exercise: Filling Data 219
Formatting Cells 220
Text Formatting 220
Cell Formatting 220
Number Formatting 220
9.6 Exercise: Formatting Cells 223
Sorting Data 223

Printing a Worksheet 224
Test Yourself 225
End-of-Chapter Project 226

CHAPTER 10 Excel 2010 Formulas, Functions, and Charts 229
Creating Formulas 230
10.1 Exercise: Create a Formula 230
Understanding Order of Operations 231
10.2 Exercise: Using Parentheses to Control Order of Operations 232
Copying Formulas 232
10.3 Exercise: Copying Formulas with Relative Referencing 233
10.4 Exercise: Copying Formulas with Absolute Referencing 234
Introducing Functions 234
Using the SUM and AVERAGE Functions 235
10.5 Exercise: Inserting a SUM Function 235
10.6 Exercise: Inserting an AVERAGE Function 236
Other Common One-Argument Functions 237
Using Financial Functions 237
10.7 Exercise: Using a Financial Function 238
Using Logical Functions 239
10.8 Exercise: Using IF Functions 239
Nesting Functions 240
Conditional Formatting 240
10.9 Exercise: Applying Conditional Formatting 241
Naming a Range 242
Creating Charts 243
Parts of a Chart 243
Showing and Hiding Optional Parts of a Chart 245
Formatting Parts of a Chart 245
Moving and Resizing a Chart 245
10.10 Exercise: Creating and Formatting a Chart 246
Test Yourself 247
End-of-Chapter Project 249
Challenge Project 249

PART VI Essentials of PowerPoint Presentations 251

CHAPTER 11 Microsoft PowerPoint 2010 253
What Is PowerPoint 2010? 254
Opening Microsoft PowerPoint 255
The PowerPoint Window 255
The Ribbon 257
The Quick Access Toolbar 258
The Mini Toolbar 259
Changing Presentation Views 260
Creating a New Presentation 260
Selecting a Layout 260
Inserting Additional Slides 261
Creating Sections for Slides 262
Entering Text on a Slide 263
Adding Pictures and Clip Art 263
Adding Clip Art to a Slide 264

Using Shapes 265
Adding Shapes to a Presentation 265
Saving a File 266
11.1 Exercise: Creating a Simple Presentation 266
Applying a Theme 268
11.2 Exercise: Changing the Presentation Theme 269
Using Color Schemes 269
11.3 Exercise: Changing the Color Scheme 270
Adding Transitions 271
11.4 Exercise: Adding Transitions Between Slides 272
Opening a File 273
Printing a File 273
Working with a Slide Master 274
Test Yourself 276
End-of-Chapter Project 277

Glossary 279
Answer Key 291
Index 299
Credits 318

Acknowledgments

I would like to thank Darril Gibson, Faithe Wempen, Kate Shoup, Jodi Paul, and Sally Slack for their hard work and attention to detail. I would like to provide additional thanks to Lawrence J. Goodrich for overseeing the authoring and editorial part of the project, and Katherine Dillin and Ruth Walker for editing and proofreading

In the Jones & Bartlett Learning camp, special thanks go to Chris Mengel for spearheading the project and effectively communicating feedback to the author. Anne Spencer provided the stunning layout design and John Garland laid out the content. Kimberly Potvin carefully reviewed all of the images and sought permissions as necessary—a feat unto itself!

Finally, thanks to Susan Schultz for keeping everyone on task and on schedule.

Introduction

This book will teach you about computers. It is one of the friendliest computer books you will ever read! The computer is the most important invention of the twentieth century. In the twenty-first century, the computer has become an absolute necessity in our everyday world. Today, it's hard to think of a job in which the computer does not play an important role. The computer is used in office technology, medicine, astronomy, music, video, art, photography, engineering, business, and more. With so many possibilities, you can see how your life will be enriched if you can use computers.

What's Covered in This Book

This book covers the following topics:

- Computer hardware
- The Microsoft Windows 7 operating system
- The Internet
- Microsoft Word 2010
- Microsoft Excel 2010
- Microsoft PowerPoint 2010

Hardware is the physical components of a computer. Although you don't need to learn much about computer hardware to use computers, we strongly suggest that you invest some time in learning the basics. You will appreciate this when someone asks you, "How large is your hard drive?" or "How much RAM do you have installed in your computer?"

The book continues with one of the most important topics you need to learn—the operating system. The operating system covered in this book is Microsoft Windows 7, released in 2010. An operating system is the program that manages computer operation. This is the first program installed in a computer. Once this program is installed, you can install other programs "on top" of it, called application programs.

The Internet is one of the most important reasons to learn to use computers. For one thing, computers let you use the Internet for an amazing service, called e-mail. This is a way of sending messages and documents to anyone who has an e-mail address, instantaneously! You can send not only text but also pictures, music, video, and many other types of files. Another important use of the Internet is research. You can obtain information on almost any topic over the Internet. You can also create your own website. This allows you to create an environment that anyone can "view" over the Internet to find out information about you or your business or organization.

Word 2010 is Microsoft's latest word processor. A word processor is an application program designed for creating and writing documents. And with Word, you can not only create documents, but also make them look appealing and professional (or friendly) with the use of fonts, color, art, graphics, and photos. You can even save documents as webpages as well.

Excel 2010 is a business application program similar to an accounting ledger that you use to keep track of data, perform calculations, and create graphs. You can also analyze your data, by, for instance, performing "what-if" analyses.

PowerPoint 2010 is an application that allows you to create professional presentations about any topic. Public speakers of all types often use PowerPoint slides as visual aids as they talk. But PowerPoint also helps you create posters as big as your printer plotter can print. Many professionals and students use PowerPoint for research projects and other presentations to colleagues, clients/customers, and classmates.

How This Book Will Help You

The strength of this book is that it combines several topics into one book. And it's written in plain English. It was created for beginners. Many people are afraid of or intimidated by computers. They may have read books that were too complicated or technical. We set out to write a book that would make it as simple as possible for the reader to understand computers. Wherever possible, this book omits technical wording that would keep you from learning.

One of the biggest obstacles to learning is fear of a topic. Another obstacle is the feeling that there's too much material. We included in this book only what's essential for beginners. We don't want to overwhelm readers with unnecessary technical information, especially at first.

Whenever possible, you should perform the exercises included in this book on a computer. This is what will give you the hands-on experience so vital to working with computers. Read slowly, and you will get more out of this book than if you try to read it as fast as possible. If you understand this, it will be much easier for you to learn. Above all, have faith in yourself!

What's New in Office 2010?

Office 2010 is the latest version of the Microsoft Office suite. A suite of programs is a set of related programs that are packaged together as one unit, such as Office 2010. Although Office 2010 looks similar to its predecessor, Office 2007, Microsoft brought back the File menu (now on a tab on the Ribbon) and eliminated the Microsoft Office button in the upper-left corner. For this, those of us who have used several versions of Office say, "Thank you, Microsoft."

Clicking the File tab opens a Backstage view that gives you all of the file-related commands in one spot—Open, Save, Print, and so on. The Backstage features an a new larger (and automatic) print preview pane on the right, which is really handy for seeing how your document will print and cutting down on wasted paper and ink or toner.

The Ribbon is still very easy to use, and looks much the same across all of the Office applications. Once you get to those chapters in this book, you will learn about new additions to each application.

Buying a Computer: Windows 7 Requirements

When you are ready to buy a new computer, you should have a good idea of some of the important specifications your computer should meet. Chapter 1, "Getting Started," includes a lot of easy-to-understand information on preparing to buy a computer.

A new personal computer that carries the Windows 7 Capable logo can run Windows 7. All editions of Windows 7 deliver core experiences, such as innovations in organizing and finding information, security, and reliability. All Windows 7 Capable PCs run these core experiences, at a minimum.

Microsoft recommends the following minimum specifications for a personal computer running Windows 7:

- **CPU:** 1 gigahertz (GHz) or faster 32-bit (x86) or 64-bit (x64) processor
- **RAM:** 1 gigabyte (GB) for 32-bit systems or 2 GB for 64-bit systems
- **Hard disk space:** 16 GB available hard disk space (32-bit) or 20 GB (64-bit)
- **Graphics/video card:** DirectX 9 graphics device with WDDM 1.0 or higher driver

To get an even better Windows 7 experience, choose a personal computer that exceeds the minimum specifications. You will have more processing power and memory to run several programs at once without the computer slowing down. You will also be able to watch videos over the Internet without experiencing choppiness. Because many computers are designed to work well with Windows 7, the computer you choose will depend mostly on your budget.

Here are some recommended hardware specifications for getting a high-quality computing experience with Windows 7:

- **CPU:** Intel-compatible Core i7-980X (3.33 GHz or greater) or AMD Phenom II X6 1090T
- **RAM:** 4GB (four gigabyte) single module
- **Hard disk space:** 1 terabyte (TB) or higher SATA, or 256 GB solid-state drive
- **Graphics card:** A dedicated graphics card with DirectX 11 support and 3D
- **DVD drive:** Blu-Ray 8x speed with DVD±RW and CD±RW
- **USB ports:** USB3.0 4.8 gigabits per second (Gbps)
- **Internet access:** Sign up with a service provider
- **Network connectivity:** Ethernet and Wi-Fi; mobile broadband optional

PART

Essential Computer Knowledge

CHAPTER

1

Getting Started

- Welcome to the world of computers! This chapter serves as a jumpstart to understanding computers, operating systems, peripherals, and accessing the Internet. The topics covered in this chapter will give you a solid foundation in personal computers, and the information learned will be especially helpful if you're planning to buy a computer.
- So as not to overwhelm you with details in any one chapter, the topics of computers and the Internet are covered in three chapters. For instance, you will learn about what's really "under the hood" of a computer in Chapter 2. You will discover the essentials of the Internet, websites, and the many things you can do on the Web in Chapter 3. For now, let's take a look at computers in general and the software that runs on them.

CHAPTER TOPICS

This chapter covers the following topics and concepts:

- What types of computers are available
- What an operating system is
- How to buy a computer
- How communications devices and connections link computers to the outside world
- What the common peripherals for a computer are
- What speakers are
- What printers, scanners, and all-in-one units are
- What digital cameras are
- What CDs, DVDs, flash drives, and external USB drives are
- What the fun stuff is, including music players, e-readers, and more
- How to get a quick start on the Internet

KEY WORDS

- Bluetooth
- Broadband
- CD
- Computer
- Desktop computer
- Digital camera
- DVD
- E-reader
- Flash drive
- iPad
- Keyboard
- Laptop computer
- Linux
- Mac OS
- Macintosh
- Modem
- Monitor
- Mouse
- Music player
- Netbook computer
- Operating system
- PC
- Printer
- Scanner
- Smartphone
- Touchpad
- Tower computer
- Wi-Fi
- Windows

What Is a Computer?

A **computer** is a machine that runs software and lets you perform computing tasks. Computers have basic components that make them work—a central processing unit (CPU), hard disk, and memory, for example. They also have components that make it possible for you to interact with them, such as a monitor, keyboard, and mouse or touchpad.

Computers come in different shapes and sizes. Some can perform any job you would expect of a computer, while others are designed for only light computing, such as checking e-mail or surfing the Internet. FIGURE 1-1 shows the different types of computers commonly used today.

Desktops and Towers

People use desktop computers at home and work to perform typical computing. For example, users run applications in Microsoft Office such as Microsoft Word to create and edit documents, or Microsoft Excel to create and edit spreadsheets. Some applications help you create and edit graphics, music, or videos. Many companies have special line-of-business applications that help them track customers and orders, handle accounting, and other tasks.

FIGURE 1-1 Types of computers.

A standard **desktop computer** sits on top of a desk with the monitor placed on top of the computer. However, because the computer takes up desk space, many people prefer a tower model to give them more room. **Tower computers** are much like desktop computers but are built to be upright. You can generally place them on the floor under or next to your desk. A tower computer's monitor sits on top of the desk. Tower models come in full, mid, and mini sizes, depending on your needs. The larger the tower computer, the more components it can hold.

Laptops

Computer engineers created **laptop computers** with mobility in mind. Today's laptop computers can do just about anything a desktop computer can do. Plus you can carry the laptop with you wherever you go. This lets you work on a paper or check e-mail from almost anywhere—a library, coffee shop, or even at the beach. Laptops are also called "notebooks."

You face a tradeoff with laptops, though. Laptop users want their computers to be lightweight, but they also want the batteries to keep the system powered on for a long time. A very small battery will make the laptop light but it will hold a charge for only a few hours. Many manufacturers offer laptop batteries that run for four, six, or eight hours, but those batteries cost a little more than a standard laptop battery.

Laptop manufacturers try to compromise between the systems' capabilities and portability. Some laptops are quite large and have 17-inch screens—you can use this type of laptop as a replacement for your desktop computer. Most others are smaller and lighter but may have limited capabilities.

Netbooks

A **netbook computer** is a very small portable computer with a screen size of about 9 to 10 inches. Netbooks have become popular in recent years because they are inexpensive, very portable, and can access the Internet for e-mail and surfing. Because netbooks don't have many extras built in, the battery can power the netbook for hours without any problem. You can even watch popular TV shows from the Internet using some of the free Internet TV websites.

Understanding PCs and Macs

Two more important categories of computers are the **PC** and the **Macintosh** (Mac, for short). The acronym "PC" stands for personal computer, which refers to ordinary computers used by business and home users. Many different manufacturers build and sell PCs, such as Dell, Hewlett-Packard (HP), Sony, and Toshiba. You can install and run a personal operating system, like Windows or Linux (covered in the next section), on a PC.

Apple manufactures and sells Mac computers, which run the Mac OS operating system by default. However, a Mac is simply a type of PC. Because Apple branded itself so well in the early days of personal computing, many people think of personal computers as one or the other—a PC or a Mac.

Now that you understand the types of computers available, let's take a look at the operating system.

What Is an Operating System?

The **operating system** is the essential software on a computer. It's the first program that is installed on a computer, and you cannot use a computer without an operating system. Popular operating systems include Microsoft Windows, Mac OS, and Linux:

- **Windows:** Microsoft creates the **Windows** operating system. It is the most widely used operating system in the world. The latest version for PCs is Windows 7, which offers many improvements over previous versions such as Windows Vista

> **Note**
>
> You can run many programs made for Windows and Linux on a Mac. You can even install the Windows operating system or Linux on a Mac. You cannot legally install the Mac OS operating system on a non-Mac computer.

> **Note**
>
> Once you've installed the operating system on a computer, you can install and run all of your other programs, called application programs. These programs include word processors, spreadsheet applications, Web browsers, games, and more.

> **Note**
>
> This book focuses on the Windows 7 operating system. Keep in mind that many of the features that are covered apply to other operating systems as well.

and Windows XP. Windows 7 comes in different "editions," such as Windows 7 Home Premium, Windows 7 Professional, and Windows 7 Ultimate. Most home users and many students get Windows 7 Home Premium. Microsoft has made Windows 7 very easy and fun to use. Every edition of Windows 7 lets you run programs, connect to the Internet, play music files, and watch videos.

- **Mac OS:** Apple provides the **Mac OS** operating system, which runs on Mac computers. The latest version is called Mac OS X. Like Windows 7, the Mac OS operating system is easy to use and offers many of the same features. However, many people believe Mac OS runs faster than Windows and is less prone to system "crashes." Mac OS also doesn't suffer from as many computer viruses as Windows. The Mac OS operating system is highly popular with students, but also with graphic artists. Graphics software was originally developed with a focus on the Mac operating system.
- **Linux:** The **Linux** operating system looks and operates much like Windows and Mac OS operating systems. It offers one major difference—the Linux operating system is free. Although you can buy a Linux package from a store, you're basically paying for the installation CDs or DVDs and user guide. You can download the Linux operating system from the Internet and install it without paying anything. There are actually many types of Linux operating systems, called "distributions." Some of the most popular distributions are Ubuntu, Fedora, Red Hat Linux, Debian, and Mandriva Linux.

Tips for Buying a Computer

With so many choices, how do you know which kind of computer to buy? Let's do a quick comparison of PCs with Macs:

- PCs are usually less expensive than Macs, but Macs are more reliable and better built than many PCs.
- You often have more flexibility when deciding which components you want to include in a PC, rather than buying only a pre-packaged system.
- Most software is designed to run in Windows on a PC; the variety of Mac software is more limited. Although you can run Windows on a Mac and run Windows-based software on a Mac, it doesn't always work as expected.
- The majority of home users and businesses use Windows-based PCs.

Once you decide whether to buy a PC or Mac, you can narrow your choice to a desktop, tower, laptop, or netbook computer. If you know you will always work at home or in a dorm room, for example, buy a desktop or tower. They are generally less expensive than portable computers. However, most people nowadays need a portable computer for use at home, school, work, or wherever! In that case, your best choice is a laptop. Netbook computers are highly portable and handy but aren't designed for heavy use like a laptop is.

It's important to understand basic computer hardware when buying a computer. For example, find out how much memory a computer holds, the size of the hard disk, and the CPU's capabilities. Although you'll learn about computer hardware in detail in Chapter 2, these are the most important computer components to know when comparing computers:

- **Random access memory (RAM):** This is the memory your computer uses to run the operating system and programs. Most computers have 2 gigabytes (GB) of RAM, which should be considered the minimum if you want to run several programs at once. It's best to buy as much RAM as you can afford, such as 4 GB or more. Find out how much RAM a computer has and the maximum amount of RAM you can install.
- **Hard disk size:** Laptop hard disks tend to be smaller than desktop or tower hard

disks. Even so, a typical laptop hard drive is about 250 GB. Desktop and tower hard disks are 250 GB to more than 1 terabyte (TB).

- **CPU:** Processors come in different speeds—the higher the number, the faster the computer will run. You measure a CPU's speed in gigahertz (GHz). Typical ratings are about 2.0 to 2.6 GHz for laptops, and 2.4 to 3.0 GHz for desktops. More importantly, find out if the processor is a 32-bit processor or a 64-bit processor. This affects how much memory your system will support. A 32-bit processor can handle a maximum of 4 GB of RAM. A 64-bit processor can handle much, much more RAM.

TIP

If you're a student buying your first computer, talk to your instructor or someone in the main office at school. Some schools require students to have access to a Mac computer, whereas other schools simply require computer access (Mac or PC). Your school may offer a computer purchase discount program, too.

Note

Throughout the rest of this book, the text will refer to both PCs and Macs as "PCs" for short.

Communications Devices and Connections

One of the great strengths of computers today is access to the Internet. Internet access allows you to connect with others using e-mail, or social media sites, such as Facebook and Twitter. You can also shop, research, learn, and explore using the millions of websites available on the Internet. However, you'll first need to connect. This section talks about the equipment to connect a computer to the Internet.

Modems

In the early days of the Internet, a dial-up connection using a **modem** was the only method available for accessing the Internet. People purchased a modem, connected it to the computer, and then connected the modem to a telephone outlet. Users would dial a telephone number provided by their Internet service provider (ISP), and if everything went smoothly, they connected to the Internet. This type of Internet connection is called "dial-up."

Although people still use modems and dial-up connections, the connections are slow. For example, if you want to send a three-minute song to your friend via a dial-up connection, it would take 20 minutes. If you use a high-speed broadband connection, the same song takes 20 seconds to transmit. A second problem with the slower type of connection is that if you only have one telephone line in your home or business, you cannot receive phone calls while connected to the Internet.

DSL and Cable Modems

Broadband Internet access is widely available if you're within or close to a city. **Broadband** is a kind of high-speed connection.

Cable is a popular type of broadband Internet access. The connection to the Internet takes place over the same lines used for cable TV through your local cable provider. The cable company provides Internet access on a different frequency or channel than TV signals, allowing both Internet and TV signals to use the same cable. This connection doesn't use the phone line, so you can be on the Internet and talk on the phone at the same time.

A digital subscriber line (DSL) uses a router to provide high-speed Internet access over a telephone line. DSL allows you to use a telephone line for both voice and data communications. It uses the unused bandwidth on your phone line that isn't tied up by traditional phones. This lets you browse the Internet and talk on the phone at the same time.

With broadband being so common in cities, it's easy to think that everyone has the same access. However, the United States is more than just cities. It also includes huge patches of countryside where millions of other people live. They don't have cable TV running to their homes, and they don't have broadband access. Instead, they use the traditional dial-up modems or a satellite provider for Internet access.

Satellite Broadband

Several different satellite providers have popped up, supplying users with many of the same choices for TV that people can get from cable TV providers in a city. Some of these satellite providers also offer Internet access. Additionally, some independent ISPs provide Internet access only through satellite connections. FIGURE 1-2 shows a satellite dish connected directly to a laptop. However, there is additional hardware required to make the connection.

FIGURE 1-2 Internet access via a satellite.

Many satellite services use a traditional phone and modem for the uplink to the satellite. The uplinks are very slow but the downlink from the satellite can be very quick. Some newer services include modems that can do direct uplinks to the satellite via the same satellite dish that receives the downlink. While these speeds aren't as fast as a broadband connection, they are much better than traditional dial-up.

Wireless Routers for Wi-Fi

Wi-Fi is a trademarked term indicating the Wi-Fi Alliance, and it's commonly used to indicate a wireless network. "Wireless" simply means that your computer is not connected to an ISP via a telephone line or cable, but instead through a wireless network.

Wireless works with radio signals. If your computer has a wireless card or "adapter," it acts like a modem. It sends out a radio signal searching for a wireless network. Once it finds service, it tries to establish a connection. A wireless access point or a wireless router like the one shown in FIGURE 1-3 provides the wireless service.

In Figure 1-3, note that the wireless router has multiple physical ports and an antenna. One port connects to a wired (cabled) network and provides access to the Internet. You can use other ports to create a wired network for computers that don't have wireless capabilities. The antenna transmits and receives the radio signals.

Many coffee shops and eateries are "hotspots," which means they provide free wireless service and access to the Internet. They install a wireless router and establish access with an ISP. You can bring in your laptop or other wireless device, connect to their wireless router, and you'll have access to the Internet.

FIGURE 1-3 Wireless router.

Additionally, many small offices and home users create the same type of wireless network. You plug the wireless router into a broadband connection, such as cable or DSL, to share access to the Internet with multiple wireless users in the office or home.

Mobile Broadband

Many communications companies sell access to their cell phone networks for wireless access. Some laptops include wireless cards that can connect to these networks. You can also purchase universal serial bus (USB) devices that connect to these cell phone networks. You subscribe to the service just as you subscribe for service on a cell phone.

Although the term "mobile broadband" is a common term, it is a bit misleading. The speed of these connections isn't close to the connection speeds you can get from broadband cable or DSL providers. However, it is very valuable to mobile users who need to stay connected. As long as cell phone service is available in their location, they can connect to the Internet.

Bluetooth

Bluetooth creates short-range networks commonly called personal area networks (PANs). For example, a user may have a cell phone and want to use a hands-free headset. Bluetooth headsets like the one shown in FIGURE 1-4 use Bluetooth technology to connect the headset to the cell phone. Both the headset and the cell phone must support Bluetooth.

FIGURE 1-4 Bluetooth headset.

You can also connect Bluetooth devices to a computer if the computer is Bluetooth enabled. For example, let's say you want to copy a file from your smartphone to your computer to print it and then store it. Once you "connect" your smartphone to your computer, you can copy the file to the computer using the Bluetooth connection. Even if your computer doesn't have Bluetooth capabilities built in, you can buy Bluetooth adapters that plug into a USB port.

Common Peripherals: Monitors, Mice, and Keyboards

A peripheral is any device you connect to a computer to provide additional capabilities. Many peripherals either let you input data into your computer, or view output from your computer. There are many different types of peripherals, and this section focuses on monitors, mice, and keyboards.

Monitors

The **monitor** is the most important output device. The monitor allows you to see what you are entering and what the computer needs to display. Two important factors are how sharp the image is and how fast the monitor displays images.

Most monitors today are liquid crystal display (LCD) flat monitors. FIGURE 1-5 shows an LCD monitor. It draws less power than older monitors, takes up less space, and provides better displays.

When purchasing a monitor, think about size. You measure a monitor's viewable area diagonally, between the upper-left corner and the lower-right corner. Make sure that the monitor will connect to your computer's video card. If you only have an older 15-pin three-row video graphics array (VGA) connector, but your LCD monitor uses a digital connector, get an adapter. (Chapter 2 provides details about video cards.)

FIGURE 1-5 LCD monitor.

> **TIP**
>
> Most laptops include a port allowing you to plug in an external monitor. This allows you to use the laptop hardware but enjoy a larger screen display when you're working at home or in the office.

LCD monitors are designed for a specific screen resolution. When you purchase a new monitor, pay attention to the resolution and ensure your computer is set for that resolution. For example, some 24-inch monitors work best with a display resolution of 1920 X 1080. If you use a different resolution, the screen images will be distorted.

Mouse and Touchpad

A **mouse** is the input device used extensively in Windows and most other graphical user interface (GUI) systems to point and select on-screen information. FIGURE 1-6 shows a wheel mouse with a USB connector. This wheel provides an easy way to scroll up or down, and also doubles as a button on some mice.

FIGURE 1-6 A USB wheel mouse.

Most mice today use optical technology. The optical mouse actually includes a tiny camera that takes 1,500 pictures every second. It works on almost any surface and uses a light-emitting diode (LED) that bounces light off that surface onto a sensor. The sensor sends each image to a processor for analysis and senses when the mouse moves. These movements are sent to the computer to move the cursor.

FIGURE 1-7 A laptop touchpad.

Laptops often include a **touchpad** you can use instead of a mouse. FIGURE 1-7 shows a touchpad. You use your finger to drag the pointer around the screen. Touchpads also have two buttons that you operate the same way you'd work the two buttons on a mouse.

Keyboard

The **keyboard** is also an input device. The keyboard and the mouse are the most widely used input devices. Most keyboards today connect to the computer using a USB or wireless connection. FIGURE 1-8 shows an ergonomic keyboard designed to place less stress on the user's wrist.

FIGURE 1-8 An ergonomic keyboard.

In addition to the standard letters and numbers, keyboards also include special function keys that usually sit across the top of a keyboard labeled F1 through F12. These function keys have unique purposes. For example, if you press the F1 key in most programs, it will launch help. In many applications, F3 launches the search feature. F5 refreshes a screen display in some applications, such as the Microsoft Internet Explorer Web browser. However, the F5 key launches a slide show in Microsoft PowerPoint.

Additionally, many applications use shortcuts with the Ctrl and Alt keys. For example, you can often save a document by pressing the Ctrl+S keys at the same time, or print a document by pressing the Ctrl+P keys at the same time.

Speakers

Computers include a built-in speaker. However, many users purchase additional speakers to provide better sound. Although most users are satisfied with two speakers to provide stereo sound, some want a more sophisticated sound.

FIGURE 1-9 A 5.1 speaker system.

FIGURE 1-9 shows a 5.1 sound system with five speakers and a subwoofer. In a typical room, you would place the two smallest speakers behind your seating area on the right and left. The two mid-size speakers would go in front of your seating area on the right and left. The biggest speaker in the middle is a subwoofer that provides heavy bass sounds. It represents the .1 in a 5.1 sound system. Position the final speaker (shown on top of the subwoofer) directly in front of the seating area—this speaker transmits spoken words. Application developers can program sound so that it comes from any direction. For example, an application can show a dog barking in front and to the right of you and the speakers cause the sound to come from the same location.

Printers, Scanners, and All-in-One Units

This section covers even more peripherals that many computer users find very important, namely, printers, scanners, and combination units referred to as "all-in-one" products.

Printers

FIGURE 1-10 Inkjet printer.

A **printer** is an output device that provides a hard copy of your documents and images. Two main types of printers fit home use: inkjet and laser. An inkjet printer, shown in FIGURE 1-10, sprays tiny ink droplets onto paper to form letters and images. A laser printer, shown in FIGURE 1-11, fuses toner onto paper to accomplish the same thing. Inkjet and laser printers connect to computers using USB and/or wireless connections. Older printers connect to a computer's parallel port.

When purchasing a printer, consider the quality, initial cost, cost of ink or toner, and speed at which it prints. This section covers common printers suitable for home use. Each printer is different, so be sure to read the owner's manual. However, once you set it up, you'll have very little to tinker with other than making sure it has paper or replacing the toner or an ink cartridge.

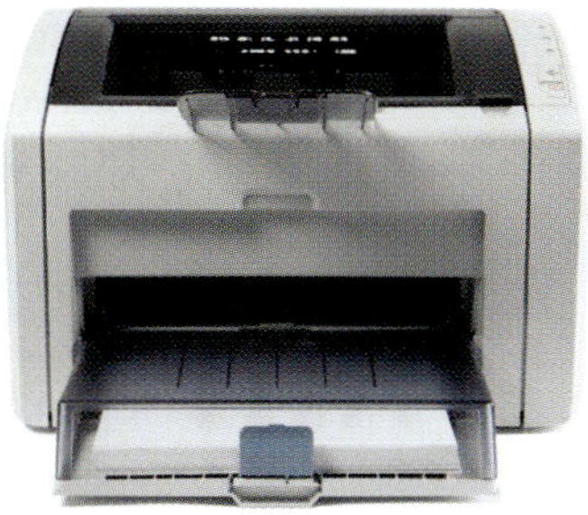

FIGURE 1-11 Laser printer.

Wired or Cabled Printers

Connecting a printer is usually a very simple process. Most printers use USB cables. You simply connect the printer to a power outlet and then connect the USB cable to both the printer and the computer. If you're using Windows 7, Plug and Play (PnP) technology takes over and you'll soon be ready to print.

Most printers today are PnP devices. After you connect the printer to the USB port, it automatically installs the correct printer driver (a small software program) and the printer is available to your programs. If you're running Windows 7, you'll see an information bubble that pops up indicating that the operating system has found and is configuring the printer.

If PnP doesn't work, use the installation software and directions from the manufacturer to install the printer. This often means that you insert the installation CD into your system and follow the prompts to install the correct drivers. Once you've installed the correct drivers, plug in the printer and PnP will then work

When you are finished, the printer appears in the Devices and Printers section in Windows 7. If you want to print a test page, first make sure your printer is turned on and then that it's ready to print.

Wireless Printers

Wireless printers are an exciting new addition to the printing world. Just like other wireless devices, you don't need to connect them to your computer. Instead, these printers connect to your wireless network. For example, you can add a single wireless printer in your home and everyone with wireless access can use it.

Tips for Buying a Printer

Although you can find many inkjet printers for under $100, you may want to think about how long the printer will last. A printer is an electro/mechanical device. It contains a lot of moving parts. If the construction is cheap, it will probably break down sooner rather than later. A more expensive inkjet has better quality color, can handle more pages at one time, and can use heavier paper.

Another cost to consider is the inkjet cartridges. Many are expensive! A color printer usually requires at least two cartridges: one cartridge for color and one with black ink. The cost of ink cartridges represents your long-term outlay. When you're purchasing a new computer, you can sometimes get a brand-new printer included for free. Although this may sound like a great deal, when you realize how much ink it uses and the cost of the ink cartridges, you might be better off purchasing a higher-quality printer.

Check to see if the printer can print on standard paper. Most do. If you have to purchase special paper on which to print, your costs can skyrocket.

If you only want to print black and white, consider a laser printer. Laser printers use toner instead of ink, which can be less expensive over the long term. However, if you want color, you may have more affordable options from an inkjet printer than from a color laser printer.

The printer's resolution determines how good the printout looks. You can get professional looking printouts with 600 dots per inch (dpi) at an affordable price. You can also choose draft quality printouts from most computer applications to save on ink or toner.

Last, consider the speed. Most printers are rated using pages per minute (ppm), and it's common to find printers that can print more than 20 ppm.

You configure a wireless printer to connect with a wireless router. Use the same settings for the wireless printer as you use for wireless laptops or other wireless devices connected to the router.

The setup can be a bit more complex than simply plugging in a printer to a USB port. However, if you already have a wireless network, it isn't much harder to set up a wireless printer than it is to set up any other wireless device on your network. In fact, Windows 7 can detect most new wireless printers and configure them automatically.

Scanners

A printer produces a hard-copy printout from a computer file. A **scanner** does exactly the opposite. It converts a document or an image from paper and converts it to a computer file. The hard-copy printout can be a text file, a picture, or a drawing. This is a great way to store receipts and printed photographs in your computer.

Some scanners can convert a document into an actual text document. When you scan a text document, the scanner actually converts the text to an image. You cannot edit the text directly on the scanned image. You must convert it to text with special software called optical character recognition (OCR). This OCR software converts the image to a simple text file that you can edit. As with any other type of software, there are many types of OCR programs, some better than others. A higher-quality OCR program converts the image to text more accurately.

Flatbed Scanners

FIGURE 1-12 shows a flatbed scanner. It allows you to place the hard copy you wish to scan on top of a flat piece of glass that is visible when you lift the top cover. You simply place the image on the glass and then use software to scan the image. The computer will show you what the scanned image looks like. You can then edit the scanned image or save it on the computer for later use. Other types of scanners include sheet-fed and handheld scanners.

FIGURE 1-12 Flatbed scanner.

Sheet-fed Scanners

A sheet-fed scanner like the one shown in FIGURE 1-13 lets you feed paper through an automatic paper feeder. The scanner moves the paper through the unit until it is completely scanned. The advantage is that you do not have to pause before feeding the next page while waiting for the scanner to finish scanning the current page. For example, if you want to scan a multiple page document, the paper feeder will send each page through one at a time.

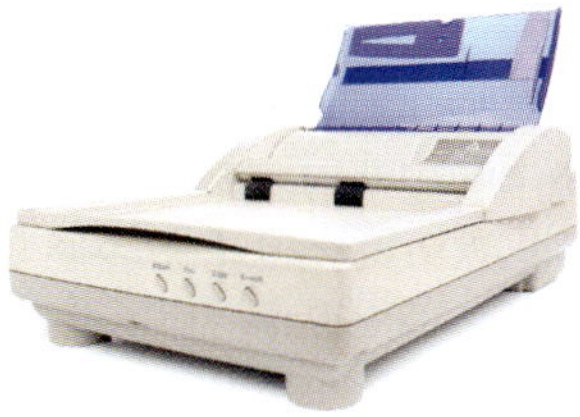

FIGURE 1-13 Sheet-fed scanner.

Handheld Scanners

Handheld scanners scan smaller images, such as barcodes. FIGURE 1-14 shows a handheld barcode scanner. Point the scanner at a barcode, and the scanner reads it. Pen-sized scanners are also available for small amounts of text. Because a handheld scanner is not as wide as the entire page, you slide the scanner over one

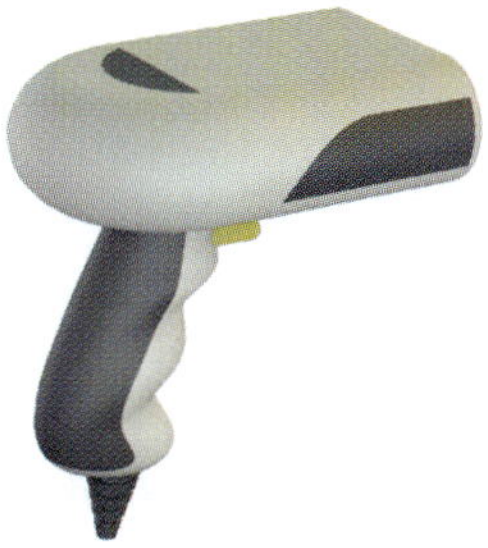

FIGURE 1-14 Barcode scanner.

▸ TIP

If the printer you choose doubles as a photo printer, make sure you can connect your camera directly to the printer. This will allow you to print photos easily without the computer.

section of a given image or area of text, then the rest of the image or text. You usually need multiple passes to scan a whole page.

All-in-One Units

All-in-one printers like the one in FIGURE 1-15 are multipurpose machines. They can print, scan, copy, and fax documents. Some all-in-one printers can also print photos.

This type of printer should be able to print documents with a resolution of at least 600 dpi. Similarly, the scanner should be able to scan documents and images with a resolution of at least 600 dpi. The copy function works just like any copier. You place the document in the scanner and press the copy button. This is actually scanning and printing the document. The fax capability lets you send and receive faxes from the system. If it uses a separate fax line modem, it can send and receive faxes even when the computer is off.

Most all-in-one printers have paper feeders that automatically feed the sheets through when you're copying or faxing them. This is very useful when you're copying or faxing multiple pages at a time.

FIGURE 1-15 All-in-one printer.

Digital Cameras

Digital cameras are another wonder from the technical world. They have become so affordable that anyone can own one. You can take a picture, connect the camera to your computer, and have the image available in seconds.

Know some of these important terms when shopping for a digital camera:

- **Pixel:** A pixel is short for picture element. A single picture contains millions of pixels. One of the main ways that manufacturers categorize their digital cameras is in terms of pixel count. This is the number of individual pixels that goes into making each image. A few years ago the standard was 3 to 4 megapixels (MP), but smartphones with built-in cameras achieve that today. Top-of-the-line digital cameras can capture 15 to 20 MPs. A single MP is equal to a million pixels. The higher the MP, the sharper the picture looks.
- **White balance:** With film you can buy daylight-balanced film for shooting outdoors or tungsten-balanced film for shooting indoors to achieve a proper white balance. Digital cameras normally have an automatic setting, and the camera decides what white balance setting to use.
- **Sensitivity:** Sensitivity settings on digital cameras are the equivalent of International Standards Organization (ISO) ratings on film. Just about every digital camera has settings with a light sensitivity equivalent to ISO 100 film and ISO 200 film. Many have an ISO 400 setting. Some digital cameras have an automatic ISO setting, where the camera will pick from ISO 100, ISO 200, and sometimes ISO 400, depending on the light level and the mode in which the camera is operating.
- **Optical zoom:** Optical zoom works just like a zoom lens on a film camera. The

lens changes focal length and magnification as it zooms and the image quality stays high throughout the zoom range.

- **Digital zoom:** Digital zoom crops the image to a smaller size, then enlarges the cropped portion to fill the frame again. Digital zoom results in a significant loss of quality.

Storage Formats

Digital cameras can use multiple picture and storage formats. The two primary types of files created by digital cameras are JPEG and TIFF.

JPEG is an acronym for Joint Photographic Experts Group. JPEG files are stored with the .jpg extension. This is a standard format for storing pictures. Saving your picture in this format compresses the file. The compression makes the file smaller but loses some quality as well. For most situations, the quality loss is negligible. TIFF is an acronym for Tagged Image File Format. TIFF files are stored with the .tif or .tiff extension. These keep all the original information, but at the cost of much bigger files.

You can store JPEG and TIFF files on different types of digital storage cards. A digital camera comes with some on-board memory, but it will fill up if you take a lot of pictures. Extend this storage capacity with memory cards.

These cards are available in many different types:

- **Compact Flash (CF):** A matchbook-sized memory card used in many digital cameras today. You can also use them for many other devices that store digital information. Compact flash cards can store digital information in some musical keyboards as well.
- **Microdrives:** The Microdrive is a miniature hard disk designed to fit in a CF Type II slot. The latest have 8 GB capacity.
- **Sony Memory Stick:** Sony was the first company to use this as a storage medium, and it currently sells memory sticks as large as 32 GB.
- **Secure Digital (SD):** This is a postage stamp-sized flash memory card. It is compatible with different digital camera brands and MP3 devices. Enhanced versions are as large as 32 GB.

FIGURE 1-16 Digital camera with LCD screen.

Most digital cameras include an LCD like the one shown in FIGURE 1-16. The LCD is a screen on the camera that displays the pictures that are currently in the camera. This is one of the best parts about digital photography. You get to see the pictures as soon as you take them. Eventually you can transfer these pictures to your computer or print them directly to your photo printer.

The most common method for transferring your digital pictures from the camera into your computer is via the USB port. Usually you install a driver that comes with your camera, and as soon as you plug the camera into the USB port, the computer recognizes it and launches an application for the camera. Regardless of how the program runs, it will display some type of interface that allows you to see the pictures in the camera, and to transfer them to the computer.

CDs/DVDs, Flash Drives, and External USB Drives

In addition to hard disk drives, other storage options are available for a computer. The primary external storage options you'll use are CDs, DVDs, flash drives, and external USB drives. The great benefit of these external options is that you can easily carry data from one system to another to share it. For example, you can create your own slide show or movie, copy it to a DVD, and give copies to your friends and family. Similarly, you can copy files onto a flash drive, slip it into your pocket, and carry it wherever you go to share the data.

CDs and DVDs

Note

You may notice a slight difference in the spelling between disk and disc. Hard disk drives are spelled as "disk," with a "k" at the end. Optical media discs are spelled as "disc," with a "c" at the end.

CDs and DVDs are generically referred to as optical media. Data is written onto these discs with a laser. A laser within an optical media reader, such as a DVD drive, reads the data. Some CDs/DVDs are manufactured to be written to (burned) only once; other CDs/DVDs can be written to many times. Rewritable CDs/DVDs usually have the letters "RW" on the product packaging.

A compact disc or **CD** can store approximately 650 to 700 megabytes (MB) of data. Companies that sell programs previously distributed their programs on floppy disks. However, as programs kept increasing in size, they could no longer fit on floppy disks. Instead, businesses and individuals began to use CDs. CDs can also hold audio files that easily play on a computer.

You must have a CD drive attached to the computer to read CDs. Access the CD drive just as you would any other drive. FIGURE 1-17 shows a CD drive in a laptop. The drive is open with a CD placed in the drive. Many laptops include built-in CD drives but you can also purchase external CD drives.

FIGURE 1-17 CD in a laptop computer.

DVD is an acronym for digital versatile disc or digital video disc. You must have a DVD drive to use a DVD. Additionally, you need a DVD burner to write data to DVDs. This can be included in the computer or an external DVD drive like the one in FIGURE 1-18.

DVDs were a significant advancement in portable storage technology. They are the same size as a CD but can store seven times more data than a CD. A CD has a capacity of 650 to 700 MB, but a DVD holds 4.7 GB or higher, depending on the type of DVD. DVDs are often used for movies, but also for software and data storage.

FIGURE 1-18 External DVD drive.

There are several different types of DVDs:

- **Single-sided single layer:** Single sided means that you use only one side of the DVD. It can store approximately 4.7 GB with an approximate movie time of 2 hours.
- **Double-sided single layer:** Double sided means that you can use both sides of the DVD. It can store approximately 9.4 GB with an approximate movie time of 4 1/2 hours.
- **Single-sided dual layer:** Dual layer means that you have two layers on one side of the DVD. It can store approximately 8.5 GB with an approximate movie time of 4 hours.
- **Dual-side dual layer:** This type allows you to use two layers on each side. It can store approximately 17 GB with an approximate movie time of more than 8 hours.

> **Note**
>
> DVD drives are backward-compatible with CDs, so they can read data from CDs and play audio and video CDs. However, you cannot read data on a DVD in a CD drive.

Flash Drives

Flash drives are one of the handiest devices to become available in the computer industry. A flash drive is a small, lightweight, removable, and rewritable data storage device using flash memory. That is, the technology allows you to read and write to it and it doesn't need power to hold the data. It comes in a variety of capacities and with multiple features. **FIGURE 1-19** shows a USB drive on a key chain.

> **Note**
>
> You can tell a DVD is dual layer because the package displays DVD+R DL or DVD-R DL. The "DL" indicates dual layer.

FIGURE 1-19 USB flash drive on a key chain.

A flash drive offers many features. Listed below are some flash drive highlights:

- **Portable:** It is very small in size. It fits in your pocket or on a key chain.
- **Capacity:** Flash drives are available in different capacities, such as 1 GB, 4 GB, 64 GB, 128 GB, and 256 GB. The capacities keep increasing and the prices keep decreasing. At this writing, you can purchase a 64 GB flash drive for $139, but a few years ago, this was the price for a 1 GB flash drive.
- **Interface:** It connects to your computer via a USB port. As soon as you plug it in, the computer recognizes it. Use it to open, save, or copy files just as if it were a hard disk attached to your system.
- **Standard:** USB flash drives have a standard connector that plugs into any USB port. Some of them have a cap you pull off to expose the connector. Others are cap free and include a slide that you push to expose the connector.
- **Security:** Some flash drives offer different types of security, such as a password, data encryption, and fingerprint security. A USB drive with fingerprint security allows one or more users to register their fingerprint on the drive. This way no one can access the data without the correct the fingerprint. Security is especially important if the flash drive contains sensitive information. If you lose a drive without built-in security, the data is not protected. Whoever finds the drive will be able to access the sensitive information.
- **MP3 flash drives:** These are flash drives that provide an MP3 player so you can play MP3 music while you're carrying the flash drive. They even include an LCD screen so you can see what's on the flash drive.

> **WARNING**
>
> When you want to remove a USB flash drive from a computer, first let the system know you're removing it. The lower-right corner of a Windows 7 system has a notification area on the task bar. Select Safely Remove Hardware from there to let the system know you're removing the flash drive. When you click this icon, it gives you the choice of ejecting the device. Once you select it, Windows 7 displays a message that it's safe to remove the flash drive. Using this method ensures that data is not corrupted when you remove the drive.

Cameras and other video devices use flash cards as opposed to flash drives. They rely on the same type of flash memory as a flash drive but are in different packages so they can easily plug into cameras. Digital cameras and the different types of flash cards were presented earlier in this chapter.

External USB Drives

External USB hard drives have become very common. FIGURE 1-20 shows a smaller model that's about the size of a wallet and can be slipped into your pocket. Others are larger and are usually kept on a computer desk. These drives have a very large capacity, such as 750 GB to more than 1 TB, allowing you to store huge amounts of data.

FIGURE 1-20 Small external USB hard drive.

One common use for these external hard drives is to back up data. They hold a lot more than CDs and DVDs, and they can easily be written and rewritten. Additionally, some wireless routers have USB ports that let you plug in an external USB hard drive directly into the router. You can then share access to the hard drive with everyone on your wireless network.

TIP

For step-by-step instructions on backing up your files and settings, see Chapter 6. You can also use online continuous backup services, such as Carbonite and Mozy Home.

The Fun Stuff

Computers aren't all work. They can be a lot of fun, too. Many computing and electronic devices add enjoyment to your work, school, and personal life. This section takes a look at some of the most popular electronic devices that can connect to your computer or work separately.

Music Players

If you love music, you're probably already using one of the many portable **music players** available on the market. Most of these are referred to as MP3 players because they play music using the MP3 format. They are small enough to slip into your pocket. Today's MP3 players include the same type of flash memory used in USB flash drives and can store thousands of songs. FIGURE 1-21 shows an MP3 player.

FIGURE 1-21 MP3 player.

One of the most popular brands of music player is Apple's iPod. In addition to selling the iPod, Apple also sells music through the Apple iTunes Store. Microsoft's version is Zune, and the company sells music through the Zune Marketplace. Both the Apple iTunes Store and the Zune Marketplace also sell other content, such as games and videos. You can even download TV shows to play on these devices. You have dozens of other MP3 player brands to choose from as well as other sources from which you can purchase music, games, and videos for MP3 players.

iPads

Tablet computers have been around for several years. Apple released its version, the **iPad**, in 2010. It's a portable computer with a touchscreen that you can use for many different purposes. The iPad includes many of the same capabilities of an iPod touch. It lets you run the same applications, watch videos, and listen to music. The iPad is also an e-book reader, so you can read digital books you purchase from Apple's iBookstore.

The iPad is Wi-Fi capable. You can connect into wireless networks to access the Internet. You can also purchase data plans for connectivity through the current iPad service provider if you don't have access to a Wi-Fi network. The iPad includes a built-in e-mail program for casual e-mail. You can also browse the Internet. As of this writing, you're not able to add common browser add-ons, such as the Adobe Flash player. Sites that use Flash won't work properly, if at all.

Shortly after Apple released the iPad, the company sold more than 1 million units. Apple fans love them, and there are a lot of Apple fans.

E-readers

An **e-reader** lets you read electronic books or e-books. One of the primary benefits is that you can carry around an entire library of books in a device smaller than a single book. The iPad functions as an e-book reader, and much more. Several other devices also function as e-book readers.

Amazon sells the Kindle. It includes free wireless access to download books directly from Amazon, which offers more than 600,000 downloadable books. Amazon also created the Kindle application that you can use to read e-books on Windows, Mac OS X, and some smartphones. Barnes & Noble sells the Nook e-book reader. The Nook includes both Wi-Fi and mobile broadband connectivity. Barnes & Noble boasts more than one million titles available for download.

Smartphones

Smartphones are cell phones with advanced features and capabilities. They usually have personal data assistant (PDA) capabilities, such as the ability to store contact information for friends, family, and business associates. They also include the ability to surf the Internet and access e-mail. FIGURE 1-22 shows a smartphone with a miniature keyboard.

FIGURE 1-22 Smartphone.

The BlackBerry has been popular in the business world for quite some time and has given employees the business applications they need. The Apple iPhone has been very popular with consumers due to its ease of use and general "cool" factor. Apple has released several versions since the original iPhone. Google created the Android operating system, which has been used on several different types of phones such as the Droid. Both the iPhone and Android-based phones have a wealth of applications that can also run on the phone, making them fun as well as increasing their usefulness. Many employees are now asking their employers for these other phones instead of the BlackBerry.

Now that you've learned about several computer-related electronics—that are useful and fun—let's move on to the last section in the chapter for a brief introduction to the Internet and e-mail.

A Quick-Start Guide to the Internet and E-mail

The Internet, sometimes called the Web, holds a wealth of information, downloadable files, interesting websites, and more. At a minimum, you need an Internet connection and a Web browser to access websites. In this section, you will learn how to use the Microsoft

> **Note**
>
> You will learn all about the Internet and e-mail in Chapter 3. This section just covers the essential information for accessing the Internet and creating a Hotmail account.

Internet Explorer Web browser to sign up for a Microsoft Hotmail e-mail account. Hotmail is a free e-mail service provided by Microsoft through the Windows Live Web site.

Let's get started. In Windows 7, follow these steps:

1. Click the Internet Explorer icon at the bottom of the window, as shown in FIGURE 1-23. If the icon doesn't appear in the taskbar, click the Start button in the lower-left corner of the window, click All Programs, and then click Internet Explorer in the programs list.

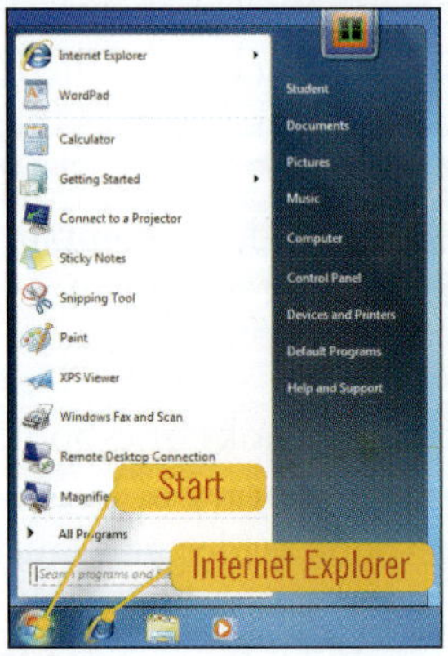

FIGURE 1-23 Starting Internet Explorer.

2. In the address bar at the top of the window, type www.hotmail.com, as shown in FIGURE 1-24.

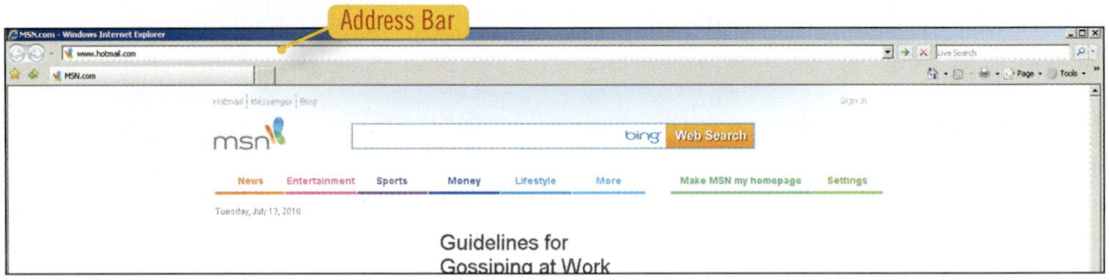

FIGURE 1-24 Entering an address in the Internet Explorer address bar.

3. To sign up for a Hotmail account, click the Sign Up button on the Windows Live sign-up/logon webpage. See FIGURE 1-25.

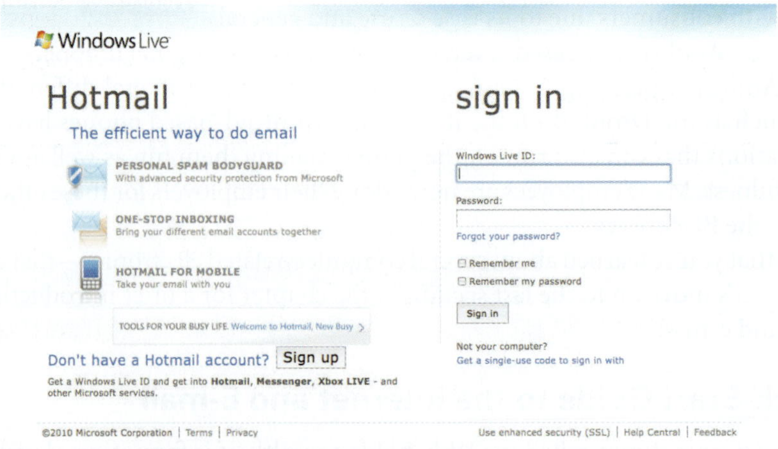

FIGURE 1-25 Click the Sign Up button.

4. On the Create Your Hotmail Account webpage shown in FIGURE 1-26, enter your information in the text boxes and then click I Accept.

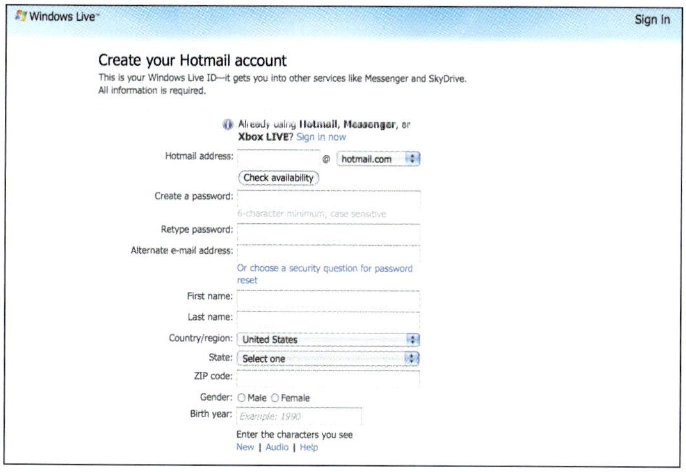

FIGURE 1-26 Creating a Hotmail account.

Windows Live creates your Hotmail account and signs you in automatically. You will see the webpage shown in FIGURE 1-27. Now let's see how to create and send a simple e-mail message using Hotmail.

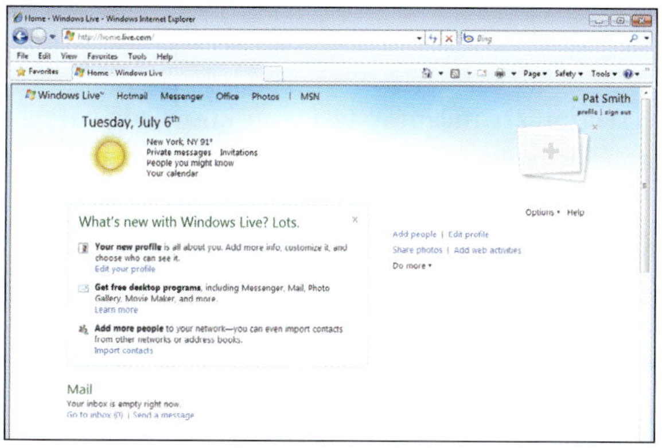

FIGURE 1-27 The main Windows Live webpage.

Composing a New E-mail Message with Hotmail

Composing a new e-mail message in Hotmail takes only a few steps:

1. Click the Hotmail link at the top of the Windows Live webpage.
2. Click the New link, as shown in FIGURE 1-28.

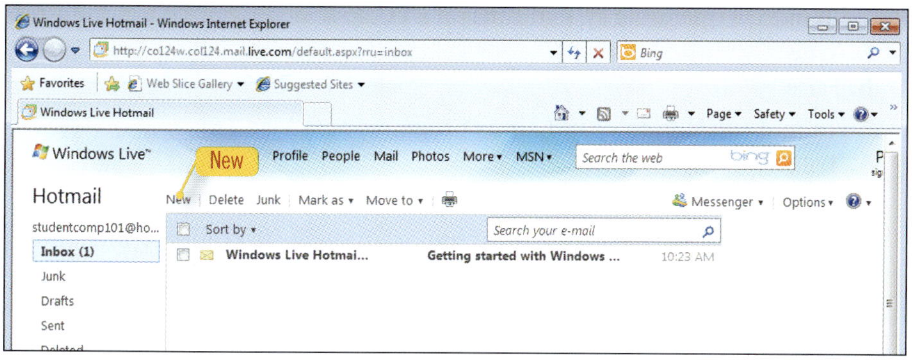

FIGURE 1-28 Clicking New to start a new e-mail message.

3. Type the recipient's e-mail address in the To field (shown in FIGURE 1-29). This is the address of the person to whom you're sending an e-mail. You need to get the address from that person.

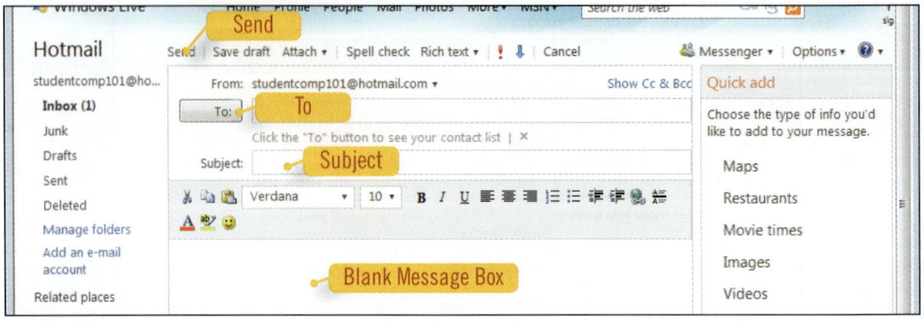

FIGURE 1-29 Composing a new e-mail message.

4. Type a subject in the Subject field, such as Hi There! or whatever is appropriate for the message.
5. Type your message in the blank message box.
6. Click Send.

That's it. You've sent your first e-mail using your new Hotmail account! You will learn more about e-mail in Chapter 3. This section simply gets you started using online e-mail.

Test Yourself

The questions in this section are meant to test your knowledge of what you read. Make sure you answer them. The page number where the answer can be found appears after each question.

1. Which of the following are types of computers for personal use? (4)
   A. Desktops
   B. Towers
   C. Laptops
   D. Netbooks
   E. All of the above
   F. A and C only
2. A netbook is a larger version of a laptop. (5)
   A. True
   B. False
3. The three primary types of computer operating systems are _______, _________, and ________. (5)
4. The Windows operating system runs on a PC. (5)
   A. True
   B. False
5. You cannot run Windows and Linux programs on a Mac. (6)
   A. True
   B. False
6. Which of the following are the most important items to compare when buying a computer? (Select three.) (6)
   A. Keyboard
   B. RAM
   C. Hard disk size

D. CPU capabilities
E. Monitor

7. When buying a computer, get a minimum of 2 GB of RAM. (6)
   A. True
   B. False
8. What type of modem provides broadband access to the Internet? (Select two.) (7)
   A. Dial-up
   B. Bluetooth
   C. Cable
   D. DSL
9. What type of Internet connection uses a wireless router? (8)
   A. Wi-Fi
   B. Dial-up
   C. Bluetooth
   D. DSL
10. You can create short-range personal area networks (PANs) with ________ technology. (9)
11. Most laptops include a device you can use in place of a mouse. You use your finger to drag the pointer around the screen. What is this? (10)
    A. Wheel mouse
    B. Touchpad
    C. Keyboard
    D. iPad
12. You have a speaker system that is identified as a 5.1 system. The .1 indicates the speaker system has a ______________. (11)
13. An all-in-one printer can usually print, copy, scan, and fax documents. (14)
    A. True
    B. False
14. Which of the following can you use to scan documents or images? (Select three.) (13)
    A. Flatbed scanner
    B. Sheet-fed scanner
    C. Handheld scanner
    D. ISP scanner
15. The two most common file formats for pictures created from digital cameras are JPEG and TIFF. (15)
    A. True
    B. False
16. A _____ is a type of optical disc that can hold 4.7 GB or more of data. (16)
17. What type of drive is portable enough to fit on your key chain and can store large amounts of data on it? (17)
    A. Optical media drive
    B. Flash drive
    C. External USB drive
    D. All of the above
18. What can you use to read books that are in a digital format? (19)
    A. MP3 player
    B. E-reader
    C. Digital camera
    D. Scanner

19. Smartphones are cell phones that have advanced capabilities, such as a built-in PDA. (19)

A. True

B. False

20. ______ is the name of a free online e-mail service provided by Microsoft. (20)

End-of-Chapter Project

You want to buy a new laptop computer and printer. Research computers and costs for three different laptop units. Get specifications and costs on three different printers: a laser printer, an inkjet printer, and an all-in-one product. Keep detailed notes while performing your research. You will use the notes later in the course.

For the laptop computers, gather the following information at a minimum:

- Manufacturer
- Model name/number
- CPU speed
- 32-bit or 64-bit system
- Amount of RAM installed
- Maximum amount of RAM that can be installed
- Hard disk capacity
- Screen size
- Price

For the printers, gather the following information at a minimum:

- Manufacturer
- Model name/number
- Pages per minute (color and/or black and white)
- Resolution (dots per inch, or dpi)
- Printer price
- Ink price for inkjet printer and all-in-one unit, toner price for toner printer

CHAPTER

2

Computer Hardware In Depth

- Computer hardware refers to all the physical components that make up a computer. Software refers to programs. The topic of hardware is very important to anyone starting out in the field of computers. Although the topic is vast, you don't have to know everything as a beginner. However, it makes sense to understand the basics of the important devices that make up a computer. No matter what you plan to do with computers, at some point, you will face certain questions about hardware.
- You learned a lot about computers and peripherals in Chapter 1. This chapter takes a deeper look at what is inside of a computer—the hardware—but it covers only the basics. It doesn't include a lot of unnecessary technical details that may overwhelm beginning computer students. It's written like the rest of the book—in an easy, plain-English manner.
- At some point in the future, you may want to know more about hardware. To learn the more advanced technical details, read books about computer hardware or take additional computer courses. For now, let's explore the basic concepts that will help you have a better understanding of computers in general.

CHAPTER TOPICS

This chapter covers the following topics and concepts:

- What the system unit and internal components are
- How a power supply provides electricity to a computer
- What a motherboard is
- Why the central processing unit is the brain of a computer
- What the Basic Input/Output System (BIOS) does
- What memory is and how much your computer needs
- Where ports are located on a computer and which devices plug into them
- What a controller is and why it's important
- How a video (or graphics) card makes images appear on your monitor
- What sound cards are for and how they work with speakers
- The importance of hard disks for storing data

KEY WORDS

BIOS
Central processing unit (CPU)
Computer port
Controller
Flash memory
Hard disk drive
Motherboard
Power supply
Random access memory (RAM)
Sound card
System unit
Universal serial bus (USB) port
Video card

Introducing the System Unit and Internal Components

FIGURE 2-1 A computer and internal hardware components.

A computer case and the components it houses are referred to as the **system unit**. Many people call the system unit the central processing unit (CPU) because the CPU is the most important component inside the system unit. However, this is not its correct name. The CPU is a separate component within the system unit. (You'll learn about the CPU later in this chapter.) FIGURE 2-2 shows a system unit for a tower computer.

FIGURE 2-2 Tower computer system unit.

Some of the most common components in the system unit are the:

- Power supply
- Motherboard
- CPU
- Slots for adapter cards
- RAM or system memory
- Graphics card
- Hard drive
- CD/DVD drive/burner

FIGURE 2-3 gives you a big-picture view of the inside of a typical system unit for a tower computer. A laptop computer or netbook have the same components but they are usually much smaller. They are also arranged differently to make everything fit. This chapter and its figures focus on components found in ordinary desktop or tower computers. However, the same concepts apply to laptop and netbook computers.

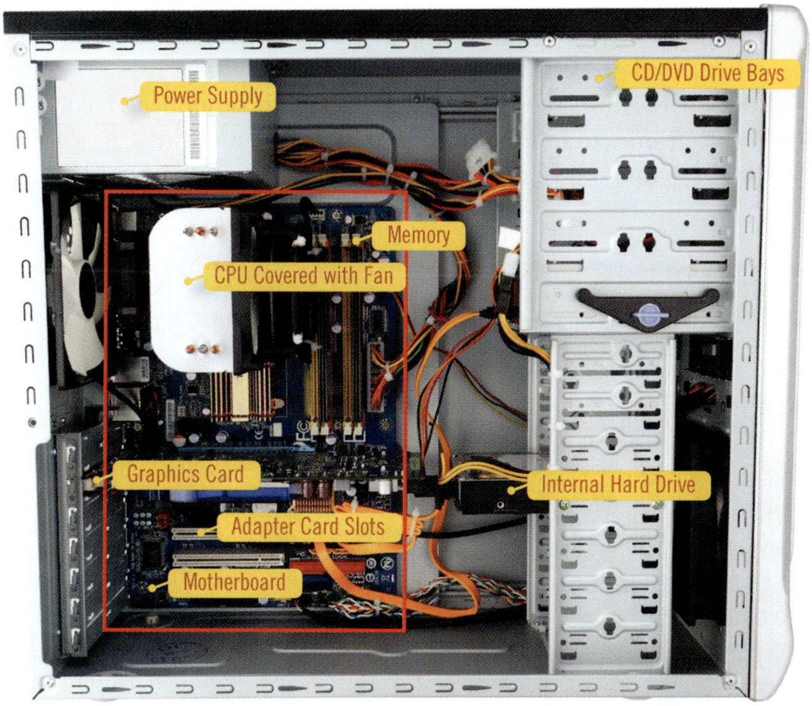

FIGURE 2-3 A look inside a computer.

Power Supply

FIGURE 2-4 Power supply.

The **power supply** provides electricity to a computer. It contains the electronic circuits that provide the power that the computer requires to operate properly. FIGURE 2-4 shows a typical power supply. Notice that the power supply has a cooling fan behind the open vent to keep it from overheating.

Heat can be the enemy of electrical components within a computer. If a system gets too hot, internal components can fail. Cooling fans pull cool air from outside the computer into and over the components that generate heat. The processor and graphics card both generate a lot of heat and sometimes have additional fans to keep them cool.

Power supplies are rated by the amount of power they can deliver. Electric power is measured in watts (W). The wattage rating sets the limit on how many options can be installed in a given computer. In the early days of personal computers (PCs), a typical power supply might have been rated at about 65 watts. Later, the power requirements increased as engineers added more components to computers, and the power supply had to provide this extra electricity. Today, a typical computer power supply has a rating of approximately 300 to 450 watts.

If you add more components to a system, make sure that the power supply will support the additional components. If you exceed your power supply's rating, the computer will not work properly or may not work at all.

Motherboard

The **motherboard** is one of the most important components in your computer system. It is the largest board inside the system unit. It lies flat against the case, and many of the internal components in the computer plug into the motherboard. Some of those components are the central processing unit, memory, and graphics card.

The motherboard is also a computer's most complex component. It contains most of the important electronic circuits that run a computer, as shown in FIGURE 2-5. All devices in a computer are in one way or another connected to the motherboard.

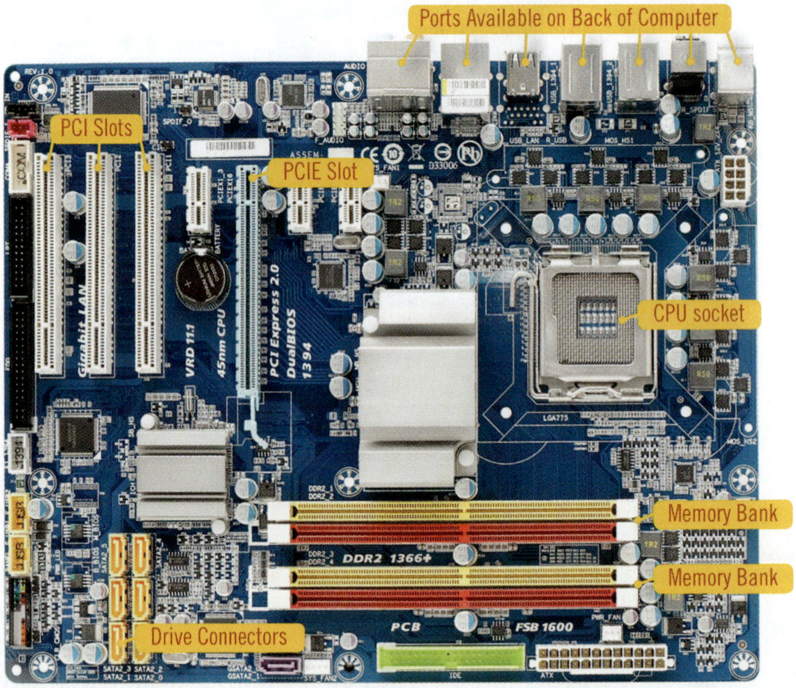

FIGURE 2-5 A motherboard with some of the larger components labeled.

Most motherboards today use one of many Advanced Technology Extended (ATX) form factors. A motherboard's form factor is its general size. The form factor determines the size of the computer case. Case manufacturers design the cases to support motherboards based on these form factors. It's also important to match the power supply to the motherboard's form factor to ensure the computer will have the right amount of electricity. If you plan on building your own PC someday, form factor is a critical first item to consider.

Most of this chapter covers components that are built into the motherboard or plug into slots on the motherboard, such as:

- **The central processing unit (CPU):** The brain of the computer system
- **The Basic Input/Output System (BIOS):** A combination of chips and software that contains hardware and system settings, and that loads the operating system
- **Random access memory (RAM):** System memory
- **Ports:** Universal serial bus (USB), video, sound, and more
- **Controllers:** For video, keyboard, disk drives, and more
- **Sound card:** Enables music, speech, and sound effects to flow through the speakers

Central Processing Unit (CPU)

The **central processing unit (CPU)** is the most important "chip" in a computer. It's the brain that controls the operations. The processor interprets and executes all the instructions that are processed on the computer. This includes math operations and logical operations. CPUs can execute millions of instructions per second.

Many different factors are responsible for a computer's speed. The CPU's clock speed is one of the most important. The speed of the CPU is measured in gigahertz (GHz). Typical ratings are about 1.6 GHz for mini computers, 2.0 to 2.6 GHz for laptops, and 2.4 to 3.0 GHz for desktops. You can find both faster and slower processors in each category.

Although the processor speed used to increase regularly, CPU manufacturers are finding it's easier to add multiple CPUs in a single package rather than increase the CPU speed. For example, a processor may be dual core or quad core. This means that a single processor package includes two processors if it is dual core, or four processors if it is quad core. Processors can then share tasks, which is more efficient than a single processor handling the entire load.

Intel and AMD Make CPUs

Intel Corporation and Advanced Micro Devices (AMD) are the two leading CPU manufacturers. These two companies are highly competitive, and they frequently improve their processors as each business tries to outdo the other.

Processor names are usually grouped in families. For example, AMD K10.5 processors come in multiple versions, including the Phenom II and Athlon II processors. Similarly, Intel has multiple versions of the Core i7 processor that include four physical cores within the same package.

It's very important to know if the CPU is a 32-bit processor or a 64-bit processor. This determines how much memory your system will support, and memory is the second most important speed factor. A 32-bit processor can address about four billion memory spaces. This sounds like a lot, but it equates to about 4 GB of RAM. Today's computers are memory hogs, and 4 GB of RAM is plenty for ordinary use but not enough for gamers and other power users.

Windows reserves some of the address space in 32-bit systems. Even if you have 4 GB of RAM installed in your computer, Windows will use only about 3.2 to 3.4 GB of the 4 GB. The rest is wasted. You don't have the same problem with 64-bit systems.

In contrast, a 64-bit processor can address about 18 exabytes (EB). You can also express this as 18,000 petabytes (PB) or 18,000,000 terabytes (TB), or 18,000,000,000 gigabytes (GB). You probably don't need an exabyte of memory in your system, but you might want to use more than 4 GB. Additionally, 64-bit processors are quicker and more efficient when running many applications.

The Chip Set

The chip set is a set of support chips that controls how the CPU communicates with your

Note

Although a CPU can fit in the palm of your hand, it contains millions of miniaturized transistors and other electronic components.

TIP

When you shop for a computer, the processor can be one of the most important parts to consider. It is the brain of the computer and directly affects the computer's speed. Identify the processor's speed, and how many cores it has. Higher speed and more cores equates to a faster computer. This will also directly translate into a higher price.

computer's other components. Many important functions are embedded in the chip set, such as support for USB devices, some disk drives, Ethernet adapters, and memory controllers. The chip set plays an important role in system performance. The lucky thing is that at this stage of your technical life you don't have to worry about this technical detail. For now, let the experts decide all this.

Basic Input/Output System (BIOS)

BIOS is an acronym for Basic Input/Output System. This is the combination of chips and built-in software that determines what a computer can do without accessing programs from a disk. On PCs, the BIOS contains all the code required to control the keyboard, display screen, disk drives, and more.

> **Note**
>
> "Booting up" means turning your computer on when it's powered off. "Rebooting" means to restart your computer while it is running.

The BIOS includes instructions on how to load basic computer hardware. The BIOS also runs a test referred to as Power-On Self-Test (POST), which ensures that the computer meets basic requirements to boot up properly. If the computer does not pass the POST, you will receive an error indicating what is malfunctioning within the computer. The following are four important responsibilities of the BIOS:

- **POST:** Tests basic computer hardware, ensuring it functions properly before starting the operating system
- **Bootstrap loader:** Locates and loads the operating system
- **BIOS software/drivers:** The interface between the operating system and the hardware
- **Setup:** A configuration program that lets you configure hardware and system settings, such as which device to boot from, and the time and date

> **WARNING**
>
> Be careful when changing BIOS settings. If you misconfigure these settings, your computer might not boot.

You press certain keys on your keyboard as the computer is booting up to access the information stored in the BIOS. For example, some systems display a message to press the F10 key or the DEL key; other systems prompt you to press any key to access the setup program. When you press the correct key, the BIOS setup program starts.

CMOS

CMOS is short for complementary metal-oxide semiconductor. That's a long term for a little chip inside the computer that stores information such as the system time and which device to boot from. CMOS works with BIOS to run a computer.

CMOS keeps its data even when you turn the computer's power off because a small battery powers the chip. The battery powers the internal clock, so even if you turn your computer off for a while, it will still have the correct time when you power it back on.

Random Access Memory (RAM)

Memory is a key component of every computer system, and it's an important consideration when buying a computer. Memory is also called "system memory" or "primary memory." The topic of memory can be technically overwhelming. Don't worry, though, most of it is for technical experts.

Random access memory (RAM) comes on small printed circuit boards that are installed on the system motherboard. These little memory boards are commonly called sticks, modules, or DIMMs (short for dual inline memory module). FIGURE 2-6 shows two sticks of RAM.

FIGURE 2-6 RAM sticks.

A computer uses RAM memory to store the programs and data that you are currently working on. For example, when you open a program, the CPU loads the program into RAM from the disk drive. When you finish, you save your data on the disk drive for long-term storage.

RAM is one of the most important components in a computer. A typical computer has at least 1 GB but more often 2 GB. Power users and serious gamers often have as much as 6 GB or 8 GB to increase the system's performance. The motherboard sets the maximum RAM you can have on a given computer. Additionally, systems with 32-bit CPUs can't access more than 4 GB of RAM.

Current versions of RAM are measured in megahertz (MHz) or GHz such as 1,066 MHz or 1.066 GHz. A higher number indicates a faster speed and better performance. RAM used to be measured and stated in nanoseconds. A nanosecond is one billionth of a second, and a typical access time was 60ns. (Access time is the amount of time it takes for the CPU to receive data from RAM.) Detailed memory specifications still list access time in nanoseconds, but RAM speed is more commonly listed in MHz or GHz.

Note

RAM is volatile. This means that RAM requires constant power. If you turn off your computer's power, this will erase RAM's contents.

RAM Jargon Buster

RAM technology is always changing. Whenever an important change takes place, manufacturers give the new technology a name. This means a new acronym. Some of the names used for RAM are:

- **Synchronous Dynamic RAM (SDRAM):** The "synchronous" part means the RAM is synchronized with the system clock so that all operations take place at the same time.
- **Double Data Rate SDRAM (DDR SDRAM):** This type of RAM is twice as fast as SDRAM. DDR SDRAM comes in even higher speeds—DDR2, DDR3, and DDR4.

2.1 Exercise: How Much RAM Does a Computer Have?

To check the amount of RAM in a computer running the Windows 7 operating system, follow these steps:

1. Click the Start menu button in the lower-left corner of the desktop window.
2. Right-click Computer in the Start menu (on the right-hand side) and select Properties.
3. In the window that appears, find the line that shows the amount of installed memory, as shown in FIGURE 2-7.

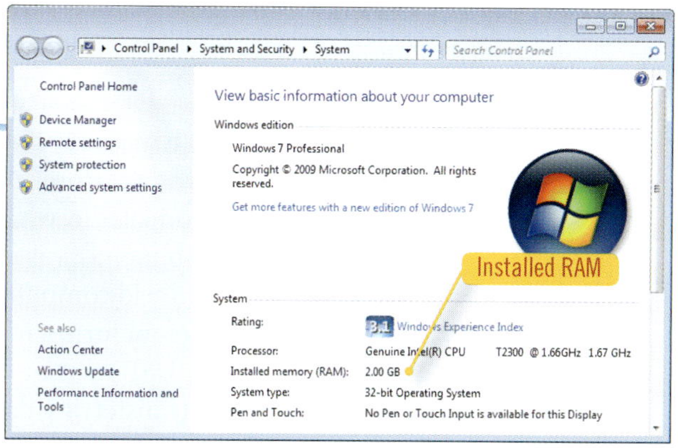

FIGURE 2-7 Viewing the amount of RAM in a computer.

Memory Banks

RAM is installed in memory banks on the motherboard. A memory bank is a group of sockets. Most computer systems have two or more memory banks, and each bank has one to three slots.

Each system has rules on how to fill memory banks. Some computers require all the sockets in one bank to be filled with the same capacity module. Other computers require the first bank to have the highest capacity modules if different modules are used. If the configuration rules aren't followed, the computer might not start up or it might not recognize all the memory in the system. These are easy fixes—just turn the computer off, read the computer's user manual, and reinsert the RAM modules as needed.

Note

If you want to upgrade the memory in your computer, follow the rules for memory banks. However, when you purchase a new computer, you only need to pay attention to the total amount of RAM. The RAM will already be installed.

TIP

If you really want to know more detail about memory, visit *http://www.kingston.com*. Select Memory Tools and then select Ultimate Memory Guide. The Ultimate Memory Guide is a wealth of information on memory.

FIGURE 2-8 shows a motherboard with two memory banks. Each bank has two slots and all four slots are filled. When the slots are filled with memory, technicians say that the bank is populated. With all banks populated, you would not be able to add additional memory without taking some out. For example, a motherboard populated with four 1 GB memory sticks has a total of 4 GB of RAM. If your motherboard can accept 8 GB of RAM and you want to increase the memory from 4 to 8 GB, you would have to replace those sticks with four 2 GB memory sticks.

FIGURE 2-8 Motherboard with two memory banks.

Flash Memory

Flash memory functions like RAM and a hard disk combined. Flash memory stores bits of electronic data in memory cells like RAM. However, like a hard disk, the data is nonvolatile, which means it isn't erased when you turn the computer or device off. Flash memory is ideal for use in flash drives, digital cameras, cell phones, printers, handheld computers, pagers, and audio recorders. Flash memory is available in many different forms, including CompactFlash, Secure Digital, SmartMedia, MultiMedia, and USB memory. Flash drives, or USB thumb drives, are very popular with users for transferring data from computer to computer.

Computer Ports

Computer ports are the points where external devices—peripherals—connect to a computer. Keyboards, mice, printers, scanners, and digital cameras are just a few examples. FIGURE 2-9 shows a motherboard with several of the ports labeled. These ports are available on the rear of the computer.

You connect peripherals to the computer with a cable that attaches to one of the ports. A port's main function is to act as the point of attachment where the cable from the peripheral device plugs into the system unit, allowing data to flow to or from the peripheral device. Ports are built into the motherboard, or they can be located on an adapter card that plugs into the motherboard. Ports come in many different varieties:

- **PS/2 port:** This is a round port for plugging in a PS/2 keyboard or mouse. Moth\

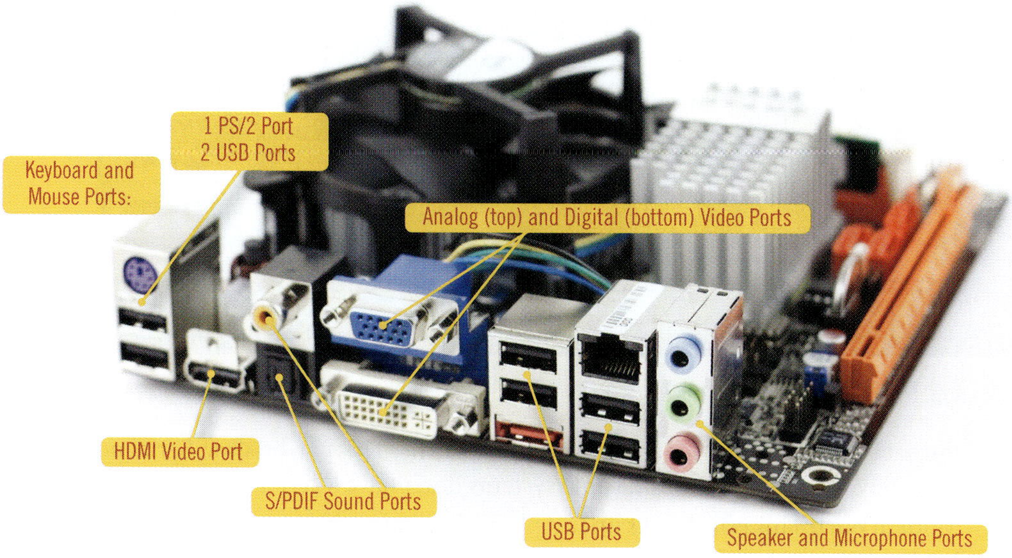

FIGURE 2-9 Motherboard with ports labeled.

erboards used to have two PS/2 ports—one for the keyboard and one for the mouse. Some systems today don't have any PS/2 ports.

- **Video ports:** This is where the external monitor plugs into the computer. Monitors have significantly improved over the years, and your computer may have multiple video ports. The traditional three-row15-pin port is for analog video (called VGA). Because most newer monitors can accept a digital signal, many computers include a digital video port. One kind of digital video port is High-Definition Multimedia Interface (HDMI), which supports a high definition monitor. Some motherboards, especially laptops, have a built-in on-board video card. However, because people often want a better monitor, the graphics adapter card on laptops has the video port available on the back of the computer where you can connect an external monitor.
- **S/PDIF sound port:** S/PDIF is an acronym for Sony/Philips Digital Interconnect Format. It includes two ports. The round port is a standard RCA jack, and it accepts digital sound input from a coaxial cable with an RCA adapter. The square port is covered with black plastic but can be opened to accept digital sound input from a fiber optic cable. For now, just know that S/PDIF is related to sound.
- **Ethernet network port:** Most computers on a cabled network connect using twisted pair cabling. The twisted pair cable connects to the computer with an RJ-45 jack. An RJ-45 jack is similar to a phone connection but is a little larger.
- **FireWire/IEEE 1394 port:** This port and connector goes by several different names. For example, Apple calls it FireWire, Sony calls it i.Link, and it has been standardized as IEEE 1394. IEEE 1394 ports and cables transmit images and video in a purely digital format between your system and video devices, such as digital camcorders and cameras. **FIGURE 2-10** shows a motherboard with a FireWire port and some other ports.
- **Parallel port:** The parallel port was historically used to connect a printer or a scanner to a computer. Most systems today use USB ports instead of the older parallel port.
- **Serial ports:** Serial ports are also called COM1 and COM2. "Serial" means that

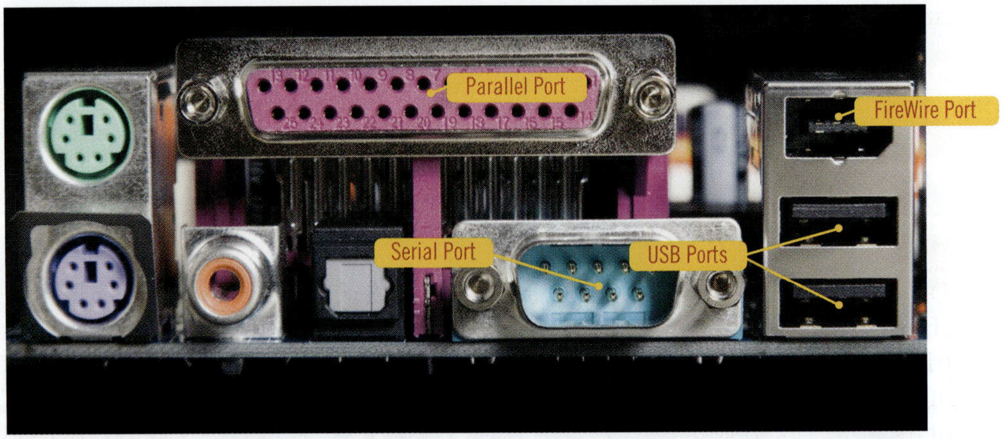

FIGURE 2-10 Motherboard with FireWire port.

the data being transmitted travels one bit at a time. This can be slow. Serial ports are rarely used these days and some systems don't have a serial port.

- **Modem port:** This port hooks up to a phone to create a dial-up connection to the Internet. This method of connecting to the Internet is all but obsolete in urban areas. However, many people outside major cities still use dial-up for Internet access.

> **Note**
>
> HDMI stands for High-Definition Multimedia Interface. This port lets you transfer video and audio signals over one cable rather than a separate cable for video and another for audio. HDMI connections are perfect for people who want to use their computer as part of a home theater with a high definition TV set.

USB Ports

The **universal serial bus (USB) port** has become so popular and widely used that it deserves its own section in this chapter. USB ports connect many different devices to your computer. One of the handiest things about USB devices is that you can connect them without turning off the computer. The computer should recognize USB devices as soon as you plug them into a USB port. If not, all you do is install a driver, which is a small computer program that instructs the CPU how to communicate with the new device. The operating system usually installs the driver automatically.

All new motherboards come with USB ports. Most computers provide USB ports on the front, back, and/or sides of the system unit. This is important because you may want to access the USB port from the front and not have to move the system unit around to access the USB port. USB 2.0 is the most popular version. However, USB 3.0 devices started to appear in 2010 and look very promising. Thankfully, USB devices are backward compatible with USB 2.0. In other words, you can plug a USB 3.0 device into a USB 2.0 port and it will still work, although not at the faster USB 3.0 speeds.

The following are some of the common devices that often connect to a computer's USB ports:

- Flash drives or USB external drives
- Digital cameras
- Printers
- Scanners
- Music players
- Smartphones

Controllers

Input/output (I/O) devices involve the transfer of data into or out of a computer. They include devices such as a display, keyboard, and disk drives. I/O devices require a controller. A **controller** is an interface circuit that connects the I/O device to the CPU. The primary job of a controller is to transmit and receive data to and from the I/O device. A controller can be built into the motherboard, on the device itself, or on a separate adapter card that you plug into the motherboard. Some examples are:

- **Built-in controller:** A keyboard's controller is built into the motherboard.
- **On the device:** An integrated drive electronics (IDE) hard drive has the controller built into the drive itself.
- **On an adapter card:** You can add a graphics card to a computer and then plug the monitor into the adapter card.

Integrated Drive Electronics (IDE)

IDE is a standard technology that interfaces the hard disk and other I/O devices, such as CD/DVD drives, to the CPU. IDE hard drives have the controller included on the hard drive itself. A ribbon cable connects the hard drive and its controller to the host adapter on the motherboard. A motherboard contains two host adapters called IDE1 and IDE2 for the primary and secondary connections. Each IDE connector can support two devices.

The IDE drives are derived from Advanced Technology Attachment (ATA) standards. They use parallel connections and are sometimes referred to as PATA for Parallel ATA.

Serial Advanced Technology Attachment (SATA)

SATA is an advanced interface that connects hard disks and other I/O devices to the computer. SATA provides several improvements over PATA or traditional IDE drives. They are faster, which can improve the overall computer performance. Their cables are smaller, which improves the airflow within the computer and helps keep the system cooler. Additionally, SATA devices are hot-swappable, which means you can swap them out while the system is powered on. Many newer computers include SATA devices inside the computer and eSATA ports to connect external SATA devices.

> **TIP**
>
> You may remember from the serial port discussion that a serial port is slower because it sends data one bit at a time. However, serial ATA is quicker than parallel ATA because of how the cabling is designed. SATA uses fewer pins and achieves significantly higher speeds.

Small Computer System Interface (SCSI)

SCSI is a parallel interface standard for attaching peripheral devices to computers. SCSI is better than IDE but more expensive. You can connect as many as 15 devices to a single SCSI port. It's usually used in servers, although some high-end workstations also use SCSI controllers.

FireWire

Apple invented FireWire for high-speed transmission of digital data. It is very popular with users transmitting video data between the computer and video devices, such as camcorders and cameras. It's also known as i.Link by Sony, and more generically as IEEE 1394. IEEE 1394a transfers data at 400 Mbit/second and IEEE 1394b transfers data at speeds up to 800 Mbit/second.

A single FireWire controller in a system can support up to 63 FireWire devices. These devices are daisy-chained together. In other words, one device plugs into the computer and the next device plugs into the first device. If you added a third device, you would plug it into the second device.

Video or Graphics Card

The **video card**, also called the graphics card, is where you plug the monitor into the system unit. This is how text, pictures, and video—and anything you do on the computer—are displayed on the monitor. LCD-type monitors connect to the graphics card using a digital visual interface (DVI) connector or an analog VGA connector. DVI is the better choice. Many computers today also include an HDMI connector that allows you to use an HDMI TV as a computer monitor.

Graphics cards usually include their own video RAM (VRAM). The more VRAM a graphics card has, the faster the images can be displayed on the monitor. VRAM also affects the number of colors a monitor can display at a given resolution. Most graphics cards have on-board RAM, and it's not uncommon to see graphics cards with 1 GB or

> **Note**
>
> "On-board" means an item is built in. On-board RAM, for example, is built into a graphics card.

more of on-board RAM. However, some low-end computers use a graphics chip on the motherboard without any dedicated RAM. These graphics chips use some of the system RAM for video. In other words, you may have 2 GB of RAM on the system, but the graphics chip will use 128 megabytes (MB) or more, reducing the amount of RAM you have for your programs to run.

The Sound Card and Speakers

Computers need both a **sound card** and speakers to hear audio, such as music, speech, and sound effects. Most motherboards provide an on-board sound card. This built-in sound card is fine for most purposes. However, if you want higher quality sound, you can add an additional sound card to the system.

Multimedia means that the computer can do more than just display text and pictures. The computer can play and record music, display videos, run games, and more. The sound card allows you to hear audio from the computer. Sophisticated sound systems include as many as seven speakers and a subwoofer. These are almost a must for music enthusiasts and dedicated gamers. They use surround sound technology to make different sounds seem as though they are coming from different directions. For example, you can hear a jet coming from behind you, fly overhead, and zip out of earshot in front of you. Explosions feel real when they boom out of the subwoofer. These sound systems can produce concert-hall-quality music from your favorite artists as well.

The same sound card and speakers can play music from the CD/DVD drive, the standard Windows sounds, and music from external devices plugged into your system. You can also plug in external devices to your sound card, record audio into the computer, and record music from your computer to the external device. Many musicians require this flexibility so that they can easily combine music from multiple sources.

The Basic Functions of a Sound Card

A sound card converts digital sound signals to analog signals for speakers. Sound cards can also amplify the audio sent to the speakers making it louder or softer. However, most speakers include their own power and can include their own volume control.

Sound cards also include a sampler. A "sampler" is a circuit that digitizes an audio waveform. This means that it converts the analog waveform to a digital waveform. You can attach a microphone or any other audio input device to the sound card and record it. Sound cards can also generate their own sounds. They include built-in synthesizers that allow them to play musical notes from a wide range of musical instruments.

Nearly all sound cards support the Musical Instrument Digital Interface (MIDI) protocol, which is a standard for representing music electronically. You may also hear the term *Sound Blaster-compatible*. This means that the sound card can process commands written for a Sound Blaster card. This is because Creative Labs, the company that took the lead in sound cards, became the de facto standard, with a product line of sound cards called Sound Blaster.

How the Sound Card Connects to Speakers

You need speakers or headphones to hear the audio from your computer. Although a sound card can power headphones, an ordinary sound card does not have the necessary power to drive anything more than the smallest computer speakers. Many computer users buy better speakers with dedicated power that can also produce superior sound.

Some systems have simple sound card ports like those shown in FIGURE 2-11. The small image to the left of the top port has an arrow pointing into the center, which means it accepts input from external devices, such as MIDI instruments. This is also called a line-in connection. The image by the middle port has an arrow pointing out from the center—you would plug your speakers into this port. This is also called a line-out connection. You plug

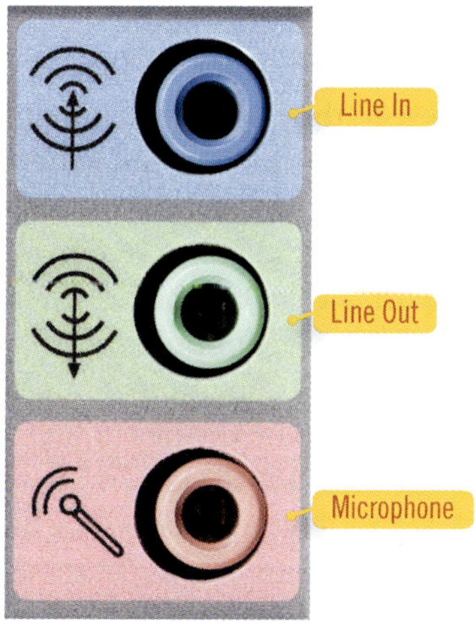

FIGURE 2-11 Simple sound card connections.

one speaker into the computer and the second speaker plugs into the first speaker. The bottom port is for a microphone.

More sophisticated sound cards and speaker systems have additional connections. They also come with detailed instructions on how to connect them.

Most of this chapter has focused on many of the components on the motherboard. By now, you should have a good idea what these components are and what they do. The last section in this chapter takes a look at hard drives.

The Hard Disk Drive

The **hard disk drive** is your primary storage device. Most of a computer's information—its data—is stored on a hard drive. In addition, all your programs, such as the operating system, application programs, and data, are stored on a hard drive. Hard drives are important for two good reasons:

- **Inexpensive:** Secondary storage on the hard drive is inexpensive when compared with primary storage in RAM. A typical hard drive can store 250 GB to more than 1 TB of data.
- **Nonvolatile:** The information on the hard drive does not get erased even when you turn off the power because it is magnetically stored. Remember that RAM is volatile, which means its contents are erased when you turn off the computer's power.

How a Hard Drive Works

A traditional hard drive is a sealed unit that contains rigid disks called platters. Computer information is stored on these platters. The platters are made of rigid aluminum that has a circular shape. Magnetic material, such as iron oxide, coats the platter so that the bits that make up the information can be written on the magnetic surface and then read at a later time.

FIGURE 2-12 Inside of a traditional hard drive.

FIGURE 2-12 shows the inside of a traditional hard drive. This drive has three platters and can write data on both sides of each platter. The arm extending over the platter holds the read/write head. An "actuator" is the mechanical system that moves the arm back and forth over the platter as it spins, allowing it to read data from the disks and write data to the disks. A spindle motor rotates the platters continuously.

The hard drive is constantly spinning, so do not move a computer while it is on. The read/write head is very close to the platter, and moving it can cause a head to crash onto the platter destroying the head, the platter, and your data.

As mentioned previously, hard drives include a controller. This is the interface circuit that allows the data to transfer between the system and the hard drive. IDE hard drives have become a standard in the PC world and are often referred to as PATA drives. However, SATA drives are becoming more popular.

Internal hard drives connect via an internal interface. This may be a traditional IDE interface using PATA. It could also be the newer SATA interface, or even SCSI. If you're purchasing a new drive to place inside the system, be sure that the new hard disk matches the internal interface. You cannot plug a SATA drive into a PATA connection. Also ensure that you have an available connection to plug in the new hard drive.

However, you can avoid the interface challenge completely by purchasing a USB hard drive similar to the one shown in FIGURE 2-13. This is an external hard drive that plugs into an available USB port. You can't use this as the primary hard drive in your computer, but you can use it for additional storage or to store backups.

Note

Each disk can be divided into one or more drives, referred to as volumes or partitions. For example, a single disk may be a single volume known to the operating system as C. It's also possible to partition a single hard disk into multiple logical disk drives that may be known as C, D, and so on.

FIGURE 2-13 External USB drive.

Hard drives spin at a steady rotational speed. The faster they spin, the faster you can get the information. Get a hard drive that spins at least 7,200 revolutions per minute (rpm). Most hard drives also include small amounts of built-in memory referred to as a "disk buffer" or "disk cache." This is used to optimize both reading from the disk and writing to the disk. Most hard drives have either an 8 MB or 16 MB disk cache. Higher numbers are better.

Newer solid-state disk (SSD) flash hard drives have become available in recent years. These work inside systems as if they were hard drives, but use flash memory instead of actual platters and spindles. They are significantly quicker than traditional hard drives and have no moving parts, which makes them less susceptible to failure. SSD drives are often configured to plug into SATA connectors.

Formatting a Disk

Formatting a disk is the process of preparing it to work with a computer. A disk must be formatted before the computer can use it. Formatting is not something you do all the time. In fact, a disk is usually only formatted when it is originally manufactured. Years ago, you had to format the disk when you purchased it. Today when you buy a disk, it is already formatted but you can reformat it if necessary.

When a disk is formatted, the operating system writes the structures necessary to manage files and data. Files are often stored in folders. A folder is a location on the disk where you can store and organize files similar to how you can store and organize paper files in a folder. For example, you can create a folder named Data on your C drive and it

Note

You'll learn the essentials of files and folders in Chapters 4 and 5.

would be accessible via C:\Data. A folder is also called a directory, although directory is an older term that is falling out of use.

It's also possible to store data directly on the drive without storing it in a folder. This is referred to as storing the data in the root. A folder named Data is referenced as C:\Data, but just C:\ by itself is referred to as the root of the C drive. The root is created automatically when a disk is formatted and cannot be erased. Although you can store files in the root, it is recommended that you do not clutter it with unnecessary files. You would instead create folders and subfolders to organize and store the information on a disk. You will learn more about the root and folders later in this book when you read about Windows 7.

How Much Disk Space Do You Need?

When buying a hard drive, consider capacity, interface, speed, and buffer. The capacity indicates how much data you can store on the system. For example, a hard drive may be able to hold 500 GB of data, 1 TB of data, or more. The amount of space you need depends on what you do with your system. If you regularly store Blu-Ray movies or HDTV shows on your system, these require a lot of space and you'll need larger hard drives. However, if you only use your computer to surf the Internet, send and receive e-mail, and write papers for school, 250 GB will be more than enough space.

2.2 Exercise: Checking Your Hard Disk Space

To check the amount of hard disk space in a computer running the Windows 7 operating system, follow these steps:

1. Click the Windows Explorer icon, which looks like a folder, on the taskbar at the bottom of the Windows 7 desktop window. See FIGURE 2-14. You can also click Start > All Programs > Accessories > Windows Explorer.

FIGURE 2-14 The Windows Explorer icon on the taskbar.

2. In the Windows Explorer window, click Computer in the left pane.
3. The main window on the right shows the amount of available disk space and the total disk space, as shown in FIGURE 2-15.

WARNING

Formatting a disk erases everything on it. Do not format a disk unless you are sure you don't need any information on the disk, or that you have already backed it up. The only time you really need to format a disk is if the disk contains a computer virus that you cannot remove through other means, or the disk's information has become corrupted and unusable. Other times you may actually want to erase everything on a disk, such as when you're installing a clean version of an operating system. In any case, be careful when formatting a disk since you'll lose all data on the disk.

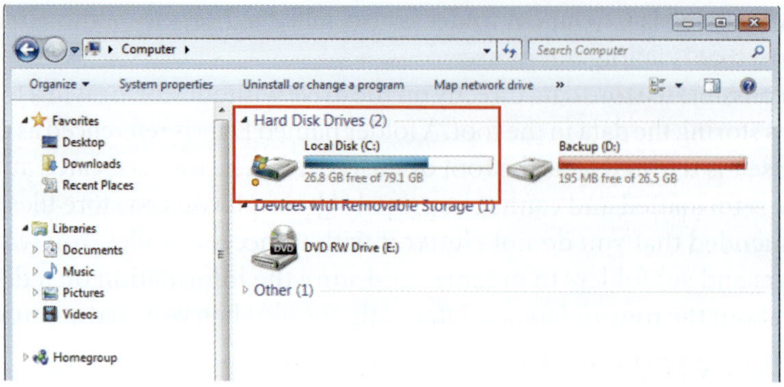

FIGURE 2-15 Checking hard disk space.

Test Yourself

The questions in this section are meant to test your knowledge of what you read. Make sure you answer them. The page number where the answer can be found appears after each question.

1. The system unit and CPU are the same thing. (26)
   - **A.** True
   - **B.** False
2. _____ is the enemy of electrical components in a computer. (27)
3. If you add more components to your computer, why do you need to check the power supply? (28)
4. Most of the hardware components of a computer are located on a specific board. What is this board? (28)
   - **A.** Fatherboard
   - **B.** Motherboard
   - **C.** ROMboard
   - **D.** IDE board
5. The ________________ is the brain of the computer system. (29)
6. A CPU can have how many bits? (Select two.) (29)
   - **A.** 16
   - **B.** 32
   - **C.** 48
   - **D.** 64
7. What is the maximum amount of RAM a 32-bit processor can handle? (29)
   - **A.** 1 GB
   - **B.** 2 GB
   - **C.** 3 GB
   - **D.** 4 GB
8. As a computer boots up, the BIOS is responsible for loading the operating system. (30)
   - **A.** True
   - **B.** False
9. What is the difference between booting up and restarting a computer? (30)
10. RAM modules are commonly referred to as ________________. (30)

11. What do you plug RAM modules into? (31)
    A. A memory port
    B. A memory bank
    C. A controller
    D. The BIOS
12. The only way to determine how much RAM your computer has is to remove the computer case and look at the RAM modules. (31)
    A. True
    B. False
13. Which of the following are ports on a computer? (33)
    A. Video
    B. Ethernet network
    C. FireWire
    D. USB
    E. All of the above
    F. A and D only
14. An HDMI port can handle audio and video signals. (35)
    A. True
    B. False
15. A controller can be found on which of the following? (Select three.) (34, 35)
    A. Motherboard
    B. Device
    C. Adapter card
    D. Computer case
16. A video card and graphics card are the same thing. (35)
    A. True
    B. False
17. What is the primary purpose of a sound card? (36)
    A. Converts the file to a hard copy printout
    B. Synthesizes the sounds with on-board samplers
    C. Converts analog signals to digital sound
    D. Converts digital sound signals to analog
18. What does a computer use to store applications and data over the long term? (37)
    A. Memory
    B. Disk drive
    C. CPU
    D. ROM
19. A solid-state drive has no moving parts. (38)
    A. True
    B. False
20. A hard disk must be formatted before you can use it. (38)
    A. True
    B. False

End-of-Chapter Project

Refer to the notes you created for the Chapter 1 project for which you researched three different laptop computers. Do the laptops have 32-bit or 64-bit processors? How much RAM does each computer have? What is the maximum amount of RAM each computer can handle? If you decided to get the maximum amount of RAM for each computer, how does that affect the cost of each unit?

11. What do you plug RAM modules into? (31)
   A. A module port
   B. A memory bank
   C. A controller
   D. [illegible]

12. One way to determine how much RAM your computer has is to remove the computer case and look at the RAM modules. (31)
   A. True
   B. False

13. Which of the following are [illegible] (31)
   A. [illegible]
   B. Ethernet network
   C. [illegible]
   D. USB
   E. All of the above
   F. A and D only

14. [illegible]
   A. True
   [illegible]

[illegible]
   C. [illegible]
   D. [illegible] card

16. A [illegible] and [illegible] are the same thing. [illegible]

[illegible]
   C. Converts analog signals to digital sound
   D. Converts digital sound signals to analog

18. What does a computer use to store applications and data [illegible]
   A. Memory
   B. Disk drive
   C. [illegible]
   D. ROM

19. A solid state drive has no moving parts. (38)
   A. True
   B. False

20. A hard disk must be formatted before you can use it. (38)
   A. True
   B. False

End-of-Chapter Project

Refer to the notes you created for the Chapter 1 project for which you researched three different laptop computers. For the laptops [illegible] How much RAM does each computer have? What is the maximum amount of RAM each computer can handle? If you decided to get the maximum amount of RAM for each computer, how does that affect the cost of each unit?

PART II

Applications

CHAPTER

3

The Internet

- The Internet is a worldwide phenomenon. More than 1 billion people interact with each other every month via e-mail, chat rooms, blogs, and social networking websites. You can research topics, get information, view pictures, listen to music, and watch videos. Organizations have websites that allow their employees and customers to gather information, buy products, get technical support, and participate in video conferencing.
- The Internet continuously evolves. Every year, people find more and more ways to communicate, collaborate, and learn on the Internet. The technologies that make all of it happen also continually advance.
- What do you need to use the Internet? How do you get to websites? What are common things you might do while "surfing the Web"? This chapter will help you answer these questions. Think of the Internet as a tool that helps you accomplish many different tasks. You can also think of it as a source of information and entertainment.

CHAPTER TOPICS

This chapter covers the following topics and concepts:

- What the Internet is
- How the Internet works
- How to connect to the Internet
- What the components of websites are
- How Web 2.0 and social media help you connect with others
- How to use Hotmail and Microsoft Outlook to send and receive e-mail
- What chatting over the Internet means
- What a blog is
- What type of music files are available on the Internet
- What some sources of entertainment are on the Internet
- How to keep your computer and data safe while using the Internet and e-mail

KEY WORDS

Attachment	E-mail	IP address	Spam
Backbone	Home page	Link	Spyware
Blog	Instant messaging	Microsoft Hotmail	Uniform resource locator (URL)
Browser	Internet	Microsoft Outlook	Uploading
Client	Internet Explorer	Phishing	Virus
Domain name	Internet router	Search engine	Web 2.0
Domain Name System (DNS)	Internet service provider (ISP)	Server	World Wid Web (WWW)
Downloading		Social media	

What Is the Internet?

The **Internet** is a global collection of networks. It is a worldwide system of interconnected computers, as shown in FIGURE 3-1, with more than a billion users. Think of the Internet as:

- The people who use it
- The protocols that govern its communication
- The computers and other hardware that make this possible

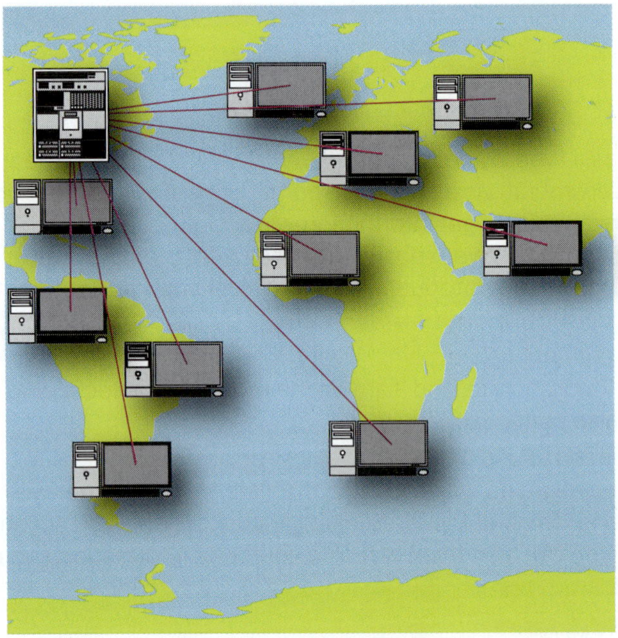

FIGURE 3-1 The Internet is a global network.

History of the Internet

The Internet began around 1969. Back then it was known as the ARPANET. It started as a research project developed by an agency called ARPA (Advanced Research Projects Agency) within the U.S. Defense Department. Its initial purpose was to set up a communications network that the government could easily re-route in case of nuclear war.

As different networks started to develop, they had a problem communicating with each other because they were all using different communications protocols, or rules for communicating. Eventually the Defense Department established a standard communications protocol, called Transmission Control Protocol/Internet Protocol (TCP/IP), which allowed different networks to communicate with each other. By early 1983, all the ARPANET hosts had switched to TCP/IP. This first TCP/IP-based wide area network would later become known as the Internet.

The network opened to commercial interests in 1988, and a wide variety of private networks and services joined in. The first Internet service providers (ISPs) were founded soon afterward. The Internet started to become known to the public in 1991, when British scientist Tim Berners-Lee began the publicized World Wide Web project, and the first Web browsers were born. By the end of the 1990s, the terms "Internet" and "World Wide Web" had become part of everyday life.

The World Wide Web (WWW)

The **World Wide Web (WWW)** is a term that defines the information available on the Internet. This implies that by using your computer you can access an astronomical amount of information from the more than a billion other computers connected to the Internet. You find this information with programs called browsers. The World Wide Web is just one of the many services that the Internet provides. Electronic mail (**e-mail**) is another example of a service provided by the Internet. It's important to know that the World Wide Web is not a synonym for the Internet. The World Wide Web is part of the Internet.

The Internet is the actual network of networks where all the information resides. Things like Telnet and File Transfer Protocol (FTP) are other services that are all part of the Internet. This technology has made it possible for data to leave one computer and travel across the world through different networks and arrive at another computer in a fraction of a second.

How the Internet Works

To access the Internet, you use an **Internet service provider (ISP)**. This is a company that has more advanced equipment and the facility to connect to other computers. Your computer connects to your ISP via cable, digital subscriber line (DSL), wireless, satellite, or dial-up, and your ISP connects you to all the other computers on the Internet.

Every computer that connects to the Internet is part of a network. When you connect to your ISP, you become part of your ISP's network. The ISP may then connect to a larger network and become part of that network, as shown in FIGURE 3-2. The Internet is simply a network of networks.

Note

Chapter 1 explained communications devices and connections.

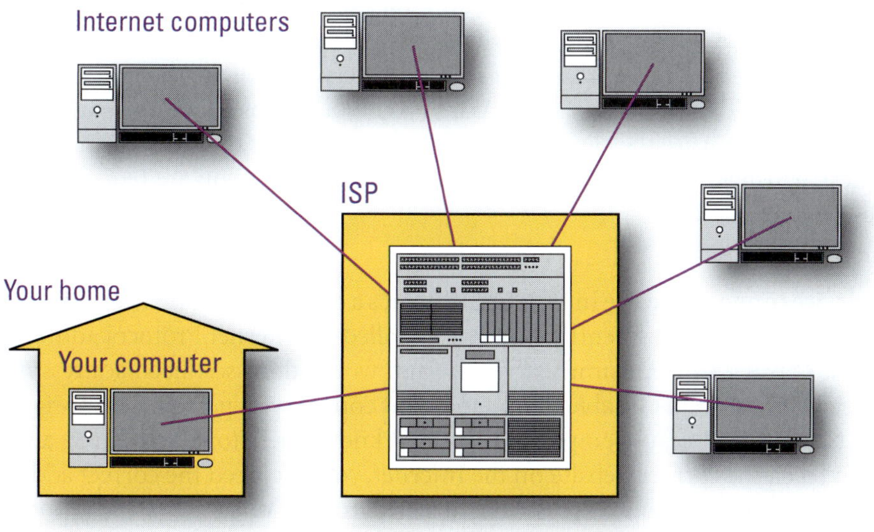

FIGURE 3-2 You access the Internet through an ISP.

Large communications companies have their own dedicated backbones. **Backbones** are high-speed communication lines that carry vast amounts of information. You may hear the term T1 line or T3 line associated with backbones; these are just different types of lines that run at different speeds. Many large companies operate their own high-capacity backbones, which connect in different regions. In each region, a communications company has a point of presence (POP). The POP is a place for local users to access the company's network. The POP then connects to high-level networks that connect to each other through network access points (NAPs), as shown in FIGURE 3-3.

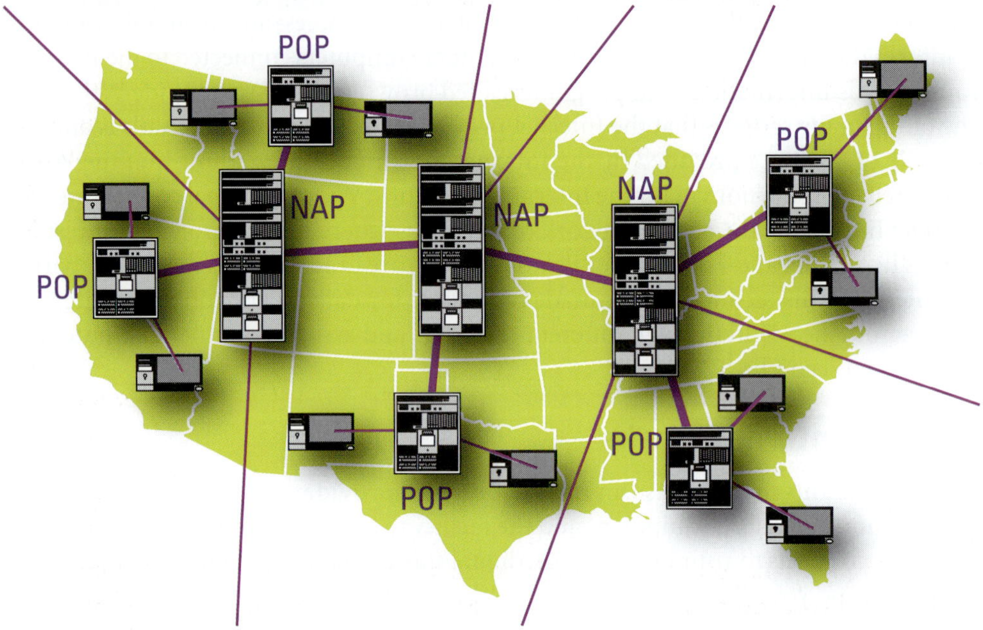

FIGURE 3-3 POPs and NAPs.

You will often hear the term "router" when discussing the Internet. **Internet routers** are computers that determine the path that the data on the Internet takes from one point to another. A router's basic job is to make sure that information makes it to the intended destination.

All of the computers on the Internet are either servers or clients. The computers that provide services to other computers are **servers**. The computers that connect to servers are **clients**. There are different kinds of servers associated with the Internet: Web servers, e-mail servers, FTP servers, and so on. When you type a website address in a browser on your computer, you are the client. The address is sent across the Internet in the form of a request, which you will learn about shortly. The computer you are requesting it from is the Web server.

Internet Protocol (IP) Addresses

Each device connected to the Internet, whether it's a computer or other communications equipment, has a unique identifying number called an Internet Protocol address, or **IP address**. This is a concept similar to home and work addresses. Each address must be unique, or you wouldn't be able to find the right company or person. The postal system would break down because employees wouldn't know where to deliver letters and packages. To reach the correct website on the Internet, you also need the correct address.

Current IP addresses are expressed in Internet Protocol version 4 (IPv4) format, which looks like 209.191.122.70. There are about 4.3 billion unique IP addresses. However, as the Internet continues to grow, eventually all those numbers will be assigned. In fact, we're almost to that point now. For new computers and devices to access the Internet, more numbers must be added to handle the additional capacity. Internet Protocol version 6 (IPv6) is the solution. It provides 3.4×1038 addresses, which is 340 trillion, 282 billion, 366 million, 920 thousand, 938 followed by 24 zeroes! With IPv6 coming on the scene, the world will never run out of IP addresses.

Domain Name System (DNS) is a system that converts text names to IP addresses automatically. This way you only need to know something like *www.yahoo.com* instead of a numbered IP address that is difficult to remember and doesn't have much meaning. Behind the scenes, DNS servers work hard as translators, turning uniform resource locators (URLs) into IP addresses to deliver webpages to your browser.

Uniform Resource Locators (URLs) and Domains

A **uniform resource locator (URL)** is the address of the website you are trying to access. When you get on the Web or send an e-mail message, you use a **domain name** to do it. For example, the URL *http://www.yahoo.com* contains the domain name *yahoo.com.* So does this e-mail address: *anyname@yahoo.com*. When you use a domain name, you use the Internet's DNS servers to translate the human-readable domain name into the machine-readable IP address.

Top-level domain names, also called first-level domain names, include .com, .org, .net, .edu, .gov, .cc, and .biz. These are the last three characters—or two characters in the case of .cc—of a URL. If you're creating a website, you can request the one you want, but top-level domain names are usually assigned based on the type of organization you have.

A second-level domain is the portion of a URL that identifies the specific and unique administrative owner associated with the Web address. Every name in the .com top-level domain must be unique. The left-most word, such as www, is the host name. It pinpoints the name of a specific machine (with a specific Web address) in a domain. A given domain can, potentially, contain millions of host names as long as they are all unique within that domain. For example, in *www.yahoo.com*, yahoo is the second-level domain name.

HTTP stands for Hypertext Transfer Protocol. This is the protocol that transfers data over the World Wide Web. That's why website addresses begin with *http://*. Whenever you type a URL into your browser and press the Enter key, your computer sends an HTTP request to the appropriate Web server. The Web server, which is designed to handle HTTP requests, then sends you the requested Hypertext Markup Language (HTML) webpage. **FIGURE 3-4** shows the parts of a URL.

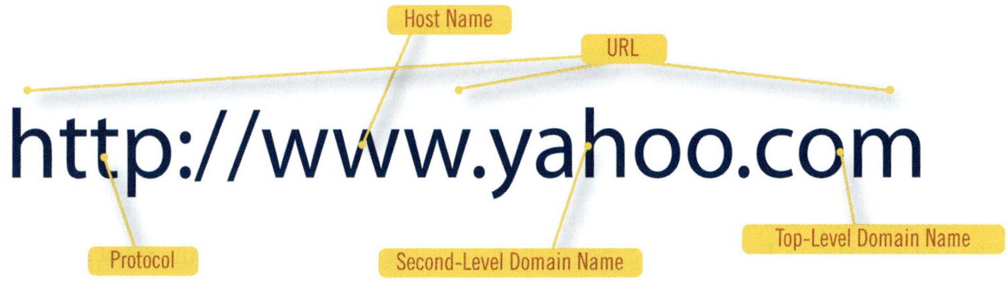

FIGURE 3-4 The parts of a URL.

Connecting to the Internet

Most computers are ready for an Internet connection right out of the box. But you need more than just a computer to access the Internet. At the very least, you need:

- A computer
- A modem (this can be a high-speed modem installed by a telephone or cable

company, a mobile broadband modem that works with your laptop computer, or a dial-up modem that connects to a standard telephone line)
- An Internet service provider account

Connections

You have many ways to connect to the Internet, and each one has different speed, capacity, or cost benefits. You read about communications devices and connections in Chapter 1, so here's a quick refresher on some of the most common ways to connect to the Internet today:

- **Broadband:** This requires a type of modem, but the connection may come from a telephone company or cable company. Broadband speeds exceed 256 kilobits per second (Kbps), which means 256 kilobits of data are transmitted per second. However, it's common for ISPs to offer speeds of 10 megabits per second (Mbps) and higher. That's much faster—1 megabit equals 1,000 kilobits.
- **Wireless:** Internet users can connect to the Internet without wires or cables using a variety of devices, including desktop and laptop computers as well as mobile devices, such as cell phones. Speeds vary widely based on a number of conditions, but wireless enables users to connect anytime, anywhere.
- **Satellite:** Just as satellite providers deliver television services, they can also supply Internet services. Satellite Internet services are common in areas where wired Internet connections are unavailable. Speeds are faster than dial-up yet slower than broadband.
- **Dial-up:** This requires an ordinary modem and a standard telephone line. Speed is limited to 56 Kbps. You have to actively connect to the Internet; it is not "always on" as broadband, home or office wireless, and satellite are.

Equipment

The basic equipment you need to connect to the Internet is a computer with a network card and some type of modem. Most computers come with a network card already installed, but if your computer doesn't have one, you can purchase one separately. You can also buy a mobile broadband modem or air card if you want to get Internet service through your cell phone service provider.

To connect more than one computer to your Internet connection at home or work, you also need a router, which allows you to share one connection with all your computers. Some routers share an Internet connection by plugging in with a network cable as well as with a wireless signal. If you plan to access the Internet wirelessly, choose a wireless router, and make sure your computers have a wireless network card. Most laptops come with wireless networking features while desktops typically connect via a network cable.

> **Note**
>
> Some mobile broadband providers offer portable routers. They look like flat squares that can fit in a shirt pocket. With a mobile router, you become your own hotspot when you're out and about. The mobile router works much like a wireless router at home or in the office, but the mobile router uses your cell phone provider's service for Internet access.

ISP Account

Just as cable TV requires a subscription to access its content, you must subscribe to an Internet service provider to access the Internet. Countless ISPs offer a variety of ways to get onto the Internet. For example, many ISPs offer different speeds at different prices. The lowest speed is the least expensive, whereas the highest speed is the most expensive. Research the options available in your area, including price and service, to find a plan that works for you.

Browser

A **browser** is a client program that accesses files from a Web server. When your computer is connected to the Internet, you use a program called a browser to view websites. You can also do online banking, chat with others, and more. A website is a file(s) on some remote server that displays information about a given topic, a company, a business, an organization, or an individual.

Microsoft Internet Explorer 8

Internet Explorer is the most popular Web browser, and it comes pre-installed on PCs that run the Windows operating system. The latest version, Internet Explorer 8, features several new privacy, security, and compatibility features to speed up, enhance, and protect your browsing experience.

Some of the best features of Internet Explorer include:

- **Tabbed browsing:** This feature allows you to keep all your favorite websites open within one Internet Explorer window, as shown in FIGURE 3-5. You can switch between websites you've already opened by clicking the tab for the website you

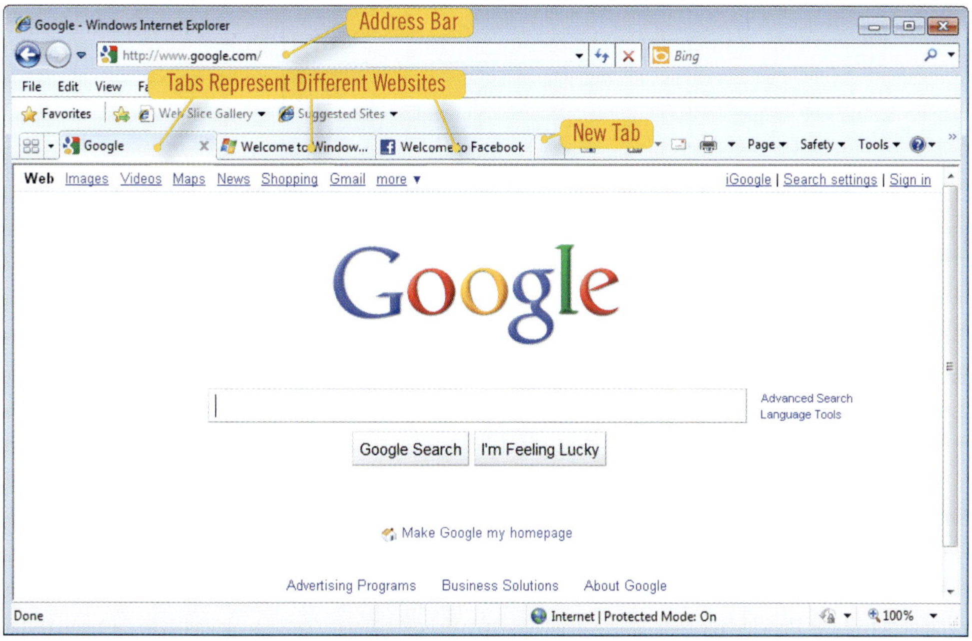

FIGURE 3-5 Tabbed browsing in Internet Explorer.

  want. To open a new tab, click the New Tab tab or press Ctrl+T. Type a new URL into the address bar on any open tab to view another website—each tab behaves as if it is its own browser window.
- **Pop-up Blocker:** Internet Explorer automatically prevents pesky pop-up windows from appearing. Advertisers usually create these small browser windows, which appear when you first load a website. Sometimes they're malicious, sometimes not. They are annoying and intrusive, so Internet Explorer prevents them from opening.
- **SmartScreen Filter:** This feature detects threats on websites and prevents them from running. If Internet Explorer 8 detects a malicious website, it blocks the entire site. It can also block malicious portions of a legitimate website without affecting the rest of it.
- **InPrivate Browsing:** This prevents Internet Explorer from storing personal information and browsing history. This feature provides peace of mind for people surfing the Web from a shared computer—at a library, an Internet café, or a friend's house. To activate InPrivate Browsing, click the Safety button in the upper-right area of Internet Explorer, and then select InPrivate Browsing.

You can change a variety of options for safety, security, and default behaviors in Internet Explorer by selecting Tools > Internet Options. The Internet Options dialog box (a dialog box is a small window), shown in FIGURE 3-6, has tabs that allow you to customize your Web browsing experience.

TIP

Find out if the ISPs in your area will let you test-drive their services for two to four weeks without committing to a long-term plan. Once you sign up for a service plan, however, you can adjust it over time to better meet your needs. That means if you initially selected a somewhat slow access speed to save money, but found you need a faster connection after using it awhile, you can usually change your plan without penalty. You will have to pay the higher service plan cost for the faster connection.

Note

Web surfing is the act of viewing websites on the Internet.

Note

In Internet terms, "malicious" means dangerous. It applies to viruses, worms, spyware, and more. You'll learn how to stay safe on the Internet later in the chapter. A pop-up blocker is one of many ways to prevent malicious stuff from invading your computer.

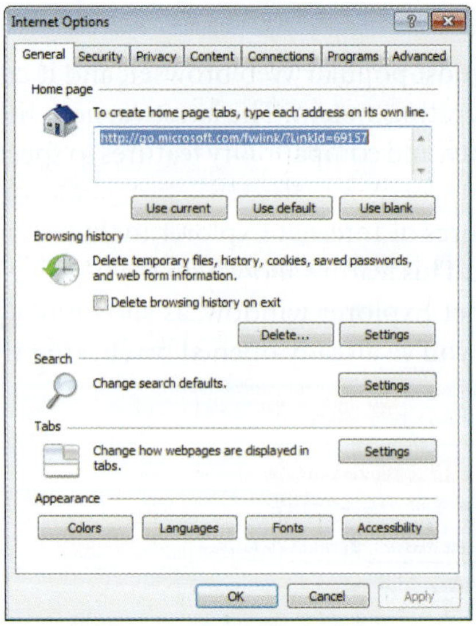

FIGURE 3-6 Internet Options dialog box.

Other Popular Browsers

A number of other Web browsers are available, each with its own set of benefits and features. Three of the most popular Web browsers currently available are:

- **Mozilla Firefox:** You can download the Firefox browser at *http://www.mozilla.com/firefox*. It's free, and like most Web browsers today, add-ons are available to customize how the browser looks, feels, and behaves.
- **Google Chrome:** Available for download at *http://www.google.com/chrome*, Google's Web browser has a minimal look and feel, as well as customizable features.
- **Opera:** Find this fast, easy-to-use browser at *http://www.opera.com*. Opera also has versions of its popular Web browser for a variety of mobile devices.

Websites

Websites are probably the most important things available on the Internet. A website is made up of one or more files (usually many files) and allows a business or an individual to provide information and services to the general public. People access a website based on whatever their needs may be. For example, your bank may have a website that allows you to view your bank account and perform different types of banking transactions. This is an example of a website that not only provides information but also services. On the other hand, if you visit research-related websites, they usually provide information only. You can even create a personal website that displays information about yourself.

To access any website, you need the site's address, called a URL. You learned about URLs earlier in this chapter. A URL looks like *http://www.yahoo.com*. Once you know the address of the website you want to access (the URL), just open your browser, type the URL in the address bar, and press the Enter key or click the Go button. When your browser finds the website, it displays it on your computer. The first page you see on most websites is usually called the **home page**.

A typical website has multiple pages. That is, when you access the initial page, it contains links to other pages. You can recognize a **link** because it's a word, phrase, or some type of image that is highlighted in some way. Text is usually underlined and/or in a different color than the body text of the rest of the webpage. Also, when your mouse passes over a link, the mouse pointer changes shape (most often to a hand).

Search Engines

A **search engine** is a program designed to find information on the Internet. Three of the most popular search engines are Google, Bing, and Yahoo. When you already know a website's URL, you simply type it into the address bar to access the website. On the other hand, if you don't already know the URL, use one of these search engines to find the information you're looking for. FIGURE 3-7 is an image of the search engine Bing. To access it, type *www.bing.com* in your browser's address bar.

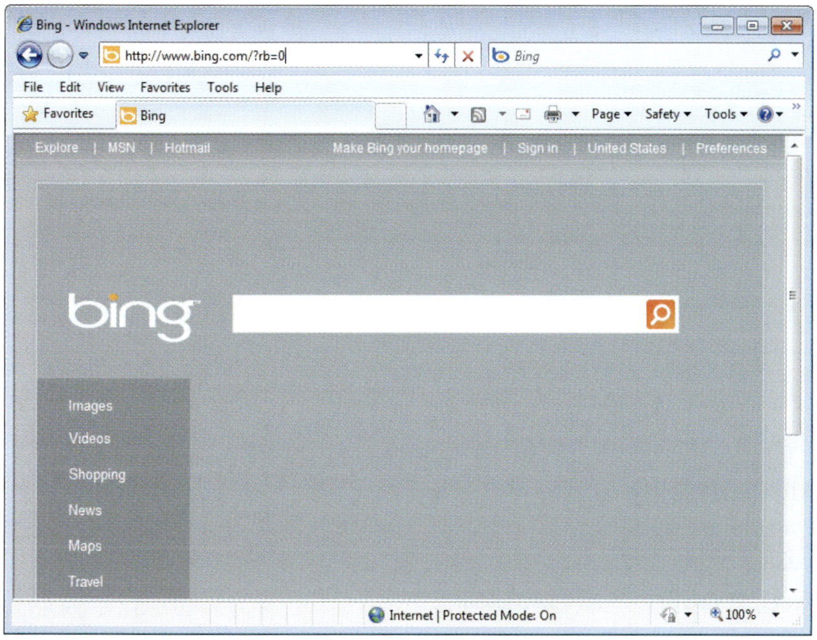

FIGURE 3-7 The Bing search engine site.

Once you access Bing, type your search terms—some words describing whatever it is you're looking for—in the text box. Then press the Enter key or click the search icon to the right. By using the search engine, you can find almost any topic you can dream of. You can also view pictures related to your search terms by clicking the Images link along the window's left side. The search engine will look for related documents and display a page with links to all the documents that meet your criteria, which is known as a results page.

A search engine works by using programs that collect related information that is available anywhere on the Internet. Because there may be thousands of documents per given topic, the search engine collects many of them. When you request a topic, you may get many pages with hundreds or even thousands of links that contain the information you requested.

The hard part is selecting the link that best fits your need; that is, the link to the website that contains the important information you're interested in. For example, if you type "penguins" in the search engine's text box, it will find millions of links that deal with that topic, as shown in FIGURE 3-8. You will then have to select (click) the link you think has the information you need. If you click the wrong one, just go back to the results page and select (click) another link.

Make it easier to find what you're looking for by using more specific search terms. Instead of searching for "penguins," try using more words that describe what you want to learn about, such as "penguin food," "penguin habitat," or "penguin cartoons." Each of those three search terms will display different results. FIGURE 3-9 shows the results for "penguin habitat." You still get more than 1.7 million hits, but the results list focuses on penguin habitat rather than anything else related to penguins.

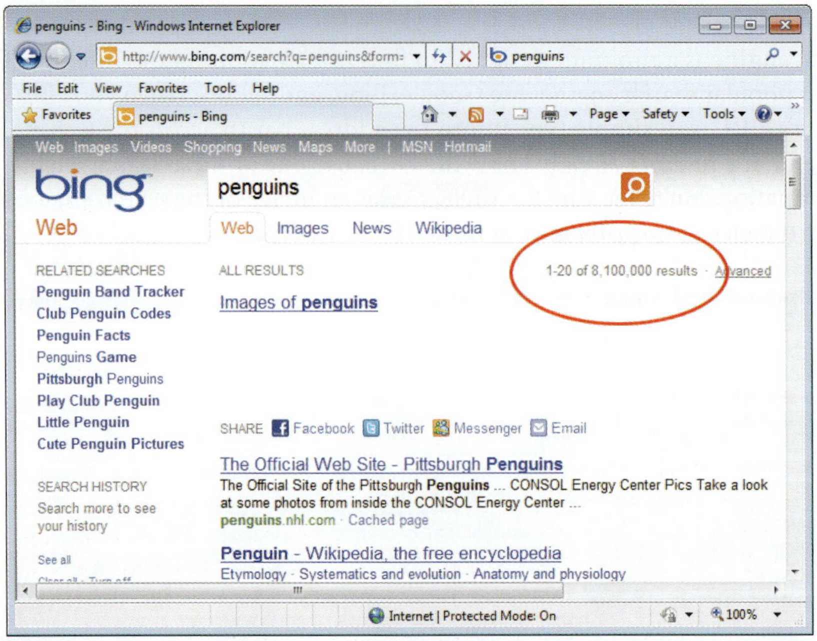

FIGURE 3-8 A search on "penguins" results in more than 8 million hits.

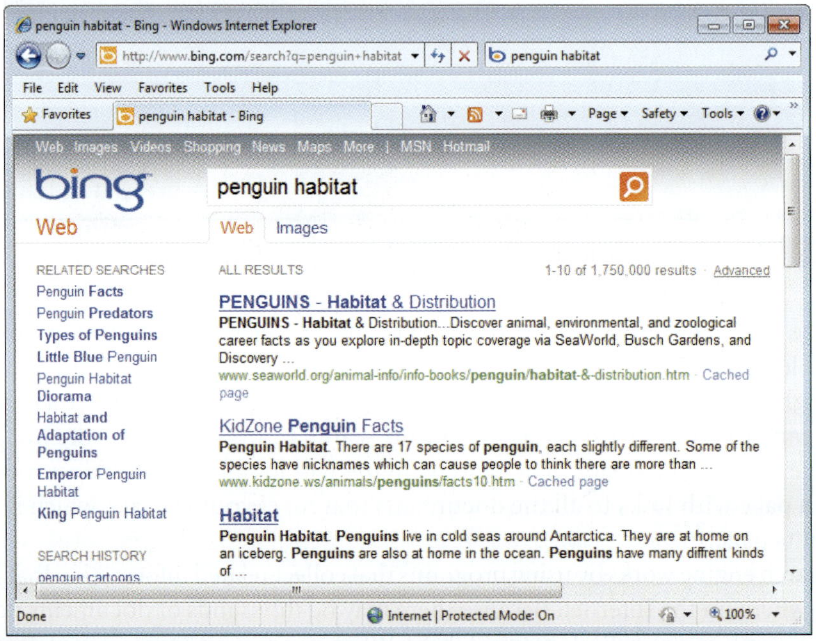

FIGURE 3-9 A search on "penguin habitat" narrows the results, a bit.

To limit the search engine's results, specify additional criteria. For example, if you want information on the rock group The Eagles and you type "eagles" in the search engine's text box, you will get many results on eagles that have nothing to do with the rock group. You will get links to websites that deal with such topics as the American eagle and birds in general. To limit your search to the rock group, type "eagles +rock group." Using the plus sign (+) with more than one search term instructs the browser to find links that relate only to the words as a group.

You can also tell a search engine to exclude one or more terms. Maybe you want to learn about all types of eagles except for Bald eagles. By typing "eagles -bald," you are instructing the search engine to create a results page that will have links about eagles, but only those that don't contain the word "bald."

TECHNICAL TIP

Speed Up Your Search! When you click on one of the many links the search engine found, the page will start loading. If it turns out that you clicked the wrong link or the link did not satisfy your need, click the Back button to return to the previous page. If you use a slow Internet connection, this can be time consuming because you have to wait for the previous page—the search engine results—to load again. You can avoid this by holding the Ctrl key when you click the link. This will open the website on a new tab. If you don't want it, just close the tab, but your search engine results will still be open and available for you to make another selection. You will not have to wait to load the results page again. This is much faster!

TIP

Check out the advanced search options for any search engine you use. You can usually find an Advanced link somewhere close to the search text box in search engines. This narrows searches even more, making your time on the Internet very efficient.

Downloading

Downloading means that you retrieve a file from another computer into yours. This is one of the most important things you can do on the Internet. Why? Because you may need a file, and the fastest way to obtain it is to download it. For example, you might need an updated driver for your scanner, printer, or sound card. The easiest and fastest way to get it is to visit the manufacturer's website and download it. Or maybe you want to save a copy of your daughter's wedding pictures to your computer. FIGURE 3-10 shows you how downloading works.

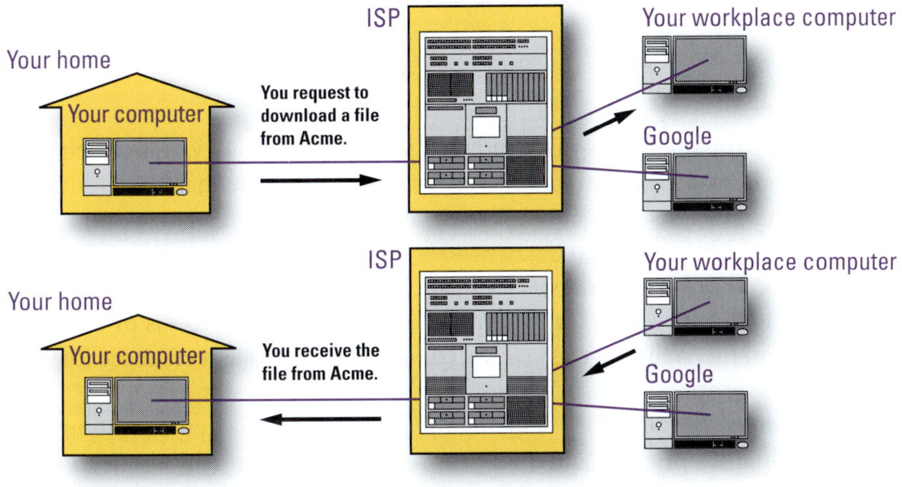

FIGURE 3-10 Downloading.

Uploading

Uploading is the reverse of downloading. Instead of requesting a file, you are sending files from your computer to some other computer. One of the most common uses of uploading is when you want to publish a website. To publish a website means to make it available to anyone on the Internet. When you first create a website, it is only on your computer. To publish one you upload it to a host computer that stays on 24 hours a day, 7 days a week. This way even when you turn your computer off, anyone on the Internet can still see your website because all are viewing it from the host, which is never turned off.

Here are the steps involved:

1. Hire a company to host your website.
2. Create your website on your home computer.
3. Upload your website to the host computer.

Once the website is available on the Internet, all you do is update it by uploading your updates whenever necessary. Good websites are constantly changing to offer new and different content or products; in fact, some companies update their websites every single day to keep the content fresh. FIGURE 3-11 shows how uploading works.

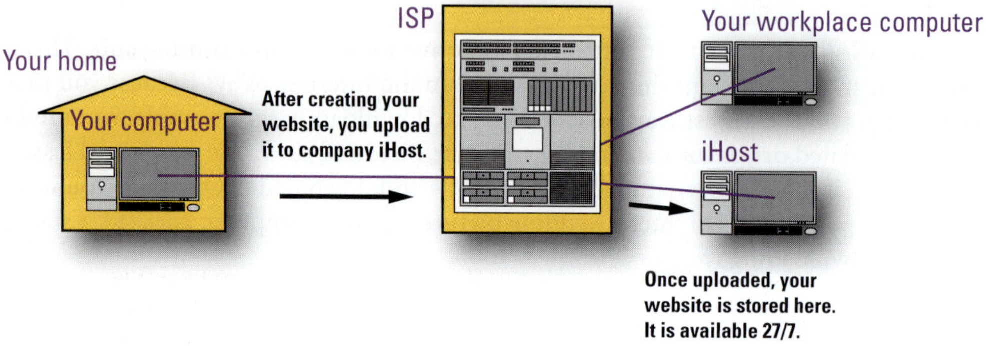

FIGURE 3-11 Uploading.

Websites of Interest to Students

In many ways, the Internet is mankind's information repository. It may help to imagine the Web as a huge decentralized library. Because the Internet has contributors creating and updating websites all over the world, you can find information on just about any subject you could ever think of.

If you need information about cinema in France, forest destruction in South America, or job vacancies in Ireland, for example, all of that information is probably available somewhere on the Web. For this reason, the Web is an excellent resource for students of all ages and education levels.

Increasingly, educators are realizing the potential of this new technology for developing learning resources that are both more interactive and contain more multimedia content than traditional lecture and textbook approaches. By combining video and sound clips with static pictures and text, it is possible to make information both clearer and more interesting to use.

In addition, the use of hypertext on the Web means that documents can be logically linked to one another. Information can therefore be presented in a non-linear format, and material can be linked to other related resources elsewhere on the Internet. The accessibility of the Web increases the potential for distance-learning and asynchronous learning, that is, freeing students to choose their own times and places for study, and to progress through the material at their own rate.

Tens of millions of documents are currently available on the Web, covering a huge range of topics. Some of the most useful for academic users include:

- **Teaching resources:** Lecture notes, interactive tutorials, discussion articles
- **Research:** Project descriptions, databases, conference proceedings, grants
- **Computing:** Software archives, tutorials, manuals, discussions

- **Administration:** Staff lists, course details, minutes of meetings
- **Government:** Legislation, political parties, United Nations, European Union
- **Environment:** Conservation, climate change, wildlife, pollution
- **Career:** Vacancy listings, career agencies, online newspapers
- **Travel:** Tourist guides, accommodation, timetables, weather
- **Culture:** Art galleries, music, cinema, literature, religion
- **Recreation:** Sport, recipes, TV listings, magazines

Of particular interest to students is the EBSCOhost Electronic Journals Service (EJS), located on the World Wide Web at *http://ejournals.ebsco.com.* It contains links to millions of articles from a wide variety of publishers. Search for journals, tables of contents (TOCs), abstracts, and articles to aid in your research.

A few other helpful reference websites include:

- **RefDesk.com:** Features a large collection of reference materials that are great for finding and checking facts. The address is *http://www.refdesk.com.*
- **ipl2 (The Internet Public Library):** An online library with free, electronic versions of dictionaries, encyclopedias, books, magazines, and newspapers. The address is *http://www.ipl.org.*
- **Encyclopedia.com:** Hosts a variety of high-quality encyclopedias, as well as dictionaries and thesauruses. The address is *http://www.encyclopedia.com.*

As you can see, the Internet is great for research, with literally billions of websites out there. Publishers of dictionaries, encyclopedias, textbooks, magazines, and more all have websites that can help you and your family research far beyond the printed materials available in a school or public library. By using the search engine skills you learned earlier in the chapter, you can use targeted search terms to find even more educational resources on the Web.

Web 2.0 and Social Media

When the Internet's popularity began to rise in the late 1990s, most websites were static. In other words, a website might contain text or pictures, but interactivity had not yet taken root. As the Internet has evolved, more and more websites now feature applications that ease collaboration or other ways for users to interact with a site, such as viewing video, downloading music, or commenting in a public forum.

The term **Web 2.0**, which is the Web you know now, is associated with websites that allow you to do more than just view information. These sites were built with participation in mind. They let you add value to a website—essentially, to enter into a type of conversation with a site's owners. Many websites offer forums that permit you to comment on a news story, or make product suggestions, for example.

Social media is an extremely popular evolution of the Web 2.0 experience. Social media websites connect friends, relatives, employees, and colleagues. They are an electronic way to stay in touch. They are tools for sharing and conversing with many people at once. By creating accounts on social media sites and connecting with others, you'll have a way to keep all your contacts up to date on your personal and/or professional life.

For example, say you've just gone on vacation. Instead of e-mailing your pictures to 10 friends and family members, add those pictures to a social media website where all your friends and family can see them and comment on them, all in one place. Many companies are using social media to communicate to customers and non-customers alike; it's often seen as a friendlier and more organic way to reach people.

Social Media Sites and Services

Each of the many social media websites and services available has its own focus or niche. For example, some social media websites focus on connecting friends and family, while others focus on professional networking. You might want to create accounts on more than one site depending on what you want to get out of social networking.

A number of topic-specific social networking websites are out there, too. There are sites dedicated to wine lovers, athletes, collectors, and more. Try typing one of your interests into a search engine to see if there are any social networking websites dedicated to your favorite hobby.

Facebook

Launched in 2004, Facebook is so popular it is currently the most used social network worldwide. When you have a free Facebook account, you add not only people but also entities (companies, musical groups, fan clubs, etc.) to your list of friends. You can notify your list about yourself, by posting notes, pictures, or links to other websites. You can also read the notifications of those on your list as well as comment on them.

Facebook offers an embedded instant messaging program to chat with your friends in real time. You can join many networks within Facebook, such as for regional areas, alumni, and professional organizations. Applications also run within Facebook; you can play games with your friends or share reviews of your favorite books and music.

Most modern cell phones have Facebook applications so you don't need to be tethered to a computer for access. Once you have a Facebook account, you can open it from any Internet-enabled device to start sharing.

MySpace

MySpace began in 2002. By 2006, it was the most popular social networking website on the Web. While Facebook has surpassed it in popularity since then, MySpace still draws in millions of visitors.

With a MySpace account, you connect to friends, family, colleagues, musical groups, or companies to see their latest notifications. You can also add blog entries, photo albums, and post links to other websites to share with your friends list.

Twitter

Twitter is one of the first, as well as the most popular, forms of microblogging. You'll learn more about blogs later in this chapter, but for now all you need to know is that a blog is a way to publicly share your opinions or observations. Microblogging is essentially a tiny blog entry consisting of no more than 140 characters. The main Twitter webpage is shown in FIGURE 3-12.

Like other social networking websites, you create a Twitter account and connect to others by sharing Twitter messages, which are known as "tweets." Twitter users often reply to each other's tweets, which can be public or private messages.

Many other social networking websites, such as Facebook and MySpace, have features that allow you to publish your tweets as your status. Because tweets must be 140 characters or less, it's convenient to use Twitter with a cell phone or other mobile device. You can choose from dozens of other ways to publish to Twitter as well, including Web browser add-ons, sidebar gadgets, and stand-alone programs.

Twitter is flexible in that it can deliver content to a cell phone just as easily as to a Web browser, a Facebook page, or a desktop program.

Classmates.com

Classmates.com is a social networking website focused on helping you reconnect with your school friends. Although other social networking websites also allow you to search for people by school and year, Classmates.com includes reunions and other helpful student and alumni information.

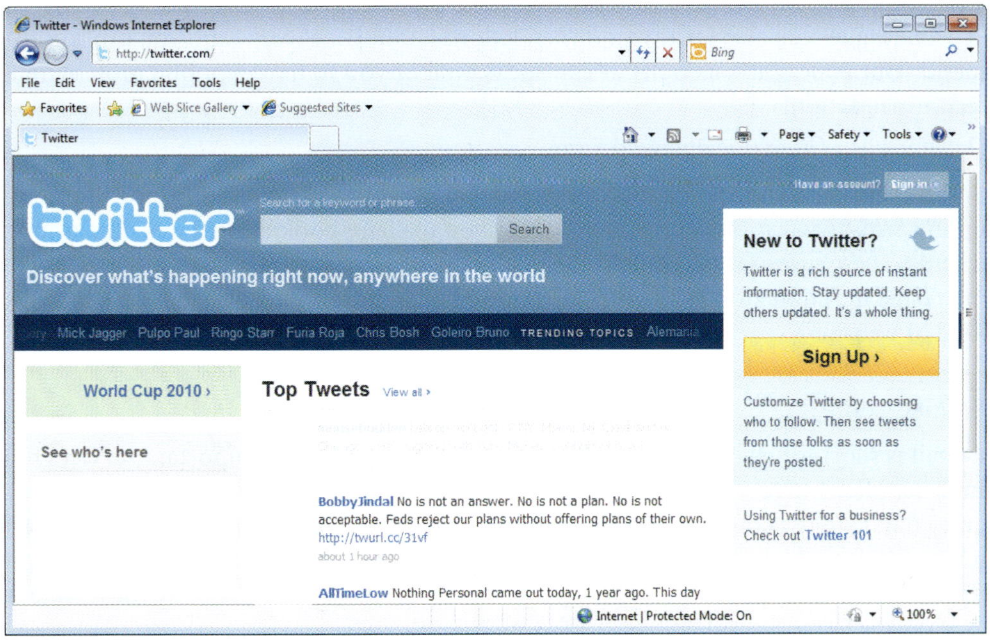

FIGURE 3-12 The main Twitter webpage.

LinkedIn

If you're more interested in professional networking than catching up with your friends, LinkedIn is the most popular business-oriented social networking website. The main LinkedIn webpage is shown in **FIGURE 3-13**.

On LinkedIn, you basically create an online resume. You can connect with former colleagues to keep up with their professional status. LinkedIn is a valuable tool for job-seekers; when you search for a job, the site can help locate your professional contacts who

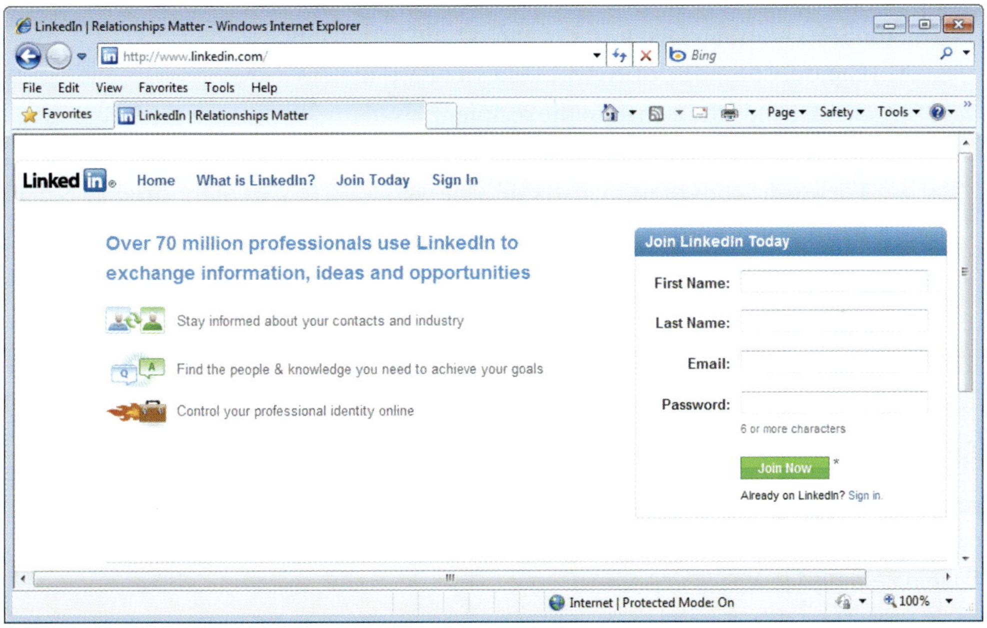

FIGURE 3-13 The main LinkedIn webpage.

may be able to make introductions to get you in the door. Professionals connect to give and receive advice on a wide variety of business topics.

Colleagues can also write recommendations about your work (and you can recommend your colleagues, as well). It can speak well of you to have a public professional recommendation!

Delicious and Other Bookmarking Sites

So-called social bookmarking sites, such as delicious (*http://delicious.com*) and Stumbleupon (*http://www.stumbleupon.com*), allow you to share bookmarked websites among friends. These sites are also good for browsing the Web for sites related to subjects you're interested in. Think of it as "if you like this kind of website, you'll probably also like this kind of website."

E-mail

E-mail is short for electronic mail. It's probably one of the most important services the Internet offers. It's certainly popular—more than 240 billion e-mail messages are sent every day. E-mail allows you to send files (usually text messages but not limited to text) to anyone else who has an e-mail address, in seconds, anywhere in the world. When you mail a letter via the post office, you have to wait at least a day or two before the recipient receives the letter. E-mail takes just a few moments.

With e-mail, not only can you send text messages to someone else, but along with the text message you can send other files, called attachments. An **attachment** is simply a file that the recipient receives at the same time with the text message. You will learn more about attachments shortly.

To e-mail someone or receive e-mail, you run an e-mail program on your computer, such as **Microsoft Outlook**. You can also use a Web-based e-mail service, such as **Microsoft Hotmail**. Different e-mail programs vary in the way they look, but they all have similar features. Most of them provide the following:

- **Inbox folder:** New messages appear in the inbox.
- **Sent items folder:** A copy of each sent e-mail is located in the Sent items folder.
- **Deleted items folder:** E-mail messages you delete sit in the Deleted items folder.
- **Menu bar:** This lets you select many different options.
- **Toolbar:** It displays icons to execute certain actions such as:
  - **Create, Compose, or New:** Creates a new e-mail message
  - **Send:** Sends the e-mail to the recipient
  - **Reply:** Sends a reply to the sender
  - **Forward:** Sends the e-mail to someone who wasn't a part of the original e-mail
  - **Print:** Prints the e-mail message to a printer
- **Address book:** It keeps track of all your e-mail addresses, plus many other features.

> **TIP**
>
> If you're using a shared computer, for security purposes, don't select the Remember Me or Remember My Password checkbox when logging on to Windows Live.

Using Hotmail

You learned how to set up a Hotmail account in Chapter 1 and send an e-mail message. Now that your Hotmail account is working, let's see how to read e-mail messages. This section will revisit how to create a new e-mail in Hotmail (as a refresher) but add an attachment this time.

To get started, open a Web browser and go to *http://www.hotmail.com*. Sign in using your Windows Live ID and password. On the main screen, click the Inbox link in the left pane. Your Hotmail inbox will appear, as shown in FIGURE 3-14.

Reading E-mail Messages in Hotmail

Reading e-mail messages in Hotmail is similar to reading e-mail messages in any other e-mail program. Hotmail displays a list of your e-mail messages in the middle pane.

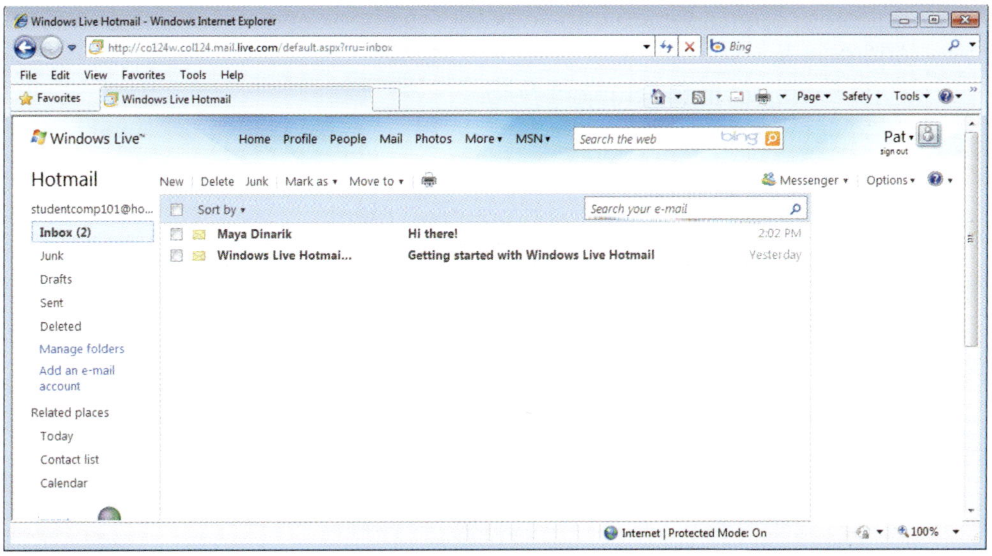

FIGURE 3-14 The Hotmail inbox.

Hotmail makes it easy to see which of your new messages you haven't read by displaying them in a bold font.

Clicking an e-mail message displays the entire message within your browser, as shown in FIGURE 3-15.

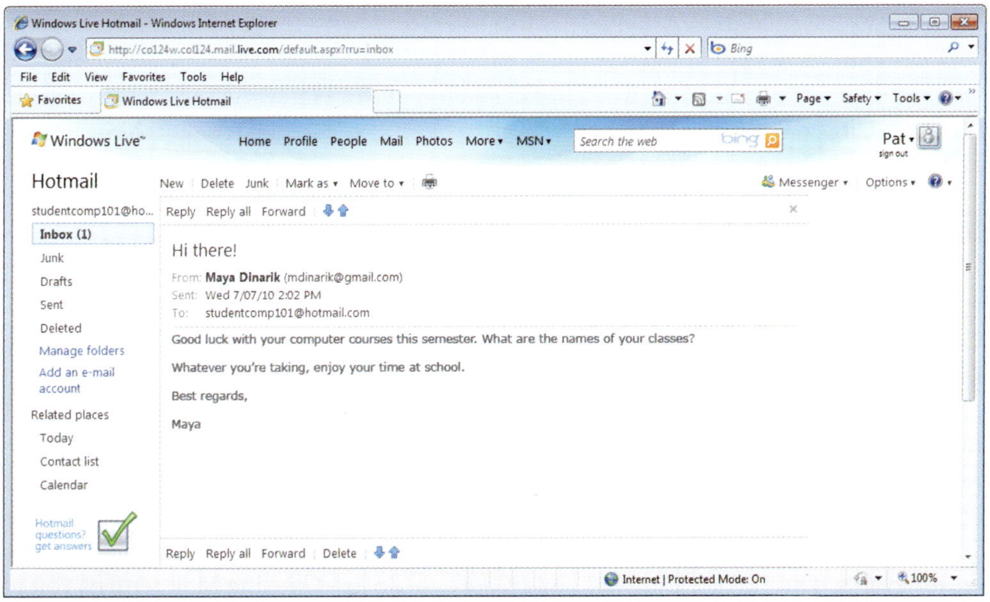

FIGURE 3-15 Reading an e-mail in Hotmail.

Composing a New E-Mail Message in Hotmail and Adding an Attachment

Now let's see how to send an e-mail to someone, with an attachment. An attachment is a file(s) that you send along with your text in the same e-mail message. For example, you have a picture you would like to send to your relatives who live across the country. Or perhaps you want to submit an assignment to your instructor.

To create an e-mail in Hotmail and add an attachment, follow these steps:

1. Click the New link at the top of the page.
2. Type the recipient's e-mail address in the To field. If you've already entered e-mail addresses in the Hotmail address book, just click the To

button to open a window to your address book and select one or more addresses.

3. Type a subject in the Subject field.
4. Type your message.
5. Click the Attach link.
6. Select File or Photo from the drop-down menu.
7. Navigate to the folder that contains the file or photo to attach, and select the file name. Click Upload Now. The file will be attached to the e-mail message, as shown in FIGURE 3-16.
8. Click Send.

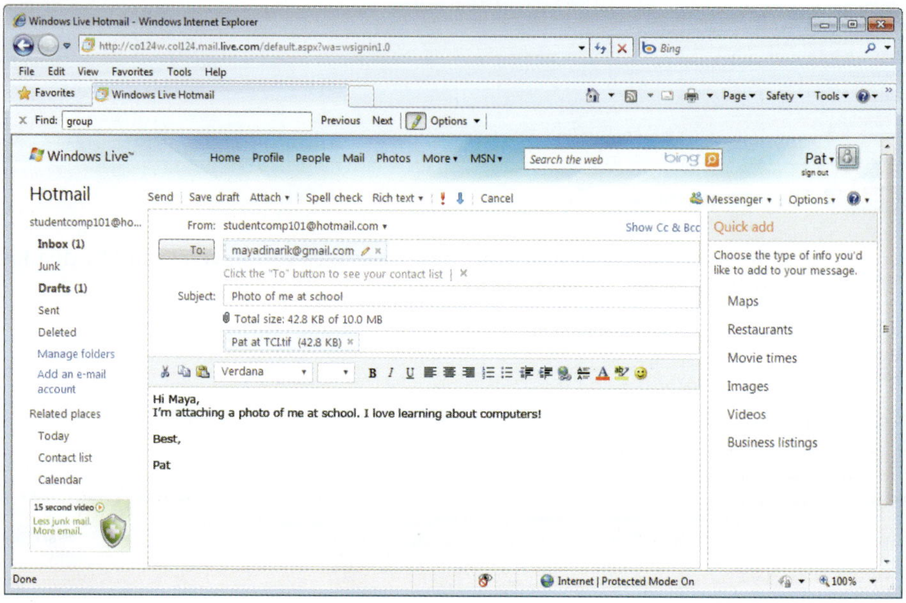

FIGURE 3-16 An attached file in Hotmail.

Using Microsoft Outlook 2010

Outlook 2010 is a popular e-mail program currently used in many businesses and homes. Many of the Outlook commands are located across the Ribbon, which is a feature found in all Office 2010 programs. FIGURE 3-17 shows the main Outlook 2010 window. Some of the important items to notice are the Inbox, Sent Items, and Deleted Items folders. You read about them in the previous list. Also notice the Mail, Contacts, Calendar, and Tasks buttons in the lower-left part of the window. The Contacts feature lets you add people to your address book. The Calendar helps you keep track of appointments and set reminders for events. The Tasks feature lets you create a to-do list. Clicking Mail returns you to the default Mail view, if you decided to work in the Contacts, Calendar, or Tasks panels.

As you use the program more and more, you will learn many of its features. For now, let's find out how to read messages in the Inbox, use the Contacts feature, create and send messages, and then use the Calendar. To get started, open Microsoft Outlook 2010:

1. In Windows 7, click the Start button in the lower-left corner of the desktop window.
2. Select All Programs > Microsoft Outlook > Microsoft Outlook 2010.

Reading E-mail Messages in Outlook

To read a new e-mail message, click the Inbox folder in the left pane. You will see your incoming e-mail in the middle pane, and a preview of the highlighted message in the right pane, as shown in FIGURE 3-18.

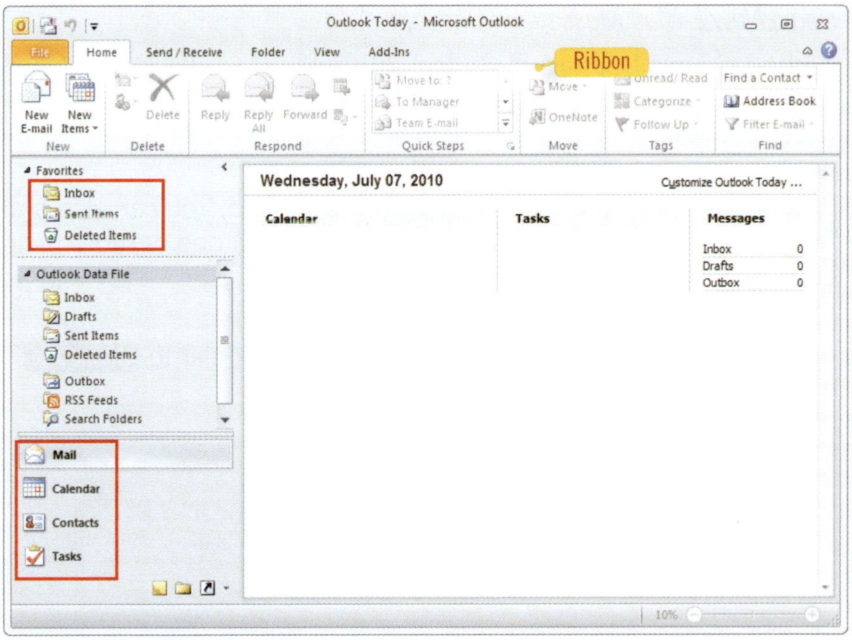

FIGURE 3-17 The Outlook 2010 window.

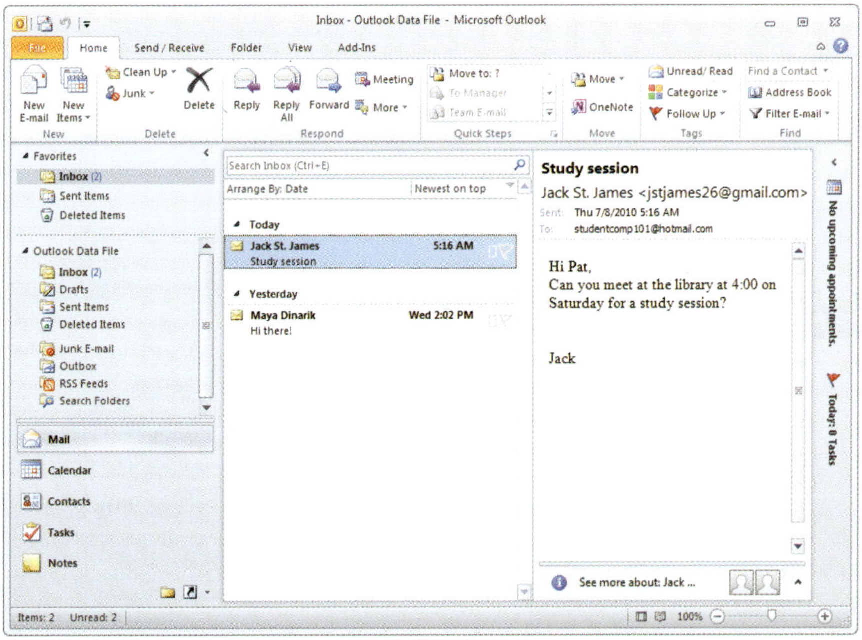

FIGURE 3-18 The Outlook 2010 inbox.

When you highlight a message (click it), Outlook previews it in the right pane. You can read it in the preview pane, or double-click the e-mail message to open it in its own window. When you finish reading it, simply close it. If you don't want to save it for later, click the Delete button on the toolbar at the top of the e-mail message.

Using Outlook Contacts

Within Outlook is an address book. Access it by clicking the Contacts link in the left pane. There, you can add contact information for your personal and business contacts. Your company may also have its own address book containing employee contact information.

The Contacts feature is a handy way to keep everything in one place, and makes it easier to send e-mail messages. When you start typing a contact's name into the To field of an e-mail message, Outlook will complete the field automatically.

Composing a New E-Mail Message in Outlook

To compose a new e-mail message in Outlook 2010 and add an attachment, follow these steps:

1. On the toolbar, click the New E-mail icon on the Ribbon. A blank e-mail window appears, as shown in FIGURE 3-19.
2. Type the recipient's e-mail address in the To field. You can also click the To button to access the address book and select one or more recipients.
3. Type a subject in the Subject field.
4. Type your message. The window should look similar to FIGURE 3-20.
5. Click the Send button.

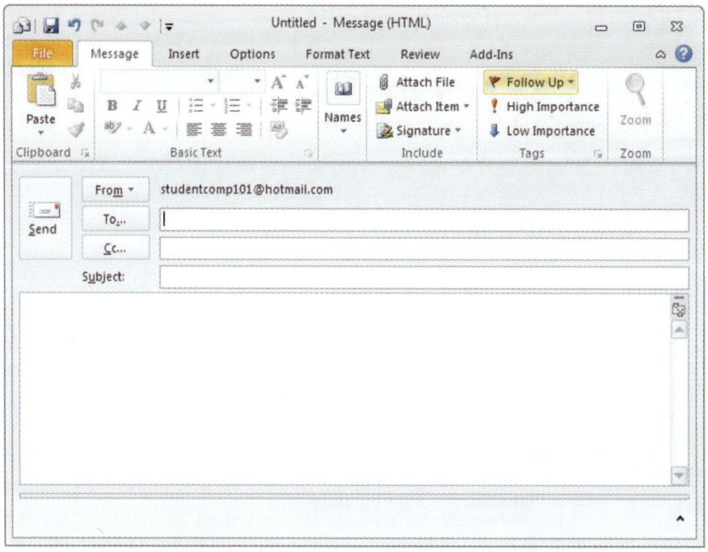

FIGURE 3-19 A blank message window.

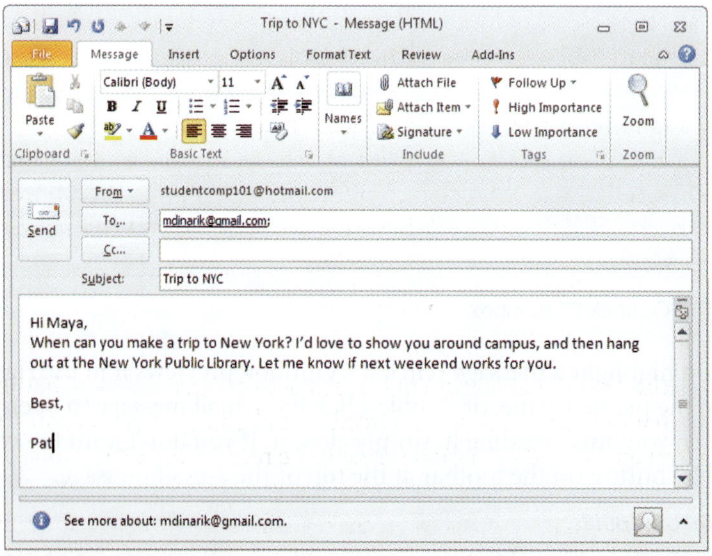

FIGURE 3-20 A message that's ready to send.

That was easy! To add an attachment, such as a file or photo, click Attach File on the Ribbon, navigate to the folder that contains the file or photo to attach, and double-click the file name. The file will be attached to the e-mail message. Click Send as usual.

Using the Outlook Calendar

Another of Outlook's productivity features is the Calendar, shown in FIGURE 3-21. Open it by clicking the Calendar link in the left pane. In the Calendar, you can schedule all your meetings and appointments, and you can even invite others to join by sending a meeting request. Your school group or department may have a shared calendar, and you can also request permission to view others' calendars.

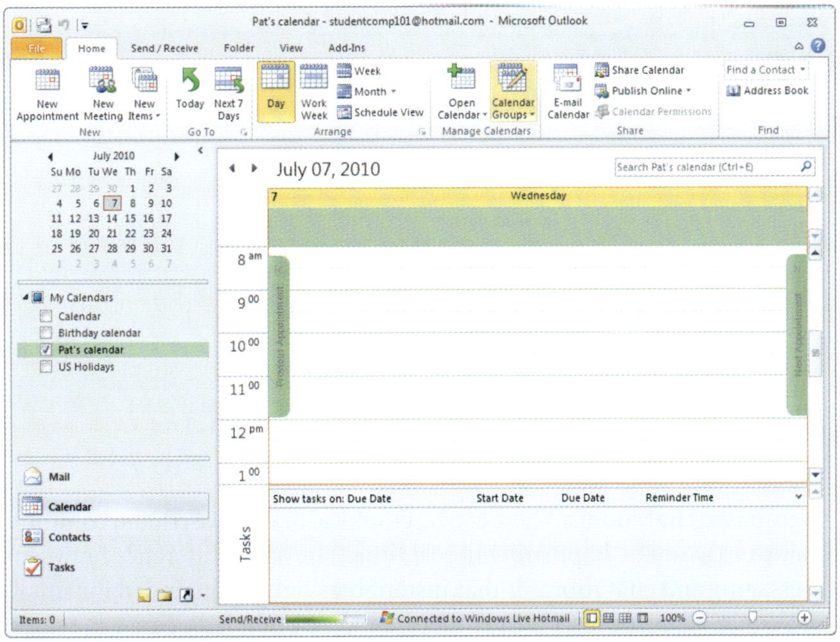

FIGURE 3-21 The Outlook Calendar.

Consolidating All E-Mail Accounts in Outlook

If you have more than one e-mail address, you can have new messages from all those accounts delivered into your Outlook inbox. Add a new account to Outlook by clicking the File tab on the Ribbon, and then click the Add Account button under Account Information, as shown in FIGURE 3-22. Type the requested information into the text fields, and Outlook will add it to a list of your e-mail accounts.

When adding a Hotmail account, you may be prompted to download and install a "Hotmail connector." Close Outlook, follow the prompts in the Microsoft Outlook Hotmail Connector dialog box, and then reopen Outlook. After that, any mail sent to your Hotmail account will appear in your Outlook inbox.

Chatting

Chatting is a method of talking to someone over a network in real time. Chatting is different from e-mail in that the messages are synchronous, or being sent at the same time. Remember, e-mail is sent and stored on a mail server to be read by the recipient at a later time.

You can chat using three basic methods:

- **Instant messaging:** This is a two-way, real-time chat with anyone anywhere in the world. **Instant messaging** usually takes place with one or more people you know. It's as timely as a telephone conversation and is a great way to communicate with someone when a telephone call might not be appropriate. Many companies also use instant messaging as a collaboration tool. It's easy to get a quick response from a coworker without having to take the time to e-mail or visit in person. Basically, you type something in a chat window and the other person responds.

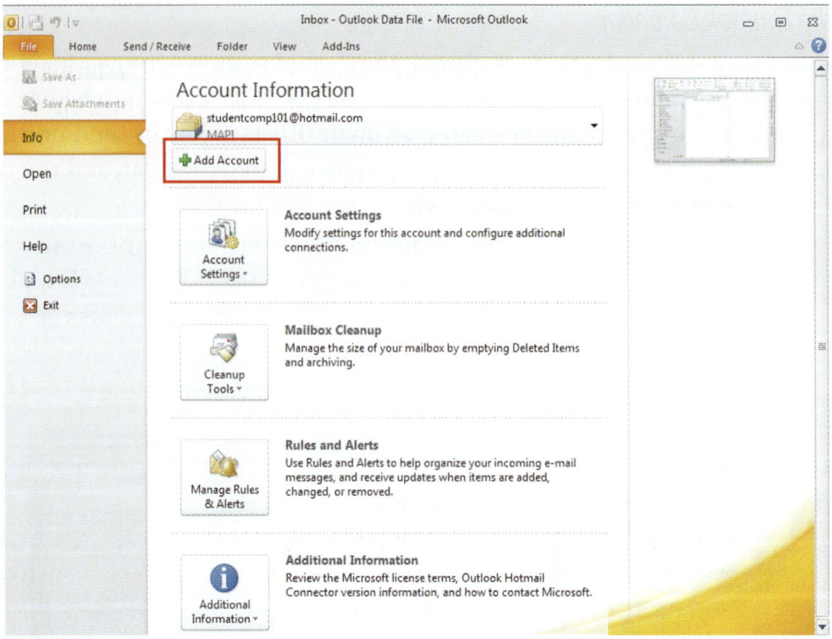

FIGURE 3-22 Adding an e-mail account to Outlook.

- **Web-based chat rooms:** These can be graphical or text-based, and communication may or may not be happening in real time. The main difference between instant messaging and chat rooms is that instant messaging is intended for small groups of people. Chat rooms, on the other hand, are intended primarily for groups of people to discuss a topic that's part of the name of the chat room.
- **Internet Relay Chat (IRC):** IRC is a mature text-based chat technology that allows users to visit existing channels or create their own. It allows people from all over the world to communicate in groups as well as on a one-on-one basis.

Chatting software usually splits your screen into two panels: one for you and the other for whomever you are chatting with. Once you're in the chat room, you introduce yourself and start communicating with someone.

Take these important precautions when chatting online:

- In general, when you're chatting, you don't always know who you're chatting with, so use caution as to how far the chat goes.
- Verify that the information you get is accurate.
- Guard your personal information. Don't give anyone passwords, financial data, or any other private information unless you are absolutely certain you know the person you're chatting with is someone you can trust with that type of material.

Blogs

Blog is short for Web log. A blog is basically a journal meant for the general public, usually representing the views or ideas of the person or company who created it. The idea is to update a blog on a regular basis, so the content is "fresh" and readers are kept up to date. A nice feature of blogs is that they're usually created and updated using software that's very easy to use and provides a professional appearance.

As an example of a blog, a musical group may state its philosophy, musical taste, musical ideas, concert reviews, concert promotions, and so on, in a blog. Fans of the musical group can view the blog to find out related information.

Music

Music on the Internet is available in many ways, including Internet radio stations. Another example is musical groups who maintain websites with biographies, tour information, samples of their music, short video clips, pictures of the bands and their concerts, and fan-based interaction. Other websites let you download music (legally, of course).

Even more important, you can send your friends and family music files via e-mail. This is especially important to musicians. Many years ago, musicians who wanted to share their music with friends and associates had to burn songs to a CD or DVD and send it via a postal service. This would take at least a few days. Now anyone can send music as an MP3 attachment via e-mail or post the files for download on a website. People who want to hear the music have access 24/7.

WAV and MP3 Files

If you're interested in music and the Internet, it's a good idea to know a little bit about two important formats that are in wide use: WAV and MP3.

WAV is short for Waveform Audio Format file. A WAV file is an audio file format created by Microsoft that has become a standard PC audio file format. The file name extension—.wav—identifies a WAV file. Used primarily in PCs, the WAV file format has been accepted as a viable interchange medium for other computer platforms, such as Mac. This allows content developers to freely move audio files between platforms for processing. Usually, when a musical piece is recorded into a computer, it records as a WAV file. The problem with WAV files is that they are usually very large. A simple 3-minute song can be 30 MB in size. This is relatively large, especially when you're thinking about transmitting it on the Internet. Not only can it take a very long time, but most ISPs place a limit on how large a file their customers can send or receive.

MP3 stands for MPEG Layer 3. (MPEG stands for Moving Picture Experts Group.) MP3 is a standard for compressing music files. Compressing means making files smaller in size. As stated before, WAV files are very large. MP3s solve the problem by taking a large WAV file and making it about 10 times smaller. This means that a 30 MB wave file can be reduced to approximately 3 MB! This is really important for transmitting music files on the Internet. Some programs can convert WAV files to MP3 files. Once you have converted a music file to MP3, you can attach it to an e-mail message and send it to anyone.

Entertainment

Entertainment on the Internet takes many forms. Thousands of websites are dedicated to entertainment alone. All you do is open a search engine and type in the name of a show you're interested in, a hobby, a game, or a place you'd like to visit on vacation, for example. The search engine will display many links that let you find what you're looking for. This short list includes entertainment information that's a few clicks away.

- For tickets to movies, show times, and general entertainment news, visit Ticketmaster.com, American Ballet Theatre, Moviefone.com, E! Online, and Broadway.com.
- For information on dining in your area, visit CitySearch.com and MenuPages.com.
- Find vacations and airline tickets, and make travel arrangements at Travelocity, Expedia, Kayak, Orbitz, and many more.
- Websites such as Amazon.com provide many different items you can buy that are a type of entertainment, such as books, music, and movies.
- Play Moonbase Alpha *(http://www.nasa.gov/offices/education/programs/national/ltp/games/moonbasealpha/mbalpha-landing-collection1-overview.html)*, a free NASA game, or find thousands of single-player or multi-player interactive games online.

- Join Internet groups, such as those at Yahoo Groups, on almost any given topic. Once you join, interact with other members, and send and receive information.

The "Down" Side of the Internet: Security Issues

This topic is last because it covers the Internet's negative aspects. As you have read in this chapter, the Internet provides many exciting and rewarding experiences. This section addresses some of the negatives associated with the Internet.

A **virus** is a program designed to interrupt or harm your computer programs and your work. A virus can transmit via the Internet right into your computer. The way to protect yourself against viruses is to install a good commercially available antivirus program. These programs do a good job of alerting you when a virus is present in your computer. If they find a virus, they can usually remove it. Keep your antivirus programs up to date because computer criminals create new viruses all the time. Most antivirus programs update themselves automatically, usually once a day. But you have to be connected to the Internet to receive the updates.

Spyware is software that gathers information about an Internet user, without his or her knowledge. Although spyware is most often used for commercial purposes (targeting you in some way to advertise or sell you a product), attackers may use it for other purposes. It may be software that collects information about your Web surfing habits. Again, you can use commercially available programs to alert you and remove these spyware programs.

Phishing is the act of tricking someone into giving confidential information. It may come in the form of an e-mail message that looks official and requests that you provide sensitive information, such as ID names and passwords. Be very cautious when providing sensitive information to anyone over the Internet.

Spam is the junk mail that fills up your e-mail inbox. Most ISPs today have spam filters installed on their servers, which catch a majority of the messages. Some e-mails will still get through to your account, though. If you use an online service, such as Hotmail, it automatically routes suspicious e-mails to the Junk folder. Microsoft Outlook has a Junk E-mail folder that works the same way.

Every computer should have a firewall enabled, which adds to the computer's overall security. Windows 7 comes with a built-in firewall that's enabled by default. Make sure you leave the firewall on at all times.

Note

Spam filters aren't perfect. Occasionally they place "good" e-mail in a junk folder by mistake. That's why you should browse the list of e-mails in your junk folder, move any messages to the inbox that aren't actually junk, and then delete the rest. Don't open any messages in your junk folder while reviewing the list—the spammers will know you opened the e-mail and send you more!

TIP

Most Internet protection suites have antivirus, antispyware, antispam, antiphishing, and a firewall all in one package. Symantec, McAfee, Kaspersky, and Webroot supply some popular Internet protection suites.

Test Yourself

The questions in this section are meant to test your knowledge of what you read. Make sure you answer them. The page number where the answer can be found appears after each question.

1. The Internet is a global collection of networks. (46)
   A. True
   B. False
2. What does WWW stand for?(47)
3. What does HTTP stand for? (49)
   A. Hyper Terminal Transfer Protocol
   B. Hypertext Transfer Protocol
   C. Hyper Terminal Text Protocol
   D. Hypertext Transport Presence
4. What does ISP stand for? (50)
   A. Internet service provider
   B. Internet service package

C. Internet service protocol
D. Intranet service provider

5. What does URL stand for? (49)
A. Uniform Realtor Location
B. Universal Resource Locator
C. Uniform Resource Locator
D. Universal Resource Location

6. An IP address is a unique ID assigned to your computer. (48)
A. True
B. False

7. What is a server? (48)
A. A computer that provides services to other computers
B. A computer often used from home to connect to the Internet
C. A subscription service you set up on your computer
D. Another name for an ISP

8. What can you do with a Web browser? (50)
A. Visit websites.
B. Perform online banking.
C. Chat with other people.
D. All the above

9. What is a search engine? (53)

10. MySpace and Facebook are the two most popular search engines. (53)
A. True
B. False

11. What is downloading? (55)
A. Retrieving a file from another computer
B. Sending a file to another computer
C. Installing a Web browser
D. Connecting to the Internet through an ISP

12. What is uploading? (55)
A. Retrieving a file from another computer
B. Sending a file to another computer
C. Installing a Web browser
D. Connecting to the Internet through an ISP

13. What is an attachment? (61, 62)

14. You should feel comfortable sharing personal information with anyone you meet on the Internet. (66)
A. True
B. False

15. What music formats are important to know? (Select two). (56)
A. JPG
B. WAV
C. DOC
D. MP3

16. Which is smaller in size, a WAV file or an MP3 file? (56)

17. To create an e-mail in Hotmail, first click the New link. (50)
A. True
B. False

18. The Internet has many practical uses for students. Name a few. (45, 46)

19. What is Facebook? (47)

- **A.** A search engine
- **B.** A class reunion website
- **C.** A social networking website
- **D.** A user guide

20. What is spyware? (57)

End-of-Chapter Project

You need to set up Internet access. Research three providers and keep detailed notes on the services' features and costs.

PART III

The Operating System

CHAPTER 4

Windows 7 Basics

- Every computer needs an operating system to function. This chapter explains how to use Microsoft Windows 7, a very popular operating system for personal computers (PCs). Here are some basic things you should know about operating systems:
  - The operating system is the first program installed on a computer, and the first to load each time the PC starts up. The operating system detects and manages the installed hardware, making sure all the components—such as disk drives, display monitor, keyboard, and mouse—work together smoothly.
  - The operating system also provides a user interface. Through the Windows interface, you can run programs, manage the contents of your drives, and change system settings, such as the color scheme and desktop background.
- Windows 7 also provides extra applications for accomplishing certain tasks. For example, it comes with Windows Media Player, a program that lets you play music and videos, and Internet Explorer, a Web browser. It also includes basic programs for writing, drawing, and backing up files.

CHAPTER TOPICS

This chapter covers the following topics and concepts:

- What the Windows desktop is
- How to size and arrange windows
- How to run programs and switch between them
- How to work with program windows
- What Windows Explorer can help you accomplish
- How to personalize Windows
- Where to get help and support
- How to turn the computer off

KEY WORDS

Address bar
Aero
Aero Peek
Aero Shake
Background
Close button
Command bar
Command button
Dialog box
File
Flip 3D
Folder
Graphical user interface (GUI)
Hibernate
Homegroup
Icon
Jump list
Lock
Log off
Maximize button
Menu bar
Minimize button
Multitasking
Navigation pane
Notification area
Path
Peeking
Pin
Preview pane
Program window
Recycle Bin
Restart
Restore button
Ribbon
Scroll bars
Search box
Shortcut
Shut down
Sleep
Snap
Start button
Start menu
Switch user
Taskbar
Theme
Title bar
Toolbar
Views button
Windows

TIP

On your mouse are at least two buttons: left and right. When this book tells you to click, it means to press and release the left mouse button. A right-click is the same thing except it uses the right mouse button. Left-clicking usually selects something; right-clicking usually opens a menu. The instructions for a mouse apply to a touchpad on a laptop computer as well.

What Is Windows 7?

Windows 7 is the latest operating system from Microsoft Corporation. An operating system is a program that manages the operation of a computer at a very basic level. It provides services that affect your computer's operation. It is the first program installed in a new computer. All other programs are called application programs. Windows 7 is the operating system you are learning in this book.

Microsoft Windows 7 provides a **graphical user interface (GUI)**, so you can interact with graphics, a mouse, and menus rather than having to type commands. You use a mouse to point at, click on, and drag the items you want. Content appears in windows, which you can open, close, and move around on the desktop.

The **desktop** is the main screen that you see when your computer boots up (turns on). When you open up programs, they are displayed in windows overlaid on top of the desktop. This is where you will do your work. FIGURE 4-1 shows the Windows 7 desktop.

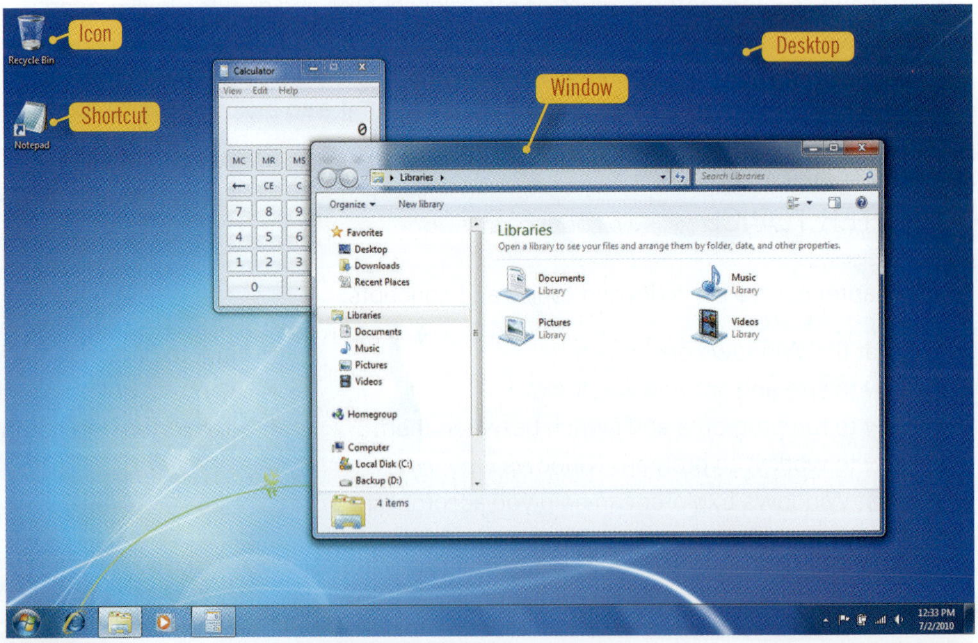

FIGURE 4-1 The desktop can contain windows, shortcuts, and icons.

An **icon** is a visual symbol of a computer resource. In Windows, icons are small pictures that represent programs, folders, files, drives, and any other computer resource. (You'll learn about files and folders later in the chapter.) To access the actual computer resource, you usually click or double-click the icon. Some icons sit directly on the desktop; others are contained in file listings or on the Start menu. Not every icon represents an actual file, folder, or program; some icons are shortcuts to other icons. A **shortcut** is a link or pointer provided for quick access to the original. There can be many shortcuts, all pointing to the same file. Deleting a shortcut, however, does not delete the original item. You can usually distinguish a shortcut icon from the original that it refers to by a small arrow in the shortcut icon's lower-right corner.

You can customize the Windows 7 interface by applying different themes. A **theme** is a collection of settings that determines the way Windows 7 looks and feels. It allows you to change the wallpaper, icons, pointers, and system sounds.

The default theme in Windows uses Aero features. **Aero** is a type of 3D theme that gives the display a three-dimensional look. When you apply an Aero theme, the borders of each window are partially transparent. This allows you to see what lies beneath. Because of this semi-transparency, Aero is sometimes referred to as "Aero Glass." Aero themes also provide for some extra animation flourishes within the interface. Run the mouse over a navigation button and the button will glow. New windows slowly materialize into existence, and, when minimized, they fade and shrink downward. Other Aero features include Snap, Shake, and Peek, covered later in this chapter.

> **Note**
>
> The **Recycle Bin** is an icon on the desktop that acts like a garbage can. When you delete (erase) a file, it gets placed in the Recycle Bin. If you change your mind, you can retrieve the file from the Recycle Bin back to the folder from which it was deleted. You will learn more about the Recycle Bin and deleting files in Chapter 5.

4.1 Exercise: Interacting with an Icon

Follow these steps on your own PC to begin exploring the Windows desktop:

1. Right-click the Recycle Bin icon on your desktop. A menu appears.
2. Click away from the menu to close it without making a selection.
3. Double-click the Recycle Bin icon. A Recycle Bin window opens.
4. Click the Close (X) button in the upper-right corner of the window. The window closes.

Using the Taskbar

The **taskbar** is the bar at the bottom of the Windows desktop, as shown in FIGURE 4-2. The taskbar contains the Start button, the notification area, and the clock. It is also the place where you will see button icons of any opened programs. If you don't see the taskbar, it may be set to be hidden. Just move the mouse pointer to the bottom of the desktop to make it appear.

FIGURE 4-2 The taskbar.

> **Note**
>
> You'll be introduced to Windows Explorer later in this chapter, and learn about it in detail in Chapter 5.

When you open programs, Windows displays an icon for each opened program on the taskbar. To switch to a program, click the icon on the taskbar. When an Aero theme is enabled, you can hover the mouse pointer over an icon in the taskbar to see a thumbnail preview of the window. This is called **Aero Peek**.

New in Windows 7, you can also **pin** certain shortcuts directly to the taskbar, so icons for them appear there even when the program is not running. By default, a Windows Explorer shortcut appears there, for example.

Also new in Windows 7 are **jump lists**. A jump list enables you to quickly open a recently used file of the same type as one that is currently open. Right-click any open program's icon on the taskbar to see a jump list for it. For example, in FIGURE 4-3, a jump list for Notepad (a text editor program) appears.

FIGURE 4-3 A jump list for Notepad.

The **Start button** is an orb with the Windows logo at the left end of the taskbar. Clicking this button opens the **Start menu**, which displays icons that represent programs, folders, and services.

The **notification area** contains icons that provide notifications (important messages) about your computer. Notifications are small pop-up windows that are displayed in the notification area of the taskbar. They provide information about a variety of things, including status, progress, and the detection of new devices. This area also shows icons for some programs that run in the **background**—that is, without an active window open, such as your antivirus software. It also shows icons for some commonly accessed settings like the volume control and, on a laptop computer, the battery indicator.

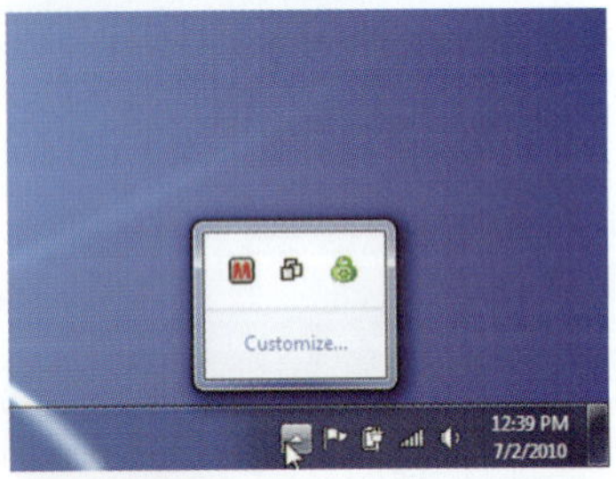

FIGURE 4-4 Hidden icons.

Because there is limited screen space, some of the items in the notification area are hidden. To display the hidden ones, click the Show Hidden Icons button (the small up arrow) to see a palette of additional icons. See FIGURE 4-4.

A clock appears at the far right end of the taskbar. The clock keeps the time on the computer not only so you can see what time it is, but to track events, such as when using calendaring programs.

4.2 Exercise: Exploring the Taskbar

Follow these steps on your own PC to try out features of the taskbar:

1. Click the Start button. The Start menu appears.
2. Click away from the Start menu to close it without making a selection.
3. Click the up-pointing arrow near the notification area. A pop-up list of hidden items appears, as in Figure 4-4.
4. Point to one of the icons in the pop-up. A small box appears telling the icon's name.
5. Click away from the pop-up to close it.

Using the Start Menu

The Start menu is where you open programs. It also provides many other services that allow you to view and access computer resources, such as disk drives, Internet Explorer, and the Help system. FIGURE 4-5 shows the Start menu and identifies the major sections of it.

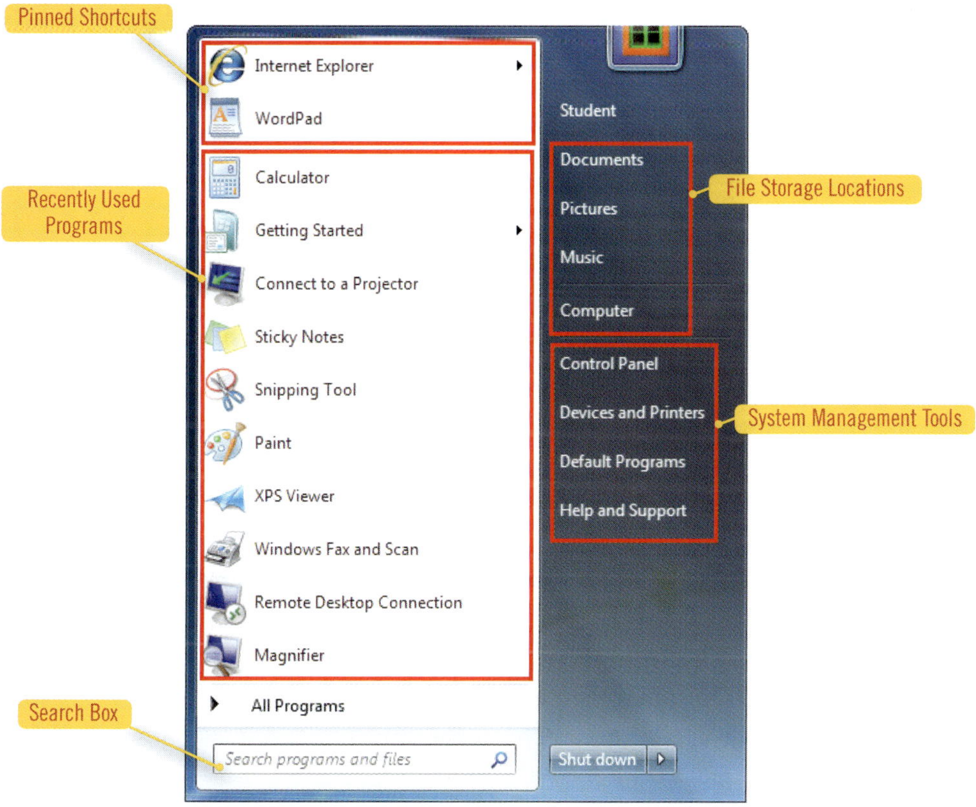

FIGURE 4-5 The Start menu.

The left side of the Start menu shows shortcuts for recently or frequently used programs; you can click any of these to start one of those programs. If you don't see the program you want listed there, click All Programs for a larger list. The All Programs menu contains both individual shortcuts and folders. Click a folder to see a list of the shortcuts it contains.

If you don't know which folder contains the shortcut for the program you want to run, here's an easy way to find it. In the lower-left corner of the Start menu is a Search box that lets you search program names incrementally—that is, as you type each letter, the list of programs displayed is immediately limited to those that match your search string of letters.

The upper-left part of the Start menu contains shortcuts that have been pinned to the Start menu. In Figure 4-5, there are two: Internet Explorer and WordPad. Pinned items are always there; you can pin the programs there that you use most frequently. To pin an item to the Start menu, right-click it and choose Pin to Start Menu.

Below the pinned items is an ever-changing list of recently opened programs. These shortcuts represent the programs that you use most often, and are there for your convenience.

The right side of the Start menu contains links to important folders and programs that provide services:

> **Note**
>
> Displaying the list of recently opened programs is optional. To turn the feature off, right-click the Start button and select Properties, and then clear the check mark for Store and Display Recently Opened Programs in the Start Menu.

- The Documents, Pictures, and Music shortcuts open folders where their respective types of files are stored by default.
- The Computer shortcut opens a folder that lists all the drives on your system; you can use this as a starting point for browsing your system's contents, as you will learn later in this chapter.
- The Control Panel shortcut opens a set of utilities for customizing Windows.
- Devices and Printers enables you to manage your hardware.
- Default Programs allows you to set up which programs are associated with which file types.
- Help and Support opens a searchable Help system for Windows 7.

4.3 Exercise: Exploring the Start Menu

Follow these steps on your own PC to try out features of the Start menu:

1. Click the Start button. The Start menu appears.
2. Click one of the program shortcuts on the left side of the menu. That program opens.
3. Close the program's window by clicking the Close (X) button in its upper-right corner.
4. Click the Start button again to reopen the Start menu.
5. Click Computer. The Computer window opens.
6. Click the Close (X) button on the Computer window.
7. Click the Start button again.
8. Type the letter **W**. A list of all programs and documents that start with that letter appears on the Start menu.
9. Type the letter **I**. The list is further refined so only items that start with "wi" appear.
10. Type the letter **N**. Now only items that start with "win" appear.
11. Press Esc. The top level of the Start menu reappears.
12. Click away from the Start menu to close it.

Sizing and Arranging Windows

As you might guess from the name, **windows** are the heart of the Microsoft Windows 7 interface. A window is a defined rectangular area in which a specific listing or activity appears. Programs run in windows, and file and folder listings appear in windows.

The **title bar** is the topmost area of any window. The title bar displays the name of the program or file you are using in that window. You can move a window by dragging its title bar. Each window has three buttons in its upper-right corner that you use to control the window's size. They are shown in FIGURE 4-6:

- The **Minimize button** collapses (shrinks) the current window to a small button on the taskbar. These buttons glow when the mouse hovers over them.
- The **Maximize button** expands the current window to its maximum size (entire screen).

- The **Restore button** (not shown in Figure 4-6) restores the window to its previous size. The Restore icon displays only when you have maximized a window. While the window is maximized, the Restore icon replaces the Maximize icon.
- The **Close button** closes the current window.

FIGURE 4-6 Control a window's size with the buttons in its upper-right corner.

> **TIP**
>
> You can resize an un-maximized window by dragging one of its borders (other than the top one, of course, because that's the title bar.)

New in Windows 7, you can use **Snap** to arrange and resize windows on the desktop. Snap can quickly align windows at the side of the desktop or maximize them to fill the desktop. To use Snap, drag the title bar of an open window to either side of the desktop to align it there, or drag it to the top of the desktop to maximize the window. To expand a window vertically using Snap, drag the top edge of the window to the top of the desktop.

Another new feature, **Aero Shake**, enables you to quickly minimize all open windows except the active one. To do this, click and hold the mouse button down on the title bar of the active window and quickly move the mouse back and forth to shake it.

To minimize all open windows at once, click the Show Desktop button as shown in FIGURE 4-7. It's the small blank rectangle at the far right end of the taskbar. If you just point at it with the mouse, a preview of the desktop appears; if you click it, all the open windows are minimized. This is also called **peeking** at the desktop, and is part of the feature called Aero Peek.

FIGURE 4-7 Click the Show Desktop button to quickly minimize all open windows.

You can arrange the open windows on the desktop so you can see them more clearly. Manually dragging the title bars to arrange them is one way. Another is to right-click an empty area of the taskbar and choose one of these commands:

- **Cascade Windows:** Arranges the windows in an orderly overlapping stack, with all title bars visible. See FIGURE 4-8.
- **Show Windows Stacked:** Tiles the windows vertically, with no overlap.
- **Show Windows Side by Side:** Tiles the windows horizontally, with no overlap.

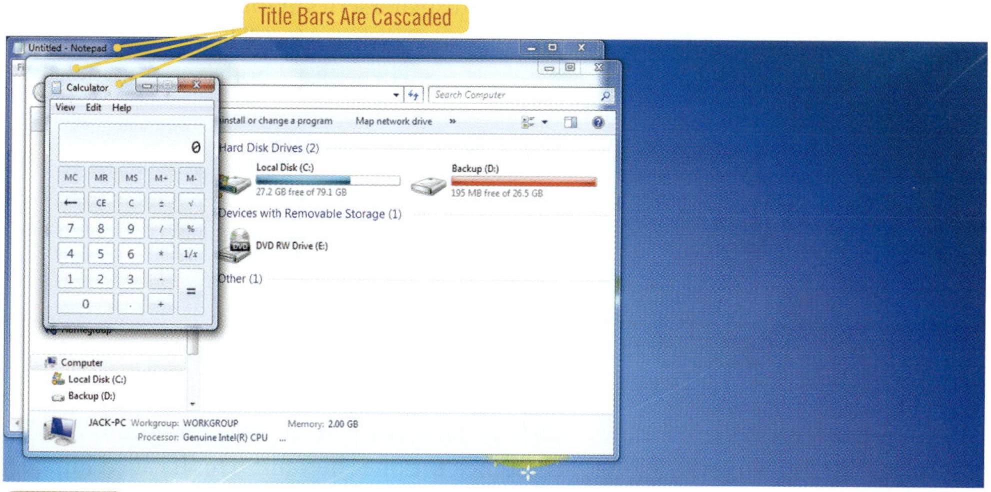

FIGURE 4-8 Cascade arranges the windows so all title bars are accessible.

4.4 Exercise: Sizing and Arranging Windows

Follow these steps on your own PC to practice working with a window:

1. Click the Start button, and then click Computer. A window opens.
2. Point at the lower-right corner of the window so the mouse turns into a double-headed arrow.
3. Click and drag inward, shrinking the size of the window by a few inches. Release the mouse button.
4. Position the mouse pointer on the bottom border of the window. The pointer turns into a double-headed arrow.
5. Click and drag downward, increasing the height of the window by a few inches. Release the mouse button.
6. Click the Maximize button. The window expands to fill the entire screen.
7. Click the Restore button. (It's where the Maximize button was previously.) The window returns to its previous size.
8. Click the Minimize button. The window disappears.
9. On the taskbar, click Computer. The window is restored to view.
10. Drag the window's title bar to the right a few inches. The entire window moves.
11. Click the Close button. The window closes, and its icon disappears from the taskbar, too.

Running and Switching Between Programs

To run a program, select it from the Start menu. Alternately, you can double-click a shortcut on the desktop for a program, or double-click a data file of a type that is associated with that program. For example, when you double-click a text file, Notepad opens, and the text file opens within it.

The ability to open and work on multiple programs at the same time is called **multitasking.** Windows 7 enables you to have many programs open at once; you can switch between them by clicking the desired program's icon on the taskbar.

There are also several other ways to switch among running programs:

- You can hold down Alt and press Tab to display a series of thumbnail images of the open windows, and then press Tab repeatedly (with Alt still held down) until the one you want is highlighted. See FIGURE 4-9. Then release both keys to switch to it.

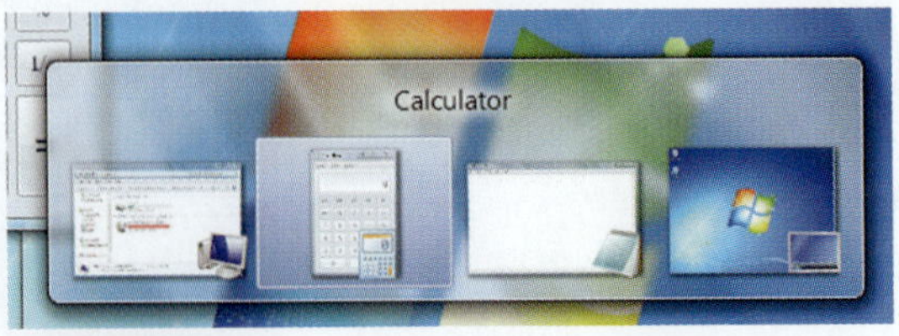

FIGURE 4-9 Alt+Tab browses the open windows.

- You can press the Windows logo key+Tab to display the open programs as a 3D stack, as shown in FIGURE 4-10. Then click the one you want. This is called **Flip 3D.** It is available only when you are using an Aero theme.

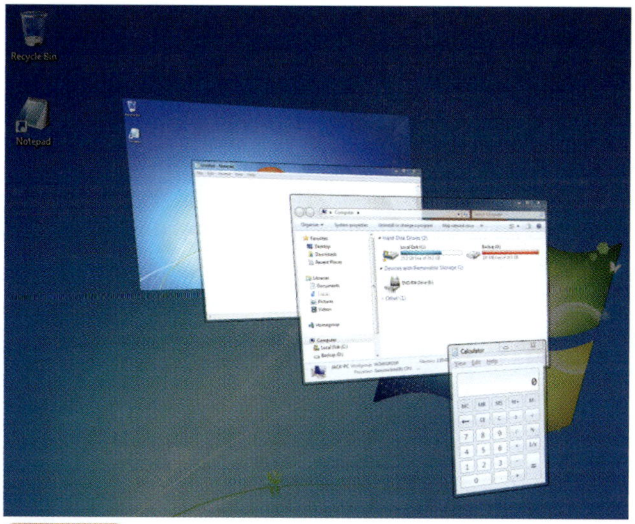

FIGURE 4-10 Windows key+Tab activates Flip 3D.

- You can point to an open program's button on the taskbar to see a preview of it (Aero Peek), and then click on that preview to switch to it.

4.5 Exercise: Running and Switching Programs

Follow these steps on your own PC to practice working with program windows:

1. Click the Start button to open the Start menu.
2. Type **note**. This filters the list to show only programs that start with those letters, as you learned earlier.
3. Click Notepad. The Notepad program opens.
4. Click the Minimize button on the Notepad window to get it out of the way.
5. Click the Start button, and click All Programs.
6. Click the Accessories folder. (You may need to scroll down to see it.)
7. Click Calculator. The Calculator program opens.
8. Hold down the Alt key and press and release Tab. (Keep holding down the Alt key.) Press the Tab key again. Notice that the selected window toggles from one to the next. When the Notepad window is selected, release the Alt key.
9. Hold down the Windows key and press and release Tab. (Keep holding down the Windows key.) Flip 3D shows the open windows. Click the Calculator window. Release the Windows key.
10. Close all open windows by clicking their Close (X) buttons.

Working with Program Windows

A **program window** is a window in which a program is running. Depending on the program, different interface options may be available in it, such as a menu bar, one or more toolbars, a status bar, scroll bars, and dialog boxes.

Many programs use menu bars and/or toolbars for command access. The **menu bar** is a thin strip at the top of a window that lists the names of menus you can open. Click a menu name to open that menu; then click a command on the menu to execute the command. The Notepad program has a menu bar, for example. Some programs have a **Ribbon** instead of a menu bar. A Ribbon is a tabbed **toolbar** that contains graphical buttons that are shortcuts for issuing different commands. The Microsoft Office programs (Word, Excel, and so on) have a Ribbon, as do the Windows 7 versions of built-in programs, such as WordPad and Paint. FIGURE 4-11 shows one program that uses a menu bar and one that uses a Ribbon.

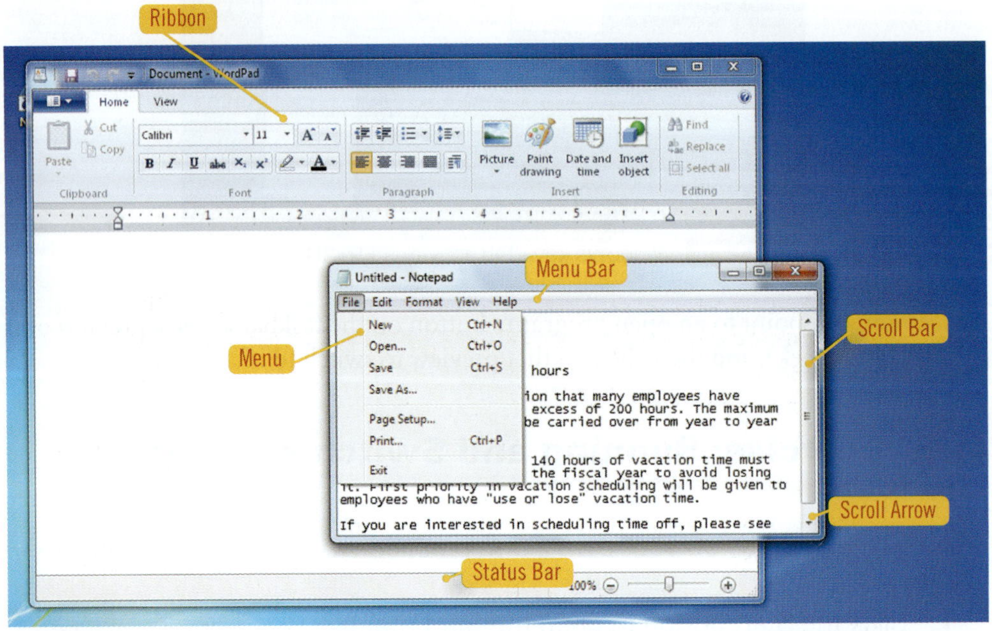

FIGURE 4-11 Program window features.

Scroll bars show up automatically when all the information in a given window cannot be seen and allow you to move vertically or horizontally. At each end of a scroll bar is a scroll arrow; click the arrow to move in that direction. In the middle of each scroll bar is a scroll box; drag the scroll box to scroll more quickly.

Learning Your Way Around Windows Explorer

Windows Explorer is the part of Windows that displays lists of folders and files. This chapter provides an overview of Windows Explorer. Chapter 5 goes into it in more detail.

A **folder** is a location where files are stored. There are already several folders on your hard disk, such as Windows, Users, and Program Files, and you can create additional ones whenever needed. Folders can be created on any drive, such as hard disks and flash drives. You can also nest folders within folders. A **file** is a collection of data stored in one unit, under a single name. This can be a document, a picture, an audio or video file, a library, a program, or other collection of data.

There are many entry points into Windows Explorer. The most basic is the Computer command on the Start menu. It opens a window that lists all the drives available on the computer, including hard disks and USB flash drives. FIGURE 4-12 shows the Computer window. From the Computer window, you can double-click a drive to see its contents, or right-click a drive and choose Properties to get information about the drive.

The Documents, Music, and Pictures links on the Start menu also open Windows Explorer windows; each opens a specific folder that contains a certain type of content. These links point to folders that are unique to the logged-in user, so each person who uses the computer can keep his or her documents, music, and pictures private.

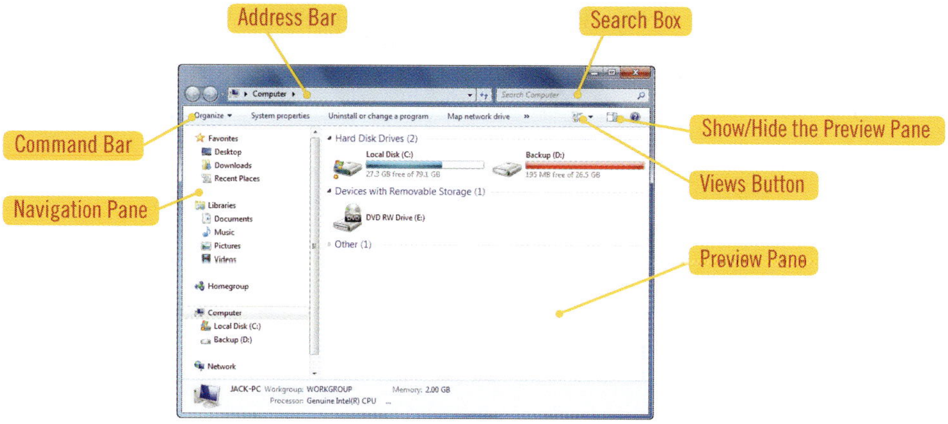

FIGURE 4-12 The Computer window shows the available drives.

Windows Explorer windows have a few special features not found in other windows:

- The **command bar** displays context-sensitive tasks, such as New Folder or Burn Disc. It also has a Views button that enables you to select the size and arrangement of the window's content.
- The **navigation pane** provides shortcuts that let you browse in several ways:
  - **Favorites:** Shortcuts to commonly accessed locations. You can put your own favorite folders here, too.
  - **Libraries:** Special-purpose folders that Windows provides and manages. You'll learn more about libraries in Chapter 5.
  - **Homegroup:** If you have a Homegroup network set up, a shortcut to it appears. A **homegroup** is a small serverless network, such as in a home or very small business.
  - **Computer:** Shortcuts to all the drives and folders on your PC.
  - **Network:** A shortcut to an interface from which you can browse the other computers on your network.
- The **address bar** displays the path to the currently displayed location. A **path** is the full instruction that uniquely points to the location, starting with the drive letter—like this: C:\Books\Chapter1\Ch01.txt.
- The **preview pane,** if you use it, displays information related to the selected item. For example, if the selected item is a document, it will display the name of the document and the program name. If the selected item is a picture, and it will display a thumbnail (scaled-down version) of the picture; and if the selected item is a video, it will display the first frame. You can toggle the preview pane on/off with the Show the Preview Pane button on the command bar.
- The **search box** allows you to search for folders or files. As soon as you type anything, it starts to search for folders or files that contain the characters that you have typed.
- The **Views button** opens a menu of viewing options that control how large the icons appear and in what layout.

Working with Dialog Boxes

When a program needs more information from you to process a command, a dialog box appears. **Dialog boxes** give you the opportunity to specify options, such as the number of copies to print or the measurements to use for document margins. Dialog boxes may have some or all of these types of controls in them, shown in FIGURE 4-13.

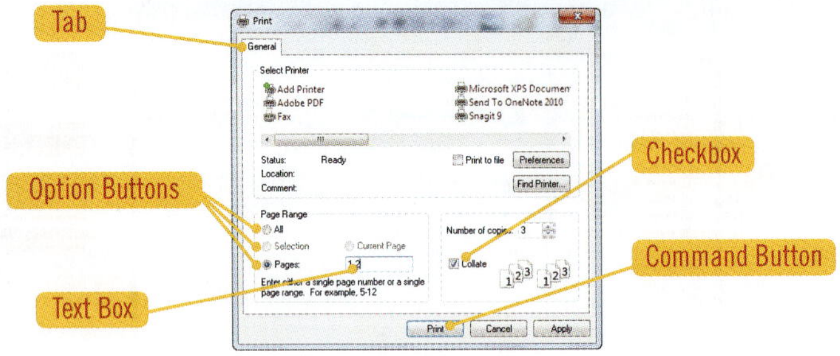

FIGURE 4-13 A dialog box asks for more information about the task you want to perform.

- **Option buttons:** A set of buttons where you can select exactly one button at a time. When you click another button, the originally selected one becomes deselected. These are sometimes called radio buttons.
- **Checkbox:** An on/off toggle that can be marked (checked) or unmarked (cleared).
- **Tab:** A flap that you can click to move to a different page of a multi-page dialog box. (In Figure 4-13 there is only one tab.)
- **Text box:** A box in which you can type a value or entry.
- **Command button:** A button that opens another dialog box, or that applies or cancels the settings you have made.

4.6 Exercise: Using a Dialog Box

Follow these steps on your own PC to practice using a dialog box:

1. Click the Start button, and then click Notepad. (It should be on the top level of the Start menu because you used it earlier. If it is not, begin typing the name until it appears at the top of the menu, and then click it.)
2. Click File on the menu bar, and then click Page Setup. The Page Setup dialog box opens.
3. In the dialog box, click the Landscape option button.
4. Click the Letter button. A list of other sizes opens. On that list, click Legal.
5. Click in the Left text box. Delete the measurement already there, and type **1** in its place.
6. Click OK to accept the settings.
7. Close Notepad by clicking its Close (X) button.

Personalizing Windows

Control Panel provides access to many different settings and options that you can configure to customize the way Windows looks and operates. Its content is broken down into categories; each category contains many different options. FIGURE 4-14 shows the options available in Control Panel.

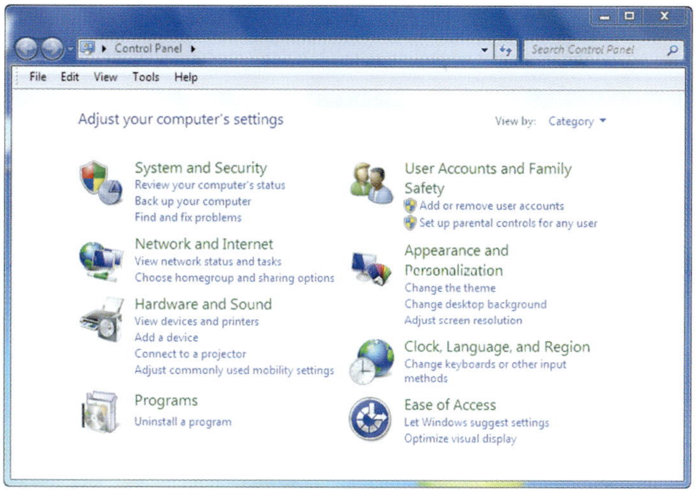

FIGURE 4-14 Control Panel enables you to customize your system.

4.7 Exercise: Changing the Desktop Background and Icon Size

The following exercise walks through a few changes you can make to personalize Windows:

1. Right-click the desktop and choose Personalize. This is an alternate way into the Control Panel that shortcuts the main screen and goes right into the Personalization category.
2. Click Desktop Background.
3. Select the background you want from the available options, as shown in FIGURE 4-15

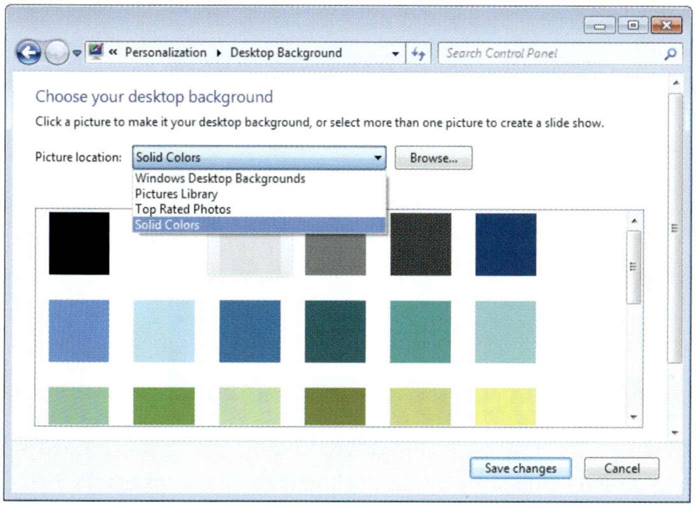

FIGURE 4-15 Selecting a different background.

TIP

You can open the Picture Location drop-down list and click Solid Colors if you want a color rather than an image.

4. Click the Save Changes button.
5. Right-click the desktop and hover the mouse over the View command. A submenu appears. See FIGURE 4-16.

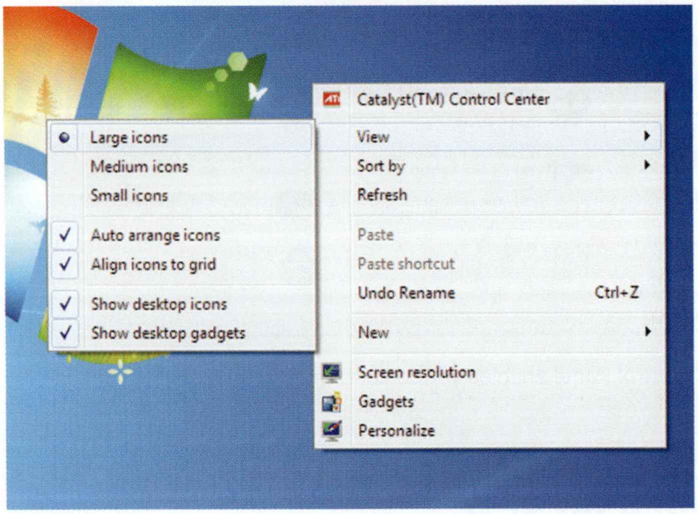

FIGURE 4-16 Adjusting the icon size.

6. Click Large Icons. The icons on the desktop become larger.
7. Right-click the desktop and hover the mouse over the View command again.
8. Click Medium Icons. The icons return to their original size.

Changing the Date and Time

When you place your mouse over the clock, the date displays. In addition, if you click the clock, a pop-up calendar and analog-style clock appears FIGURE 4-17.

From there, you can optionally click Change Date and Time Settings to open the Date and Time dialog box, where you can change the date and time, switch to a different time zone, and more.

FIGURE 4-17 View a calendar and clock by clicking the time on the taskbar.

4.8 Exercise: Changing Your Time Zone

Follow these steps to learn how to change your time zone. This is important to know if you travel, for example:

1. Notice the time shown on the clock in the taskbar.
2. Click the clock, and click Change Date and Time Settings. The Date and Time dialog box opens.
3. Click Change Time Zone. The Time Zone Settings dialog box opens.
4. Click the current time zone. A menu of zones opens.
5. Click the (UTC-6:00) Central Time (US & Canada) time zone.
6. Click OK.
7. Click OK to close the Date and Time dialog box.
8. Notice the time shown on the clock in the taskbar.
9. Repeat Steps 2 through 7, choosing your own time zone in step 5.

Getting Help and Support

One other important item on the Start menu is Help and Support. There may be times when you don't know how to accomplish a task. Other times you may have forgotten how to do something. Using Help is one way to get the knowledge you need.

When you click Help and Support on the Start menu, the Windows Help and Support window opens. To search for help on a certain topic, type a word or phrase in the Search Help text box and press Enter. Windows displays a list of matching articles. Click an article to read it. For example, FIGURE 4-18 shows a list of articles found by searching for the word "icon."

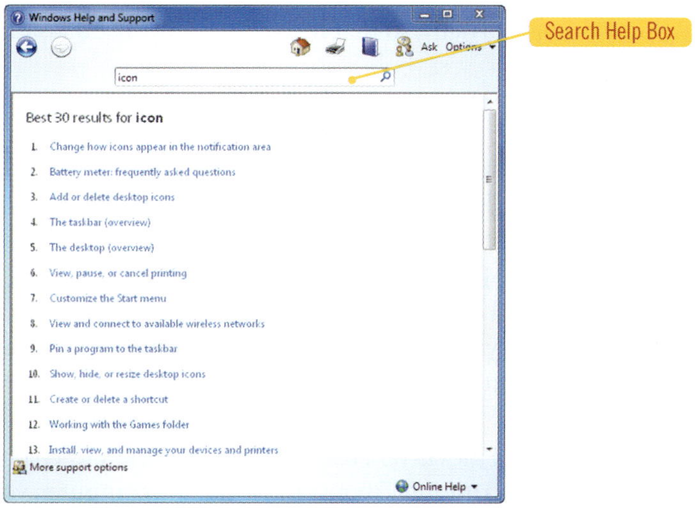

FIGURE 4-18 Search for help articles by keyword.

4.9 Exercise: Getting Help

Follow these steps to practice using the Help system:

1. Click the Start button, and then click Help and Support.
2. In the Search Help box, type **music** and press Enter. A list of articles appears.
3. Click the article titled "Managing your music" and read it.
4. Close all the open windows when finished.

Turning the Computer Off

Windows 7 offers different options when you finish working on the computer. You can shut the computer down completely (that is, turn its power off), or restart it (that is, reload Windows into memory).

To **shut down**, click the Start button and click Shut Down. To **restart**, click the arrow button to the right of Shut Down, and then click Restart on the menu that appears as shown in FIGURE 4-19.

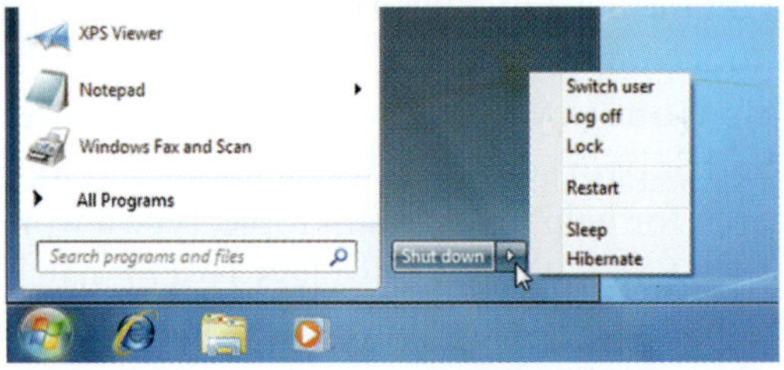

FIGURE 4-19 The Shut Down button's menu offers several choices for logging off, restarting, locking, and so on.

Using that same menu, you can also choose any of several other actions that shut the computer down only partially, so that it starts back up again faster when you are ready to resume your work:

- **Sleep:** Places the computer in a low-power state that is very close to being entirely off. Only enough electricity is used to keep the random access memory (RAM)—the computer's memory—powered. When you resume from Sleep, the computer starts up almost immediately, and all the programs and files that were previously open are still open, just as you left them.
- **Hibernate:** Copies the contents of RAM to a hidden area of the hard disk for safekeeping, and then shuts the computer's power off, so that it uses no electricity at all. When you resume from Hibernate, the previous contents of RAM are recopied back into RAM, and the computer starts up with everything just as you left it. Hibernate takes slightly longer to resume than Sleep.
- **Log Off:** Logs off the current user, shutting down any open programs and files, but leaves Windows running. To resume using the computer, you must log back on.
- **Switch User:** Returns to the logon screen, and allows another user to log on. The previously logged-on user is not logged out, though, so you can switch back and forth between user accounts without closing open programs and files. You might use this option when someone else who has an account on the computer wants to use the computer for a few minutes while you are in the middle of something.

- **Lock:** Returns to the logon screen without logging off. The logged-on user account cannot be accessed until you type its password (if it has one). You might use this option when you step away from your computer with private files open, for example.

Test Yourself

The questions in this section are meant to test your knowledge of what you read. Make sure you answer them. The page number where the answer can be found appears after each question.

1. Which of these is *not* a function of the operating system? (73)
A. Detects and manages the installed hardware
B. Provides a user interface
C. Runs programs
D. Sends and receives e-mail

2. You can pin shortcuts to which two areas? (76, 77)
A. Start menu
B. Control Panel
C. Taskbar
D. Title bar

3. A(n) ____________ is a collection of settings that determines the way Windows 7 looks and feels. (75)

4. If the taskbar doesn't appear, it may be hidden. How can you make it appear? (75)
A. Move the mouse pointer to the bottom of the desktop.
B. Press Ctrl+T.
C. Triple-click the desktop.
D. Tap the Alt key.

5. When you right-click a program's icon on the taskbar, a list appears of other recently opened files associated with that program. What is the list called? (76)
A. Task manager
B. Jump list
C. Peek view
D. Aero list

6. Which window control button appears only when a window is maximized? (79)
A. Maximize
B. Minimize
C. Restore
D. Close

7. Aero Shake minimizes all open windows except the active one. How do you activate it? (79)
A. Click and drag the title bar to the top of the screen.
B. Click and then drag the title bar back and forth quickly.
C. Right-click the active window on the taskbar and click Shake.
D. Point the mouse at the window's icon on the taskbar.

8. Where is the Show Desktop button located in the Windows interface? (79)
A. Far left end of the taskbar
B. Far right end of the taskbar
C. Upper-right corner of the desktop
D. Left column of the Start menu

9. A ________ is a location where files are stored. (82)

10. In the navigation pane, Windows Explorer displays a list of shortcuts to commonly accessed locations. What are the shortcuts called? (83)
    A. Directories
    B. Favorites
    C. Bookmarks
    D. Groups

11. Which of the following appear in a program window when all the information cannot be seen at once? (Hint: They allow you to move the window's content vertically or horizontally.) (82)
    A. Menu bars
    B. Scroll bars
    C. Toolbars
    D. Title bars

12. Which requests extra information about a command by providing option buttons, checkboxes, and other controls? (83)
    A. Menu option
    B. Taskbar command
    C. Dialog box
    D. Toolbox

13. Which command copies the contents of the computer's memory to the hard disk and then shuts off the computer's power? (88)
    A. Hibernate
    B. Sleep
    C. Log off
    D. Restart

14. A __________ is a link or pointer that provides quick access to the original file. (75).

15. The area of Windows where the background graphic appears is called the ____________. (74)

16. ____________ is a type of 3D theme that gives the display a three-dimensional look, gives window borders transparency, and adds animation flourishes within Windows. (75)

17. The __________ is the bar at the bottom of the desktop that contains the Start button, the notification area, and the clock. (75)

18. The ________________ shows important messages concerning your computer and displays icons for some programs that run in the background. (76)

19. The topmost part of a window is called the ________________. (78)

20. Flip 3D shows all open windows in a 3D stack. To activate it, press the Windows logo key+ _____. (80)

End-of-Chapter Project

In this project, you will practice some of the skills you learned in this chapter.

1. Open Windows Explorer and maximize the window.
2. In the navigation pane, under Libraries, click Documents. Click each of the other folders under Libraries, in turn, to see what they contain.
3. In the navigation pane, under Computer, click the C: drive. Double-click the Windows folder to view its contents. Then close Windows Explorer.

4. Open Control Panel, click System and Security, and then click Action Center. Review the recommendations there. (Do not make the recommended changes unless your teacher tells you to.)
5. Click Control Panel Home in the left pane to return to the top level of the Control Panel.
6. Click System and Security, and then click System. Information about your computer appears, including the type of processor and the amount of random access memory (RAM), which is the computer's memory.
7. Click the Start button, and click Help and Support. In the Search Help box, type colors and press Enter. A list of articles appears.
8. Click the article titled "Change the colors on your computer." Follow the instructions in the article, in the section "To change colors manually," to change the colors on your computer.
9. Close all open windows, and either shut down your PC or log off, per your teacher's wishes.

CHAPTER

5

Windows 7 Files and Folders

- Chapter 4 introduced you to Windows Explorer. This chapter will teach you how to use Windows Explorer to manage files and folders. When you're on a computer, you constantly work with files and folders. You use folders to store and organize files so you can more quickly find what you need. Working with files and folders includes many management tasks, such as renaming, deleting, moving, and copying. This chapter shows you how to do all of these things in Windows Explorer.

CHAPTER TOPICS

This chapter covers the following topics and concepts:

- What files and folders are
- How to navigate in Windows Explorer
- How to customize Windows Explorer
- How to create folders
- How to manage files and folders
- How to search for files and folders

KEY WORDS

- Clipboard
- Destination
- Details pane
- Drag and drop
- File extension
- File list
- File path
- Library
- Library pane
- Metadata
- Parent folder
- Properties
- Source
- Subfolder

Files and Folders

As a refresher from Chapter 4, a "folder" is where you store files. A "file" is a collection of data stored in one unit, under a single name. This can be a document, a picture, or a program, for example. If you organize your folders properly, you will discover that finding the one you need is a snap.

Exploring File, Folder, and Other Properties

Files, folders, drives, and other items displayed in Windows Explorer have **properties**, which control their behavior. To access these properties, right-click the item in Windows Explorer and select Properties from the menu that appears. A dialog box with item-specific property settings appears, as shown in FIGURE 5-1.

Although Windows makes it easy to access properties, do not change an item's properties settings unless you are sure you know what you're doing. Changing these settings can cause an object to behave differently—and you may not like the results!

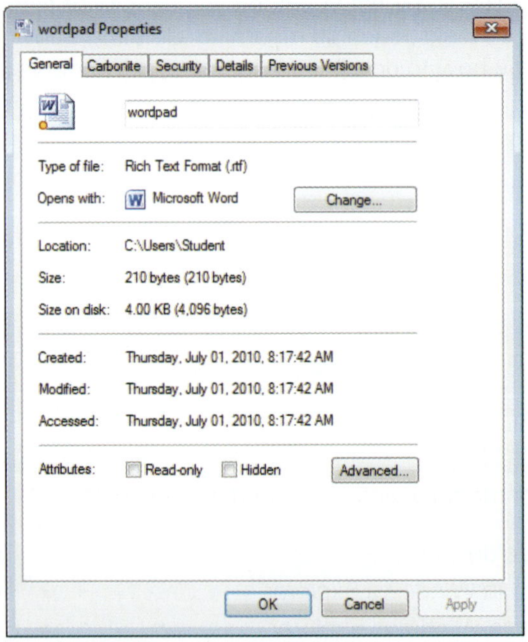

FIGURE 5-1 A file's Properties dialog box.

Note

In Windows 7, a **library** is a virtual folder that can display content from different locations on your computer. A library looks like an ordinary folder but simply points to files and folders that can be located anywhere on your computer's hard disk.

Windows 7 includes several virtual folders, also called libraries. These include a:

- Documents library, where word processing files, spreadsheets, and similar files are stored by default
- Music library, where audio files that you've downloaded or ripped and saved appear

- Pictures library, which acts as a repository for digital image files
- Videos library, where videos are stored by default

You can create folders whenever you need to. You can also nest folders within folders. For example, FIGURE 5-2 shows a folder named Book Project, which contains several nested folders called **subfolders**. In the Windows Explorer navigation pane, subfolders are indented to set them apart from the **parent folder** (in this example, the Book Project folder).

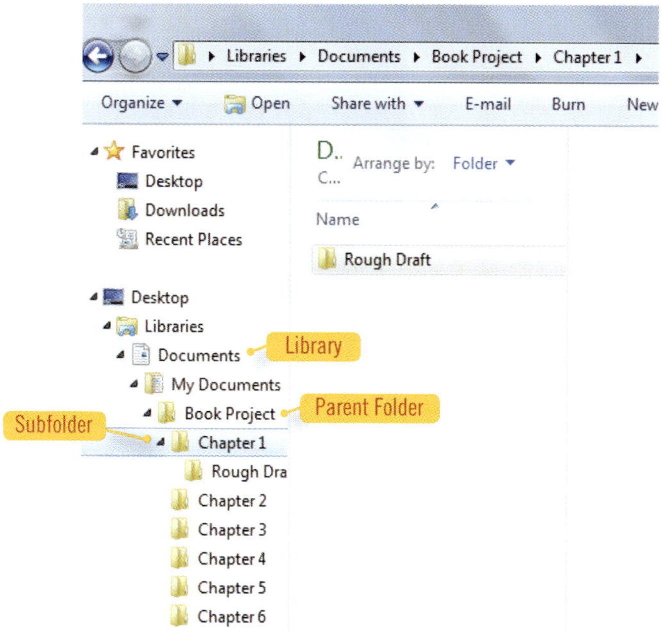

FIGURE 5-2 You can nest folders within folders.

Note

You can have many levels of subfolders. For example, in the Book Project folder, you might have a Chapter 1 folder; within the Chapter 1 folder you might have a Rough Draft folder; and so on. In Windows Explorer, the Chapter 1 folder appears indented under the Book Project folder, and the Rough Draft folder appears indented under the Chapter 1 folder.

In addition, you can create folders on any drive, whether it's a hard drive, a flash drive, or some other type of storage medium. Recall from Chapter 2 that, in Windows, letters represent drives. The letter C is generally used to represent the main hard drive. Any other drives take the next available letter.

Navigating in Windows Explorer

FIGURE 5-3 Click the Windows Explorer button on the taskbar to launch Windows Explorer.

Before you can get any meaningful computer work done, you must learn how to navigate your system. Since you save files to folders, one of the most important things to learn is how to locate specific folders so you can access the files you need. That is, you will navigate to the folder in which you saved your file.

The easiest way to navigate your system is to use the file manager program Windows Explorer. To open Windows Explorer, click the Windows Explorer button in the Windows 7 taskbar, as shown in FIGURE 5-3. Alternatively, to go directly to a specific library within Windows Explorer, click the Start button and select Documents, Pictures, or Music from the menu that appears.

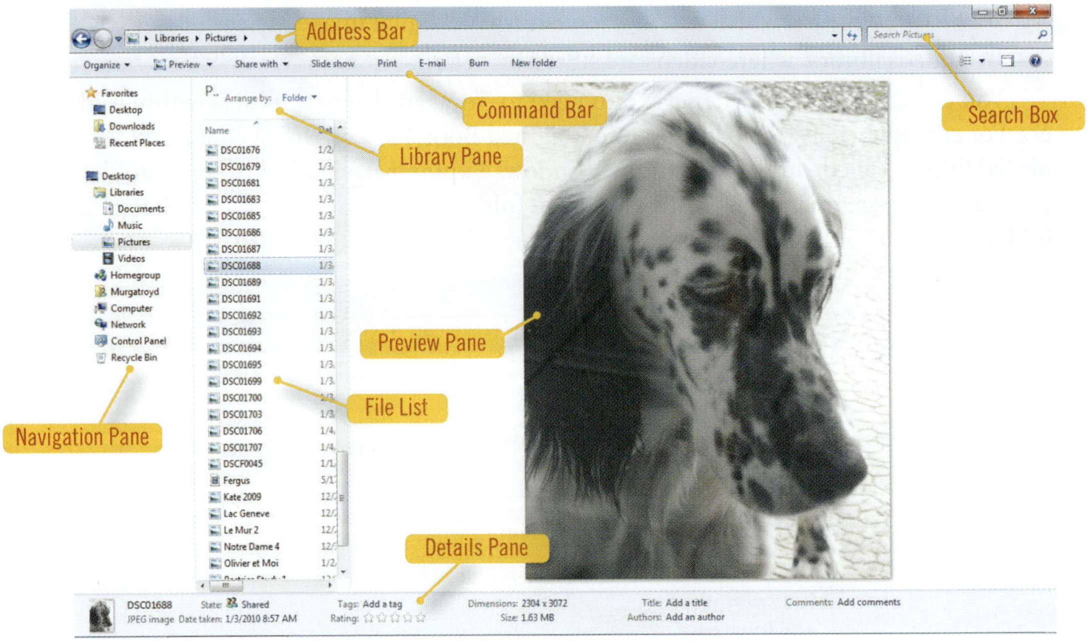

FIGURE 5-4 Use Windows Explorer to navigate your system.

As shown in **FIGURE 5-4**, the Windows Explorer window is divided into several panes and contains various tools to make it easier to find files and folders:

- **Navigation pane:** The navigation pane contains clickable links to the folders on your computer.
- **File list:** Subfolders and files in the selected folder appear in the **file list**.
- **Library pane:** Options in the **library pane** let you specify how items in the file list should be sorted. Options include by folder, author, date, type, and name.
- **Preview pane:** When you select a file in the file list, a preview of it appears in the preview pane.
- **Details pane:** The **details pane** lets you view information about the selected file. (The details that display differ depending on what type of file you select.)
- **Address bar:** The address bar shows the file path.
- **Search box:** Type a search term here to locate an item in the current folder. (You'll learn more about searching later in this chapter.)
- **Command bar:** Access various Windows Explorer tools and commands using this toolbar.

Windows rarely offers only one way to accomplish a task. For example, you can navigate folders and files in Windows Explorer using one of several methods.

Double-Clicking Through Folders

Perhaps the easiest way to navigate folders in Windows Explorer is by double-clicking folders in the file list. When you double-click a folder, the contents of that folder are then displayed in the file list.

To navigate Windows Explorer by double-clicking through folders:

1. Click the Windows Explorer button in the taskbar to launch Windows Explorer.
2. Double-click the library containing the file or folder you seek—in this example, the Documents library.

3. Windows Explorer displays a list of top-level folders in the Documents library. Double-click the folder containing the file or folder you need—in this example, the Book Project folder (see FIGURE 5-5).

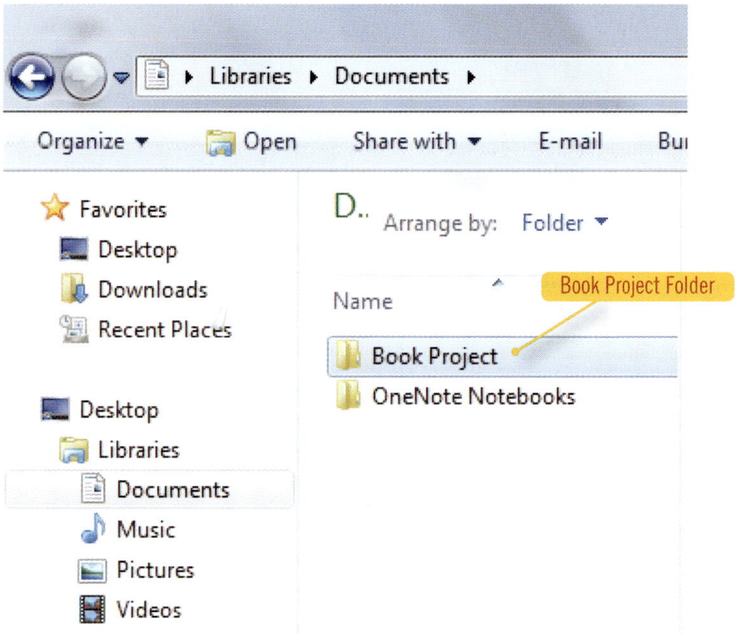

FIGURE 5-5 Double-click the Book Project folder.

4. Windows Explorer displays a list of subfolders and files in the selected folder. If the file you want to open is listed in the file list, double-click it to open it. If the file you want to open does not appear, double-click the subfolder containing the file or folder you seek, repeating as needed until the desired folder appears.

Using the Navigation Pane

In the previous section, you learned how to navigate Windows Explorer by double-clicking folders in the file list, but you could just as easily use the navigation pane to achieve the same goal. These are the steps:

1. Click the Windows Explorer button in the taskbar to launch Windows Explorer.
2. Place your mouse pointer in the navigation pane. Right-pointing arrows appear, as shown in FIGURE 5-6:
   - If the right-pointing arrow next to a folder is clear, it means the folder or library contains subfolders, but those subfolders are not displayed in the file list. Put another way, that folder is currently collapsed.
   - If the right-pointing arrow next to a folder is black and angled down, it means the folder contains subfolders, and those subfolders are displayed in the file list. In other words, the folder is expanded.
   - If there is no arrow next to a folder, it means the folder contains no subfolders.
3. Click the clear right arrow to the left of the Documents entry in the navigation pane.
4. The clear right arrow changes to a black right arrow, and a list of folders in the Documents library appears. Click the right arrow next to the folder containing the file or folder you seek—in this example, the My Documents folder.

TIP

In addition to providing easy access to libraries on your computer—Documents, Music, Pictures, and Videos—the navigation pane also allows you to access drives on your computer as well as network resources. Just click Computer or Network in the navigation pane.

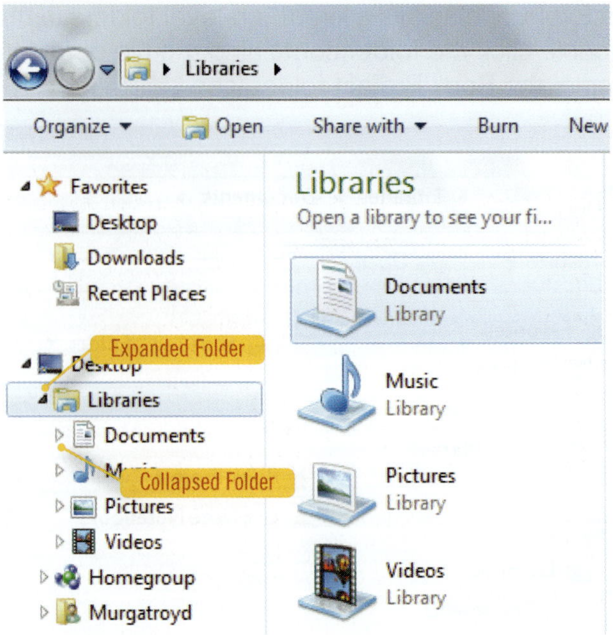

FIGURE 5-6 When you place your mouse pointer in the navigation pane, right-facing arrows appear.

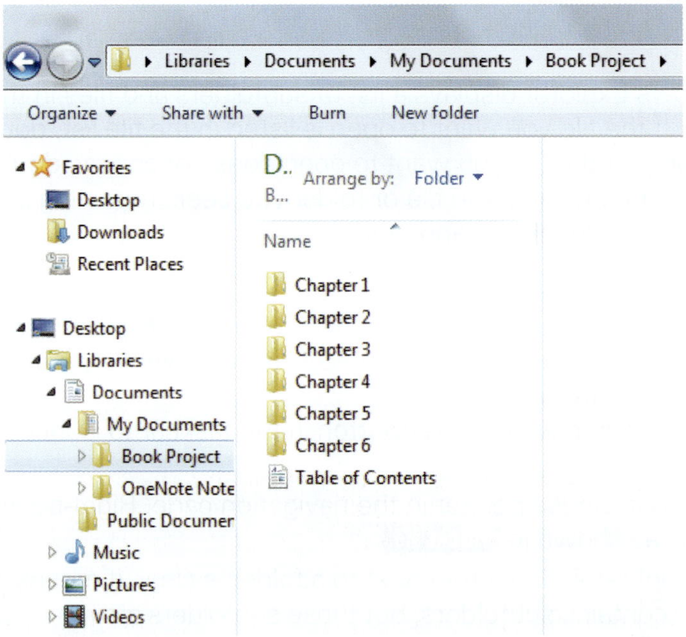

FIGURE 5-7 Click the desired folder in the navigation pane to display its contents in the file list.

5. Windows Explorer displays a list of subfolders in the selected folder. If the subfolder containing the file you seek is listed, click it, as shown in FIGURE 5-7. Its contents appear in the file list. If the folder doesn't list the desired subfolder, click the right arrow for the subfolder containing the correct file or folder, repeating as needed until the right subfolder appears.
6. In the file list, double-click the file you want to open.

Using the Address Bar

You have seen two methods for navigating to a specific folder in Windows Explorer. A third method is to use the Windows Explorer address bar. Follow these steps:

1. Click the Windows Explorer button in the taskbar to launch Windows Explorer.
2. Click the black right arrow next to the Libraries entry in the address bar.
3. A list of available libraries appears.
4. Click the black right arrow next to the Documents entry in the address bar and select My Documents in the list that appears.
5. Click the black right arrow next to the My Documents entry in the address bar. A list of subfolders in the My Documents folder appears.
6. Select the folder containing the file or folder you seek—in this example, the Book Project folder (see **FIGURE 5-8**).

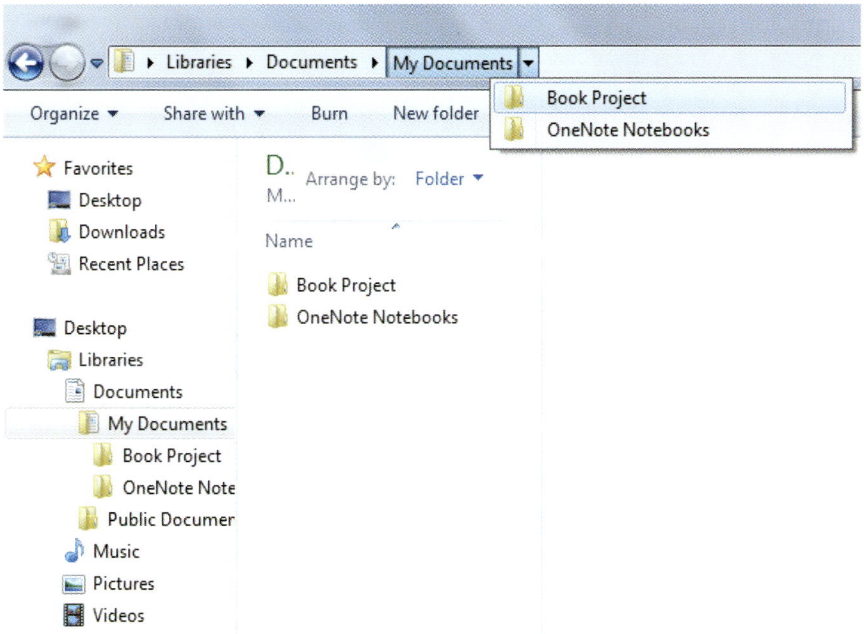

FIGURE 5-8 Select the Book Project folder.

Understanding the File Path

The term "file path" has been used a few times in this chapter. What does it mean? In plain English, the **file path** is the route to a specific folder. For example, the file path to the Book Project folder is Libraries > Documents > My Documents > Book Project. That is, to access the contents of the Book Project folder, you had to launch Windows Explorer with the Libraries window displayed, open the Documents library, open the My Documents folder, and then open the Book Project folder. Each of these is displayed in the address bar.

7. If the file you want to open is listed in the file list, double-click it to open it. If not, click the right arrow next to the Book Project folder and select the desired subfolder from the list that appears, repeating as needed until the file you want to open is listed in the file list.

TIP

As you navigate Windows Explorer, if you lose track of which folder you have open, simply look at the address bar. The address bar always displays the file path, with the currently open folder being the last folder listed.

5.1 Exercise: Navigating Windows Explorer

You aren't limited to a single method to navigate Windows Explorer. Use a combination of the methods discussed. To experiment, follow these steps:

1. Click the Windows Explorer button in the taskbar to launch Windows Explorer.
2. Click the clear right arrow to the left of the Libraries entry in the navigation pane. (If the Libraries entry is already expanded, skip this step.)
3. Click the Pictures folder in the navigation pane.
4. Click the black right arrow next to the Pictures entry in the address bar.
5. Select a folder from the list that appears—for example, the Public Pictures folder.
6. Double-click the Sample Pictures folder to display its contents, as shown in FIGURE 5-9.

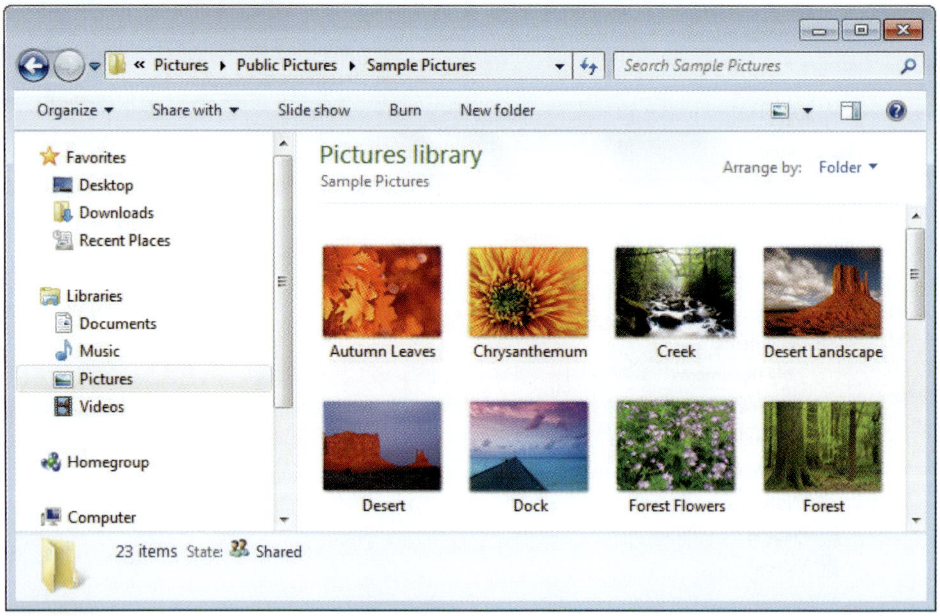

FIGURE 5-9 You can navigate Windows Explorer in a few different ways.

Customizing Windows Explorer

When you open a folder in Windows Explorer, you can control what you see and how you see it. For example, you can specify whether the Windows Explorer window displays certain panes. To do so, click the Organize button on the Windows Explorer command bar and point to Layout. As shown in FIGURE 5-10, panes currently displayed in Windows Explorer have a check mark next to their name; select the pane you want to hide or display.

You can also change file views—that is, how Windows Explorer displays folders and files in the file list. Options include Extra Large Icons, Large Icons, Medium Icons, and Small Icons, as shown in FIGURE 5-11.

Other options include the following (see FIGURE 5-12):

- **List:** In List view, you can view more files at a time in the file list.
- **Details:** Details view is similar to List view, but with Details view, the file list displays more information about each file—such as the file type and size.

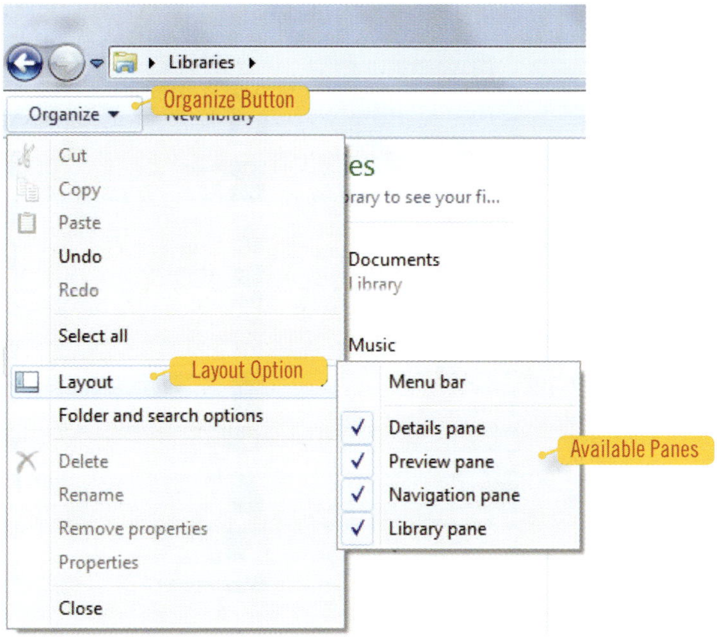

FIGURE 5-10 Choose which panes appear in Windows Explorer.

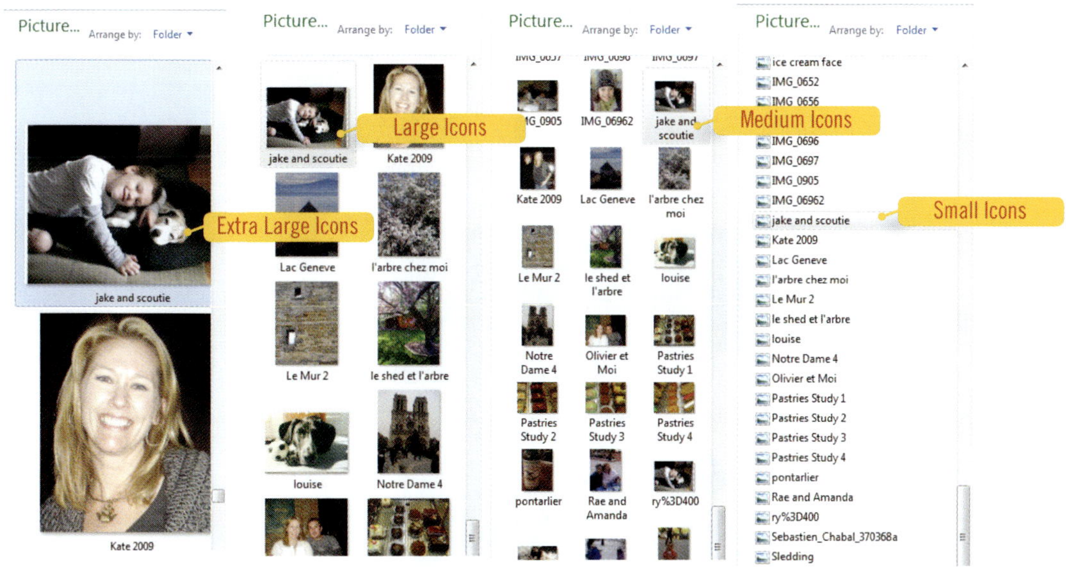

FIGURE 5-11 The larger icon views are excellent for locating photos in Windows Explorer.

- **Tiles:** This view merges Medium Icons view with Details view, showing both an image of the file or folder and information about it.
- **Content:** This view includes an image of the file or folder but places greater emphasis on its name.

To change the file view, click the Change Your View button on the right side of the Windows Explorer command bar (see FIGURE 5-13). Clicking it repeatedly cycles through the available views. Alternatively, click the down arrow to the right of the Change Your View button and select the desired view from the list that appears. If you like, use the slider bar to fine-tune your selection. Experiment with this until the Windows Explorer window looks the way you want it to.

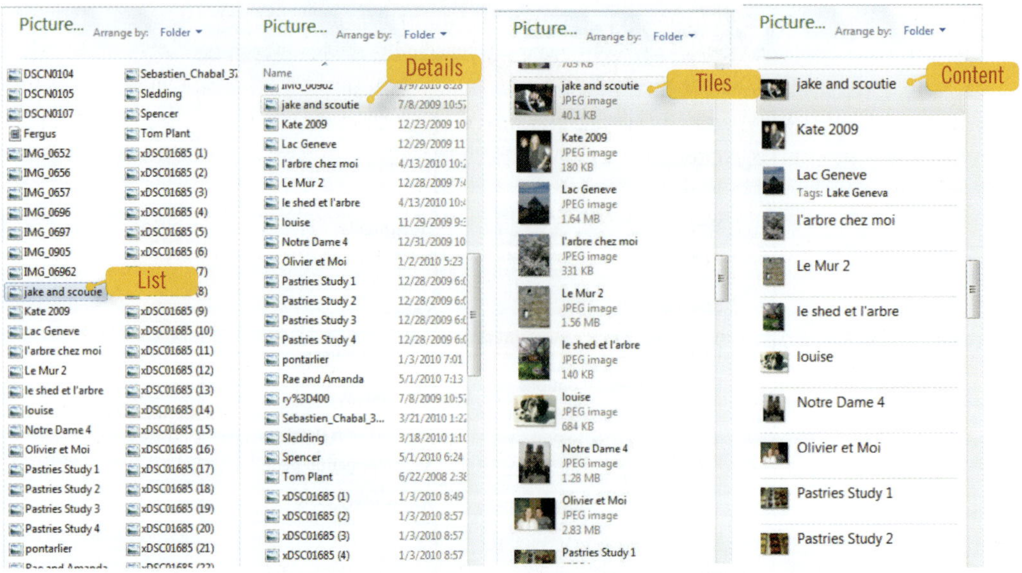

FIGURE 5-12 View information about files using various views.

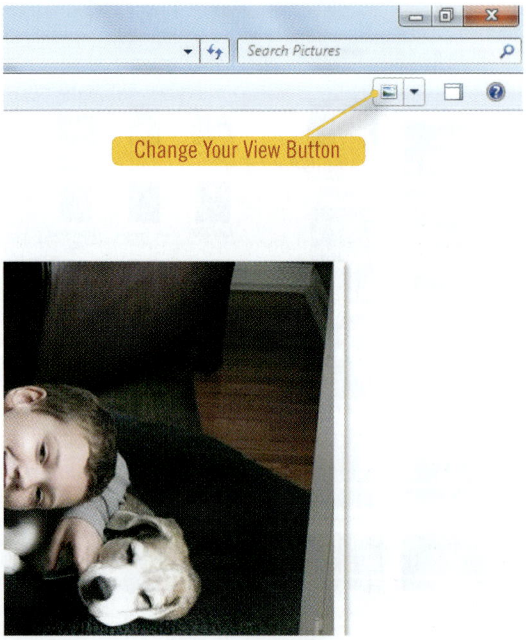

FIGURE 5-13 Changing the file view.

Creating Folders

It is vital that you organize folders on your computer in a logical manner, especially as the number of files grows. Why? Because any file you work on will have to be stored in a folder. Keeping your files and folders organized will make it much easier to find files when you need them.

A key part of keeping your files organized is creating folders and subfolders to store them, much as you use file folders to keep your paper files organized in your filing cabinet. As you begin a new project (or any other type of undertaking), make it a practice to create a new folder for that project in Windows Explorer. Then, anytime you receive or generate a file for that project, you can store it in the project's folder. If the project is a complex one, create subfolders within the main project folder as needed to keep files related to that project organized.

You have a few different ways to create a new folder. One approach is to right-click the library or folder in the navigation pane in which you want to create the new folder, select New, and then select Folder. Alternatively, you can open the library or folder in which you want to create the new folder and click the New Folder button in the Windows Explorer command bar.

Creating a Shortcut for Convenience

If you regularly access a particular folder, create a shortcut to that folder on the desktop. That way, instead of having to launch Windows Explorer and navigate to the folder to open it—which can be especially time consuming if the folder is a subfolder of a subfolder of a subfolder—you need only double-click the desktop shortcut icon once.

To create a shortcut:

1. Launch Windows Explorer.
2. In the navigation pane, right-click the folder for which you want to create a shortcut icon, select Send To, and select Desktop (Create Shortcut). A shortcut icon for the folder appears on the Windows 7 desktop.

In addition to creating shortcut icons for frequently used folders, you can create them for files, programs, or just about anything else on your Windows 7 system.

5.2 Exercise: Creating Folders

To create a folder—in this example, a folder named Taxes—follow these steps:

1. Click the Windows Explorer button in the taskbar to launch Windows Explorer.
2. Right-click the Documents library in the navigation pane, select New, and then select Folder, as shown in FIGURE 5-14.
3. A new folder appears in the navigation pane with its name, New Folder, highlighted. Type the folder's name—in this case, **Taxes**—and press Enter.

That's all there is to it. You can actually create a folder in about five seconds! Now let's create some subfolders—that is, folders that reside within the Taxes parent folder. Follow these steps:

1. Open the Taxes folder.
2. Click the New Folder button in the Windows Explorer command bar (see FIGURE 5-15).
3. A new folder appears in the file list with its name, New Folder, highlighted. Type the folder's name—in this case, **Income**—and press Enter.
4. Repeat Steps 1 through 3 to create another subfolder called **Expenses**.
5. Repeat Steps 1 through 3 to create a third subfolder called **Royalties**.

As you can see in FIGURE 5-16, the Documents library contains a Taxes folder, which itself contains three subfolders: Expenses, Income, and Royalties. Notice how in the navigation pane, the subfolders are indented under the Taxes folder; this indicates that they are subfolders.

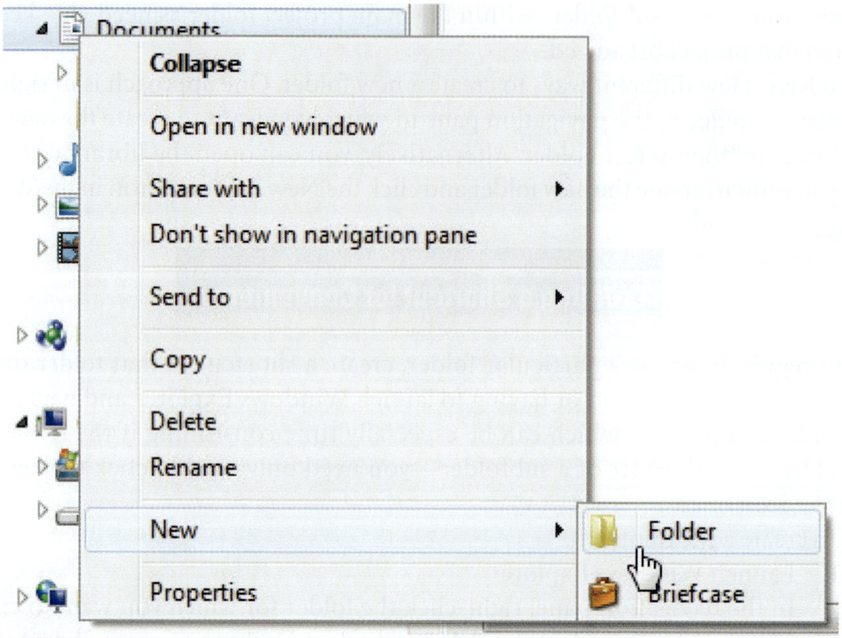

FIGURE 5-14 Creating a new folder.

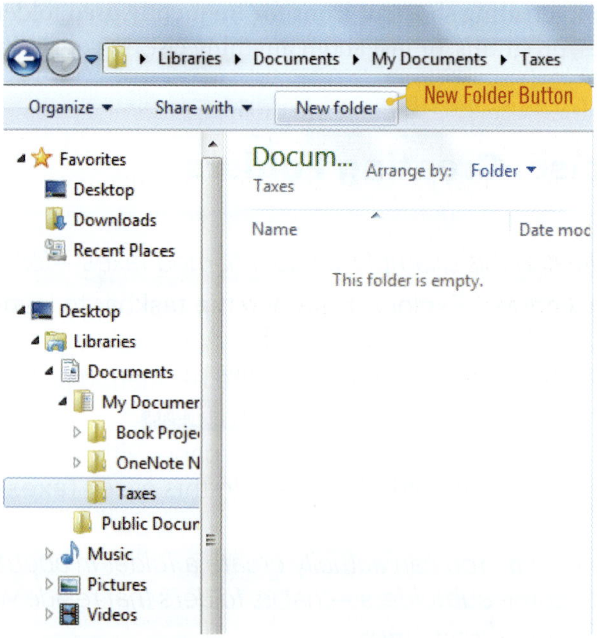

FIGURE 5-15 Creating a subfolder.

Managing Files and Folders

As you get more involved with computers, you will start performing more advanced tasks. Some of these tasks may require you to rename, copy, move, or delete files—sometimes multiple files at once. In this section, you will learn the following:

- Selecting files and folders
- Renaming files and folders
- Copying files and folders
- Moving files and folders
- Deleting and restoring files

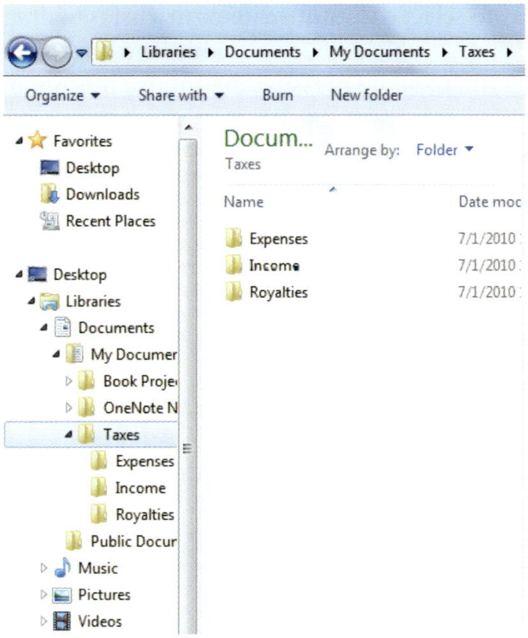

FIGURE 5-16 The Taxes folder with its subfolders.

Selecting Files and Folders

Before you can perform any action on a file or folder—rename it, copy it, move it, or delete it—you must select it. Selecting a single item is easy—you simply click it in the file list. Note that if the item you have selected is a file, a preview of that file will appear in the Windows Explorer preview pane. Selecting multiple files at once involves a bit more know-how.

Selecting Consecutive Items

If you want to select multiple items that appear consecutively in the file list—that is, one after the other—click the first item in the list that you want to select. Then, while pressing the Shift key on the keyboard, click the last item in the list that you want to select. As shown in FIGURE 5-17, the first item, the last item, and all the items in between are selected.

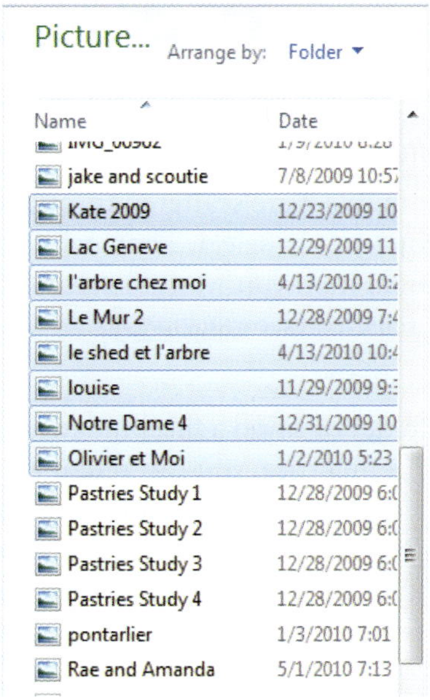

FIGURE 5-17 Selecting consecutive items.

An even easier way to select consecutive items in a list is to drag a selection rectangle around them. To do so, click a blank area in the file list above and to the left of the first file you want to select; then, while pressing the mouse button, drag down and to the right until your mouse pointer covers the last item you want to select. All files within the rectangle will be selected, as shown in **FIGURE 5-18**.

> **TIP**
>
> To select all items in a folder, open the folder in Windows Explorer, click the Organize button, and choose Select All. Alternatively, an even quicker approach is to simply press Ctrl+A (that is, press the Ctrl key and the A key at the same time).

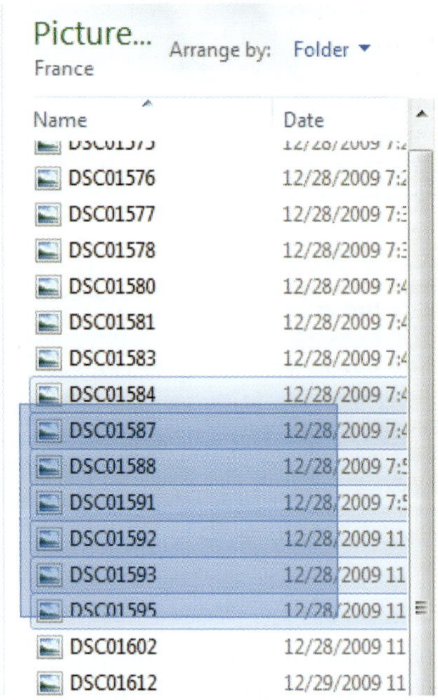

FIGURE 5-18 Drag a selection rectangle around the items you want to select.

Grouping Files for Selection

Suppose you want to move all files of a certain type from one folder to another. Or maybe you want to delete all files generated on a certain date. If so, you could group the files in the file list by type or date respectively; that way, the file list will display them consecutively, making it easier to select them. To group files in this manner, click the Arrange By down arrow in the library pane and choose the desired grouping parameter from the list that appears, as shown in **FIGURE 5-19**.

Selecting Non-Consecutive Items

Suppose the items you want to select are scattered throughout the file list. In that case, simply click the first item you want to select. Then, while pressing the Ctrl key on the keyboard, click each additional item you want to select. Each item you clicked while pressing the Ctrl key will be selected (see **FIGURE 5-20**).

> **TIP**
>
> Deselecting items is as easy as selecting them. To deselect all selected items, simply click an empty area of the Windows Explorer file list. To deselect one of several selected items, press the Ctrl key as you click the item you want to deselect.

Renaming Files and Folders

Suppose you created a new folder or saved a file, but later decided that a different name would be more descriptive. In that case, you can rename it. To rename a file or folder, select it in Windows Explorer, click the Organize button, and select Rename. Alternatively, right-click the file and select Rename from the menu that appears. The name of the folder appears highlighted; simply type the new name and press Enter.

Be aware that you can't use the following characters in a file name:

< > , ? : \ *

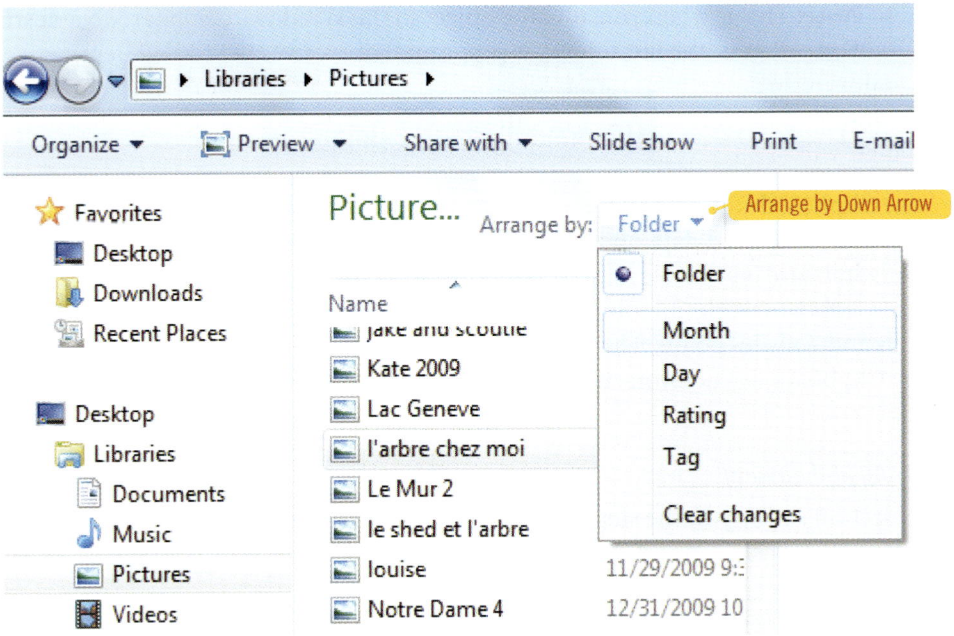

FIGURE 5-19 Group files for selection.

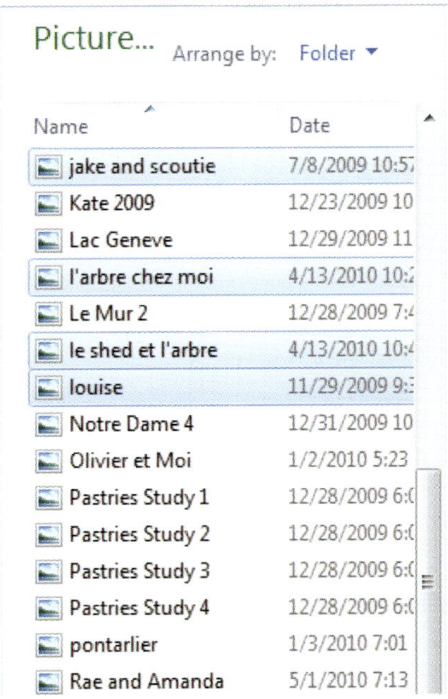

FIGURE 5-20 Selecting non-consecutive items.

If you do use an illegal symbol, Windows will display a warning message.

Note, too, that all file names in Windows are followed by a period and a **file extension**, which indicates what type of file it is. For example, document files created in WordPad have an .rtf extension, many digital image files have a .jpg extension, and some music files have a .wav extension. When renaming a file, take care to avoid changing this file extension, as doing so may render the file unusable.

Copying Files and Folders

To copy a file or folder means to create a duplicate of it. A copy operation involves two main steps:

- **Copy:** This is when you copy an object from its **source**—that is, the file, folder, or program where it resides—to the Windows Clipboard.

- **Paste:** This is when you affix the object in the Windows Clipboard to a **destination**—that is, the file, folder, or program that receives the copied item.

Understanding the Clipboard

The **Clipboard** is an area of memory (RAM) where Windows stores data temporarily. Once you've placed data on the Clipboard, you can transfer it to another location. The Clipboard is available in most Windows programs, including Windows Explorer. The Clipboard works invisibly. That is, when you copy an object to the Clipboard, no bells and whistles go off. The only proof you'll have that you copied the object into the Clipboard is when you successfully perform the paste operation.

Copying and Pasting

This section shows you the steps for copying an item from one folder to another. Once you learn this basic concept, you will be able to perform many other types of copy and paste operations:

1. In the Windows Explorer file list, click the item you want to copy to select it—in this example, the Sales Conference Expense Report file in the Documents library.
2. Click the Organize button.
3. Select Copy, as shown in FIGURE 5-21. The item you selected is copied to the Clipboard.

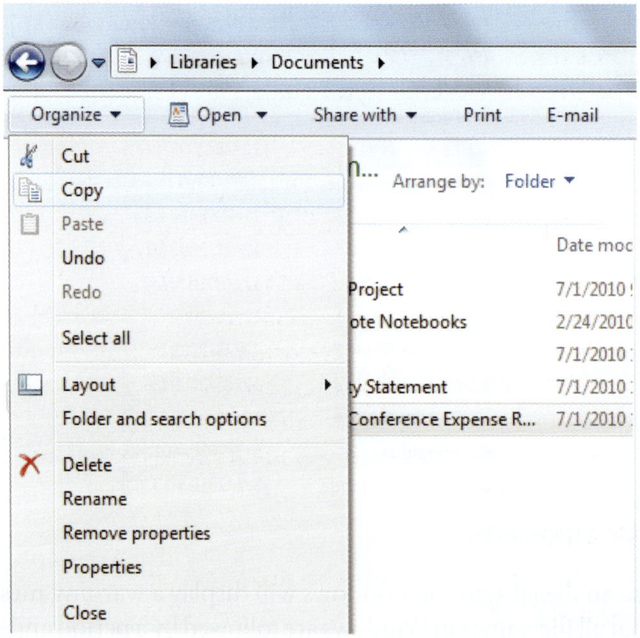

FIGURE 5-21 Copying the item.

4. In Windows Explorer, open the destination folder—that is, the folder where you want to paste the item currently on the Clipboard. In this example, the destination folder is the Expenses folder, which is a subfolder of the Taxes folder.
5. Click the Organize button.
6. Select Paste to place the item into the folder. Notice that because the

item was copied rather than moved, it appears both in the Documents library and the Expenses folder (see FIGURE 5-22).

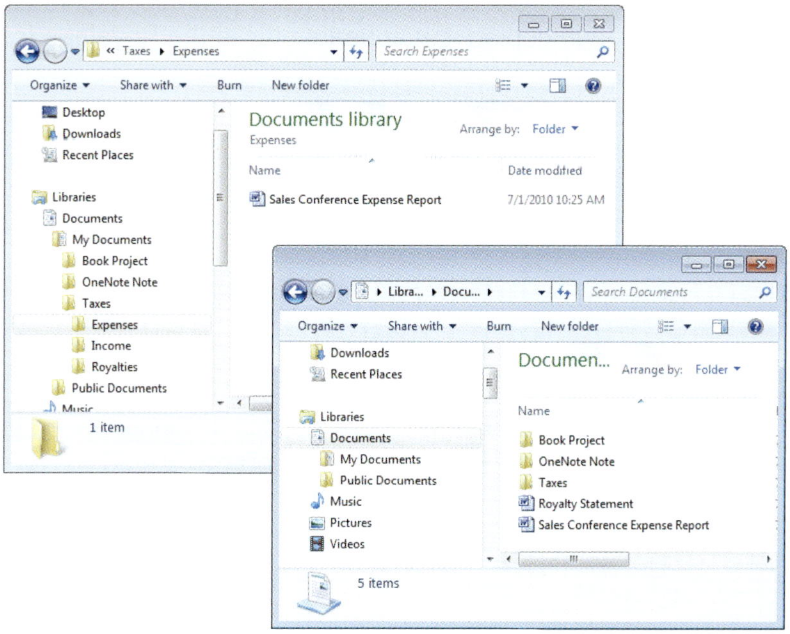

FIGURE 5-22 The item appears in both the source folder and the destination folder.

▸ TIP

An even faster way to copy an item to the Clipboard is to right-click it and select Copy in the menu that appears.

This set of steps showed you how to copy just one file. You can, however, copy multiple files at the same time. Simply select all the files you wish to copy before launching the copy operation. You can also copy entire folders and their subfolders at one time.

Moving Files and Folders

Copying and moving are not the same action. If you copy a file or folder, you create a duplicate. If you move a file or folder, you simply place that file or folder in a different location.

The easiest way to move a file or folder is to drag it from one folder and drop it in another, a method called **drag and drop**. This is a little bit risky, however, because you can drop the item by accident while you are dragging it. If you drop the item but you aren't sure where, you may have a hard time finding it—especially if you don't remember its name! A safer—although slower—approach is to cut the item from the source folder and paste it into the destination folder. If you are moving multiple files, this approach is the better option.

Moving a File with Drag and Drop

The following steps show you how to move an item from one folder to another using the drag-and-drop method:

1. Open the folder containing the item you want to move—in this case, the Royalty Statement file in the Documents library.
2. Reveal the destination folder in the Windows Explorer navigation pane. In this example, click the Documents right arrow, the My Documents right arrow, and the Taxes right arrow to reveal the Expenses, Income, and Royalties folders.
3. In the file list, click the item you want to move (here, the Royalty Statement file).
4. While pressing the mouse button, drag the item to the destination folder (here, the Royalties folder).

5. When you see the destination folder become highlighted, as shown in FIGURE 5-23, drop the item into the folder by releasing the mouse button. You have moved the item to the folder. Note that because you moved the item rather than copied it, it appears only in the Royalties folder (see FIGURE 5-24).

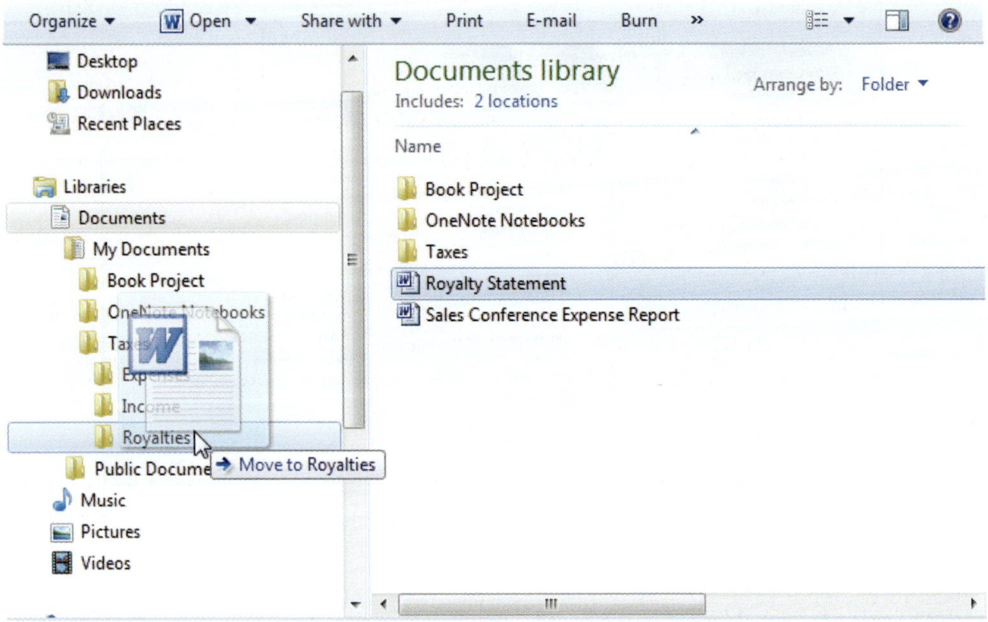

FIGURE 5-23 Drop the item when the destination folder becomes highlighted.

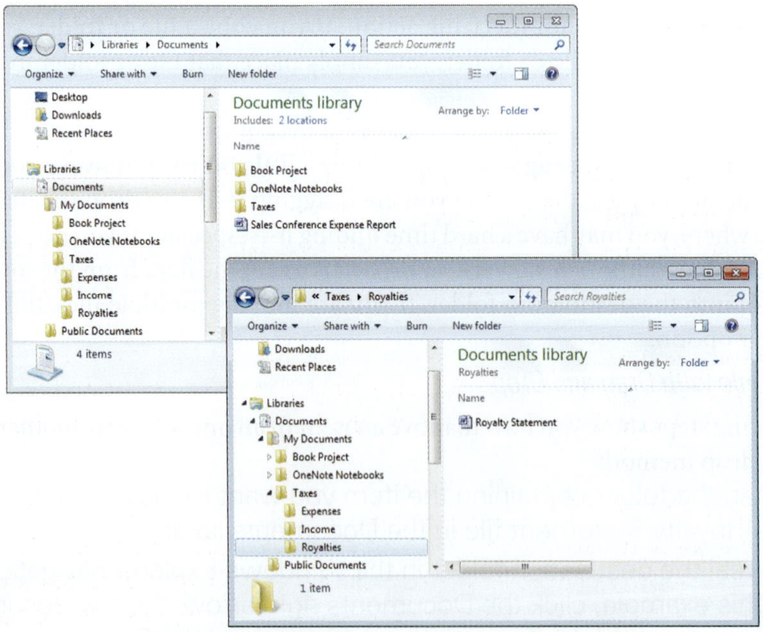

FIGURE 5-24 The item appears only in the destination folder.

5.3 Exercise: Moving a Folder with Cut and Paste

In this exercise, you will learn how to move an item from one folder to another using the cut-and-paste method. Follow these steps:

1. In the Windows Explorer file list, click the item you want to move to select it—in this example, the Royalties subfolder in the Taxes folder.
2. Click the Organize button.
3. Select Cut. The item you selected is copied to the Clipboard.
4. In Windows Explorer, open the destination folder—that is, the folder in which you want to paste the item currently on the Clipboard. In this example, the destination folder is the Income folder, which is a subfolder of the Taxes folder.
5. Click the Organize button.
6. Select Paste. You have now pasted the item into the folder. Note that because you cut and pasted the item rather than copied it, it appears only in the Income folder.

> **TIP**
>
> An even faster way to paste the item into the destination folder is to right-click the folder and select Paste in the menu that appears.

Just as you can copy more than one item at once, you can move multiple items at a time. Simply select all the files you wish to move before launching the move operation.

Deleting Files and Restoring Files from the Recycle Bin

Deleting an item means to erase it. Use the same process to delete files, folders, or just about anything else on your computer. As usual, Windows offers many ways to perform this task:

- You can click the item to select it and then press the Del key on your keyboard.
- You can click the item to select it, click the Organize button, and select Delete from the menu that appears.
- You can right-click the item and select Delete from the menu that appears.

After you delete the item, Windows prompts you to confirm the deletion; click Yes.

When you delete an item in Windows, it is not immediately removed from your computer. Instead, Windows places it in the Recycle Bin. As you learned in Chapter 4, the Recycle Bin is similar to a garbage can; it holds the items that you delete, or throw away. This is a safety measure. If, after you delete an item, you realize you have done so in error, you can restore it—that is, retrieve it from the Recycle Bin and return it to its original location.

If you need to make room on your hard drive for new files and folders, empty the Recycle Bin. Emptying the Recycle Bin permanently removes any items it contains from your system. Be aware that after you empty the Recycle Bin, you can no longer restore any files it once contained.

Deleting and Restoring Items

Now let's see how to delete an item and restore it from the Recycle Bin:

1. In the Windows Explorer file list, click the item you want to delete to select it—in this example, the Sales Conference Expense Report file in the Documents library.
2. Click the Organize button.
3. Select Delete.
4. Windows prompts you to confirm the deletion. Click Yes. Windows removes the item from its original location and places it in the Recycle Bin.

5. To restore the item, double-click the Recycle Bin icon on the Windows desktop. (To view the desktop, click the Show Desktop button on the far right of the taskbar.)
6. The Recycle Bin window opens. Click the file you want to restore to select it.
7. Click the Restore This Item button. This removes the item from the Recycle Bin and restores it to its original location.
8. To confirm that you've restored the item, display the Documents library in Windows Explorer. The item appears in its original location.

Emptying the Recycle Bin

As mentioned previously, it's a good idea to empty your Recycle Bin occasionally. This lets you permanently delete files or folders, which gives you more available hard disk space.

To empty the Recycle Bin:

1. On the Windows desktop, double-click the Recycle Bin icon.
2. Browse the contents of the Recycle Bin to be sure you want to permanently delete everything it contains.
3. Click Empty the Recycle Bin on the command bar.
4. Windows prompts you to confirm the operation. Click Yes. Windows empties the Recycle Bin.

Searching for Files and Folders

If you are careful about keeping your files and folders organized, you should not lose track of them. Inevitably, however, sometimes you will. Either you will forget where you stored a file or you may drop it in the wrong folder by accident when performing a drag and drop.

Fortunately, Windows features a robust Search feature. You can use this feature in a couple of different ways:

- If you have a general idea where your item may be—for example, you're pretty certain it's in your Documents library—use the Windows Explorer search box to find it.
- If you have no clue where your item is, use the Windows Start menu's search box to scour your computer's entire hard drive.

When searching for an item in Windows, you can search for its name, its file type, the author, the date you last modified the file, or even any words or phrases contained within the file.

How Does the Search Feature Work?

The Windows 7 Search feature uses metadata. **Metadata** is essentially data about data. Put another way, metadata is information about a file's contents. For example, an image file might include metadata that describes how large the image is, the color depth, the image resolution, when the image was created, who created it, and other data. A text document's metadata might contain information about how long the document is, who the author is, when the document was written, and a short summary of the document.

Check a file's metadata by opening the file's Properties window and clicking the Details tab.

5.4 Exercise: Searching for an Item Using Windows Explorer

To search for an item using Windows Explorer, follow these steps:

1. Open the folder you think contains the item you want to find.
2. Type your search criteria in the search box in the window's upper-right corner. As you type, Windows Explorer displays items that match your criteria, as shown in FIGURE 5-25.

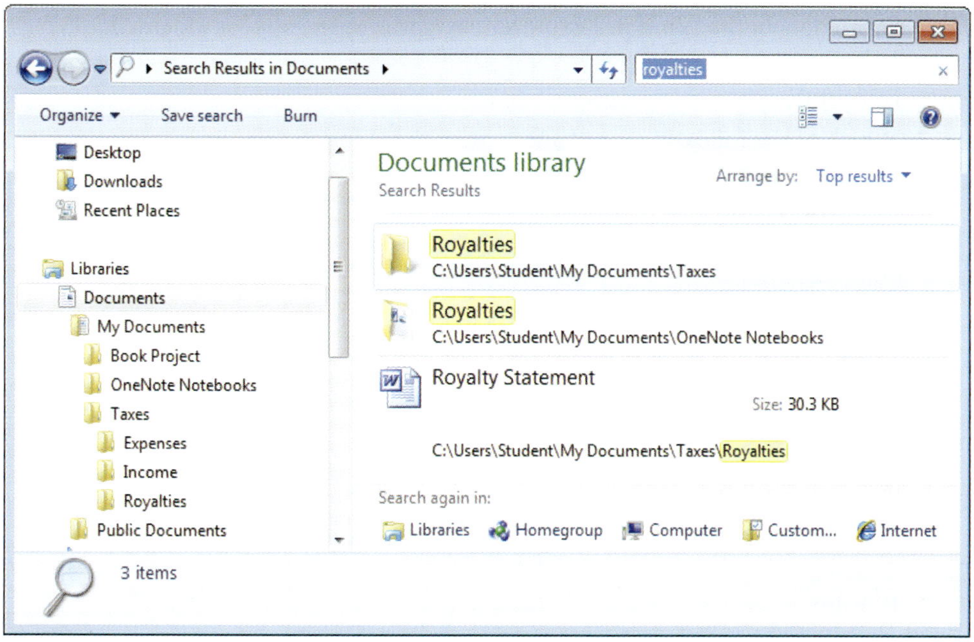

FIGURE 5-25 As you type, Windows Explorer displays items that match your criteria.

5.5 Exercise: Searching for an Item Using the Windows Start Menu

To search for an item using the Windows Start menu, follow these steps:

1. Click the Start button.
2. Type your search criteria in the search box. As you type, the Start menu displays items that match your criteria, as shown in FIGURE 5-26.

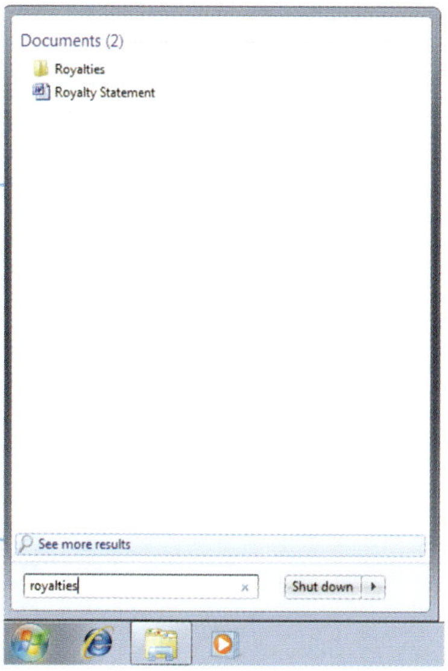

FIGURE 5-26 As you type, the items that match your criteria appear in a list.

At this point you've completed two of the three Windows 7 chapters in this book. You'll continue your learning of the Windows 7 operating system in Chapter 6 by exploring Windows programs and how to use them. Before you move on, be sure to take the quiz in the Test Yourself section and complete the project.

Test Yourself

The questions in this section are meant to test your knowledge of what you read. Make sure you answer them. The page number where the answer can be found appears after each question.

1. What program does Windows 7 provide to manage folders and files? (93)
   A. Internet Explorer
   B. Windows Explorer
   C. Folder Explorer
   D. File Manager
2. Subfolders in the Windows Explorer navigation pane appear indented. (95)
   A. True
   B. False
3. Which of the following is not a feature of the Windows Explorer window? (96)
   A. Library pane
   B. Preview pane
   C. Address bar
   D. Recycle Bin
4. When you open a folder in Windows Explorer, the contents of that folder appear in what portion of the window? (96)
   A. Navigation pane
   B. Details pane
   C. File list
   D. Preview pane
5. You cannot navigate folders and files via the address bar. (99)
   A. True
   B. False
6. Which button cycles through the available file views? (101)
   A. The Change Your View button
   B. The Layout button
   C. The Switch Icon button
   D. The Icon Layout button
7. You cannot create new folders in Windows Explorer. (102, 103)
   A. True
   B. False
8. What key must you press if attempting to select multiple files that appear consecutively in the file list? (105)
   A. Ctrl
   B. Shift
   C. Alt
   D. Caps Lock
9. What key must you press if attempting to select multiple files that appear nonconsecutively in the file list? (106)
   A. Ctrl
   B. Shift
   C. Alt
   D. Caps Lock
10. Which of the following characters can't you use in file names? (Select two.) (106)
    A. ,
    B. +

C. !
D. ?

11. When renaming a file, you must change the file extension. (107)
    A. True
    B. False
12. When copying in Windows Explorer, what is the source? (107)
    A. The item you want to copy
    B. The folder containing the item you want to copy
    C. The folder that will receive the item being copied
    D. The navigation pane
13. When copying in Windows Explorer, what is the destination? (108)
    A. The item you want to copy
    B. The folder containing the item you want to copy
    C. The folder that will receive the item being copied
    D. The navigation pane
14. What is the Windows Clipboard? (108)
15. You can only copy files one at a time. (109)
    A. True
    B. False
16. Which method for moving items is considered risky? (109)
17. Where does Windows 7 place deleted files? (111)
    A. The Garbage icon
    B. The Deleted Items folder
    C. The Waste Basket
    D. The Recycle Bin
18. You can restore deleted items in most cases. (111)
    A. True
    B. False
19. What special type of data does the Windows 7 Search feature use? (112)
    A. Metadata
    B. Source data
    C. Micro data
    D. Property data
20. You can search for files in Windows Explorer but not using the Start menu search box. (113)
    A. True
    B. False

End-of-Chapter Project

Now you will practice some of the skills you learned in this chapter by creating a folder for your course files. Follow these steps:

1. Click the Windows Explorer button in the taskbar to launch Windows Explorer.
2. Right-click the Documents library in the navigation pane, select New, and then select Folder.
3. A new folder appears in the navigation pane with its name, New Folder, highlighted. Type a name for the folder—in this case, **Class Research**—and press Enter.

4. Repeat Steps 1 through 3 to create another new folder. Name this new folder PC Basics.
5. Click the Class Research folder to select it.
6. Click the Organize button.
7. Select Cut. The item you selected is copied to the Clipboard.
8. Double-click the Introduction to PC Basics folder to open it.
9. Click the Organize button.
10. Select Paste to place the item into the folder. Note that because you cut the item rather than copied it, it appears only in the PC Basics folder.

CHAPTER

6

Windows 7 Programs

- So far, you've learned how to perform many basic tasks in Windows, such as managing your files and folders to keep things organized. In this chapter, you will learn how to use Windows programs. Windows 7 comes bundled with many useful programs. At its most basic level, a **program**, also called an **application**, is computer software designed to help the user perform a task. Two of the most useful programs in Windows 7 are **WordPad**, a word processing program, and **Paint**, which you use to create simple drawings.
- In this chapter, you will learn how to open and close a Windows 7 program; how to create a file, save it to a specific folder, print it, and close it; how to use WordPad to create simple documents; and how to operate Paint to create a simple drawing. You'll also see how to embed a drawing you create in Paint in a WordPad document, and how to apply the Windows 7 Snipping Tool to capture a screen shot or snip—that is, a copy of the contents of your computer screen, saved as a graphics file. Later in the chapter, you will be introduced to **Windows Media Player**, which lets you enjoy music, photos, and videos on your computer. To ensure you don't lose any of your files, you will find out how to back up your files using Windows 7 **Backup and Restore**. Finally, you will get some tips for installing new programs on your computer.
- Once you learn these basics, you will be able to apply them to almost any program you work with in Windows. Let's get started!

CHAPTER TOPICS

This chapter covers the following topics and concepts:

- How to open a program
- How to navigate program windows
- How to use dialog boxes
- How to use WordPad to create, save, and print a file
- How to do basic word processing in WordPad
- How to use Paint to create and modify graphics
- How to copy, move, and embed text and objects
- How to capture screen shots
- How to use Windows Media Player for music, videos, and photos
- Why backing up data is important and how to use Windows 7 Backup and Restore
- How to install new programs

KEY WORDS

Application
Aspect ratio
Backup and Restore
Checkbox
Cursor
Drop-down list box
Embed
Insertion point
Object
Option button
Paint
Pixel
Program
Ribbon
Rip
Screen shot
Scroll box
Snip
Tabs
Text box
Windows Media Player
WordPad
Work area

Opening a Program

Before you can work with a program in Windows 7, you must open, or launch, it. As you've learned already, you'll often find many ways to accomplish the same task in Windows 7, and launching programs is no exception. Open a program in Windows 7 by doing one of the following:

- Click the Windows 7 Start button and select the program from the menu that appears, as shown in FIGURE 6-1.

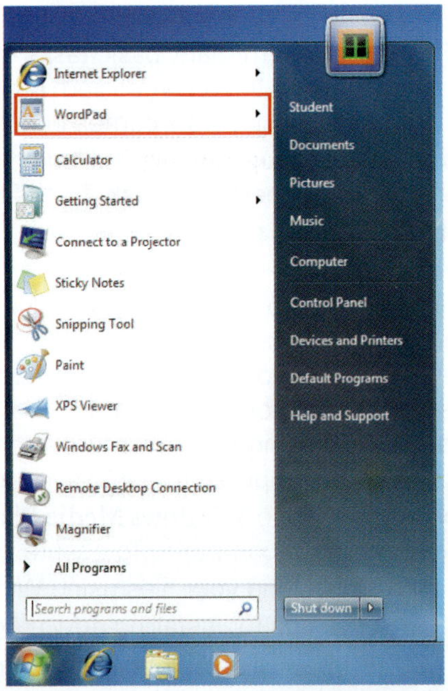

FIGURE 6-1 Select the program from the Start menu.

- Click the Windows 7 Start button, type the program name in the Start menu's Search box, and click the link for the program that appears in the Start menu, as shown in FIGURE 6-2.
- Click the program's button on the Windows 7 taskbar (assuming a button for the program is present), as shown in FIGURE 6-3.
- Double-click the program's shortcut icon on the Windows 7 desktop (assuming a shortcut icon is present), as shown in FIGURE 6-4.
- Double-click a file associated with the program you want to open in the Windows Explorer file list, as shown in FIGURE 6-5. For example, start WordPad by double-clicking a Rich Text format (RTF) file in Windows Explorer.

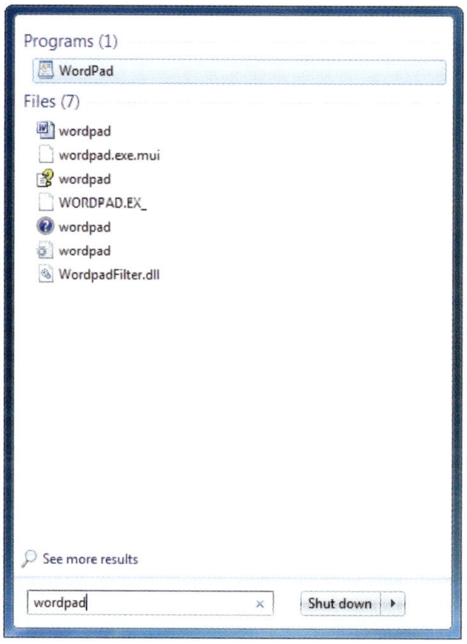

FIGURE 6-2 Search for the program in the Start menu.

FIGURE 6-3 Click the program's button in the Windows 7 taskbar.

FIGURE 6-4 Double-click the program's shortcut icon on the Windows 7 desktop.

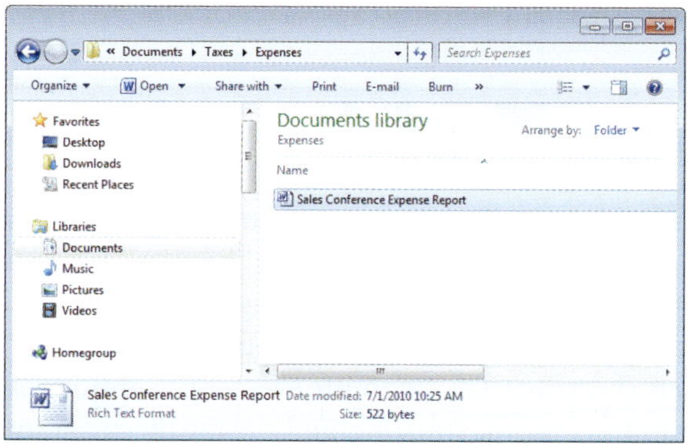

FIGURE 6-5 Double-click a file in Windows Explorer.

TIP

To add a button for a program to the Windows 7 taskbar, locate the program in the Windows 7 Start menu, right-click it, and choose Pin To Taskbar in the menu that appears.

When you open a program in Windows 7, a button for that program appears on the Windows 7 taskbar. To open a second instance of the program—for example, to work on two documents in WordPad at the same time—right-click the button and select the program's name from the list that appears, as shown in FIGURE 6-6.

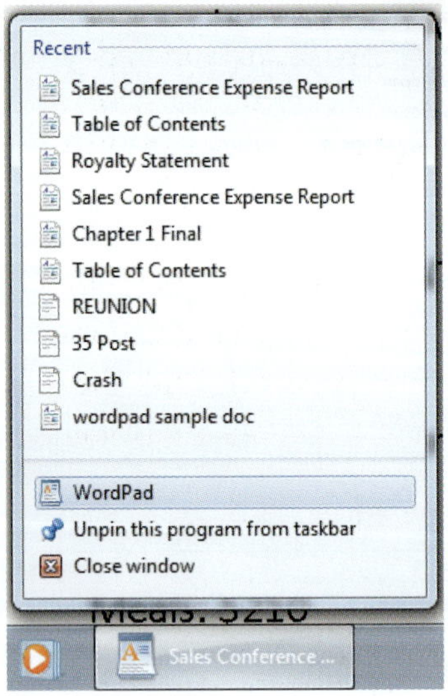

FIGURE 6-6 You can open multiple instances of a program.

Left Click Versus Right Click

By now, you have read enough to start realizing that the left and right mouse buttons perform different tasks. To summarize, you usually use the left button to select an item or start some kind of process. You press the right button to display menus and properties.

6.1 Exercise: Opening WordPad

In this exercise, learn how to open WordPad via the Windows 7 Start menu. Follow these steps:

1. Click the Start button.
2. If WordPad appears in the Start menu's left pane, click it to open it. If not, select All Programs.
3. Select Accessories.
4. Select WordPad. The WordPad window opens.

Navigating Program Windows

As you saw in the previous exercise, when you open a program in Windows 7, a window for that program appears on the desktop. Although not all program windows are the same, many Windows 7 programs have certain navigation elements in common. Chapter 4 introduced you to program windows, but this refresher adds a few details:

- **Window menu button:** Click this button to access commands for restoring, moving, sizing, minimizing, maximizing, and closing the program window. (Be aware that this button's appearance changes depending on the program that is running.)

- **Quick Access toolbar:** Click the buttons in this toolbar to quickly save a file or launch the Undo or Redo command. Note that you can customize this toolbar to include different buttons.
- **Title bar:** The name of the program and the name of the file open in the program window appear in the title bar.
- **Window controls:** Program windows include a Minimize button, a Maximize or Restore button, and a Close button. Use these to clear the program window from the desktop without closing it, enlarge the program window to cover the entire desktop, return the window to its original size, or close the program window, respectively.
- **File tab:** Click the File tab to view options for creating a new file, opening an existing file, saving a file, printing a file, and more.
- **Ribbon:** Some Windows programs include the **Ribbon** in lieu of traditional pull-down menus and toolbars. The Ribbon displays groups of related buttons and options in tabs.
- **Work area:** Files you open in the program appear in the program window's **work area**.
- **Scroll bars:** A vertical and/or horizontal scroll bar appears in the program window if your file is too large to view in its entirety in the work area. To view parts of the file not currently on screen, click the **scroll box** in the scroll bar and drag in the desired direction.
- **Zoom controls:** To zoom in or out of the file displayed in the work area, use the Zoom In button, the Zoom Out button, or the Zoom slider.

FIGURE 6-7 shows where to find all of these elements using WordPad as an example.

> **Note**
>
> You will see the Ribbon often in this and the remaining chapters of this book—it's an important part of some Windows 7 programs and Office 2010.

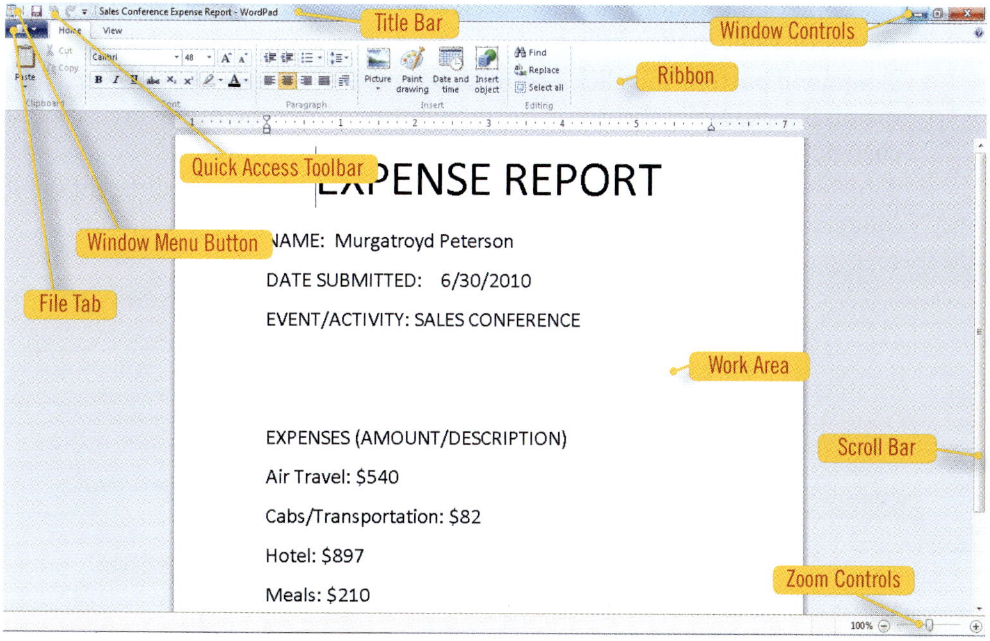

FIGURE 6-7 Common program window elements.

Understanding Dialog Box Options

Chapter 4 also introduced you to dialog boxes. Now that you're beginning to work with actual programs, it's important to revisit dialog boxes and explain some of the options you'll see frequently.

When a program requires user input—that is, it needs you to supply information—it displays a dialog box. For example, when you save a file for the first time, a Save As dialog box appears in which you choose the folder where you want to save the file, enter a name for the file, and make other choices.

Dialog boxes feature different types of input controls. These include the following (see FIGURE 6-8):

- **Option button:** Clicking an **option button** enables or disables the feature associated with it. When an option button is colored in, its associated feature is enabled; when it appears empty, the feature is disabled. Note that you can select only one option button in a group. Option buttons are often called "radio buttons."
- **Checkbox:** A **checkbox** is similar to an option button in that clicking a checkbox enables or disables the feature associated with it. The difference? You can select multiple checkboxes in a group at once. When you've selected a checkbox, it contains a check mark; deselected checkboxes are empty.
- **Text box:** You enter text in a **text box**. To do so, click inside the text box. When the blinking vertical bar (called a **cursor** or **insertion point**) appears, delete any existing characters in the text box by pressing the Backspace or Delete key on your keyboard; then type your text. The address bar in a Web browser is an example of a text box.
- **Drop-down list box:** A **drop-down list box** has a down arrow on the far right side. You change the setting in a drop-down list box by clicking the down arrow and selecting the desired setting from the list that appears. A drop-down list box is also called a "drop-down list."
- **Spin button:** You use a spin button to set a numeric value. To increase the value that appears in the text box next to a spin button, click the top arrow on the spin button; click the bottom button to decrease it. Alternatively, you can simply type a numeric value in the text box.
- **Command button:** You click a command button to execute its associated command. For example, clicking the Cancel button closes the dialog box without changing the settings.
- **Tab:** Some dialog boxes feature **tabs**, with each tab displaying a different set of input controls. To switch to a different tab in a dialog box, simply click it.

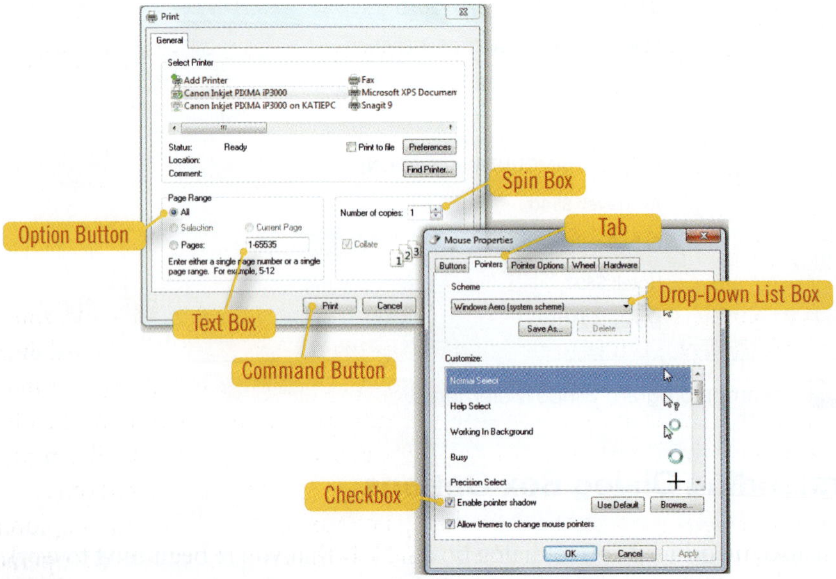

FIGURE 6-8 Windows 7 dialog boxes.

Creating, Saving, and Printing Files

When you open a program, such as WordPad or Paint, a new, blank file appears in the work area, ready for you to begin work. You don't need to open a new instance of the program window to create a new file, however. Instead, you use the New command on the File tab to create a new file, as shown in FIGURE 6-9. Alternatively, you can press the Ctrl+N keyboard shortcut. That is, while holding down the Ctrl key, press the N key.

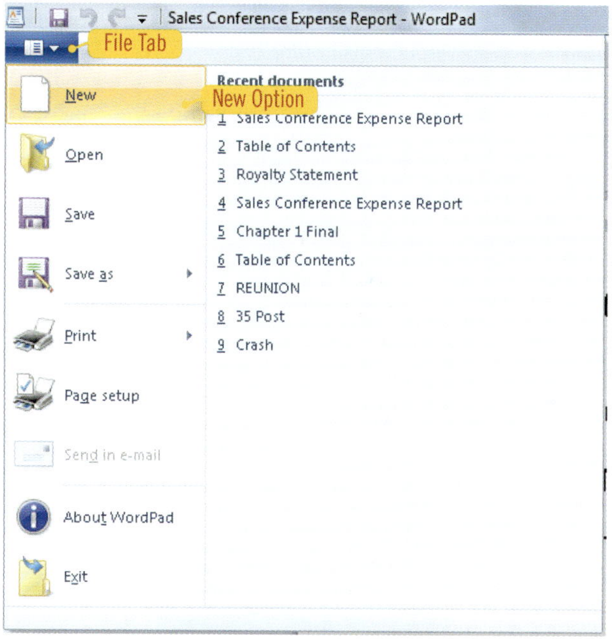

FIGURE 6-9 Create a new WordPad document.

When you create a new file, its name, which appears in the title bar, is Untitled. That's because you haven't saved it yet. Once you save the file, as discussed in the next section, the title bar will display whatever name you assigned to the file.

> **TIP**
> Some programs require that you take additional steps when creating a new file. For example, if you want to create a new file in Microsoft Word (available as part of the Microsoft Office suite of products), you must indicate what type of file you want to create—a blank document, a fax, or some other format.

6.2 Exercise: Creating a New WordPad File

In this exercise, learn how to create a new WordPad file. Follow these steps:

1. In the WordPad window, click the File tab.
2. Click New. A new, empty file appears in the work area.
3. Type some text in the file.

Saving a File

If you want to refer to the data you enter in a file at some later time, save the file. You save a file by selecting the Save option on the File tab or by pressing the Ctrl+S keyboard shortcut.

When you save a file for the first time, Windows 7 opens a Save As dialog box in which you specify where you want to save the file and enter a descriptive name for the file. The next time you save the file, Windows 7 will not open this dialog box; it will simply save the file again in the same place, replacing the existing file with the current one.

As shown in FIGURE 6-10, the Save As dialog box is similar to Windows Explorer—it features a navigation pane, an address bar, a search box, and a file list—and it operates in much the same way. That is, you can access the folder in which you want to save your file by double-clicking, using the navigation pane, using the address bar, or some combination

> **TIP**
> Frequently save a file as you work on it. That way, if your computer experiences a crash or other failure, you won't lose the work you've done on the file.

of the three. In addition, the Save As dialog box includes a File Name text box, where you type a descriptive name for the file, and a Save As Type drop-down list box, where you can choose a different file type for the file. When you've made the necessary selections in the Save As dialog box, click the Save button to complete the operation.

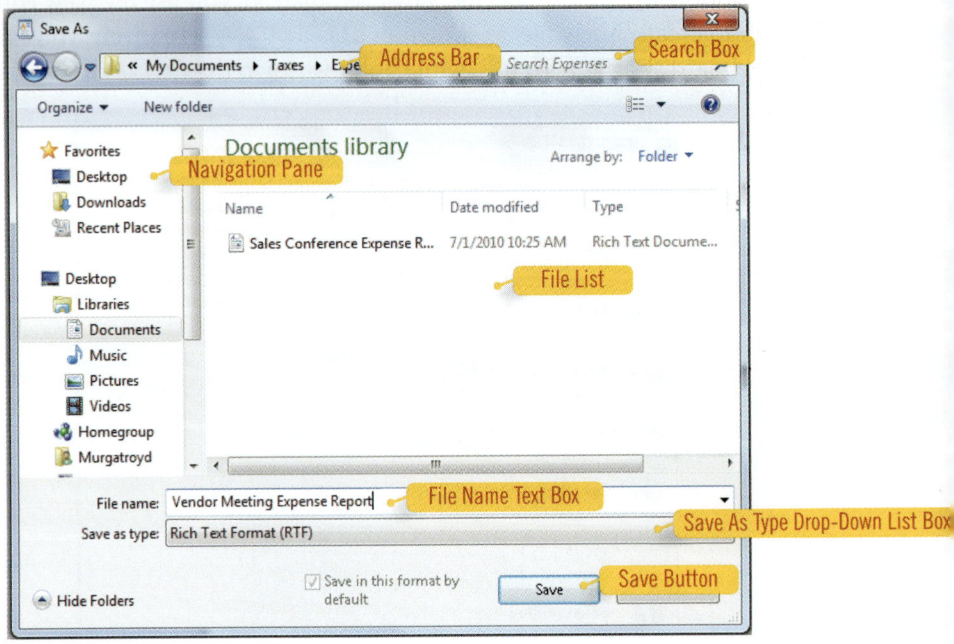

FIGURE 6-10 The Save As dialog box.

Save Versus Save As

In addition to including a Save command, Windows 7 programs also support the use of a Save As command. What is the difference between them? If, after having saved a file, you select the Save command, Windows 7 will simply replace the existing file with the current version. If, however, you select Save As, Windows 7 launches the Save As dialog box, enabling you to save a copy of the file with another name, in the same location or in another location. You might use the Save As command if you make changes to a file, but you want to keep a copy of the original version intact.

6.3 Exercise: Saving a WordPad File

In this exercise, learn how to save a WordPad file for the first time. Follow these steps:

1. In the WordPad window, click the File tab.
2. Click Save.
3. The Save As dialog box opens. Open the folder in which you want to save your file—in this example, the Expenses subfolder in the Taxes folder.
4. Type a descriptive name for the file—for example, **July Expenses**—in the File Name field.
5. Click the Save button. Windows saves the file in the folder you chose, with the name you entered.

Closing a File or Program

When you have finished working with a file or program, you can close it. When you do, the program window closes and its taskbar button disappears. If you have made changes to the file you are attempting to close since the last Save operation, Windows 7 will prompt you to save these changes.

You have a few ways to close a file or program:

- Click the Close button in the upper-right corner of the program window, as shown in FIGURE 6-11.

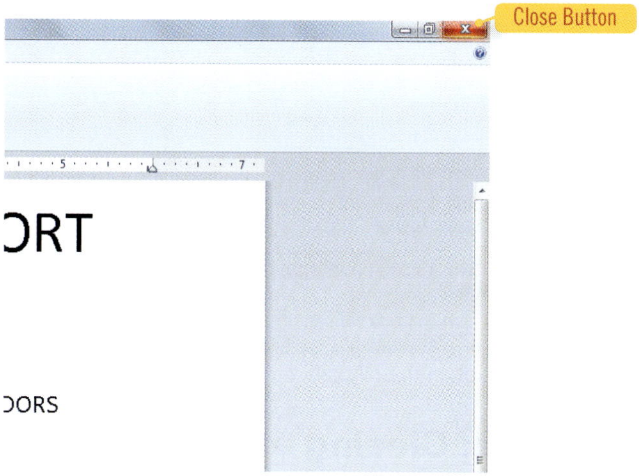

FIGURE 6-11 The Close button.

- Hover your mouse pointer over the file's program button in the taskbar. In the list that appears, hover your mouse pointer over the file you want to close, and then click the Close button, as shown in FIGURE 6-12.
- In some programs, you can click the File tab and select Exit from the list of options that appears, as shown in FIGURE 6-13.

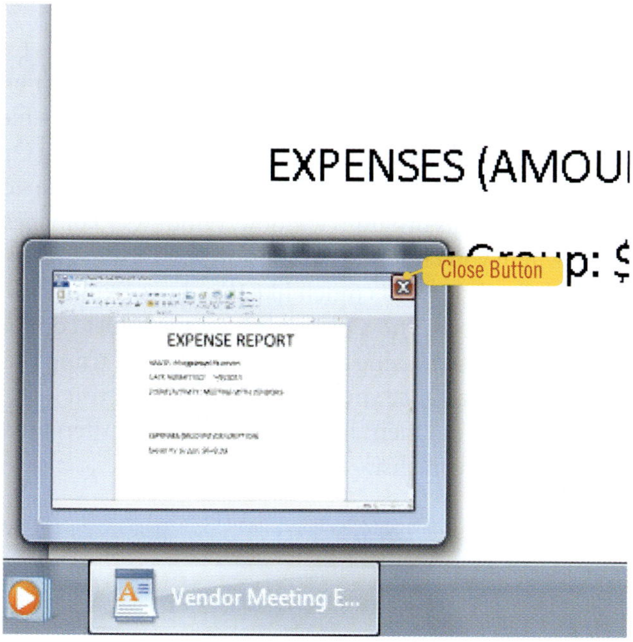

FIGURE 6-12 Click the Close button that appears over the program icon in the taskbar.

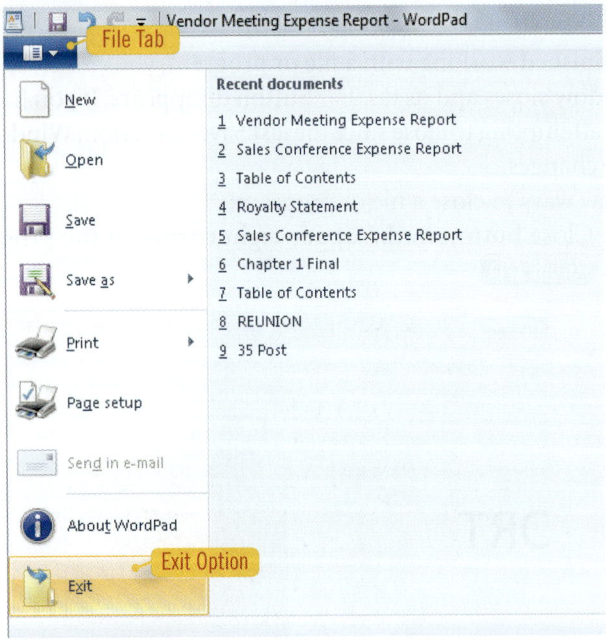

FIGURE 6-13 The Exit option in the File tab.

6.4 Exercise: Closing a WordPad File

In this exercise, learn how to close a WordPad file. Follow these steps:

1. Click the Close button in the upper-right corner of the program window containing the file.
2. If you've made any changes to the file since the last Save operation, Windows 7 will prompt you to save the file. Click Yes. Windows saves your changes and closes the file.

Opening a File

As you learned in Chapter 4, you can open a file from within Windows Explorer. Another way to open a file is from within its associated program window. For example, you can open any RTF file from the WordPad program window or a graphics file from the Paint program window. You open a file by clicking the File tab and selecting Open from the list of options that appears. Alternatively, press the Ctrl+O keyboard shortcut.

When you open a file from its program window, Windows 7 launches an Open dialog box (see FIGURE 6-14), where you choose what file you want to open. As with the Save As dialog box, the Open dialog box works much like Windows Explorer, with a navigation pane, an address bar, a search box, and a file list. Access the folder containing the file you want to open by double-clicking, using the navigation pane, using the address bar, or some combination of the three. Once you have located the file you want to open, simply click it in the file list to select it and then click the Open button. Alternatively, double-click the file you want to open in the file list.

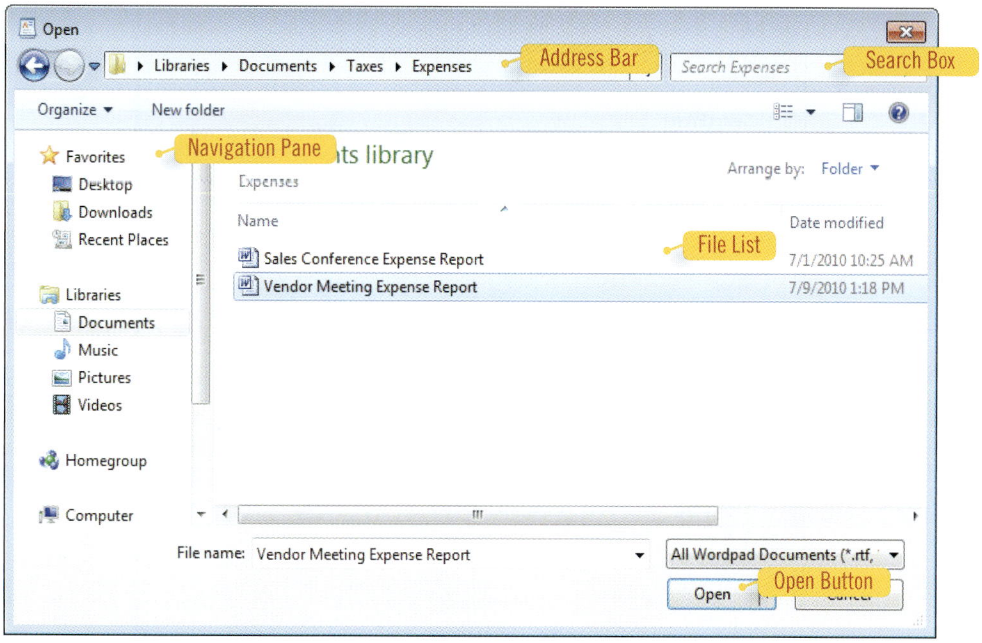

FIGURE 6-14 The Open dialog box.

6.5 Exercise: Opening a WordPad File

In this exercise, learn how to open a WordPad file. Follow these steps:

1. Start the WordPad program, and then click the File tab.
2. Click Open.
3. The Open dialog box appears. Open the folder that contains the file you want to open—in this example, the Expenses subfolder in the Taxes folder.
4. Click the file you want to open.
5. Click the Open button. The file opens in the program window.

Printing a File

Suppose you are finished working with your file and you want to make a printout of it. Assuming you have a printer connected to your computer or can access a computer over a network, you can easily do so.

Printing a file is a simple matter. Click the File tab and select the Print option, or press the Ctrl+P keyboard shortcut. When you do, Windows displays the Print dialog box (see **FIGURE 6-15**), where you can choose from various print options:

- **Select Printer:** If your computer is connected to multiple printers, choose the printer you want to use for this print job.
- **Page Range:** By default, the All option button is selected, meaning the entire document will be printed. If you prefer, however, you can choose Selection to print only a selected item in the file, Current Page to print only the page where the insertion point is located, or Pages to select a range of pages to print.
- **Number of Copies:** Windows prints one copy of the file by default, but you can change this setting to print as many copies of the file as you want. If you opt to print multiple copies of the file, Windows gives you the option of collating them.

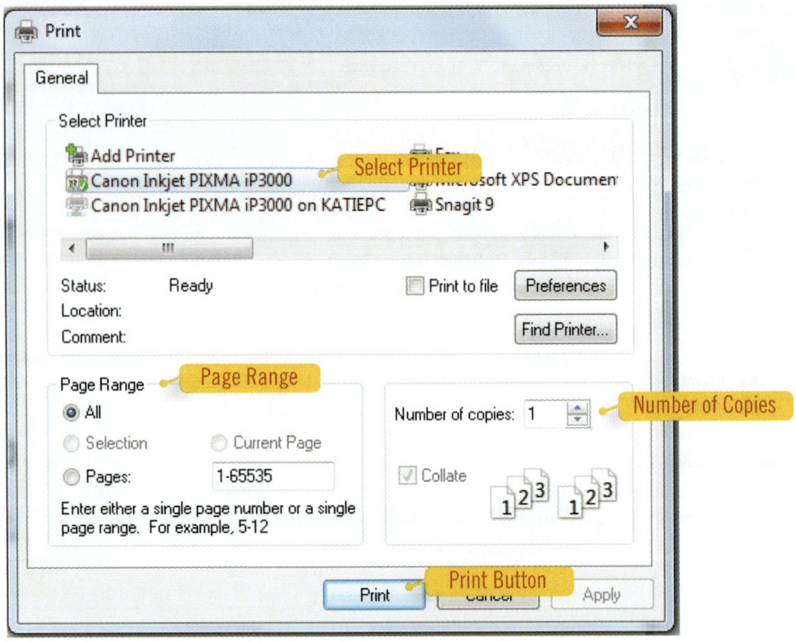

FIGURE 6-15 The Print dialog box.

After you make your selections, click the Print button to print the file.

Print Preview

Many programs offer a Print Preview option, which lets you see exactly how the file you have open in your program window will appear when printed. This can save you a lot of time and aggravation—not to mention money in the form of wasted ink and paper. To use Print Preview, click the File tab, click the arrow to the right of the Print option, and select Print Preview, as shown in **FIGURE 6-16**.

Windows displays the open file in a special Print Preview window, as shown in **FIGURE 6-17**. Note that in WordPad, the Print Preview window allows you to print directly from the Print Preview window, change the page setup, change the zoom setting, and navigate from page to page. To close Print Preview and return to the regular program window, click Close Print Preview.

6.6 Exercise: Printing a File

In this exercise, learn how to print two copies of a WordPad file. After making sure your printer is turned on, follow these steps:

1. In the WordPad window, click the File tab.
2. Click Print.

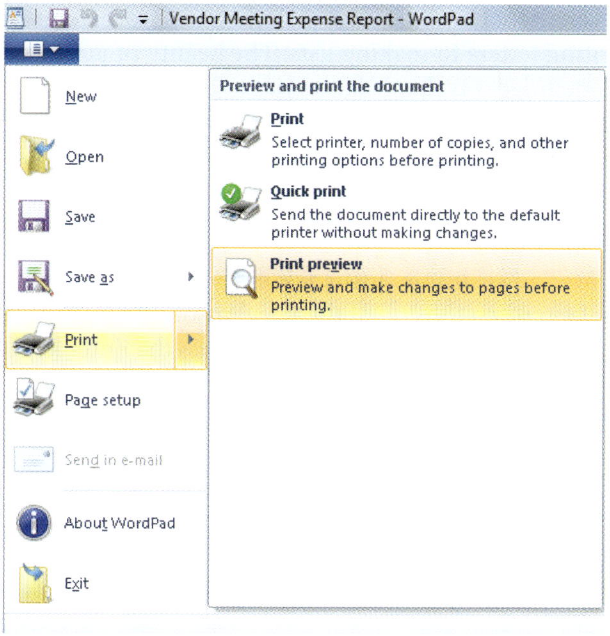

FIGURE 6-16 Select the Print Preview button

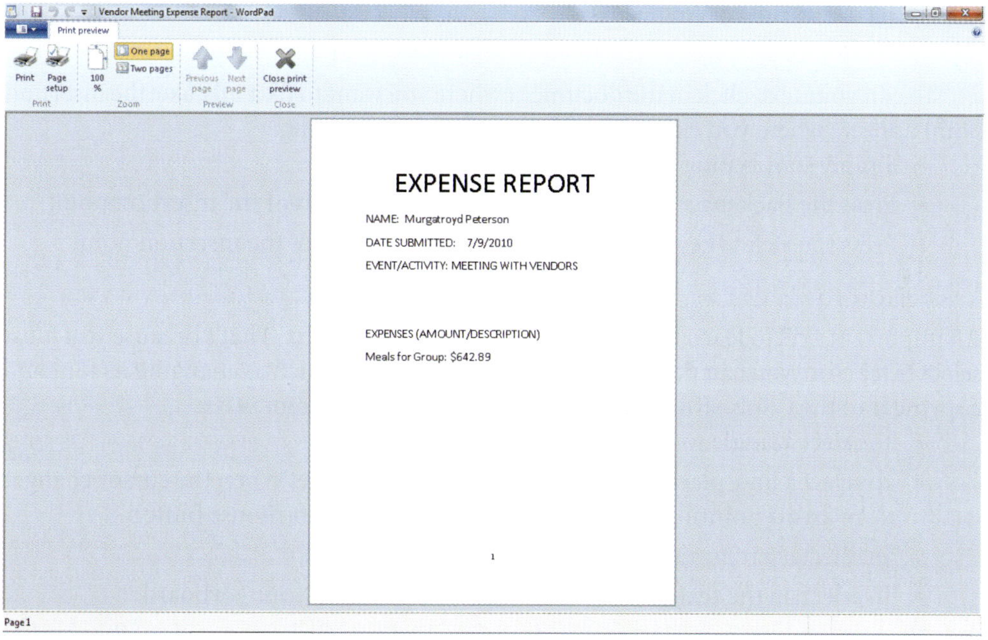

FIGURE 6-17 The Print Preview window.

3. The Print dialog box opens. If necessary, select the printer you want to use from the Select A Printer list.
4. Click the up arrow in the Number of Copies spin box one time to change the value in the associated field from 1 to 2.
5. Click the Print button. The file prints.

Basic Word Processing in WordPad

As you've seen, Windows 7 includes a simple word processing tool called WordPad, which functions like a "lite" version of a commercial word processing program, such as Microsoft

Word. WordPad is great for handling all your basic word processing needs, from viewing documents to writing letters to making lists. The beauty of any word processing program—WordPad included—is that it allows you to easily edit your text after you type it. You can also apply different fonts and colors to the text in your WordPad documents as well as adjust spacing, indents, and other page properties using the various tools found in the WordPad Ribbon.

Adding and Editing Text

Typing text in WordPad is simple. Just click in the document and begin typing (see FIGURE 6-18). When you reach the end of the line, WordPad automatically wraps the text to the next line for you. To start a new paragraph, press the Enter key on your keyboard.

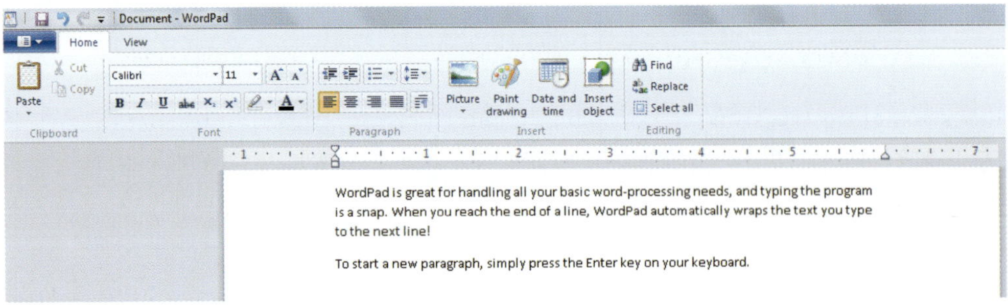

FIGURE 6-18 Adding text in WordPad is a snap.

To edit your text, click in the document where you want to fix a mistake; the insertion point appears where you clicked. Then do one of the following:

- Simply start typing to add text.
- Press the Backspace key to delete characters to the left of the insertion point.
- Press the Delete key to delete characters to the right of the insertion point.

> **TIP**
> You can also delete selected text; just select the text and press the Delete or Backspace key.

Selecting Text

An important skill to learn for word processing is selecting text. That's because you must select text before you can perform certain operations on it, such as changing its font and copying it to the Clipboard. You can select text in a few different ways:

- To select a single word, double-click it.
- To select a line, place your cursor to the left of the line. When the cursor changes to an arrow pointing up and to the right, press the left mouse button.
- To select a paragraph, triple-click anywhere within it.
- To select all the text in a document, press Ctrl+A on your keyboard.

Alternatively, you can select text by dragging. To do so, click to one side of the word or character you want to select and then drag the cursor across the text that you want to select.

> **TIP**
> To deselect selected text, simply click anywhere outside the text.

Changing the Font

Alter the appearance of a document in WordPad by changing the text font, size, and color. For example, if you are using WordPad to create a report, you might use a different font, size, and color for the report's title than for the information contained in the report. You can also apply WordPad's basic formatting commands—Bold, Italic, Underline, Strike through, Subscript, and Superscript—to your text. To change these text attributes, first select the text as described in the preceding section. Then choose the desired font, size, color, or formatting option from the Font group on the Home tab (see FIGURE 6-19).

Aligning Text, Indenting Text, and Changing the Spacing

WordPad's alignment commands let you change how text is positioned horizontally on a page. Specifically, you can left-align text (the default), center it, right-align it, or justify

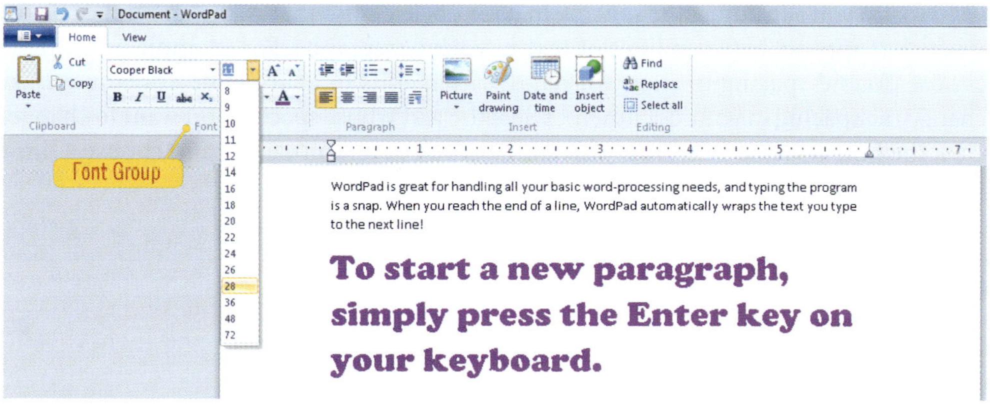

FIGURE 6-19 Use options in the Font group in the Home tab to change text attributes.

it. To change the text's alignment in your document, select the text you want to align and click an alignment button in the Paragraph group on the Home tab (see **FIGURE 6-20**).

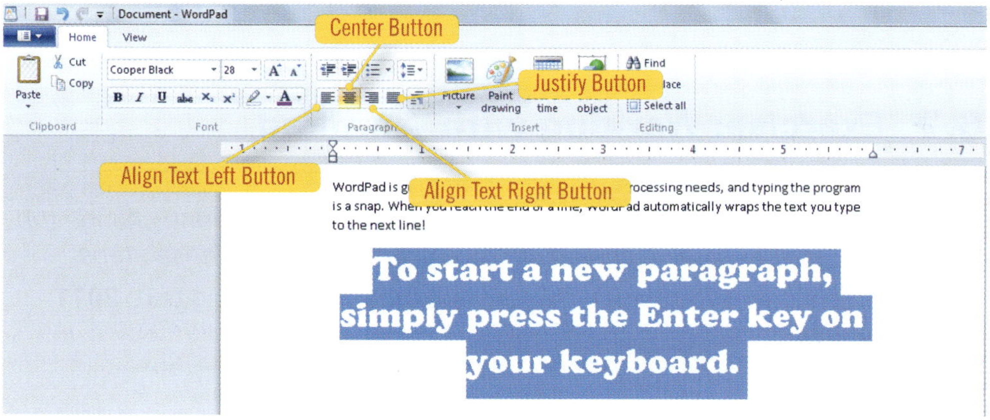

FIGURE 6-20 Use the alignment buttons in the Home tab's Paragraph group to change text attributes.

Another way to control the positioning of text in a document is to use indents. For example, you might indent a paragraph to set it apart from the rest of the text on a page. To indent a paragraph, select it, and click the Increase Indent button in the Home tab's Paragraph group (see **FIGURE 6-21**). To remove an indent from a paragraph, select the indented paragraph and click the Decrease Indent button.

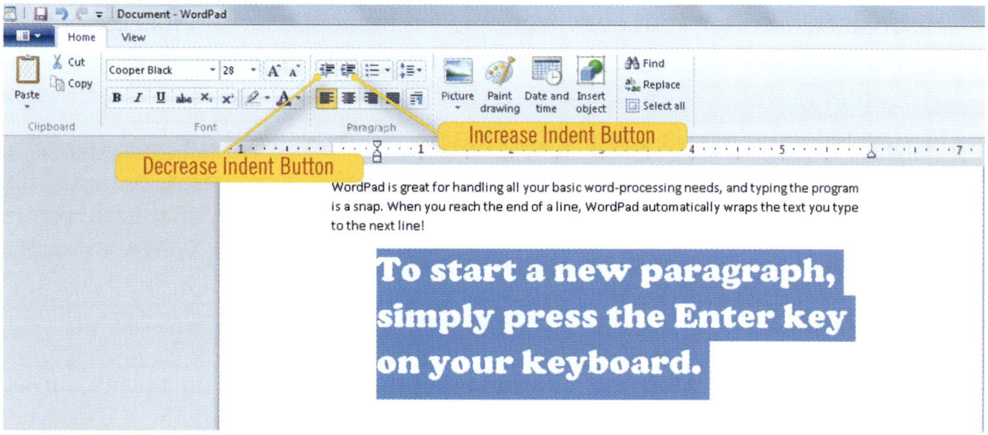

FIGURE 6-21 Increase or decrease the indent as needed.

TIP

If you make a change to your WordPad document that you want to undo, click the Undo button in the Windows 7 Quick Access toolbar. If, after undoing a change, you realize you want to reapply it, click the Quick Access toolbar's Redo button. Not sure which button is which? Just hover your mouse pointer over each icon in the Quick Access toolbar. A tooltip appears, which gives you the button's name.

Finally, you can adjust the spacing in your document—that is, the amount of blank space that appears between lines of text in your paragraphs. For example, you might choose double-spacing to allow for handwritten edits in your printed document. To change the spacing in your document, select the text whose spacing you want to change, click the Line Spacing button on the Home tab's Paragraph group, and choose a line-spacing option from the list that appears (see FIGURE 6-22).

FIGURE 6-22 Change the spacing in your document.

6.7 Exercise: Working with WordPad

In this exercise, learn how to enter text in a WordPad document, change the text's font, size, and color, and adjust its alignment. Follow these steps:

1. Create a new WordPad document and type the following text: **2011 Expenses**
2. Select the text you typed.
3. If necessary, click the Home tab.
4. Click the down arrow next to the current font name.
5. Select a different font from the list that appears, such as Arial or Times New Roman.
6. The new font is applied to the selected text. With the text still selected, click the down arrow next to the current font size.
7. Select a different font size from the list that appears—in this case, 48.
8. WordPad changes the size of the selected text. With the text still selected, click the down arrow to the right of the current font color.
9. Select a different font color from the list that appears—in this case, red.
10. The selected text changes color. With the text still selected, click the Center button.
11. The selected text is centered on the page. To deselect the text, click a blank area in the work area.
12. Close WordPad without saving the document.

Using Paint

Paint is a program for creating doodles and other simple drawings on a blank canvas. You can also use Paint to open digital photos and rotate, crop, or resize them.

The Ribbon in Paint includes various drawing tools, including the following (see FIGURE 6-23):

- **Pencil:** Select this tool to draw free-form lines.
- **Brushes:** Choose from several brushes to draw free-form lines with different textures. Options include paintbrushes, two calligraphy pens, an airbrush, a crayon, a marker, and a natural pencil.
- **Shapes:** Paint includes several ready-made shapes, which you can insert in your picture, including curves, rectangles, callouts, triangles, arrows, stars, and hearts.

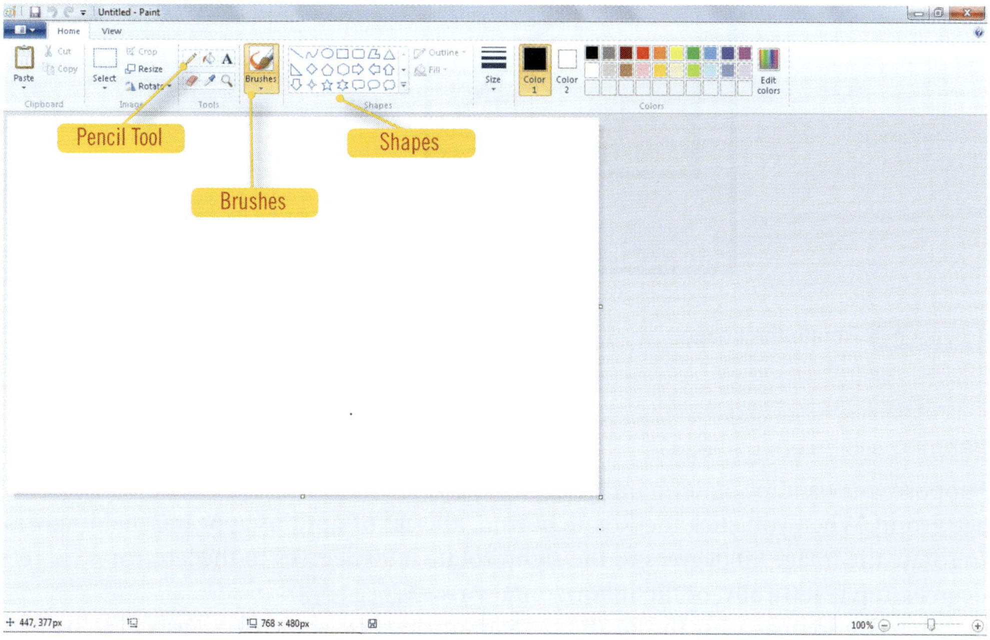

FIGURE 6-23 Paint includes various drawing tools.

The best way to become familiar with the tools in Paint is to experiment with them. Just click a tool's button to select it. Next, click the Size button and choose a line width from the list that appears. Then click the Color 1 button and choose a color from the palette. Finally, click in the work area and draw away.

TIP

Holding down the Shift key on your keyboard as you draw with the Line, Oval, or Rectangle tool lets you create a perfectly straight horizontal or vertical line, a perfect circle, or a square.

In addition to these tools for drawing, Paint includes the following (see **FIGURE 6-24**):

- **Fill With Color tool:** Pick this tool to fill a shape with color.
- **Text tool:** Use this tool to type text. When you select this tool and click in the Paint work area, a Text tab appears on the Ribbon, where you can change the text's font, size, color, and other attributes.
- **Eraser tool:** To erase part of your image, use the Eraser tool.

FIGURE 6-24 Paint's other tools.

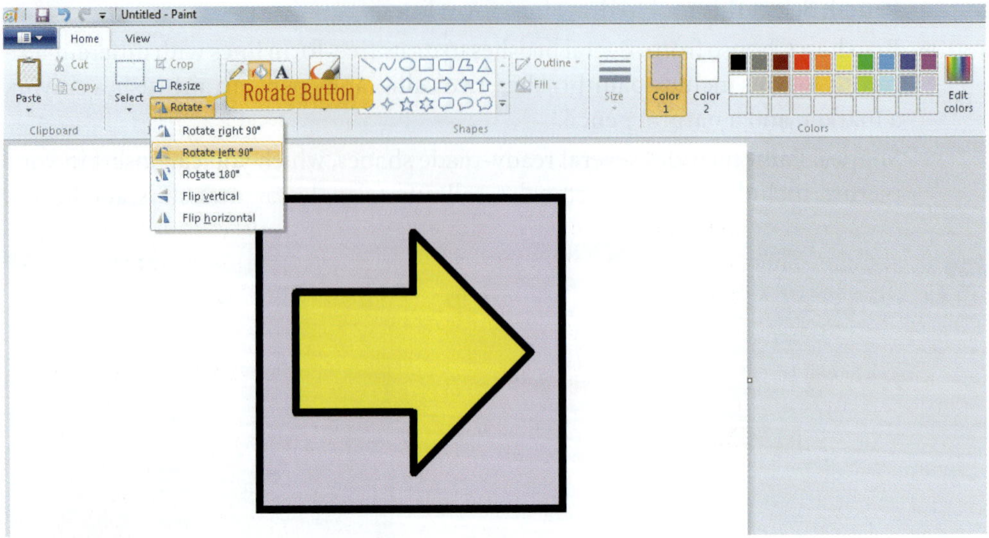

FIGURE 6-25 Rotate the image.

Rotating and Resizing Images

Suppose you want to rotate an image in Paint. Use the Rotate tool in the Home tab's Image group. When you click the Rotate button, a series of options appears, enabling you to rotate the image 90 degrees to the right, rotate it 90 degrees to the left, rotate it 180 degrees, flip it vertically, or flip it horizontally (see FIGURE 6-25).

To resize an image, use the Resize and Skew dialog box, shown in FIGURE 6-26. To open this dialog box, click the Resize button in the Home tab's Image group. Indicate whether you want to resize by a percentage or by a specified number of pixels, enter the desired values in the Horizontal and Vertical text boxes, specify whether the **aspect ratio** should be maintained (that is, whether the ratio between the horizontal and vertical values should remain the same), and click OK.

Note

What's a **pixel**? It's a tiny dot. Certain kinds of images, like those you create in Paint, are actually made up of tiny dots that, together, create the image you see. A single image can contain hundreds to millions of pixels. A pixel is also a standard unit of measurement used for images. Let's say an image is 5 inches by 5 inches. Its pixel ratio might be something like 486 x 486. It's just another way to measure the size of an image.

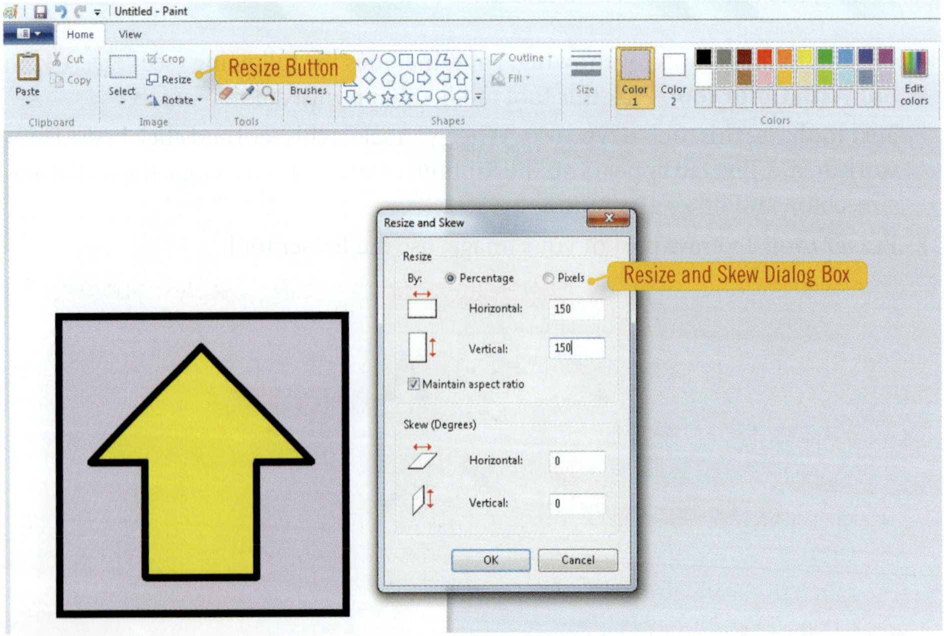

FIGURE 6-26 Resize the image.

Selecting and Editing Objects

In addition to rotating and resizing an entire image, you can also apply these changes to a specific area in the image, called an **object**. As with text in WordPad, select the object in Paint before you change it.

To select an object, use the Select tool. This tool has a few different shapes (see FIGURE 6-27):

- **Rectangular Selection:** Choose this shape if the object you want to select is rectangular. Then, click in the upper-left corner of the object you want to select and drag down and to the right, releasing the mouse button when you reach the object's bottom-right corner.
- **Free-Form Selection:** Pick this shape if the object you want to select is not a rectangle.
- **Select All:** Go for this option if you want to select the entire image.

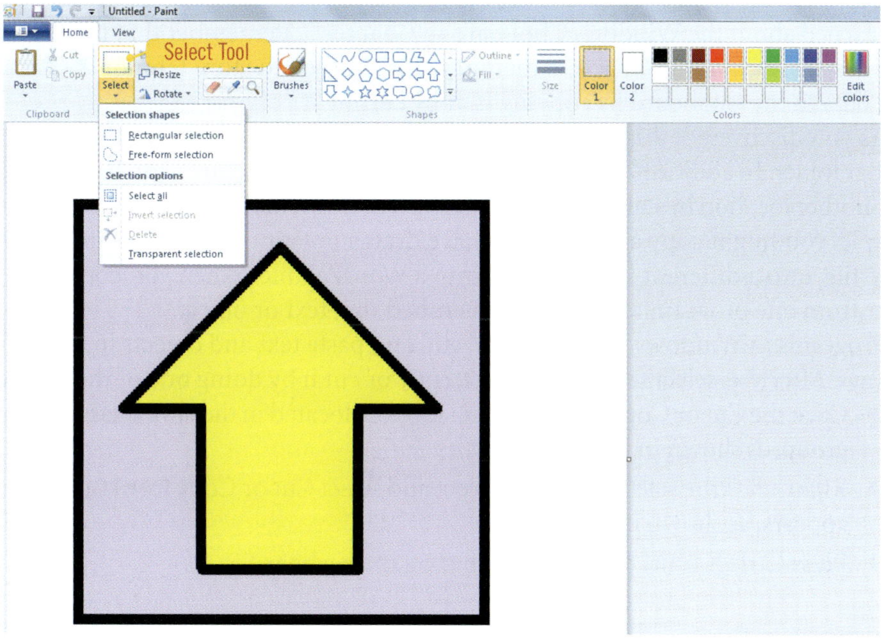

FIGURE 6-27 Paint's selection options.

6.8 Exercise: Working with Paint

In this exercise, learn how to create an object using Paint's drawing tools and crop the image.

1. With a blank canvas open in the Paint window, click the Rectangle tool in the Home tab's Shapes group.
2. Click the Size button and select a line width from the list that appears—in this case, the widest line.
3. Click the Color 1 button.
4. Click a color in the palette, such as green.
5. While holding down the Shift key on your keyboard, click in the canvas and drag down and to the right to draw a square. When the square is the size you want, release the mouse button.
6. Click the Fill With Color tool.
7. Click the Color 1 button.

TIP

Paint doesn't limit you to rotating and resizing objects. You can also crop an object—that is, alter the picture to include only the area you selected. To crop an object, select the portion you want to keep, and then click the Crop button in the Home tab's Image area.

8. Click a color in the palette, such as purple.
9. Click inside the green square. The inside of the square is colored purple.
10. Click the arrow along the bottom of the Select button.
11. Select Rectangular Selection.
12. Click in the upper-left corner of the square and drag down and to the right, but don't cover the entire square. When you reach the opposite corner, release the mouse button. A portion of the square is selected.
13. Click the Crop button. Paint crops the image to contain only the selected area.
14. Select File > New > Don't Save to close the file without saving it.

Copying, Moving, and Embedding Text and Objects

You learned about the Windows Clipboard in Chapter 5. Remember that the Clipboard is a storage area in random access memory (RAM) used to store temporary data. You place data in the Clipboard by copying it or by cutting it.

As you discovered, this temporary data can be a folder, which you then paste into another folder. In addition, temporary data can be text or a picture, which you can paste into another location in a file, into a different file, or into a file in a different program. For example, you might copy an object you have drawn in Paint and paste it into the same image file, into a different image file, or into a WordPad file. When you copy text or an object from one program to another, you **embed** that text or object.

Programs in Windows 7 let you copy, cut, and paste text and objects in a few different ways. After you select text or an object, copy or cut it by doing one of the following:

- Click the Cut or Copy button on the Ribbon, located in the Home tab's Clipboard group, as shown in FIGURE 6-28.
- Right-click the selected text or object and select Cut or Copy from the menu that appears, as shown in FIGURE 6-29.
- Press Ctrl+X (cut) or Ctrl+C (copy) on the keyboard.

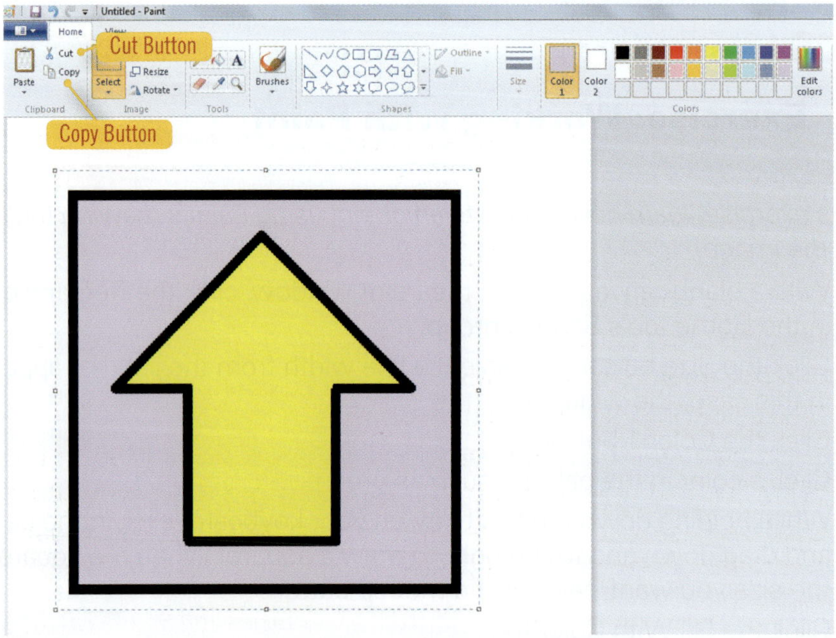

FIGURE 6-28 The Cut and Copy buttons.

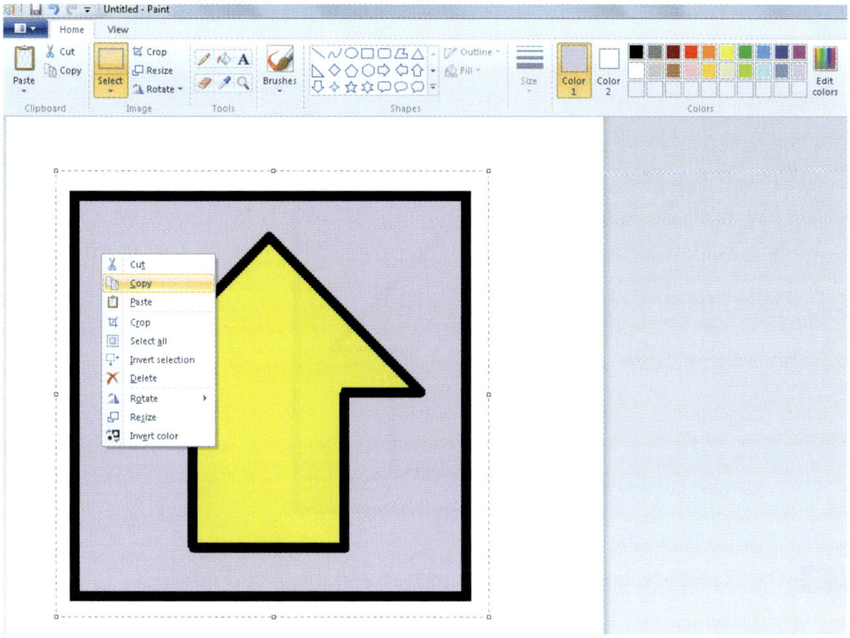

FIGURE 6-29 Select Cut or Copy from the shortcut menu.

To paste text or an object you have cut or copied, open the file in which you want to paste the item. This can be the same file from which it was cut or copied, a different file of the same type, or a file in a different program. Then click the spot where you want to paste the item and do one of the following:

- Click the Paste button in the Ribbon, located in the Home tab's Clipboard group.
- Right-click the spot where you want to paste the item and select Paste from the menu that appears.
- Press Ctrl+V on the keyboard.

6.9 Exercise: Embedding a Paint Object into a WordPad File

In this exercise, learn how to copy an object you create in Paint and embed it into a WordPad file. Follow these steps:

1. With a blank canvas open in the Paint window, draw anything you like.
2. Click the Select button and choose a selection tool.
3. Select the object you drew.
4. Click the Copy button, located in the Home tab's Clipboard group.
5. Create a new file in WordPad.
6. Type a line or two of text in the WordPad file.
7. Press the Enter key two times. The insertion point will appear two lines below the text; this is where you will embed the object you copied.
8. Click the Paste button, located in the Home tab's Clipboard group. The object you copied in Paint is pasted into the WordPad file (see **FIGURE 6-30**).

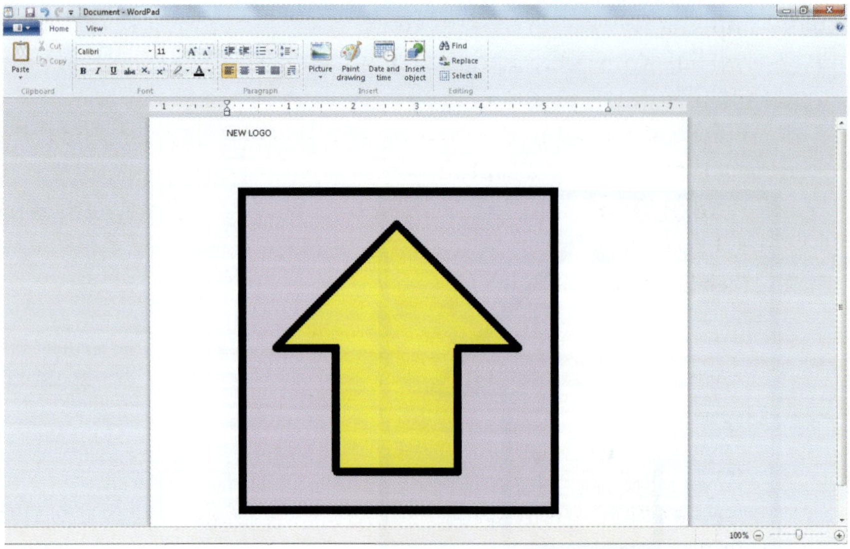

FIGURE 6-30 The object you copied in Paint is pasted into the WordPad file.

Capturing Screen Shots

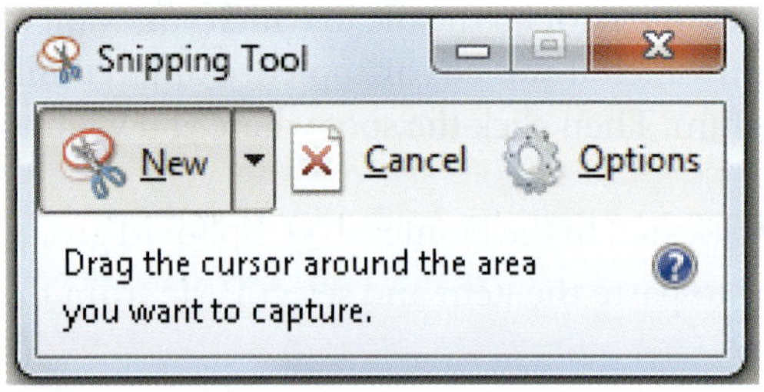

FIGURE 6-31 Snipping Tool.

Windows 7 provides a special program for capturing screen shots: the Snipping Tool, shown in FIGURE 6-31. A **screen shot**, or **snip**, is a snapshot of whatever is on the computer screen. You might take a screen shot if, for example, you receive an error message in a program you are working on and you want to be able to refer to it later when attempting to resolve the problem. You might also capture a screen shot of an image to use in a report.

When you capture a screen shot, the Snipping Tool displays it in a special window (see FIGURE 6-32) and copies it to the Clipboard; you can then paste it into a file, such as a document file. Alternatively, you can save the screen shot as a graphics file. If you wish, annotate the screen shot before pasting or saving it.

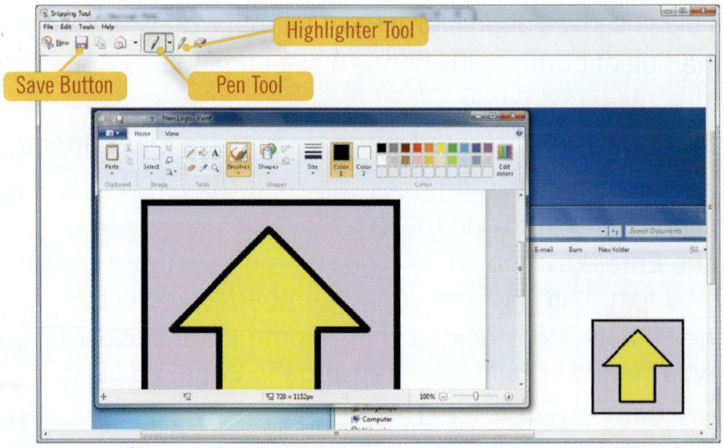

FIGURE 6-32 The screen shot appears in a special window.

With the Snipping Tool, you have a few options when capturing screen shots:

- **Free-form Snip:** Select this option to draw a free-form shape around the part of the screen that you want to capture.
- **Rectangular Snip:** Use this tool to draw a rectangular shape around the part of the screen that you want to capture.
- **Window Snip:** To select a window on your screen for capture, such as a dialog box, select this option.
- **Full-screen Snip:** Select this option to capture the entire screen.

TIP

Another way to capture a screen shot is to press the Print Screen (Prt Scr) key on your keyboard. When you do, Windows copies an image of whatever is on your screen to the Clipboard; you can then paste it into a Paint file, a WordPad file, or another file. If you just want to capture the active window, press and hold the Alt key as you press Prt Scr.

6.10 Exercise: Capturing and Saving a Screen Shot

In this exercise, learn how to capture a screen shot and save it as an image file. Follow these steps:

1. Open the Snipping Tool by selecting Start > All Programs > Accessories > Snipping Tool.
2. Click the down arrow next to the New button.
3. Select Full-screen Snip from the menu that appears.
4. The Snipping Tool captures the screen shot and displays it in a special window. Optionally, use the Pen or Highlighter tool to annotate the screen shot.
5. To save the screen shot, click the Save button.
6. A Save As dialog box opens. Find and select the folder in which you want to save the screen shot.
7. Type a name for the screen shot in the File Name field.
8. To change the file type—options are PNG, GIF, JPG, and HTML—click the Save As Type down arrow and select the desired option from the list that appears.
9. Click Save. The screen capture is saved as a graphics file.

The Fun Stuff: Using Windows Media Player

Some programs, such as Paint and WordPad, are designed to help you create and edit files—in their case, image files or text files, respectively. Still others are designed to play back or view certain kinds of files. For example, Windows Media Player, shown in FIGURE 6-33, lets you play back music and video files and view photos. Files stored in your Music, Pictures, and Videos libraries appear in the Windows Media Player file list by default. To open Windows Media Player, click its icon in the taskbar, or click the Start button, select All Programs, and then select Windows Media Player near the top of the programs list.

Listening to Music

To play back music files in Windows Media Player, click the Music library in the navigation pane, click the file you want to hear in the file list, and click the Play button along the bottom of the window. After the file has finished playing, Windows Media Player will automatically play the next file in the list. Another option is to click the Play tab in the upper-right corner of the Windows Media Player window, drag the songs you want to hear to the Play tab, and then click the Play button.

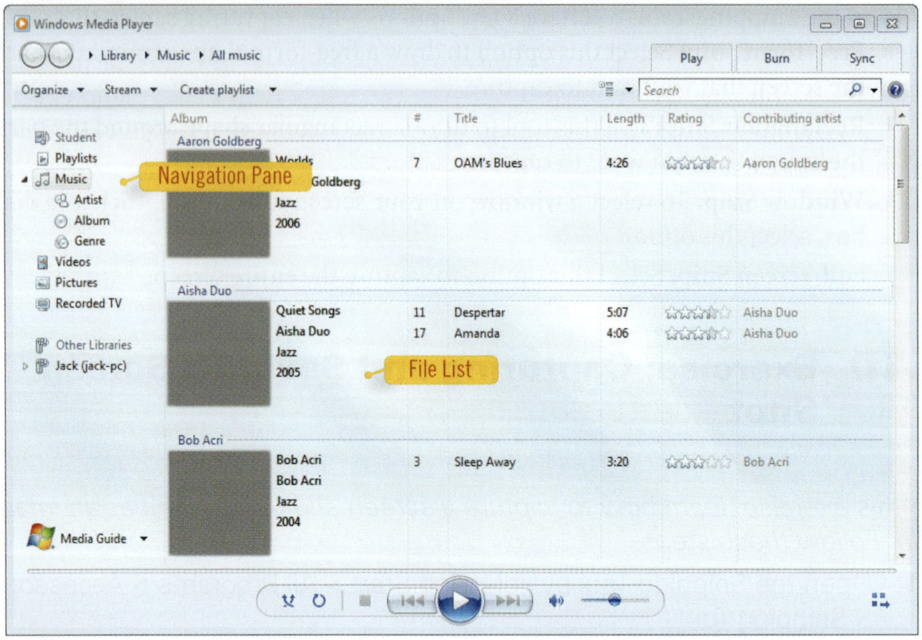

FIGURE 6-33 Windows Media Player. Notice that the program window resembles the Windows Explorer program window, with a navigation pane and file list.

In addition to the Play button, Windows Media Player includes other playback controls (see **FIGURE 6-34**):

- **Shuffle button:** Click the Shuffle button to shuffle the order in which songs in the list are played.
- **Repeat button:** Click the Repeat button to repeat the current song.
- **Stop button:** To stop playback, click the Stop button.
- **Previous button:** Click the Previous button to hear the previous song in the list.
- **Next button:** To move to the next song in the list, click the Next button.
- **Volume slider:** Drag the Volume slider left or right to decrease or increase the volume, respectively.

FIGURE 6-34 Windows Media Player playback controls.

Use Windows Media Player to do the following as well:

- **Listen to CDs:** Just insert the CD you want to hear into your computer's CD/DVD drive. Assuming Windows Media Player is your default music player, it will begin playing back the CD automatically.
- **Copy, or rip, music from CDs to your computer:** Insert a CD and, when a list of its tracks appears in the Windows Media Player window, click the Rip CD button. Windows Media Player **rips** the tracks on the CD to your Music library.
- **Burn CDs:** Use Windows Media Player to burn a collection of your favorite songs to a CD (assuming your computer's CD drive is a recordable drive). To do so, click the Burn tab in the Windows Media Player window; then drag the songs you want to include in the playlist from the file list to the Burn tab. Finally, insert a blank CD into your CD drive and click Start Burn.

Watching Videos

To watch a video in Windows Media Player, click the Videos library in the navigation pane, click the file you want to view in the file list, and click the Play button. Windows Media Player launches a special viewing window and plays back the video, as shown in FIGURE 6-35. Notice that when you place your mouse pointer over this window, playback controls appear that are similar to those in the main Windows Media Player window.

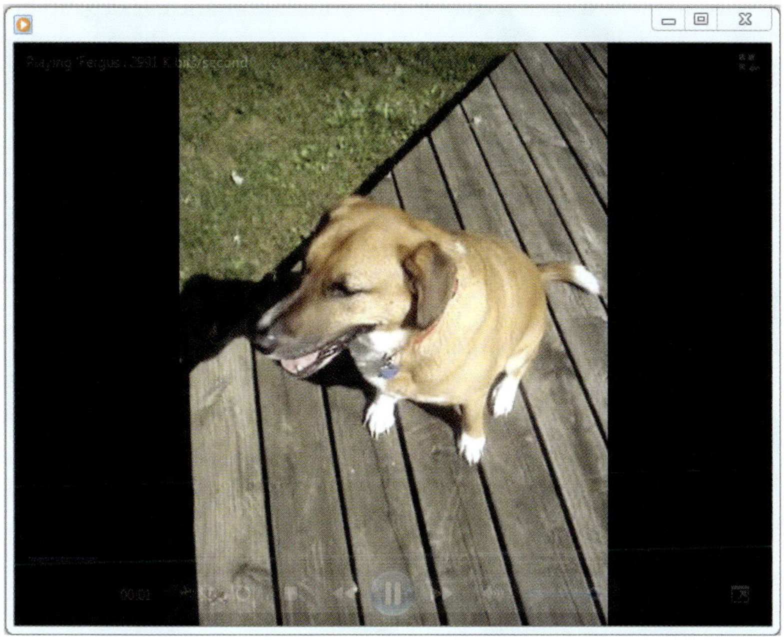

FIGURE 6-35 The Now Playing window, in which videos are played back by default.

Looking at Photos

Although other Windows programs are better suited to working with image files, you can use Windows Media Player to view them. To do so, click the Pictures library in the navigation pane. Thumbnails of the photos in your Pictures library appear. To view all of the photos as a slide show, click the Play button. Windows starts the slide show in its own window, as shown in FIGURE 6-36. Notice again that when you place your mouse pointer over the window, playback controls appear.

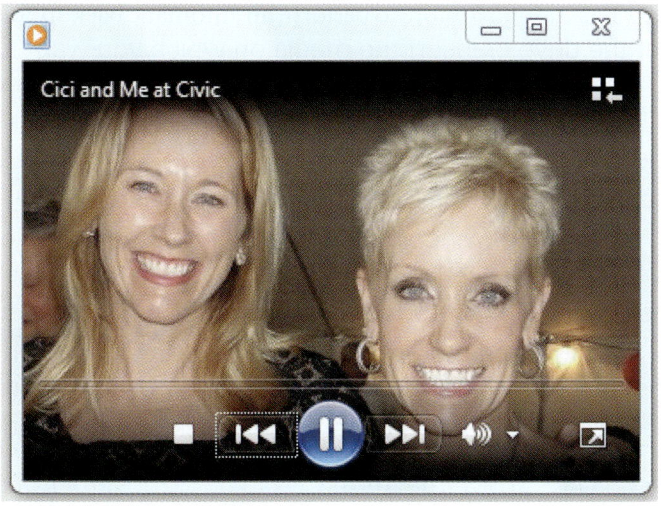

FIGURE 6-36 View photos in Windows Media Player.

The Serious Stuff: Backing Up Files

What if a disaster were to strike your computer, such as theft, loss, breakage, or a virus attack? No doubt, certain files would be extremely difficult—if not impossible—to replace. For this reason, back up your files to an external hard drive or other storage medium.

An easy way to back up files is to use the Windows 7 Backup and Restore feature. Set up Backup and Restore to perform backups automatically on a set schedule. In addition, if you need to make a system change or if your automatic backup did not occur as scheduled—for example, if you forgot to connect your storage drive to your computer or insert a DVD—run a manual backup. In the event disaster does strike your computer, you can perform a restore operation to access your backed up files.

Backing Up Files Online

In addition to using Backup and Restore to back up your files, you can turn to any number of services, such as Carbonite or Mozy Home, to back up your files online. Many services let you store up to 2 gigabytes of data for free, always. If you need more data backed up, you pay about $5 per month. The services constantly monitor your computer, backing up files as you create new files or modify existing files. Once you sign up for the service, you never have to remember to back up again—the service does it automatically in the background.

Backing up files online offers even more advantages:

1. You can access the backed-up files from anywhere, as long as you have an Internet connection. It's like having file storage on the Internet that you can access from wherever you might be.
2. You don't need storage media, such as an external flash drive or DVDs, to store your backup. This is useful if, for example, your home burns to the ground, along with your computer and storage media.

For maximum coverage, consider using Windows Backup and Restore to back up to a local storage medium and backing up online.

Setting Up an Automatic Backup

To set up Window Backup and Restore to perform an automatic backup, follow these steps:

1. Connect the drive or insert the media on which you want to save your backup to your computer. This may be an external flash drive, or even just a CD or DVD.
2. Click the Start button.
3. Click Control Panel in the Start menu.
4. In the Control Panel window, under System and Security, click Back Up Your Computer.
5. The Backup and Restore window appears. Click Set Up Backup.
6. Windows 7 launches the Set Up Backup Wizard, as shown in FIGURE 6-37. Click the drive on which you want to store the backup, and click Next.
7. Click Let Windows Choose to perform a backup on a standard set of folders, as shown in FIGURE 6-38. Click Next.
8. Your files will be backed up every Sunday at 7:00 p.m. by default. If you frequently use your computer at that time, you may want to change the

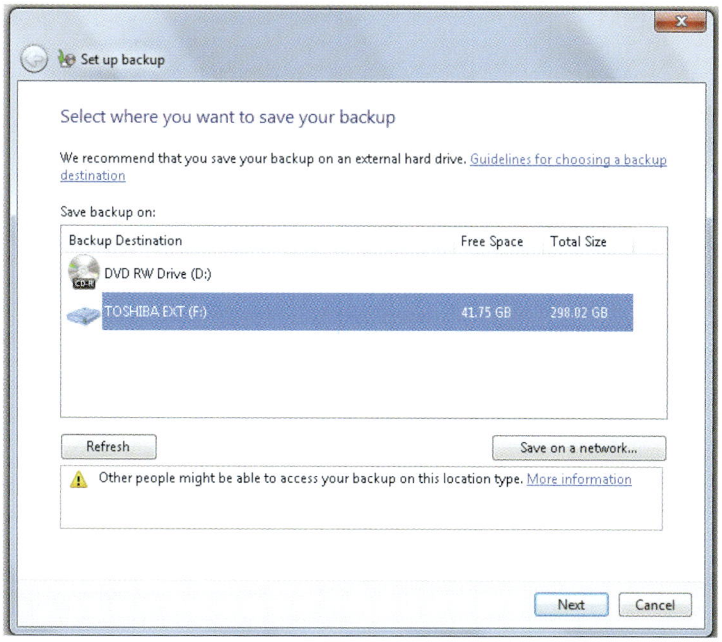

FIGURE 6-37 Choose where you want to store the backup.

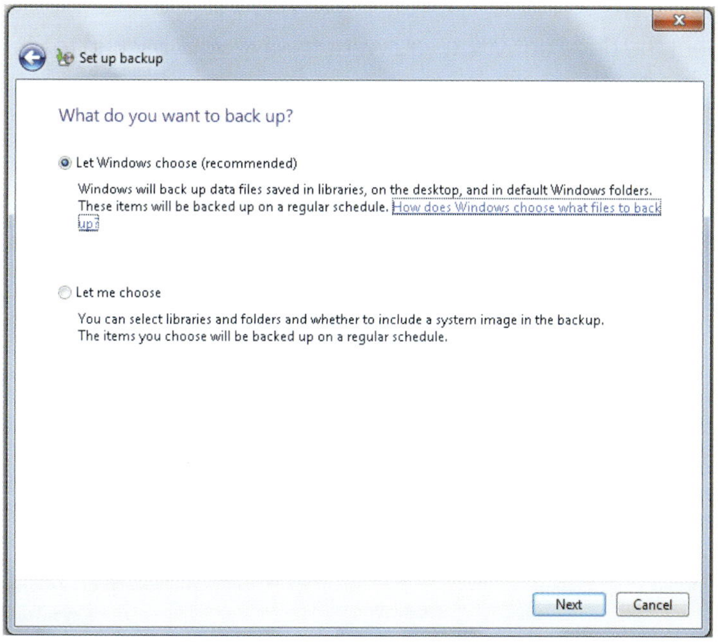

FIGURE 6-38 Select Let Windows Choose to perform a standard backup

backup schedule. Click Change Schedule. Make any necessary changes using the drop-down menus and click OK (see **FIGURE 6-39**).

9. Click Save Settings and Run Backup. Windows immediately launches a backup operation; subsequent backups will occur on the schedule you set (assuming your backup medium is connected to your computer).

Performing a Manual Backup

Run a manual backup with Backup and Restore. You might do a manual backup if, for example, you're about to make a system change or if your automatic backup did not occur as scheduled. To run a manual backup, follow these steps:

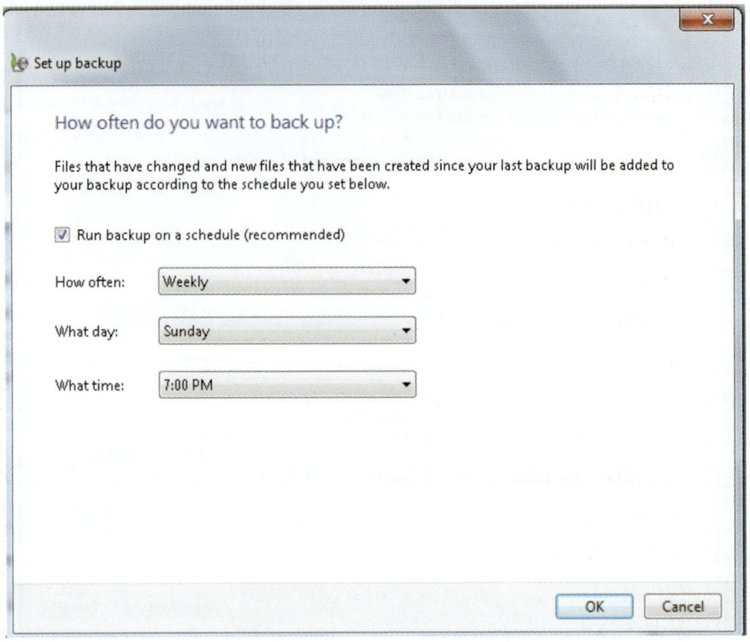

FIGURE 6-39 Adjust the backup schedule, if needed.

> **Note**
>
> You can only run a manual backup if you have already set up Backup and Restore to perform automatic backups.

1. Connect the drive on which you want to save your backup to your computer.
2. Click the Start button.
3. Click Control Panel in the Start menu.
4. In the Control Panel window, under System and Security, click Back Up Your Computer.
5. The Backup and Restore window appears. Click the Back Up Now button, as shown in **FIGURE 6-40**. Windows launches a backup operation.

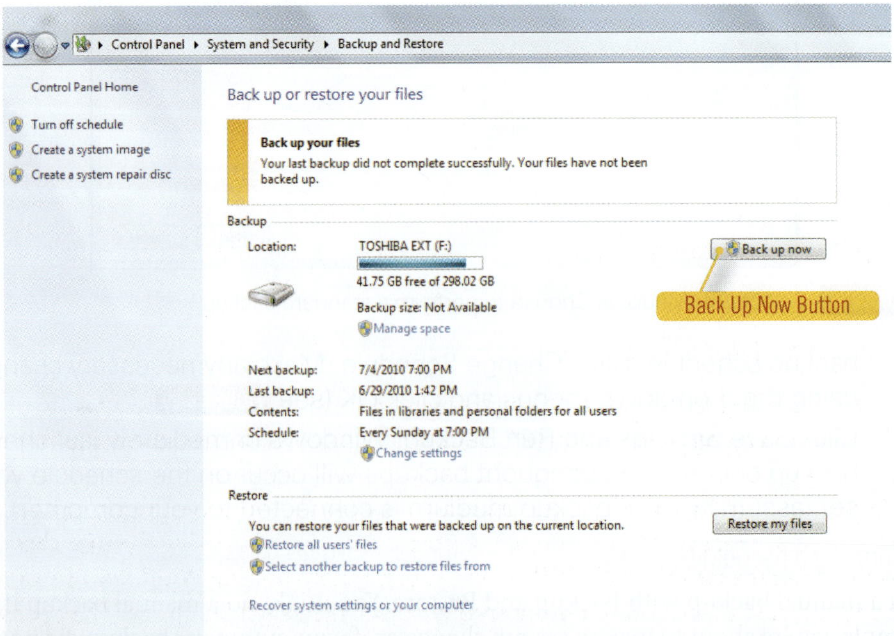

FIGURE 6-40 Click Back Up Now to run a manual backup.

Restoring a Backup

In the event disaster does strike your computer, perform a restore operation to access your backed-up files. Follow these steps:

1. Connect the drive on which your backed-up files are saved to the computer on which you want to access your files.
2. Click the Start button.
3. Click Control Panel in the Start menu.
4. In the Control Panel window, under System and Security, click Back Up Your Computer.
5. In the Backup and Restore window, click Restore My Files.
6. Windows 7 launches the Restore Files wizard (see FIGURE 6-41). To restore all folders and files in your system, click Browse For Folders.
7. Find and select the folder containing the backup of your hard drive.
8. Click Add Folder and click Next.
9. Click In the Original Location.
10. Click Restore. Windows 7 restores the files.
11. Windows 7 notifies you when the restore operation is complete. Click Finish.

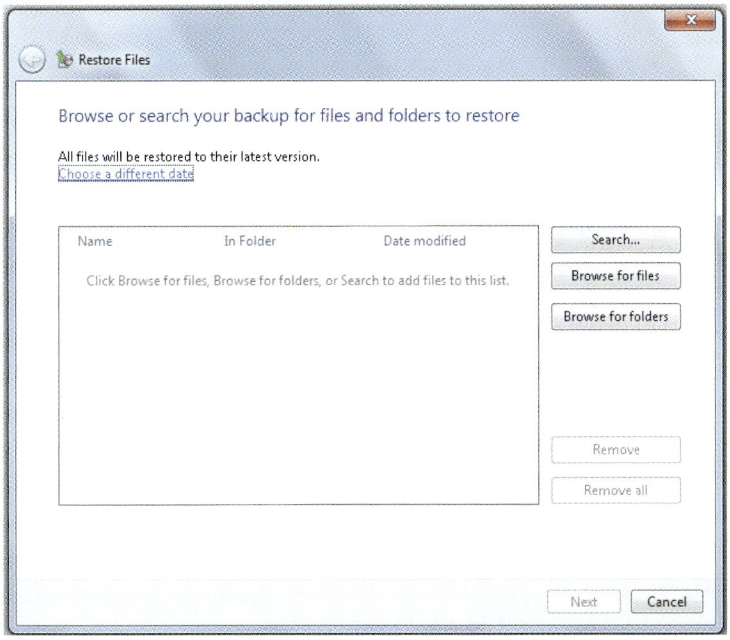

FIGURE 6-41 Click Restore My Files to launch the Restore Files wizard.

Installing New Programs

You are not limited to using the programs that come bundled with Windows 7. You can install additional programs on your PC, assuming they are compatible with the Windows 7 operating system.

When you purchase a program, you need to install it in your computer. This sounds like a complex process, but it's actually a simple matter of inserting the disc that contains the program into the CD/DVD drive. A computer running Windows 7 recognizes that you inserted a disc, and it automatically runs a file called Setup.exe. The operating system installs the program but might prompt you for some information to get started. Just follow the onscreen prompts.

> **TIP**
>
> You can also download software over the Internet to your computer. It's convenient to download software to your Downloads folder so you know where to find it. Then, the process works very much the same as installing software from a disc. Just locate the Setup.exe file in the Downloads folder, double-click it, and follow the prompts.

Some programs, such as the Office 2010 applications, require a "key" or product ID to start the installation. A key is a long string of characters that you receive when you buy software online or purchase a program from a computer store. It is a license number that means you legally acquired the software. Without this key, you will not be able to install the program.

When you install programs, the operating system stores them on your computer's hard drive. To see which programs are installed on your computer, just click Control Panel in the Start menu, click Programs, and then click Programs and Features. A list of all of the software installed on your computer appears. To remove a program, click it and then select Uninstall from the toolbar.

Now that you've reached the end of the chapter, hopefully you are feeling more confident about using programs in Windows 7. The remaining chapters in this book focus on program use, namely Office 2010 applications, such as Word, Excel, and PowerPoint. Before you start learning about Word 2010 basics (the next chapter), be sure to take the quiz in the Test Yourself section and complete the project for this chapter.

Test Yourself

The questions in this section are meant to test your knowledge of what you read. Make sure you answer them. The page number where the answer can be found appears after each question.

1. What is another word for program? (117)
   - **A.** Device
   - **B.** Gadget
   - **C.** System
   - **D.** Application
2. What kind of program is WordPad? (117)
   - **A.** A word processing program
   - **B.** A graphics program
   - **C.** A calculator
   - **D.** An e-mail program
3. You are limited to using the programs that come pre-installed with Windows 7. (145)
   - **A.** True
   - **B.** False
4. You have multiple ways to launch a program in Windows 7. (118)
   - **A.** True
   - **B.** False
5. All programs contain a Ribbon. (121)
   - **A.** True
   - **B.** False
6. Which of the following types of input controls is similar to an option button? (122)
   - **A.** A text box
   - **B.** A checkbox
   - **C.** A command button
   - **D.** A spin button
7. The New command is found under which tab on the WordPad Ribbon? (123)
   - **A.** The Home tab
   - **B.** The View tab
   - **C.** The Options tab
   - **D.** The File tab

8. Windows 7 launches the Save As dialog box whenever you select the Save command. (124)
   A. True
   B. False
9. The Open dialog box is similar to the Save As dialog box. (126)
   A. True
   B. False
10. The ________ feature lets you see exactly how a file you have open in a program window will appear when printed. (128)
11. The Print dialog box lets you print multiple copies of a file. (127)
    A. True
    B. False
12. Which of the following actions lets you select a paragraph in WordPad? (130)
    A. Clicking in the paragraph
    B. Double-clicking in the paragraph
    C. Triple-clicking in the paragraph
    D. Placing the cursor to the left of the paragraph and clicking
13. An easy way to back up your files is to use the Windows 7 Backup and Restore feature. (142)
    A. True
    B. False
14. The name of the simple graphics program that is bundled with Windows 7 is ____________. (117)
15. In Paint, a specific area of an image is called ______________. (134)
16. Embedding is when you insert text or an object from one program into another program. (135)
    A. True
    B. False
17. Which of the following is another word for "screen shot"? (138)
    A. Snippet
    B. Snip
    C. Snap
    D. Swatch
18. Which of the following is the program included with Windows 7 for capturing screen shots? (138)
    A. Snapshot
    B. Snippet
    C. Capture-It
    D. Snipping Tool
19. Which of the following files cannot be viewed in Windows Media Player? (139)
    A. Document files
    B. Image files
    C. Music files
    D. Video files
20. The process of copying music files from a CD is called ______________. (140)

End-of-Chapter Project

The projects for Chapters 1, 2, 3, and 5 of this book have built on the scenario that you are interested in buying a new laptop computer and printer, and you need to sign up for Internet access through a service provider. You researched specifications, plans, and costs, while keeping detailed notes along the way. For this project, enter your notes into a WordPad document and save the file in your Class Research folder (created in the Chapter 5 project). Name the file PC Basics Research.rtf.

Challenge Project

This project is optional but is provided if you want additional practice with programs in Windows 7. Perform the following steps:

1. Launch Paint.
2. Click the Heart tool in the Home tab's Shapes group.
3. Click the Size button and select a line width from the list that appears—in this case, the widest line.
4. Click the Color 1 button.
5. Click a color in the palette—here, pink.
6. Click in the canvas and drag down and to the right to insert a heart. When the heart is the size you want, release the mouse button.
7. Click the arrow along the bottom of the Select button.
8. Select Free-form Selection.
9. Click in the canvas and drag around the heart to select it.
10. Click the Copy button, located in the Home tab's Clipboard group.
11. Launch WordPad.
12. Type the following text in the WordPad file: **You Can Do It!**
13. Select the text you typed.
14. Click the down arrow next to the current font name.
15. Select a different font from the list that appears—in this case, Cooper Std Black.
16. The new font is applied to the selected text. With the text still selected, click the down arrow next to the current font size.
17. Select a different font size from the list that appears—in this case, 48.
18. WordPad changes the size of the selected text. With the text still selected, click the down arrow to the right of the current font color.
19. Select a different font color from the list that appears—in this case, red.
20. The selected text changes color. With the text still selected, click the Center button.
21. The selected text is centered on the page. To deselect the text, click to the right of the exclamation point.
22. Press the Enter key once.
23. Click the Paste button, located in the Home tab's Clipboard group. The object you copied in Paint is pasted into the WordPad file.
24. Click the object to select it, and then center it if it's not already centered.
25. Click the File tab.
26. Click Save.
27. The Save As dialog box opens. Open the folder in which you want to save your file—in this example, the Book Project.
28. Type a descriptive name for the file—here, **Inspiration**—in the File Name field.
29. Click the Save button. Windows saves the file in the folder you chose, with the name you entered.

PART

IV

Essentials of Word Processing

CHAPTER 7

Microsoft Word 2010 Basics

- A word processor is a program specifically designed for typing and creating documents. Microsoft Word 2010 is the latest version of Microsoft's word processor. You can use Word to accomplish more than just typing and simple document creation: You can also insert clip art, embed objects, create flyers, split a document, compare documents, add WordArt, and more. This entire book was written using Word.
- The key to using Word is learning how to navigate the Ribbon and tabs, which is where you perform most of the common word processing tasks. As you work through this chapter, you will notice many similarities to WordPad, which was covered in Chapter 6. Think of WordPad as a scaled-back version of Word.
- In this chapter, you will learn about the Word 2010 Ribbon and tabs, creating documents, applying basic formatting techniques, spell-checking your documents, and finding and replacing text. These essential skills will prepare you for Chapter 8, in which you put Word to work.

CHAPTER TOPICS

This chapter covers the following topics and concepts:

- What's new in Word 2010
- How to open Word in Windows 7
- What features are available on the Ribbon
- What the Ribbon tabs contain
- What the purpose is of the Quick Access toolbar
- When to use the Mini toolbar
- How to create and format a document in Word
- How to add a picture to a Word document
- How to save a Word file
- How to preview fonts before applying them
- How to create bulleted and numbered lists
- How to set margins
- How to set tab settings
- How to spell-check your documents
- How to find and replace words or phrases
- How to print a document

KEY WORDS

Alignment buttons
Bold
Bulleted list
Find
Font
Formatting
Indentation
Italic
Margins
Mini toolbar
Numbered list
Quick Access toolbar
Replace
Spell check
Tab stop
Tooltip
Underline
Undo

What's New?

Microsoft Word 2010 is the latest release of this powerful and flexible word processing software. It includes many new features. One of the main changes is the new File tab, which replaces the Microsoft Office button in Word 2007. You use the File tab to create, save, open, and print documents, among other tasks. Clicking the File tab opens the Backstage view window, shown in FIGURE 7-1, which displays all of the most commonly used file commands in the left pane.

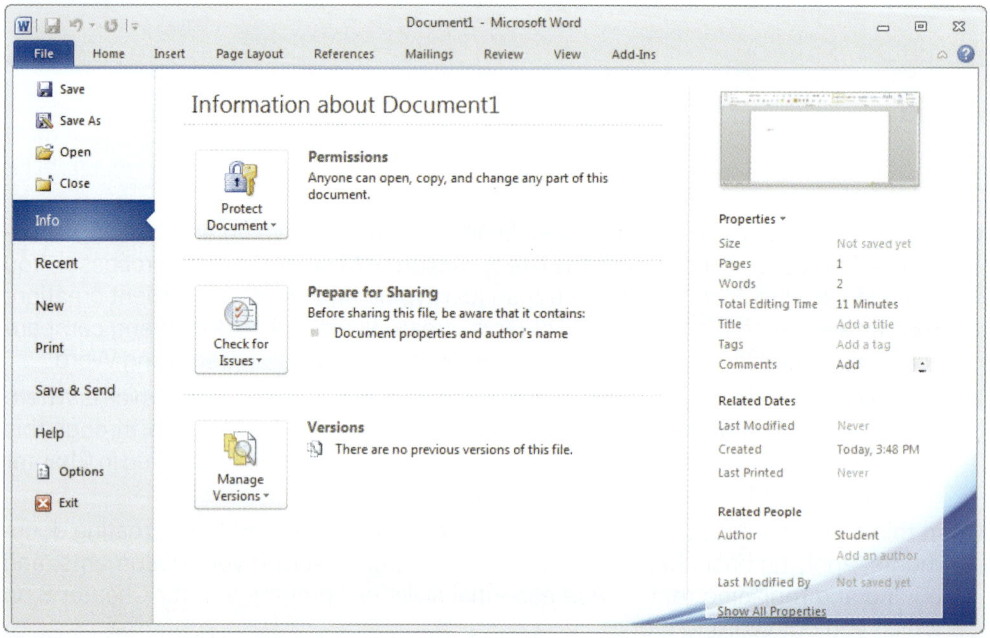

FIGURE 7-1 The Backstage view window appears when you click the File tab.

The information in the middle pane changes depending on which command you've selected in the left pane. For example, if you select the New command, the available templates appear, as shown in FIGURE 7-2.

Microsoft also added a lot of image and drawing tools for graphics enthusiasts. These include enhanced artistic effects you can apply to images (see FIGURE 7-3), picture effects, such as Glowy Edges, and the ability to remove a background from an image. Another new feature is a built-in screen capture tool, which you will learn about in Chapter 8.

Opening Word 2010

You open Word much like any other program in Windows 7. Just click the Start button, and then select All Programs > Microsoft Office > Microsoft Office Word 2010. You can also click the Start button, type "word" in the Start menu search box, and then select Microsoft Word 2010 in the results list.

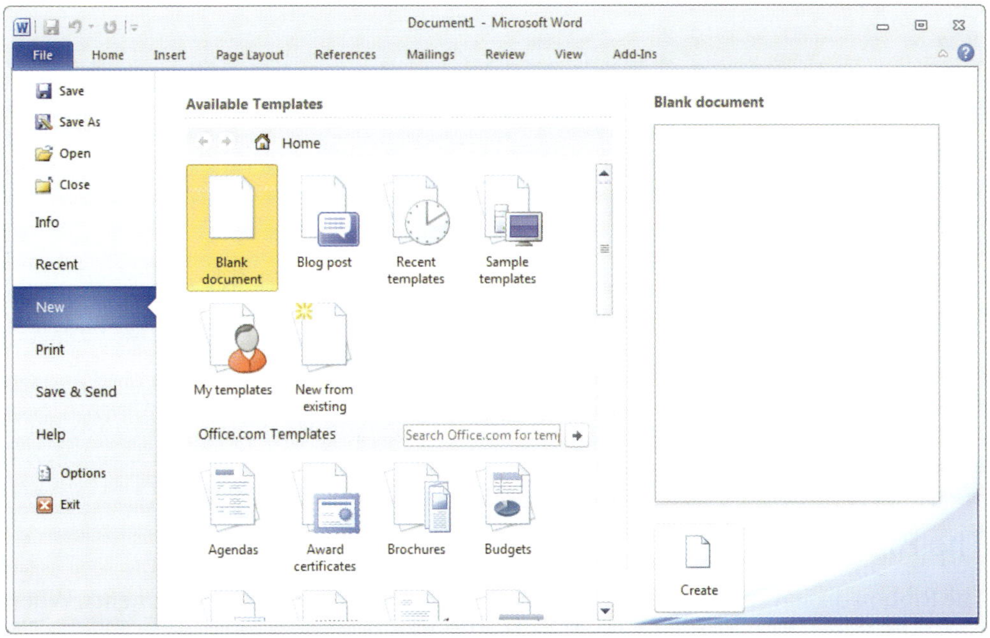

FIGURE 7-2 Available templates for creating new documents.

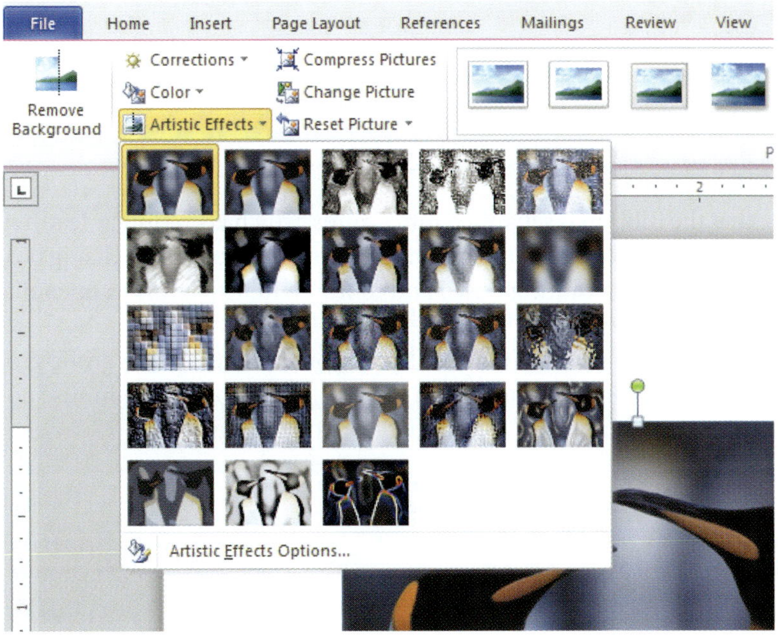

FIGURE 7-3 Artistic effects in Word 2010.

Word opens to a blank document, as shown in FIGURE 7-4. The large blank part of the window is the work area, where you type text and spend most of your time in Word. Remember from Chapter 6 that the insertion point is a blinking vertical line that lets you know where to type. The Ribbon, which you also read about in the last chapter, is across the top of the window. It contains tabs that group commands. The Quick Access toolbar is in the window's upper-left portion. You will learn more about the Ribbon, tabs, and Quick Access toolbar in the following sections.

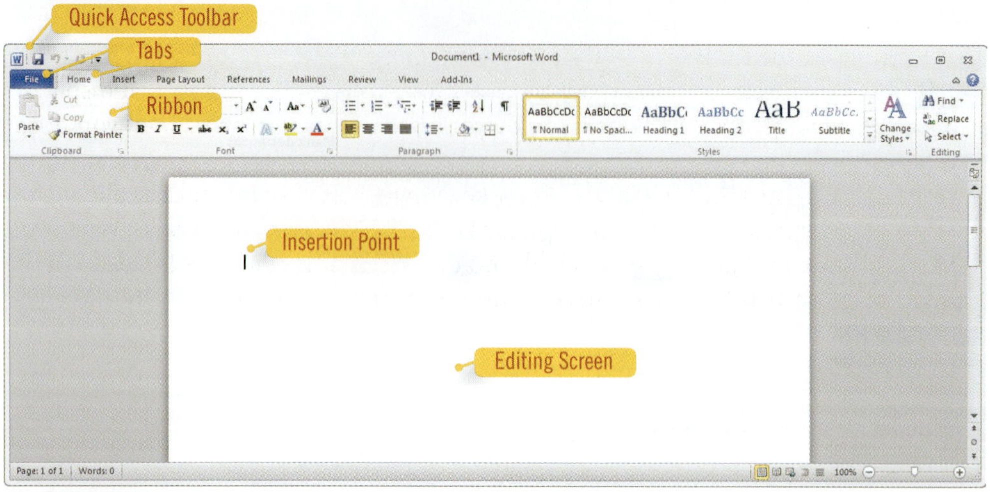

FIGURE 7-4 The main Word window.

The Ribbon

The Ribbon displays all of the basic features you use to create and edit documents. When you open Word 2010, the default tab on the Ribbon is Home, as shown in FIGURE 7-5. Features such as font and font size, bold, underline, italic, alignment, bullets, numbering, and font color are at your fingertips on the Ribbon. Once you are familiar with these features, you'll better understand what a powerful tool Word 2010 can be.

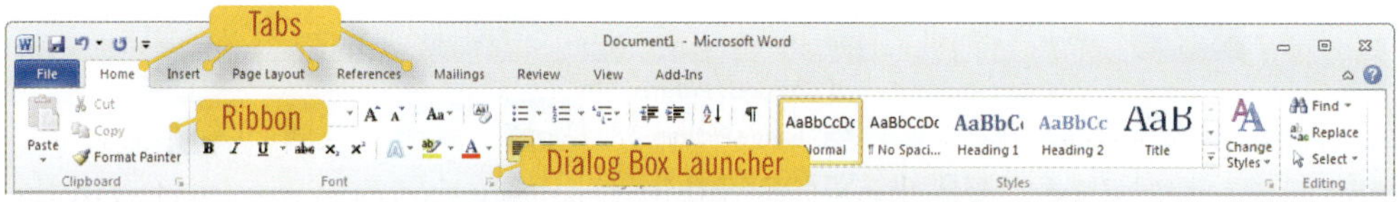

FIGURE 7-5 The Word Ribbon with the Home tab displayed.

Notice that the Ribbon is separated into groups, which keep similar features together. A group often has a dialog box launcher in the lower-right corner. A dialog box launcher looks like a small arrow pointing down and to the right. Click this to open dialog boxes that give you more options.

One other trait associated with the Ribbon: Some of the Ribbon groups contain galleries that provide live previews, as shown in FIGURE 7-6. Hover your mouse pointer over a gallery element to temporarily apply whatever you've selected.

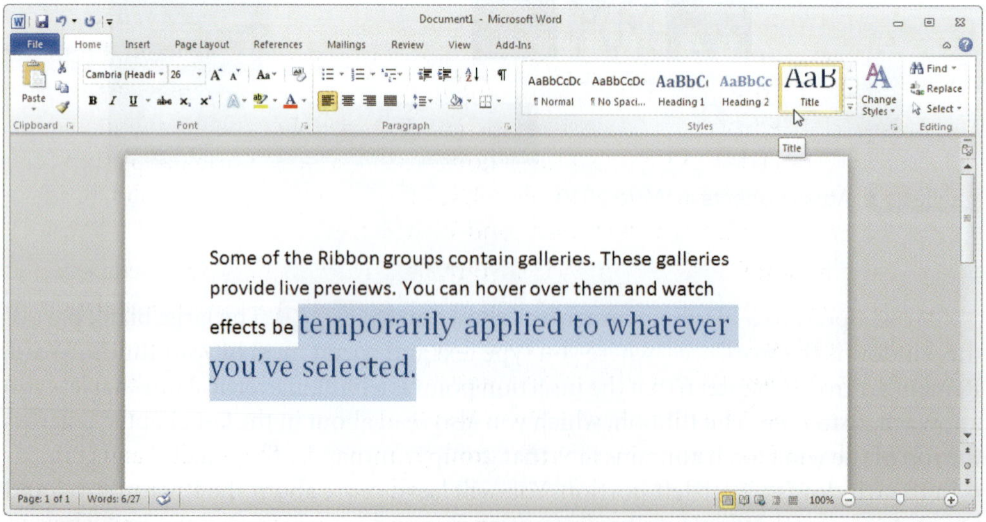

FIGURE 7-6 Live preview.

When using the Ribbon, if you don't know what a certain feature does, just hover the mouse over the icon to display a tooltip. A **tooltip** is a small window that displays a descriptive message. For example, if you're working with the Home tab and you hover your mouse over the button with a B, the tooltip shown in FIGURE 7-7 appears. Notice that the tooltip displays that tool's shortcut key (Ctrl+B). This shortcut key allows you to execute the command's function using the keyboard instead of the mouse. When you highlight some text that you want to make bold, instead of clicking the B button in the Ribbon, press Ctrl+B on the keyboard. This is a shortcut. Shortcuts usually allow you to work faster.

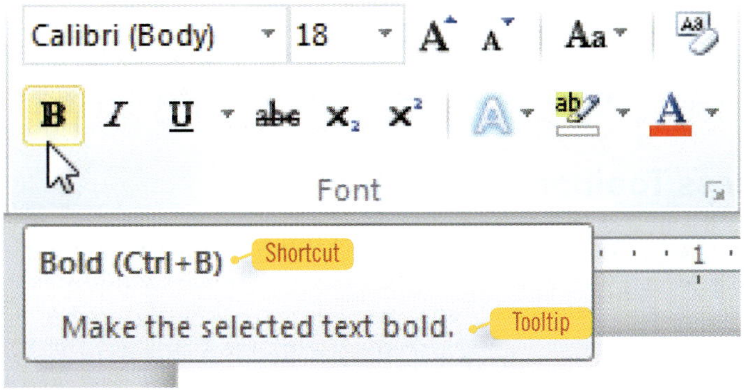

FIGURE 7-7 A tooltip.

Tabs

At the top of the Ribbon is a series of tabs, including ones labeled File, Home, Insert, and Page Layout. Word uses tabs to organize groups of commands. When you select a tab, the Ribbon changes. The reason it changes is to display the features associated with that tab. For example, if you want to insert a picture, that feature is on the Insert tab.

This section will give you an overview of some (but not all) of the available features in the various tabs in Word. As you get more practice, you will eventually learn many other features, but for now, familiarize yourself with the basics:

- **File:** The File tab is new in Word 2010 and replaces the Office button. It consolidates a variety of tools in one place. These tools let you open, save, and close files, print or share documents, open recently edited documents, view and define document properties, set permissions, and more.
- **Home:** The Home tab is the default tab (the one selected when you open Word 2010). It contains the basic features required to format a document. From the Home tab, you can also access the Clipboard, and apply fonts and styles.
- **Insert:** The Insert tab has icons related to inserting objects and other items in a document. For example, the Illustrations group allows you to insert pictures, clip art, shapes, and many other images. Use other groups to insert tables, headers, footers, page numbers, text boxes, and WordArt.
- **Page Layout:** The Page Layout tab lets you change a document's margin settings, select Portrait or Landscape orientation, and format columns, line numbers, and indents.
- **References:** The tools on the References tab let you add a table of contents, footnotes, bibliography information, citations, indices, and more. These tools are especially helpful for business and academic users.
- **Mailings:** The Mailings tab contains tools primarily for the creation and printing of mailouts. Two tools in particular are handy for just about anyone: Envelopes and Labels. With these tools, you can design and print envelopes and labels of any size or type.

- **Review:** When it's time to finalize your document, use the items on the Review tab. Here you can do things such as run the Spelling and Grammar checker, use a thesaurus, add comments to documents, and get a count of all the words in your document.
- **View:** The tools on the View tab let you see your documents in different ways. You can preview how they will look before you print them as well as how they might look on the Web. On the View tab, turn on the ruler or gridlines to align elements in your document. You can also change how documents appear on the screen: Zoom in or out, display more than one page, or even display more than one document.
- **Add-Ins:** You can add certain programs to Word to give it even more functionality. These items appear on the Add-Ins tab. The tab's content varies from user to user, based on any add-ins you installed on your computer.

Quick Access Toolbar

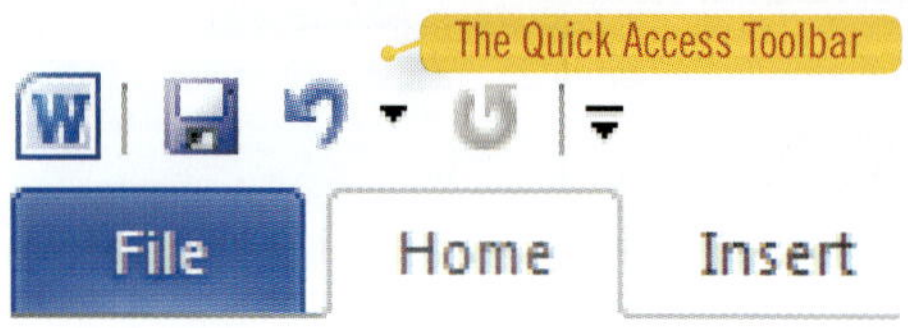

FIGURE 7-8 The Quick Access toolbar.

The **Quick Access toolbar** is in the upper-left corner of the Word window. It has icons for the most often-used tasks, such as Save, Undo, and Repeat/Redo, as shown in FIGURE 7-8. You can also customize it so that it contains many other icons for other tasks. However, try to keep it simple so that it does not become overcrowded. Remember, it is supposed to be a toolbar for the most often-used tasks.

Undo Your Changes

While working on a document, you might apply some formatting that produces an undesired effect, or you might just make a mistake. In either case, the **Undo** button will be your best friend. For example, if you highlight text and select the wrong font color, click Undo. Or, if you accidentally delete some text, click Undo instead of retyping it.

When you click the Undo button, the last change you made is undone. Click the Undo button again to undo the previous change.

The Mini Toolbar

One of the productivity tools in Word 2010 is the **Mini toolbar**, which displays automatically when you've selected text. The Mini toolbar remains transparent yet visible until you move the mouse pointer away from it. It provides the most frequently used formatting options, such as font formatting and alignment. FIGURE 7-9 shows you what the Mini toolbar display looks like after you highlight text.

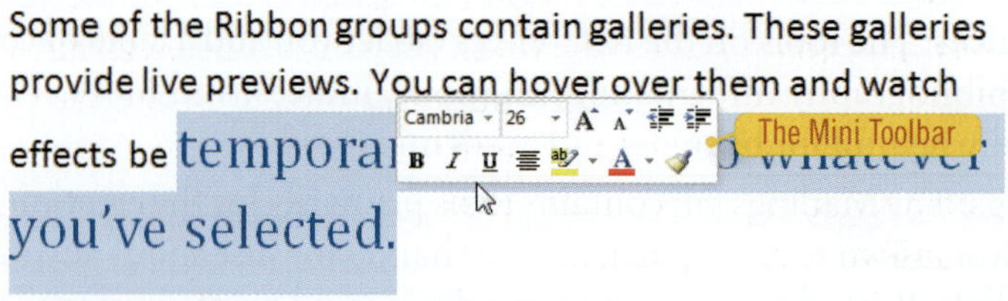

Some of the Ribbon groups contain galleries. These galleries
provide live previews. You can hover over them and watch
effects be temporar
you've selected.
Cambria
26
The Mini Toolbar

FIGURE 7-9 The Mini toolbar.

Getting Help

Help is readily available in Word 2010. Press the F1 key on the top row of your keyboard to display the Word Help dialog box, as shown in FIGURE 7-10. Alternatively, you can click the Help icon (a blue circle with a question mark) under the Exit button in the upper-right corner of the Word window. When the Help window opens, you will see different topics that you can select. The search text box lets you fine-tune the information you're looking for. If you need help on a specific topic, just type a word or phrase in the search text box and press Enter.

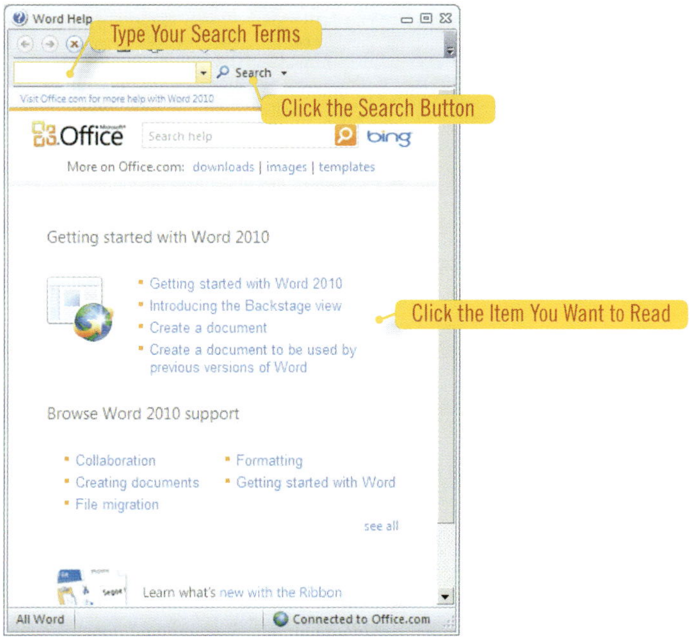

FIGURE 7-10 Using Help.

Creating and Formatting a Document

Now that you're familiar with the Word window's main parts, you're ready to create and format a document. **Formatting** a document means to make the document look the way you want. Word 2010 is so powerful that you can format the document in almost any way you can imagine. You will learn more about this in the next few pages.

Formatting Now or Later

One important feature in Word is that you can format a document as you type, or after you are finished—it depends on how you like to work. Decide what works best for you as you use Word more often. If you type a document and decide to format it later, you may have to highlight whatever you want to format. For example, if you type an entire page and later decide you want to change the font of the second paragraph, you first have to highlight the second paragraph and then apply the new font. (Remember, to highlight means to select. One way to highlight text is to click and drag the mouse over it.)

Creating a New Document

When you open Word, the screen displays a new blank document so you can start creating a document immediately. If for some reason a blank document is not displayed (you may have closed it by accident), click the File tab, and then select New > Blank Document.

Applying Fonts

A **font** or font face means the style of characters. Font size simply means the size of the characters in any given font face. Change the font as often as you wish in any document. FIGURE 7-11 shows you how to select the font and its size. You can also select text and use the Mini toolbar that appears.

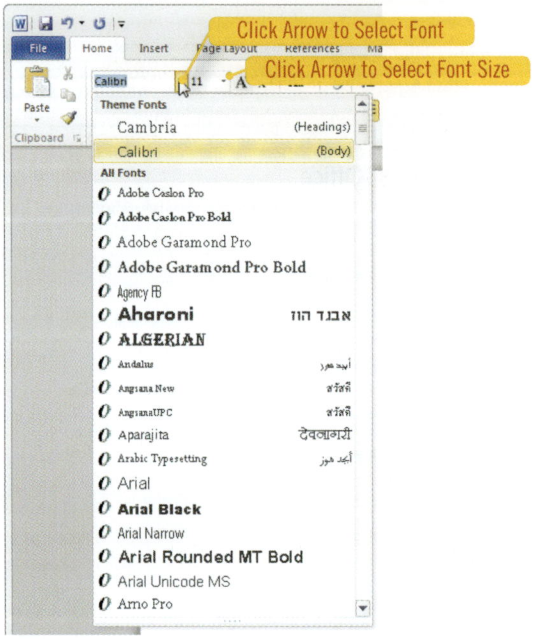

FIGURE 7-11 Selecting the font and font size.

Using Bold, Italic, and Underline

Bold, italic, and **underline** are common formatting features. Bold makes text darker, italic slants text for a special effect, and underline places a line under the text. The following examples show the three effects:

- **This is what bold looks like.**
- *This is what italic looks like.*
- This is what underline looks like.

These buttons, shown in FIGURE 7-12, work like on/off buttons, or toggle buttons. That is, to turn them on you click them and to turn them off you click them again. Remember, you can apply these effects as you type or wait until after you're done.

- **To apply as you type:** Click the button to turn the effect on, type your text, and then click the button again to turn the effect off.
- **To apply afterward:** Highlight your text, and then click the button to apply the effect.

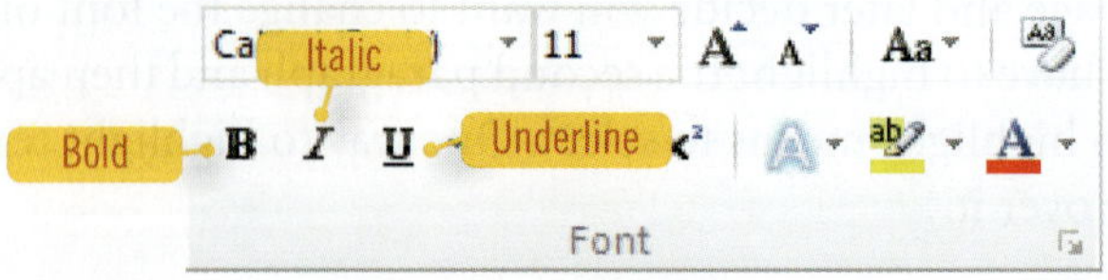

FIGURE 7-12 The Bold, Italic, and Underline buttons.

Changing Font Color and Adding Text Highlight Color

As with other tools, you can change the font color at any time. Clicking the Font Color button allows you to choose any color of the rainbow to apply to your text. Highlight the text, click the Font Color button, and choose the color you want. If you select text and click the Text Highlight Color button, color will be applied behind the font, just as if you had used a highlighter pen. The buttons are shown in FIGURE 7-13.

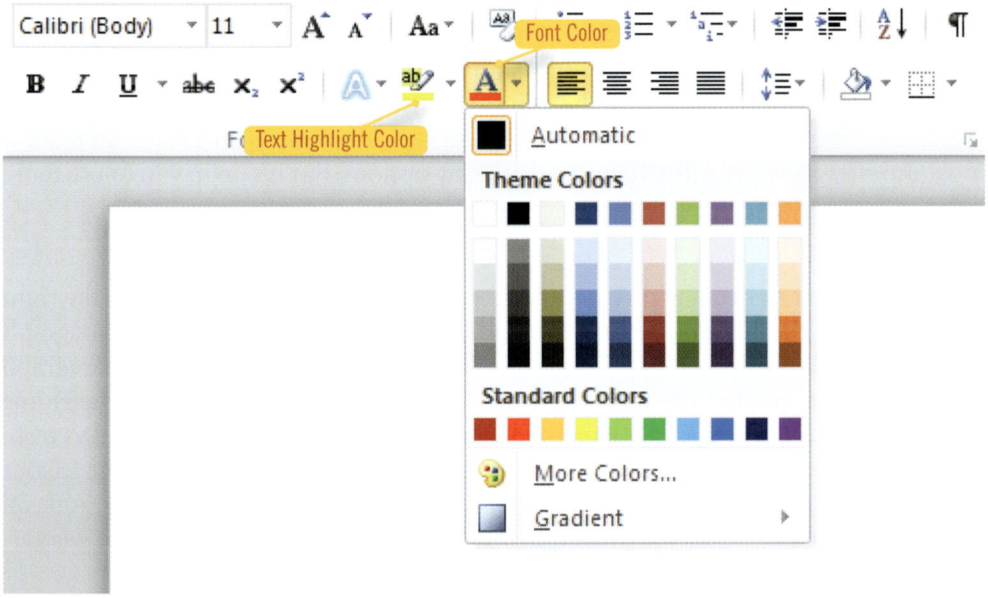

FIGURE 7-13 The Font Color and Text Highlight Color buttons.

Aligning Text

Text alignment deals with how the text edges are aligned. Align your text in four ways:

- **Left:** Only the left text edges are aligned.
- **Center:** Text is horizontally centered on the page.
- **Right:** Only the right text edges are aligned.
- **Justify:** The left and right edges are both aligned.

FIGURE 7-14 shows the four alignments.

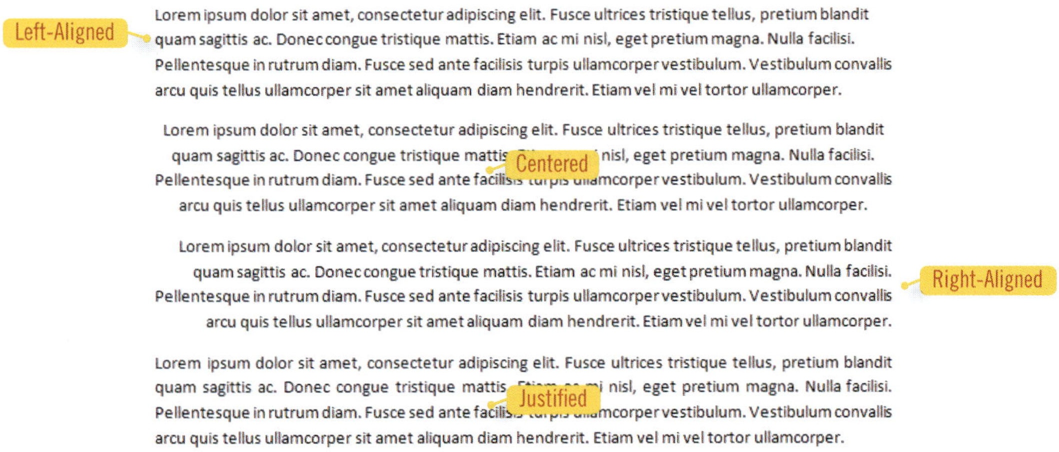

FIGURE 7-14 Text alignment.

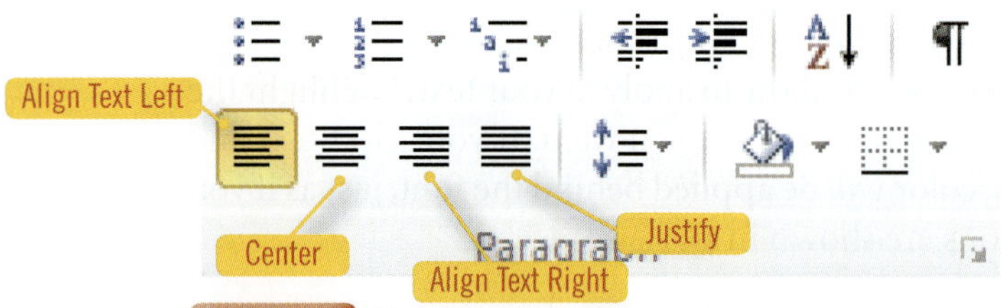

FIGURE 7-15 The alignment buttons.

The **alignment buttons** are in the Paragraph group on the Home tab, as shown in FIGURE 7-15. To use the buttons, highlight a paragraph of text and then click one of the buttons. You can also just click in a paragraph and then click an alignment button—the alignment will apply either way.

As you can see, aligning text is really simple. You can combine different alignments on the same page, as well as within the same document. Remember, though, that a document's look is important. Mixing different paragraph alignments on a page can make it look unprofessional. Word 2010 offers you many options, but it's up to you to use those options sparingly and creatively.

Indenting

Indentation determines the distance of the paragraph from either the left or the right margin. Within the margins, you can increase or decrease the indentation of a paragraph or group of paragraphs. Indentation is an effect to call attention to a specific paragraph or group of paragraphs. The indent buttons are in the Paragraph group on the Home tab, as shown in FIGURE 7-16. To use them, click in a paragraph and then click the Decrease Indent or Increase Indent button. To adjust an indentation's size, click the Page Layout tab; in the Paragraph group, enter the size in the Indent Left and Right boxes. You can enter numbers or just click the up or down arrows to set the size.

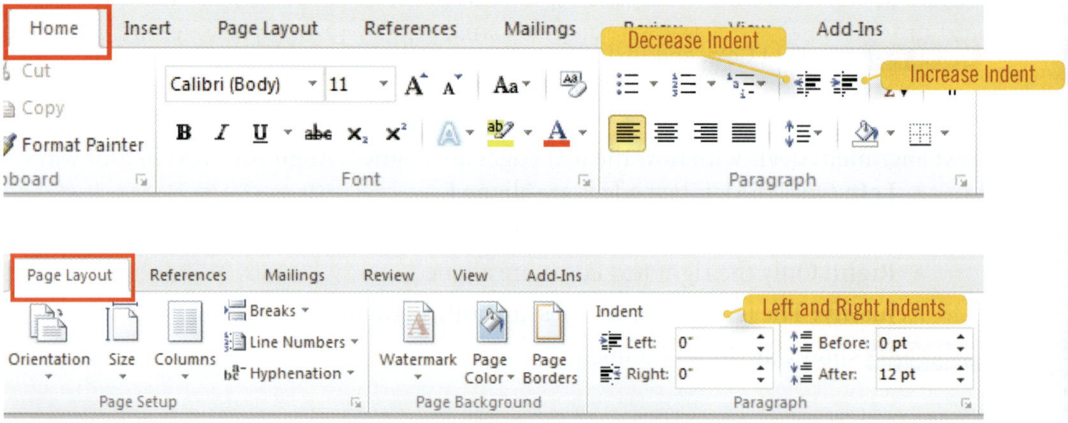

FIGURE 7-16 The indent buttons (Home tab) and indent settings (Page Layout tab).

Inserting the Date

Very often in documents, you will need to display the date. You don't have to type it! The Date & Time button on the Insert tab, as shown in FIGURE 7-17, allows you to insert the date and/or time in a number of formats. One important option is whether you want Word to update the date automatically. By default, Word does not update it automatically. If you want Word to display the current date no matter when you open the document, not when you originally created it, place a check mark in the Update Automatically checkbox in the lower-right corner of the dialog box.

Adding a Picture

You've probably heard the old saying "a picture is worth a thousand words." For this reason, you will find situations where adding pictures to your document makes a lot of sense. For example, this book has many pictures to illustrate what you are learning.

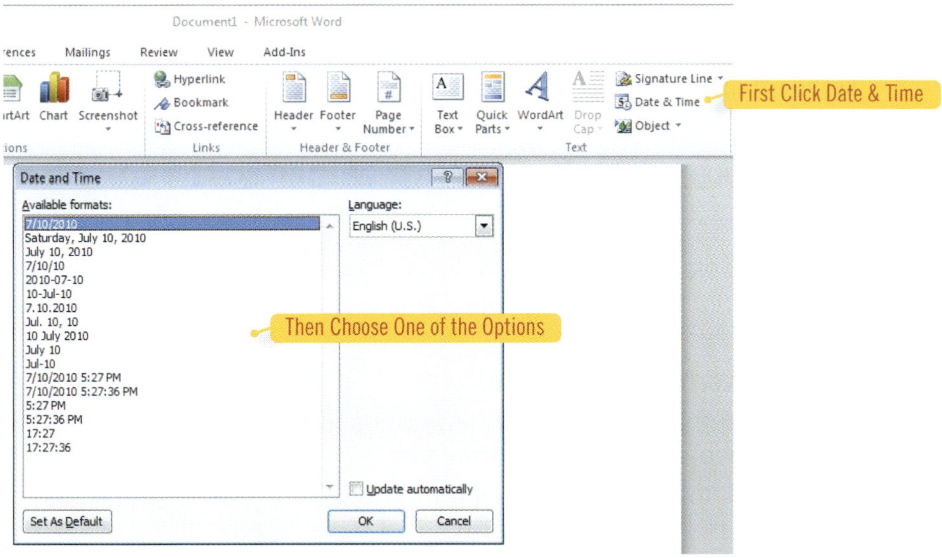

FIGURE 7-17 Inserting the date and/or time.

To insert a picture into your document, perform the following steps:

1. Click the Insert tab.
2. Click the Picture button.
3. Navigate to the picture you want to insert, select it, and click the Insert button.

If you want to resize your picture, grab one of the picture's resizing handles (circles) and drag it to make the picture larger or smaller. The resizing handles are shown in **FIGURE 7-18**.

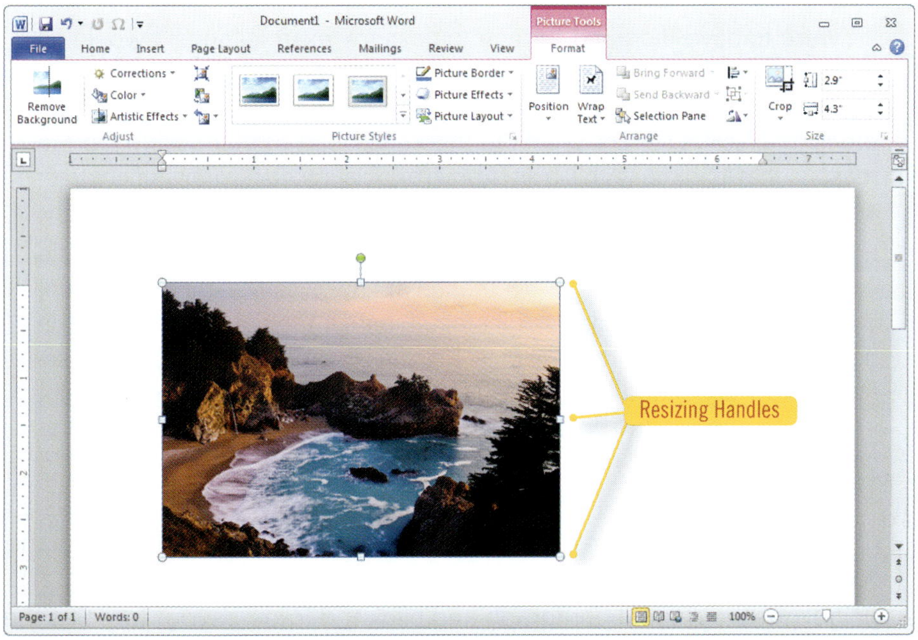

FIGURE 7-18 Resizing handles for an image.

Saving a File

To save a file in Word, click the Save button on the Quick Access toolbar. It looks like a small floppy disk. When the Save dialog box opens, specify the folder in which you want to save your file, enter the file name, and click Save. If you do not see the Save button on the Quick Access toolbar, click the File tab and then click Save or press the Ctrl+S keyboard shortcut.

7.1 Exercise: Exploring Microsoft Word Basics

Now let's practice some of the Word techniques covered so far in this chapter. In this exercise, you will create a simple memo. To work through the exercise, follow these steps:

1. In Word, open a new document.
2. On the Home tab, select the Berlin Sans FB font (or any font of your choice) and a 12 point font size.
3. Click the Insert tab, click the Date & Time button in the Text group, select the second date format in the dialog box, and click OK. Press Enter.
4. Type **From:** and then type your name. Press Enter.
5. Type **To:** and then type a friend's name. Press Enter.
6. Type **Subject: Einstein**. Press Enter.
7. Type the following text:

   In 1894, Einstein's family moved to Milan, but Einstein remained in Munich. In 1895, Einstein failed an examination that would have allowed him to study for a diploma as an electrical engineer at the Eidgenossische Technische Hochschule (ETH) in Zurich. Following the failing of the entrance exam to the ETH, Einstein attended secondary school at Aarau, planning to use this route to enter the ETH in Zurich. While at Aarau, he wrote an essay about his plans for the future:

   If I were to have the good fortune to pass my examinations, I would go to Zurich. I would stay there for four years in order to study mathematics and physics. I imagine myself becoming a teacher in those branches of the natural sciences, choosing the theoretical part of them. Here are the reasons that lead me to this plan. Above all, it is my disposition for abstract and mathematical thought, and my lack of imagination and practical ability.

   Einstein succeeded with his plan, graduating in 1900 as a teacher of mathematics and physics. One of his friends at ETH was Marcel Grossmann, who was in the same class as Einstein. Einstein tried to obtain a position but nothing came of it. Three of Einstein's fellow students, including Grossmann, were appointed assistants at ETH in Zurich. Clearly, Einstein had not impressed enough. In 1901, he was still writing universities in the hope of obtaining a job, but without success.

8. Click the Home tab. Highlight the three paragraphs (click and drag the mouse over them) and click the Justify button. You should see all the text edges aligned on both sides.
9. Highlight the middle paragraph and click the Page Layout tab. Set the right and left indents at 1 inch each.
10. Italicize the school's name in the first paragraph of the body of the memo. Because you already typed the text, remember to highlight the text you want to format before you click the Italic button.
11. Bold this sentence in the indented paragraph: "Here are the reasons that lead me to this plan."

12. Apply underlining to this sentence in the third paragraph: "Clearly, Einstein had not impressed enough."
13. Save your file as Einstein.docx in your Class Research folder. Your memo should look similar to **FIGURE 7-19**.

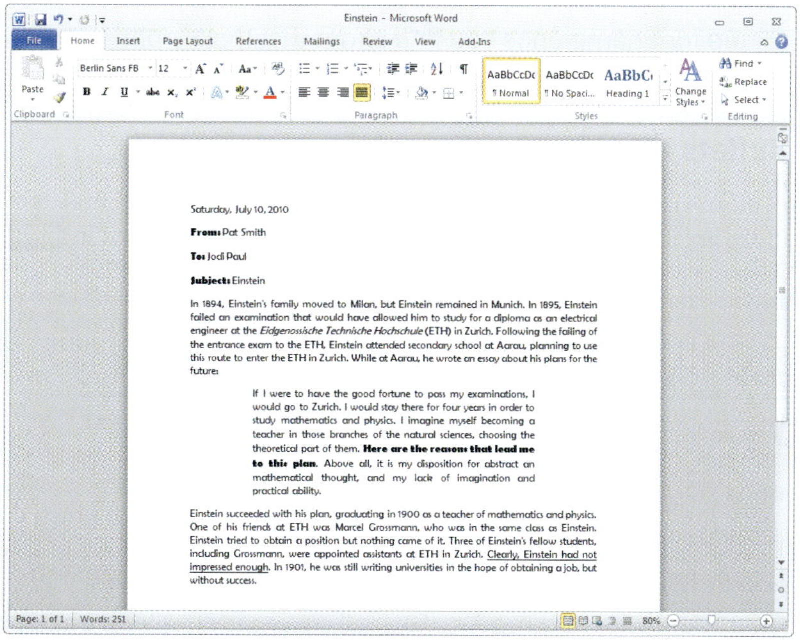

FIGURE 7-19 The finished memo.

Congratulations! You have just learned some of the most basic but important formatting features in Word 2010. If you do not feel comfortable with them, repeat the exercise until it becomes easy to do.

Previewing Fonts

Word 2010 allows you to preview what your text will look like before you apply a new font. Make sure you highlight the text first. **FIGURE 7-20** shows you how this works.

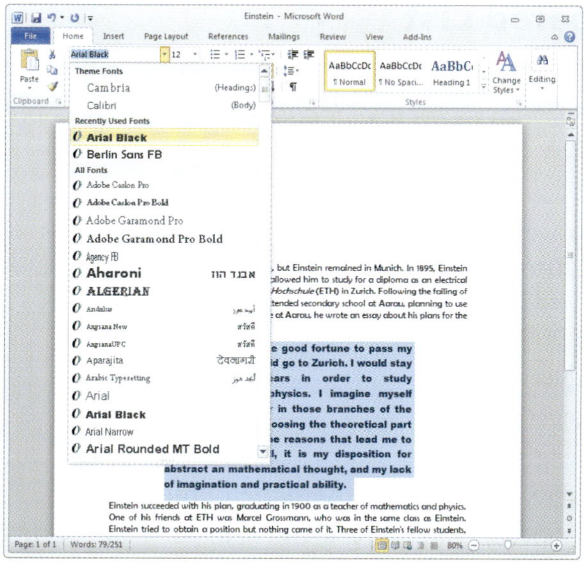

FIGURE 7-20 Previewing a font.

To preview a font, perform the following steps:

1. Highlight the text you want to change.
2. Click the dialog box launcher (small arrow) to display your list of fonts. As you highlight different fonts, you will see the highlighted text change fonts!
3. Click the font name once you find a font that looks right. You will see the new font displayed on your document.

Using Bullets and Numbering

Bullets and numbering are effects you use for lists in a document. The Bullets and Numbering buttons are in the Paragraph group on the Home tab, as shown in FIGURE 7-21.

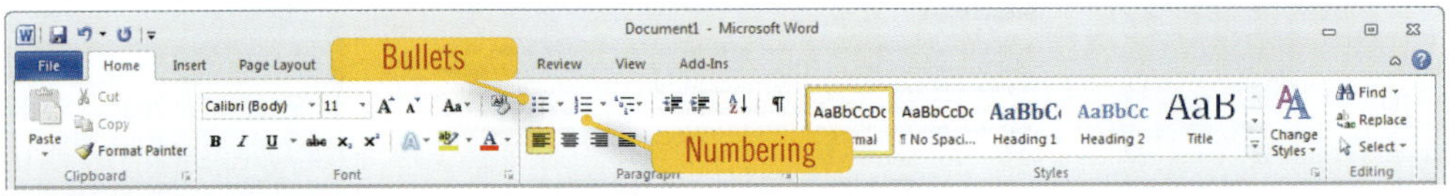

FIGURE 7-21 Bullets and Numbering buttons.

To create a **bulleted list** or **numbered list**, start on a blank line and then do the following:

- Click the Bullets button or the Numbering button.
- Type text and press the Enter key. This will create a new bullet or a new numbered entry.
- Press Enter twice to stop the automatic bullet or numbering feature.

Learn these tips as well to better customize bullets and numbers:

- When you turn on bullets or numbering, Word automatically indents the list. You can accept this indent or change it. Change the indent by using the Decrease Indent or Increase Indent buttons (shown back in Figure 7-16).
- If you want a space between each bullet (number), hold the Shift key then press the Enter key once.

7.2 Exercise: Creating a Bulleted List and a Numbered List

In this exercise, you will create a document that contains bulleted and numbered lists. Follow these steps:

1. Type the following paragraph:

Hi Jodi, I think we need a third CD. Let's start recording it as soon as possible. We should have about 10 to 12 songs on the CD. Let's try to have the CD out by October. The following people need to be contacted soon:

2. Create the bulleted list shown below:
   - Music producer
   - Music arranger
   - Recording engineer
3. Add the following text and create the numbered list:

Also, let's plan to record these three songs first:

1. Fields of Athenry

    2. The Kesh Jig
    3. The Wild Rover

4. Highlight the numbered list, and click Increase Indent. You should see the numbered list move to the right.
5. Save your file as Music in your Class Research folder.

That's how simple it is. If you did everything right, your document should look very similar to FIGURE 7-22.

> Hi Jodi, I think we need a third CD. Let's start recording it as soon as possible. We should have about 10 to 12 songs on the CD. Let's try to have the CD out by October. The following people need to be contacted soon:
>
> - Music producer
> - Music arranger
> - Recording engineer
>
> Also, let's plan to record these three songs first:
>
> 1. Fields of Athenry
> 2. The Kesh Jig
> 3. The Wild Rover

FIGURE 7-22 An exercise in using bullets and numbering.

Setting Margins

Page **margins** are the blank space around the edges of a page. In general, you insert text and graphics in the printable area between the margins. By default, Word 2010 sets the margins on any new document to 1 inch. The four margins are: Top, Left, Bottom, and Right. You can change any margin's width to suit your needs.

To change the margins, click the Page Layout tab, click Margins, and then click Custom Margins. The Page Setup dialog box appears, as shown in FIGURE 7-23, allowing you to enter your own margin settings.

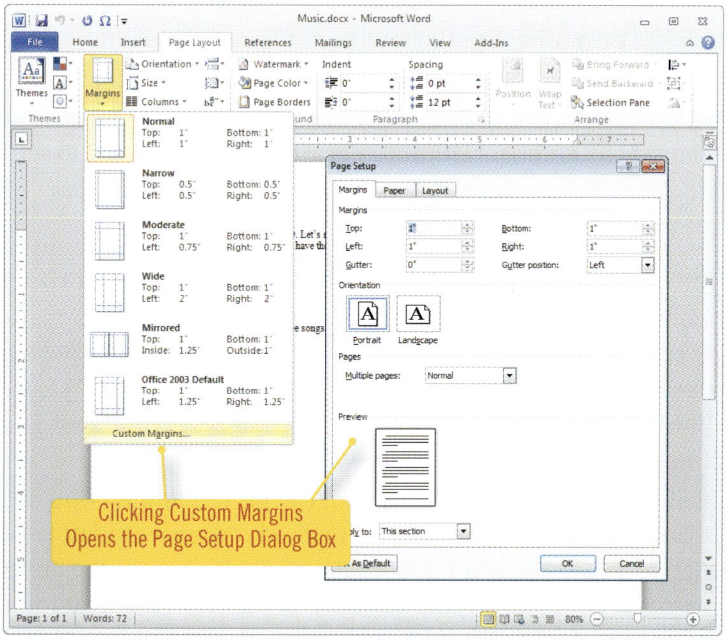

FIGURE 7-23 Setting margins.

The margin settings you enter apply only to the current document. Although you can make these changes affect all new documents, you probably should leave the default margins at 1 inch for all new documents, and change them whenever you need to. One-inch margins are standard in the business world, and that's why the default is set to 1 inch in the first place.

Why might you change margins? Let's say you created a resume, which turns out to be a little more than one page, with only two lines on the second page. It doesn't make sense to have a second page with just two lines. Adjust the margins by making them smaller than 1 inch. This creates more space on the page, and allows your resume to fit on that one page.

Setting Tab Stops

A **tab stop** is a quick way to move the insertion point to the right, and to indent only the first line of a paragraph. The Tab key is on the keyboard's far left side, just above the Caps Lock key. Every time you press the Tab key, the insertion point moves to the right by one-half inch.

Change the tab settings if you like. When you do, the tab symbols display on the ruler. If you have not noticed it by now, Word displays a ruler across the top (just under the Ribbon) and along the left side of the document window. If you don't see it, click the View tab, and then check the Ruler checkbox in the Show group. For purposes of illustration, a variety of tab stops are shown in FIGURE 7-24.

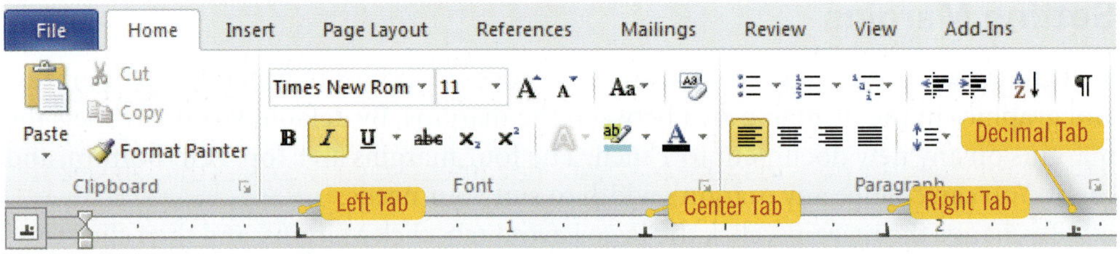

FIGURE 7-24 Tab stops on the ruler.

The tab stops are as follows:

- **Left:** Sets the start position of the text that will then run to the right as you type.
- **Center:** Sets the position of the middle of the text. The text centers on this position as you type.
- **Right:** Sets the right end of the text. As you type, the text moves to the left.
- **Decimal:** Aligns numbers around a decimal point. Also used to separate text.

Changing Tab Settings

By default, the ruler on a new document doesn't display tab stops because default tabs are set every one-half inch. If you change the tab stops, however, the horizontal ruler will display them. Change your tab stops two ways:

1. Click the positions of the tab stops on the horizontal ruler. For example, if you want a left tab stop at 1.5 inches from a document's left edge, click the ruler at that position.
2. Double-click a tab stop on the ruler.

The problem with the first method is that it can be inaccurate—you might not click exactly at 1.5. The other problem is that this method only places a left tab character on the ruler—what if you want a right tab stop? Below the Ribbon, in the upper-left corner where the horizontal and vertical rulers intersect, you'll see the icon for a left tab (by default). To create a right tab (or any other type of tab), click the icon until it changes to the kind of tab stop you want. Then click the ruler to place the tab stop.

The second method for changing tab stops—to double-click a tab stop on the ruler—opens the Tabs dialog box, as shown in FIGURE 7-25. You can change existing tabs from one type to another, or set new tabs by typing in the number where you want the tab to appear. Once you finish setting tabs, click Set, then click OK. The ruler will display your tab stops.

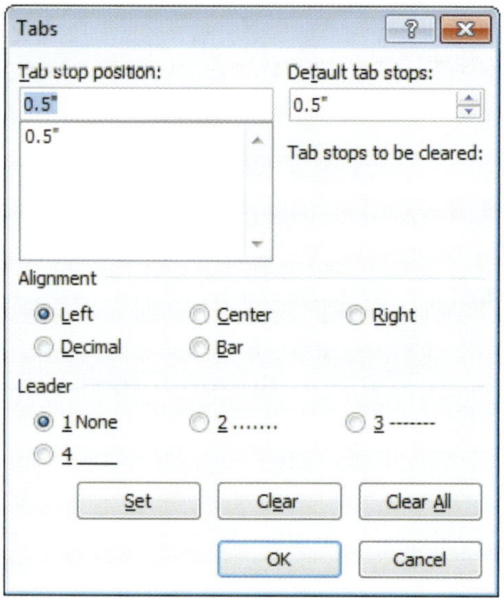

FIGURE 7-25 Tabs dialog box.

The decimal tab deserves some additional explanation. A dot leader is a dotted line that you use to connect related tab stops. You can select it as one of the options in the Tabs dialog box. The example in FIGURE 7-26 shows what a dot leader looks like. Once you've set a decimal tab, the dots will appear in your document when you press the Tab key. You often use dot leaders in a table of contents to draw the eye from the headings listed along the left to the page numbers on the right.

Mary Brown ....President

FIGURE 7-26 A dot leader.

7.3 Exercise: Setting Tab Stops

This exercise will help you learn how to set tab stops and how to create a dot leader. The finished assignment should look similar to FIGURE 7-27*. You'll use the figure as a guide in this exercise.*

Here's the step-by-step procedure:

1. Open a new blank Word document. If the ruler isn't visible, click the View tab and check the Ruler option. On the Home tab in the Paragraph group, click the dialog box launcher.
2. In the Paragraph dialog box that appears, click the Tabs button. The Tabs dialog box appears.
3. Enter 1.5 and click the Set button to set the left tab stop. Type **5**, select the Right option, and click Set. This sets the right tab stop. Your Tabs dialog box should look like FIGURE 7-28. Make changes, if necessary; otherwise click OK.

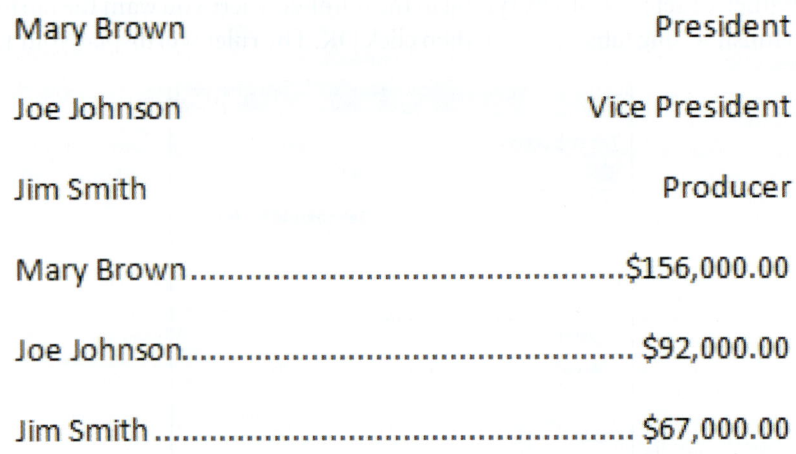

Mary Brown President
Joe Johnson Vice President
Jim Smith Producer
Mary Brown..$156,000.00
Joe Johnson..$92,000.00
Jim Smith..$67,000.00

FIGURE 7-27 Completed assignment.

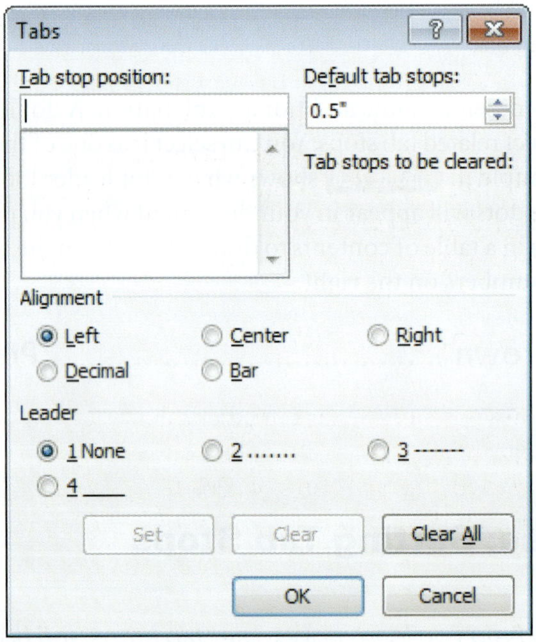

FIGURE 7-28 Tabs dialog box.

4. In your document, press the Tab key (on the keyboard) once. You should see the insertion point jump to position 1.5. Type **Mary Brown**.
5. Press the Tab key again. The insertion point jumps to position 5 on the ruler. Type **President** and press Enter. Notice how the word "President" appeared as you typed it at the right tab stop.
6. Repeat Steps 4 and 5 for the other two names—**Joe Johnson** and **Jim Smith**. At this stage, your document should resemble **FIGURE 7-29**.

Now you'll make two changes. You will keep the left tab stop exactly as before, but you will change the right tab stop to a decimal tab stop with a dot leader. For this part of the exercise, make sure the insertion point is below the section you have already created (below Producer):

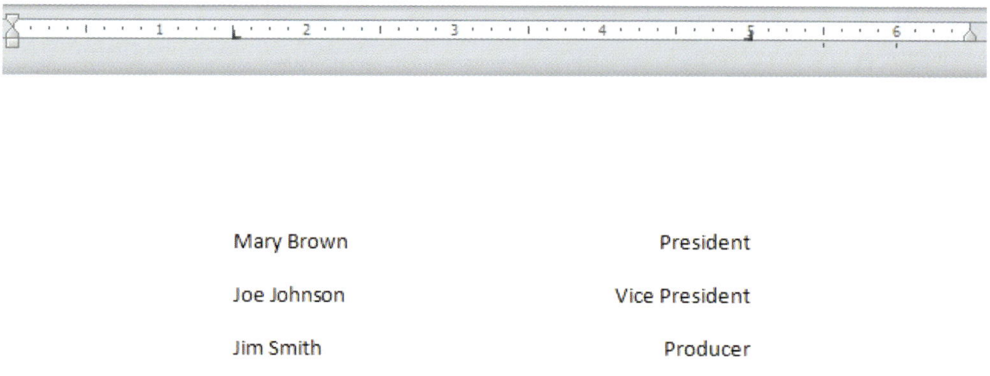

FIGURE 7-29 Your practice document so far.

> **Note**
>
> You can change tab stops at any time. Just make sure you have the insertion point in the right place before you make changes.

7. Open the Tabs dialog box again (if you forgot, review Step 1). Click the number 5 and click the Clear button to clear the right tab stop. Type **4.8** and click the Decimal option.
8. In the Leader group, click option 2 and click Set. This sets the decimal tab stop. Click OK.
9. In your document, press the Tab key once. The insertion point should jump to 1.5 on the ruler. Type **Mary Brown**. Press the Tab key again to jump to 4.8 on the ruler. You should also see the dot leader! Now, type **$156,000.00** and press Enter.
10. Repeat Step 9 for the rest of the names and salaries.

If you did everything correctly, your document should look like Figure 7-27. Notice that the decimal places are lined up, and that dots are displayed from names to salaries. This is because you selected a decimal tab stop. Practice changing tab stops until you feel comfortable with how to use them.

Spell Checking

Word can check spelling and grammar. It will check spelling as you type or you can run the checker manually. To spell-check your document, click the Review tab and then click the Spelling & Grammar button. The button has a check mark and the letters ABC on it.

FIGURE 7-30 shows a **spell check** in progress. It shows the options you can choose while checking the spelling in your documents.

As mentioned, Word 2010 automatically checks spelling as you type. The spell check feature underlines any words that are possibly misspelled with a wavy red line. Word also checks grammar automatically. A wavy green line indicates possible grammatical errors. We use the word "possibly" because Word doesn't have every word in the world in its dictionaries, nor does it always recognize grammar properly.

To eliminate the red and green wavy lines in your documents, click the File tab, and then click the Options button. In the Word Options dialog box, click Proofing in the left pane. Scroll

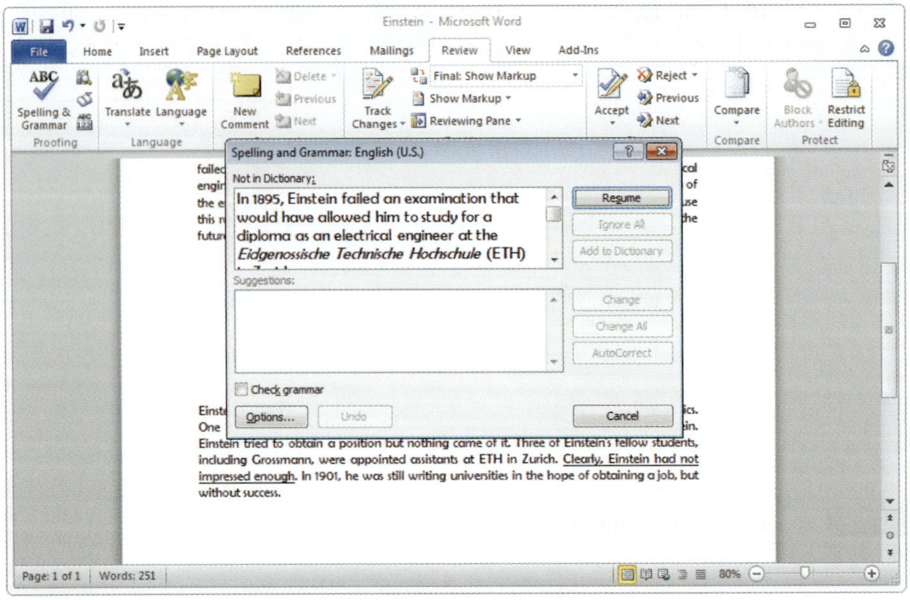

FIGURE 7-30 A document being checked for spelling errors.

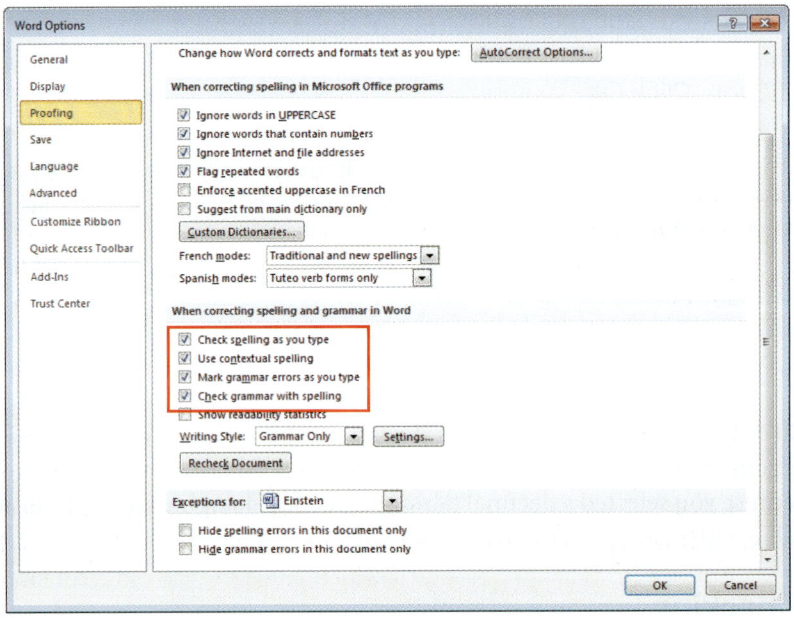

FIGURE 7-31 Changing default spelling and grammar settings.

down and clear the checkboxes highlighted in FIGURE 7-31. If you take this step, remember to run the spelling and grammar checker manually before sharing your document with others.

Using Find and Replace

Find and **Replace** are really neat features in Word. In other words, you don't have to read through your whole document looking for a certain term. If it's in the document, Word will find it.

Find allows you to enter search terms (a word or phrase), and Word will search the document for them. Replace is a similar feature, but Word replaces the search term you specify with a new word or phrase you spell out.

Word 2010 introduced a new Find feature that opens in the left pane. To use it, from the Home tab in the Editing group on the far right, click Find. The navigation pane opens on the window's left side. In the navigation pane search box, enter the word or phrase you wish to find in your document. Word automatically lists the results below the search box and highlights each found word in the document, as shown in FIGURE 7-32.

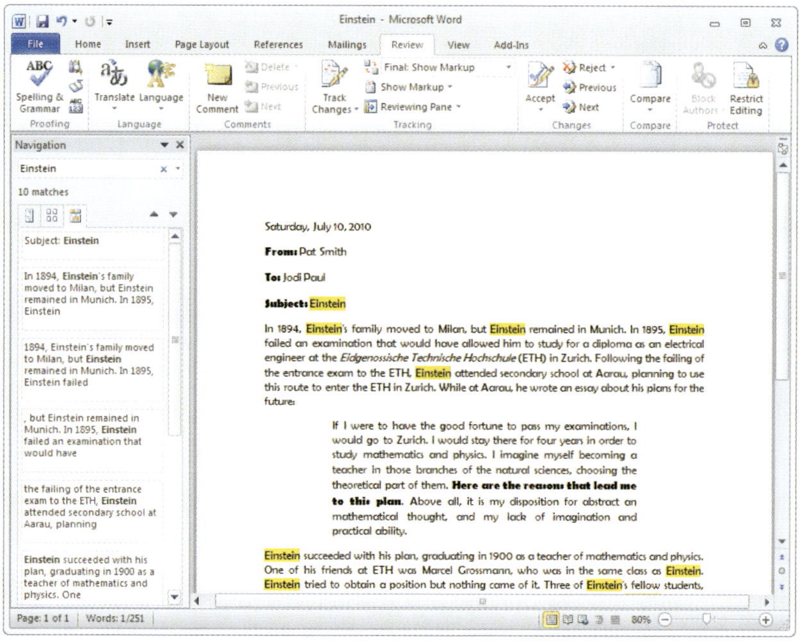

FIGURE 7-32 Using the Find feature.

Replace is another feature that will come in handy. It replaces a word or phrase with another word or phrase. You may need to replace a word or phrase with another for any number of reasons. For example, you may need to change all instances of the term "hard disk" in your document to "flash drive" instead. Rather than searching for each occurrence of "hard disk" and manually typing "flash drive," use the Replace command.

To use Replace, click the Replace button on the Home tab in the Editing group. The Find and Replace dialog box appears, as shown in FIGURE 7-33. Enter the word or phrase you want to replace in the Find What text box. Enter the replacement word or phrase in the Replace With text box. Click the Replace button. Word finds the first occurrence of the word or phrase and redisplays the dialog box. If you want to replace it, click Replace. The process continues until every occurrence of the word or phrase has been checked.

You can also click the Replace All button, which performs the replacement operation all at once.

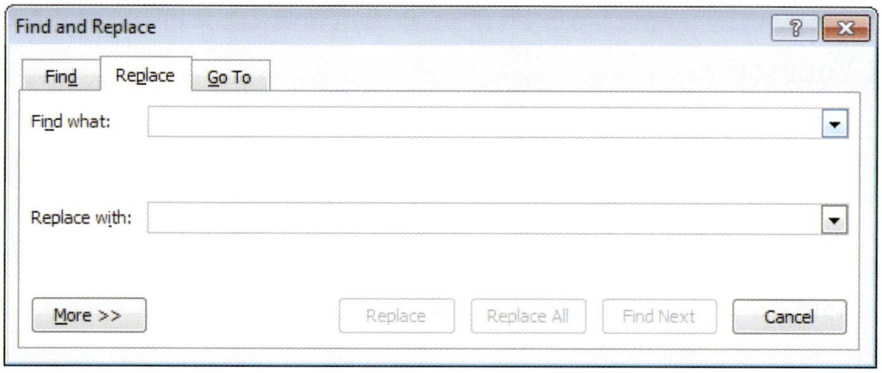

FIGURE 7-33 The Find and Replace dialog box.

Printing a Document

To print a document, click the File tab and then click the Print button. The Print window appears, as shown in FIGURE 7-34.

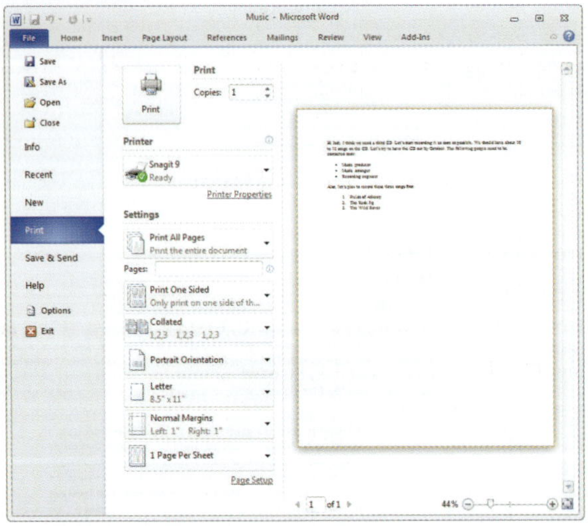

FIGURE 7-34 Print options.

Select how many copies of the document you want to print. In the Copies spin box near the top of the window, use the arrows to choose a number or double-click on the number already in the box and change it to a number you prefer.

Under Printer, select the printer you want to send the document to for printing. To switch to another printer, click the arrow to open a list of printers available on your computer or network.

Under Settings, you can select whether to print all pages in your document or just certain ones. When you click the arrow next to the default (Print All Pages), a list appears with the following options:

- Print All Pages
- Print Selection
- Print Current Page
- Custom Range

If you choose Custom Range, Word will prompt you to enter the specific page numbers (for example, 1,2,5) or the specific range of pages (6-9) that you want printed.

This chapter has exposed you to a lot of details about word processing. In Chapter 8, you will learn more advanced concepts, tasks, and features of Word 2010. Hopefully you are having fun learning all of this material. It might seem like a lot, but once you're comfortable using Word, it can help you do a lot of very handy things.

Test Yourself

The questions in this section are meant to test your knowledge of what you read. Make sure you answer them. The page number where the answer can be found appears after each question.

1. What is the purpose of a live preview in a gallery? ________________ (154)
2. How do you access the basic file task commands in Word 2010? (152)
   A. Use Windows Explorer.
   B. Click the View tab.
   C. Click the File tab.
   D. Click the Review tab.

3. What is the purpose of tabs on the Word 2010 Ribbon? (153, 155)
   A. To allow you to search for terms within the document
   B. To group similar tools together
   C. To make words appear in bold
   D. To let you open and close documents
4. Ribbon tabs display groups that display related features. (155)
   A. True
   B. False
5. What is the easiest way to discover what an unknown icon does? (155)
   A. Ask a friend.
   B. Send an e-mail to Microsoft.
   C. Click the icon multiple times.
   D. Hover your mouse pointer over the icon to read the tooltip.
6. What is the shortcut for bolding text? (155)
   A. Ctrl+B
   B. Ctrl+V
   C. Alt+B
   D. Ctrl+Alt+B
7. Which tab contains features such as Font, Bullets, and Numbering? (158, 164)
   A. The Page Layout tab
   B. The View tab
   C. The Home tab
   D. The Insert tab
8. Which tab allows you to insert a picture in a document? (161)
   A. The Page Layout tab
   B. The View tab
   C. The Home tab
   D. The Insert tab
9. Which tab allows you to set the margins? (165)
   A. The Page Layout tab
   B. The View tab
   C. The Home tab
   D. The Insert tab
10. Which tab allows you to zoom in and out of a document? (156)
    A. The Page Layout tab
    B. The View tab
    C. The Home tab
    D. The Insert tab
11. Once you create and save a document, you can return to the document and underline a sentence or make other formatting changes. (157)
    A. True
    B. False
12. What does "highlight" mean? (157)
    A. To change the font of some text
    B. To select some text using the mouse or keyboard
    C. To view a live preview
    D. To delete some text

13. Whoops! You made a small error while formatting a document. What should you do immediately? (156)
   A. Close the document without saving it.
   B. Save the document.
   C. Click Undo.
   D. Start a new document.
14. Name the four ways you can align text: ______________________ (159)
15. What does justify mean? (159)
   A. Text is aligned on the left.
   B. Text is aligned on the right.
   C. Text is aligned on both sides.
   D. Text is indented on both sides.
16. What are the default margins in a new document in Word 2010? (165)
   A. 1.5 inches
   B. 0.75 inches
   C. 0.5 inches
   D. 1 inch
17. If you spell-check as you type, how can you detect a word that's possibly misspelled? (169)
   A. Words are underlined with a wavy blue line.
   B. Words are underlined with a wavy green line.
   C. Words are underlined with a wavy red line.
   D. Words are underlined with a wavy purple line.
18. What feature in Word lets you locate a specific word or phrase? (170)
   A. Search
   B. Find
   C. Zoom In
   D. Change
19. The Replace feature can replace only one word at a time. (171)
   A. True
   B. False
20. You are not sure how to accomplish a task. How do you access Help? (Select two.) (157)
   A. Press the F1 key on your keyboard.
   B. Press the F10 key on your keyboard.
   C. Click the icon that looks like a blue circle with a question mark in it.
   D. Click the dialog box launcher in the Help group.

End-of-Chapter Project

In this project, you will transfer the research information you typed in the Chapter 6 project into a Word document. Follow these steps:

1. Open the PC Basics Research.rtf document in Word 2010.
2. Save the file in Word format: Click File, click Save As, select Word Document (*.docx) in the Save As Type drop-down list, and click Save. Click OK in the warning dialog box that appears.
3. Format the document using two different fonts: one for the headings and one for the body text.
4. Convert any lists of specifications to bulleted lists.
5. Save your work, and close Word.

CHAPTER

8

Microsoft Word 2010 Formatting, Tables, and More

- In Chapter 7, you learned many of the fundamental concepts required to perform the most basic tasks in Microsoft Word 2010, from document creation to creating bulleted lists to spell-checking your work. In this chapter, you will learn more advanced concepts. Knowing how to apply features such as headers and footers, page numbers, columns, and tables will help you produce more professional-looking documents. Diving into images, shapes, and WordArt will make your documents more lively and fun as well.
- Once you master this chapter's techniques and exercises, you will more fully realize the power of Word. The process of formatting documents, too, will become easier and more creative.

CHAPTER TOPICS

This chapter covers the following topics and concepts:

- How to split a document and how to compare two documents side by side
- Where to place headers and footers in a document
- How to insert page numbers into a document
- How to create a title page for a document, such as a report
- Where to find images, drawings, clip art, and other art
- How to insert text boxes
- How to create and format tables
- How to create and format columns
- How to insert symbols
- When to use Microsoft Equation rather than entering equations manually

KEY WORDS

Callout
Clip art
Columns
Footer
Header
Microsoft Equation
Row
Shapes
Symbol
Table
Title page
WordArt

Document Views

When working in Word, you ordinarily see a single document on the screen. It sits in a setting called Print Layout view. This means your document will print very much like what you see on the screen. However, you can view your document in many different ways using the options on the View tab on the Ribbon, shown in FIGURE 8-1.

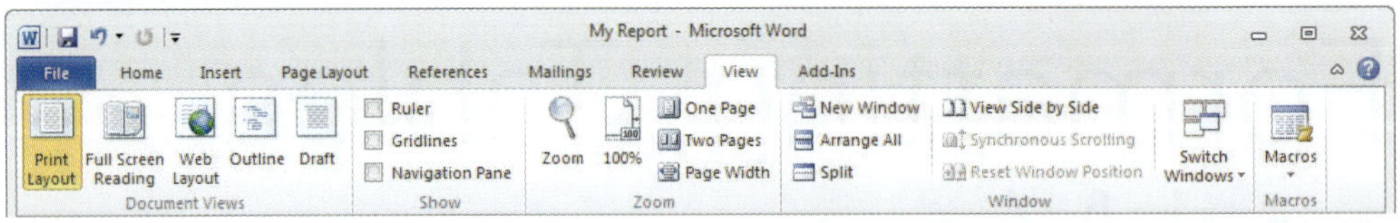

FIGURE 8-1 The Word 2010 View tab.

Several figures in this chapter will show you documents in different views. For example, you will see a document displayed with two pages side by side. This is so you can easily see how some new formatting feature affects multiple pages. You get this view by using the Two Pages command in the Zoom group on the View tab.

Other ways to use the View tab options include:

- Clicking the Full Screen Reading, Web Layout, or Outline view buttons
- Zooming in on your document
- Splitting a document
- Viewing two documents side by side

Feel free to experiment with the View tab options on your own. For now, let's take a look at the last two features in more detail.

Splitting a Document

Splitting a document allows you to see two parts of the same document at once. That is, you can split the screen in two, and see one part of the document on the top half and another part of it on the bottom half. To split a document, open any document, click the View tab, and then click Split. A divider line appears on the screen. Wherever you click becomes the split point. You can now scroll the top or bottom half of the screen independently of each other. Notice that each portion of the screen has its own set of scroll bars, as shown in FIGURE 8-2.

View Side by Side

The View Side by Side feature lets you study two different documents at the same time. Both documents must be open. To view a list of the documents you have open, select the View tab and click View Side by Side. When you do this, Word tiles the two documents vertically, which means each will take up half the screen vertically, as shown in FIGURE 8-3.

By default, Word selects synchronous scrolling. This means that scrolling one document up or down makes the other document also scroll up or down. To turn synchronous scrolling off, click Synchronous Scrolling.

Now that you understand document views, let's move on to headers, footers, and page numbers.

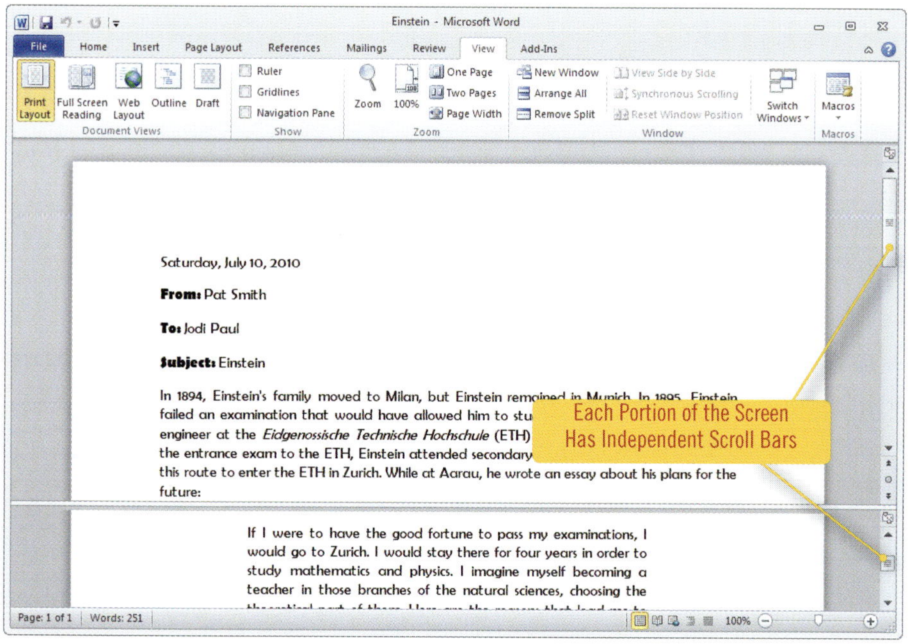

FIGURE 8-2 A split document.

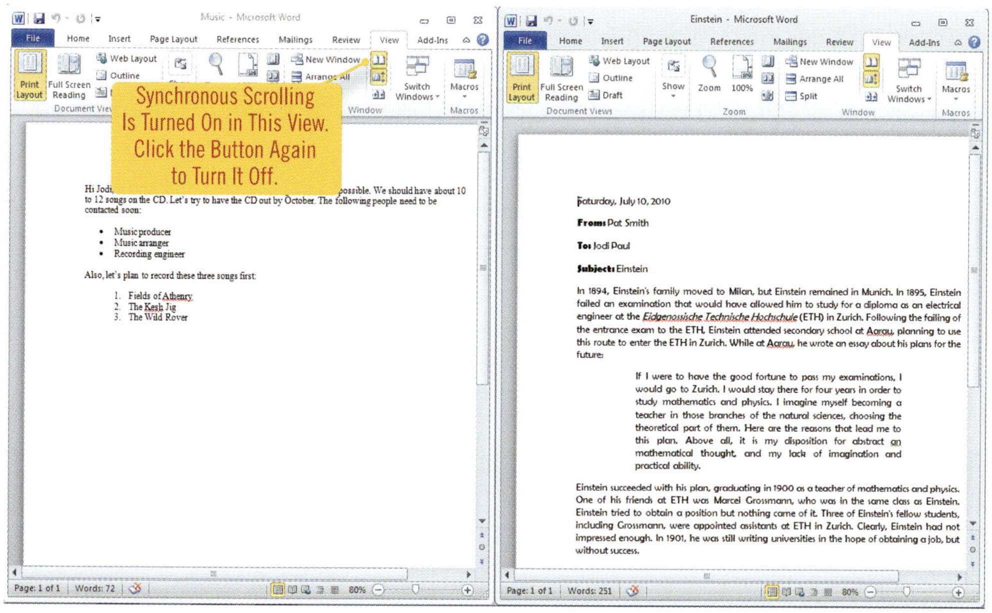

FIGURE 8-3 Two documents side by side.

Working with Headers and Footers

A **header** is text that is placed at the top of every page in a document. A **footer** is text that is placed at the bottom of every page. An example of a header and a footer is shown in **FIGURE 8-4**. For example, if you are writing a book, each chapter may have a different header and/or footer that needs to appear at the top and bottom of every page. The great thing about headers and footers is that you only type them once, and Word automatically places them on every page in a document. You can also place different headers and/or footers on odd and even pages. If you look at the top of the pages in this book, you will see a different header on the odd and even pages in each chapter.

FIGURE 8-4 A header and a footer in a document.

Headers

To insert a header into a Word document, follow these steps:

1. Click the Insert tab.
2. In the Header & Footer group, click Header. A drop-down menu appears, as shown in FIGURE 8-5.

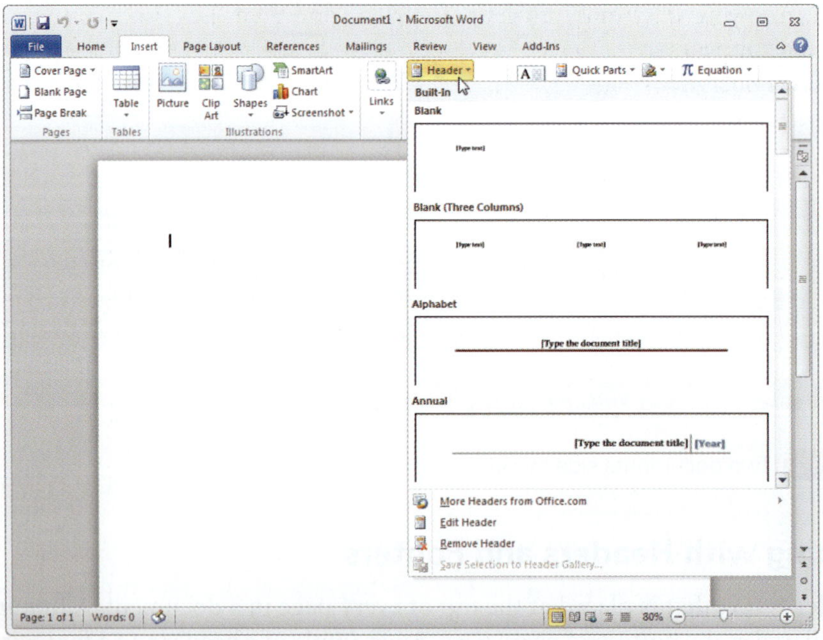

FIGURE 8-5 The header drop-down menu.

3. Select one of the many different predefined headers. If nothing is the right style for your document, click Edit Header at the bottom of the menu. The header area in the Word document opens, as shown in FIGURE 8-6, allowing you to create a custom header.

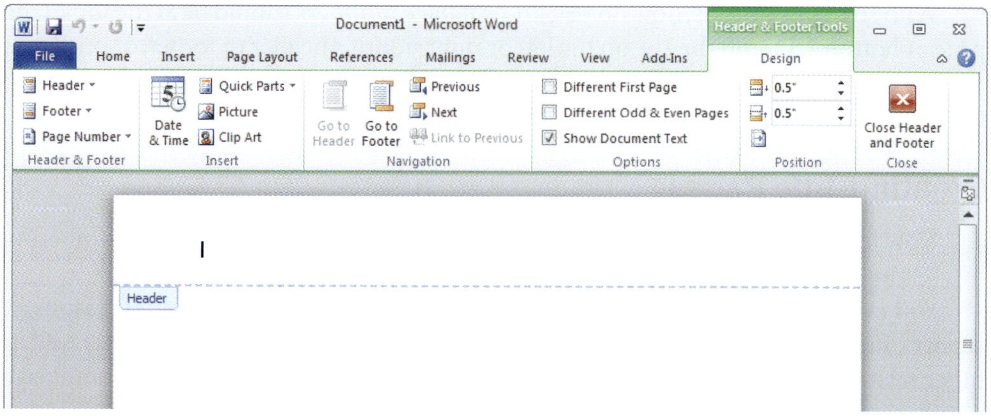

FIGURE 8-6 The header area in a Word document.

4. Notice that Word shows a blue dotted line. The header will appear above this dotted line. Just type the header in this area, and click the Close Header and Footer button when you're done. You can also double-click anywhere in the document to close the header.

Footers

You create footers the same way. Instead of clicking Header in the Header & Footer group of the Insert tab, you click Footer. The footer area shows up at the bottom of the page. Type the footer text, and then click Close Header and Footer.

Adding Page Numbers

The Word Page Number feature places page numbers in your document. To insert page numbers into your document, click the Insert tab and then click Page Number. A drop-down menu appears that offers several options for inserting page numbers, such as Top of Page and Bottom of Page. Point to any of the menu items to open a larger list of options, as shown in FIGURE 8-7.

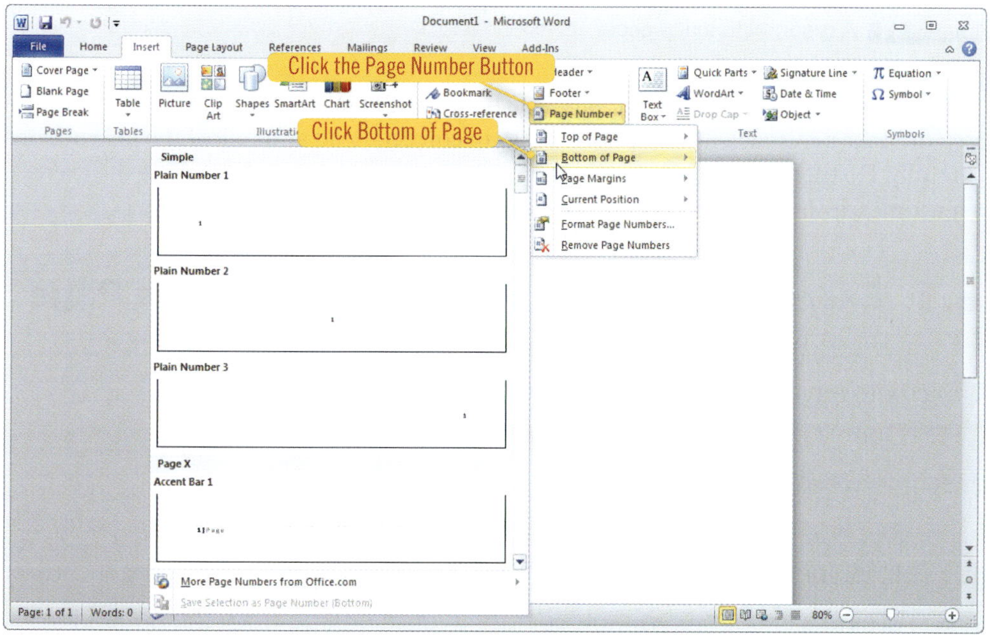

FIGURE 8-7 Page numbering options.

With so many options, how do you know if page numbers should be at the top of the page or bottom? Should they be on the left or right side of a header or footer, or centered? Should they be fancy or simple? For the most part, the answers to these questions are up to you. Select the format that looks best for your document.

Creating Title Pages

Now let's practice what you've learned about headers, footers, and page numbering by creating a report with a title page and ordinary report pages.

You might need to create a report for school, work, or just for personal reasons. A report often contains a title page. A **title page** contains the title of the report as well as other related information. The body of the report usually has a header, footer, and page numbering. The title page, however, usually does not have those elements. In the following exercise, you will learn how to add a title page, and a header, footer, and page numbers to ordinary report pages. FIGURE 8-8 shows what you will accomplish in this exercise.

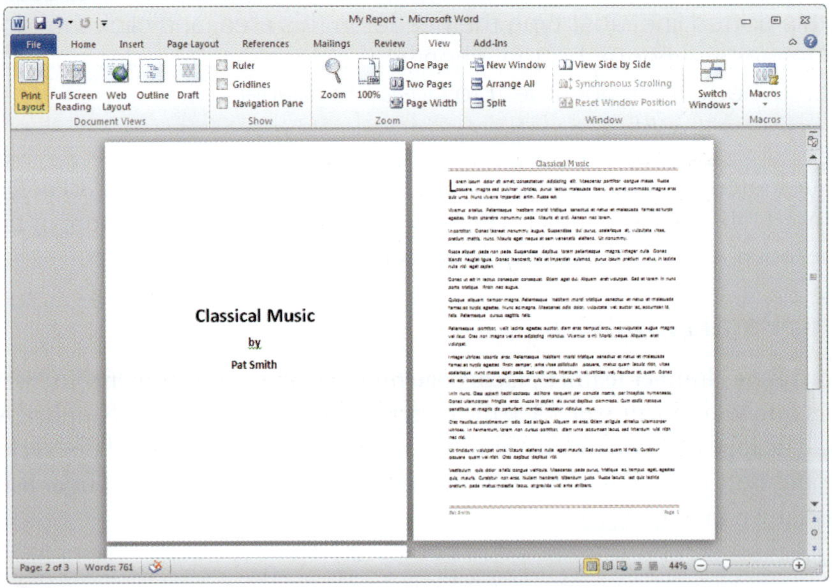

FIGURE 8-8 A report with a title page.

This exercise requires a bit of patience because it involves many steps. If you miss a step or make a mistake, it might not be easy to correct. Read and follow the instructions carefully. Do them slowly, and repeat them if necessary. After you have done the exercise a few times, it should become easier for you.

8.1 Exercise: Creating a Report with a Title Page

To create a practice report, perform the following steps:

1. Open a new blank document in Word.
2. To create the title page:
   a. Type a title for the report, such as **Classical Music**. Press Enter.
   b. Type by and press Enter. Type your name and press Enter.
3. Create a section break to separate your title page from the pages that will follow. To do so, on the Page Layout tab, click Breaks and then select Next Page, as shown in FIGURE 8-9. This action instructs Word to create a page in a new "section" of the document.

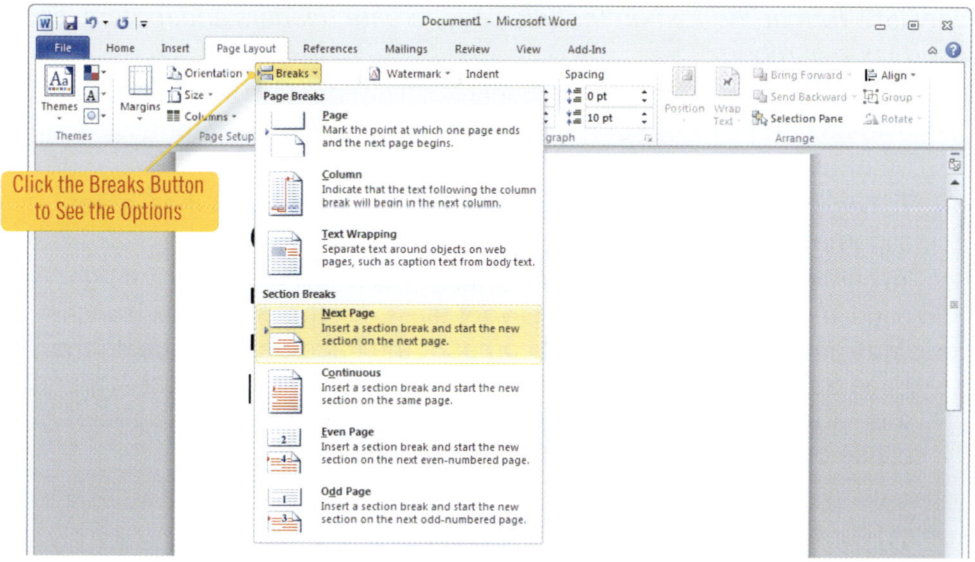

FIGURE 8-9 Break options.

4. At this point you need a few pages of text to make your report look more "report-ish." Instead of typing text, Word has a function that generates sample or dummy text for just these kinds of projects. At the top of the second page, type **=lorem(24,5)** and press Enter. The first number in the parentheses is the number of paragraphs you want; the second number is the desired number of lines per paragraph. Two pages of dummy text appear.
5. To give your report a little polish, create a drop cap. Select (or highlight) the first letter of the dummy text on page 2. On the Insert tab, click Drop Cap, and then select Drop Cap Options. The Drop Cap dialog box appears. In the Position section, click Dropped. In the Options section, click the down arrow next to Lines To Drop to select 2 lines. Click OK.
6. The report now consists of a title page, and a few pages of sample text with a drop cap. At this stage, your report should look similar to **FIGURE 8-10**.

Note

By using a section break, you are separating the title page from any report body pages you add. You can apply different formatting to one section of a document without affecting other sections. For example, you can make the margins different in each section or change from Portrait to Landscape.

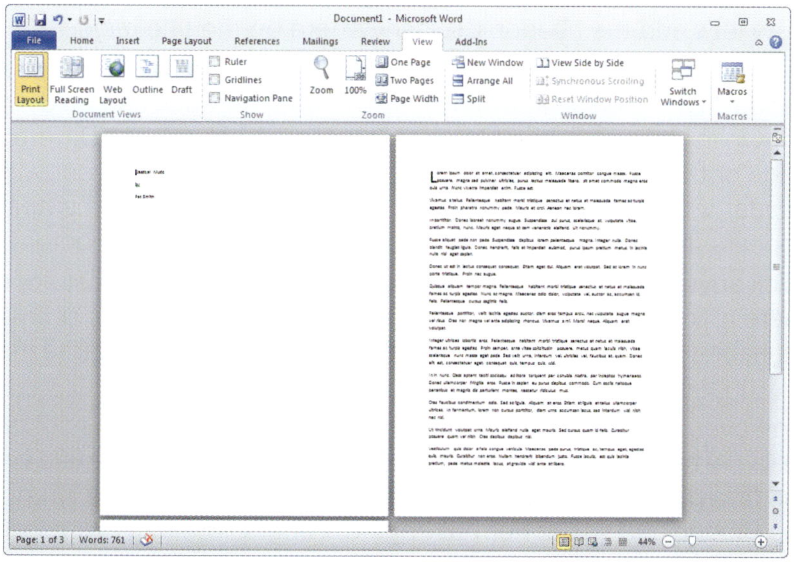

FIGURE 8-10 The draft report.

Now let's format the text on the title page, create headers and footers, and insert page numbers:

1. To format the text on the title page, highlight the text and bold it. Apply a 40-point font size to **Classical Music**. Apply a 24-point font size to the other text.
2. To center the text horizontally, highlight all text and click the Center alignment button on the Home tab.
3. To center the text vertically on the page, click anywhere on the title page and then click the Page Layout tab. Click the dialog box launcher (little arrow) in the lower-right corner of the Page Setup group. In the Page Setup dialog box, click the Layout tab. Open the Vertical Alignment drop-down menu and select Center. FIGURE 8-11 shows the Page Setup dialog box with the Center option selected. Click OK.

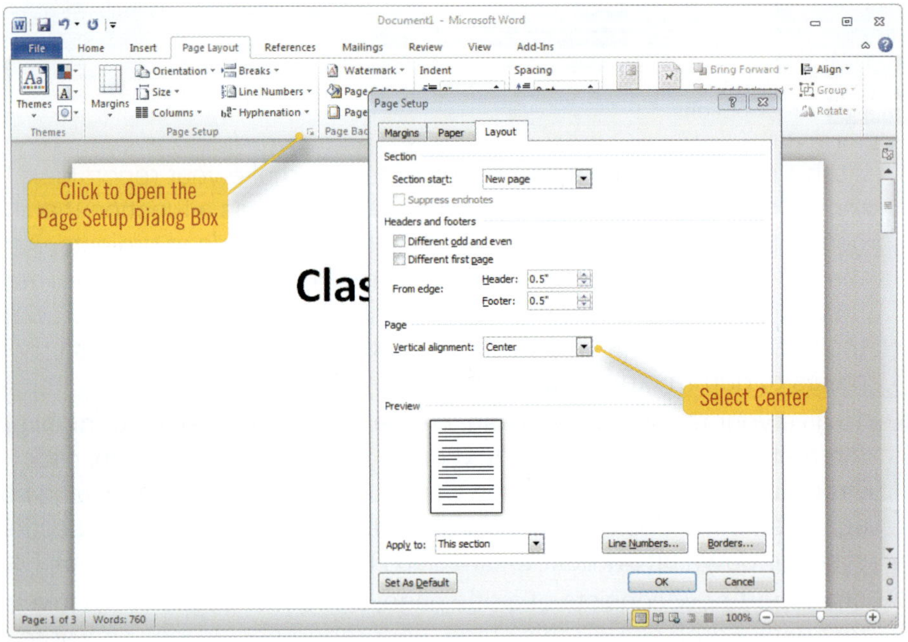

FIGURE 8-11 Selecting Center in the Page Setup dialog box.

4. Now let's add the header. Click anywhere on the title page.
5. On the Insert tab, click Header. Scroll down and select the Alphabet header. Type **Classical Music** in the header text box and bold it, as shown in FIGURE 8-12. **Important:** Make sure to check the Different First Page option. This instructs Word that you do not want to show the header on the title page. Once you check the checkbox, the header disappears from the title page. Click the Close Header and Footer button.
6. Click anywhere on the second page. Notice that the header appears there. Click Footer on the Insert tab. Select a footer style, such as Alphabet, which has a page number built in. Enter your name in the text box on the left side of the footer, as shown in FIGURE 8-13.
7. However, notice that the page number is wrong! It shows a 2 rather than 1. This is because you are technically on page 2 (the title page is the first page in the document). To correct this, click Page Number on the Ribbon and select Format Page Numbers. The Page Number Format dialog box appears. In the Page Numbering group, type 1 in the Start At box. Click OK. This will correct the problem; you should now see the

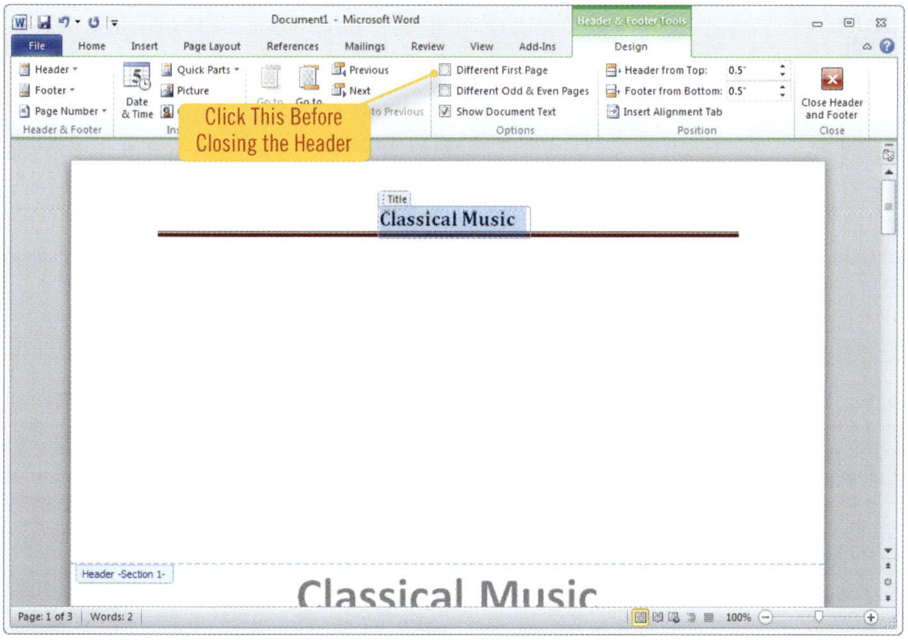

FIGURE 8-12 The Different First Page checkbox on the Insert tab.

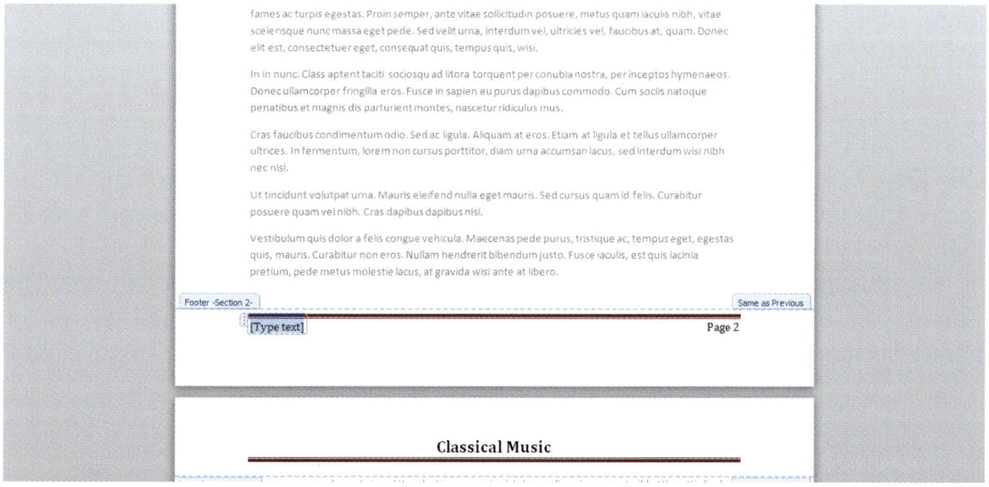

FIGURE 8-13 Adding a footer with a page number.

correct page numbers. Click the Close Header and Footer button.

8. Scroll back to the title page. Notice that it does not have a header or a footer with a page number, which is exactly what you want.
9. Save the file as My Report in your Class Research folder.

And with that you're finished! If you did everything correctly, your document should look similar to **FIGURE 8-14**. *Select File and then Print to see how your document will look when printed.*

Working with Images and Drawings

Word offers a wide variety of ways to add and edit pictures, drawings, and other graphics to your documents. In fact, all of the Word 2010 graphics features combined begin to blur the lines between Word being a "word processing package." It's beginning to look like graphics software, too.

TIP

You need to know how to copy and paste text and objects to work through some of the remaining exercises in this chapter. See those discussions in Chapters 5 and 6 if you need a reminder on how to use the Copy and Paste features. They work the same in Windows 7 and Office 2010.

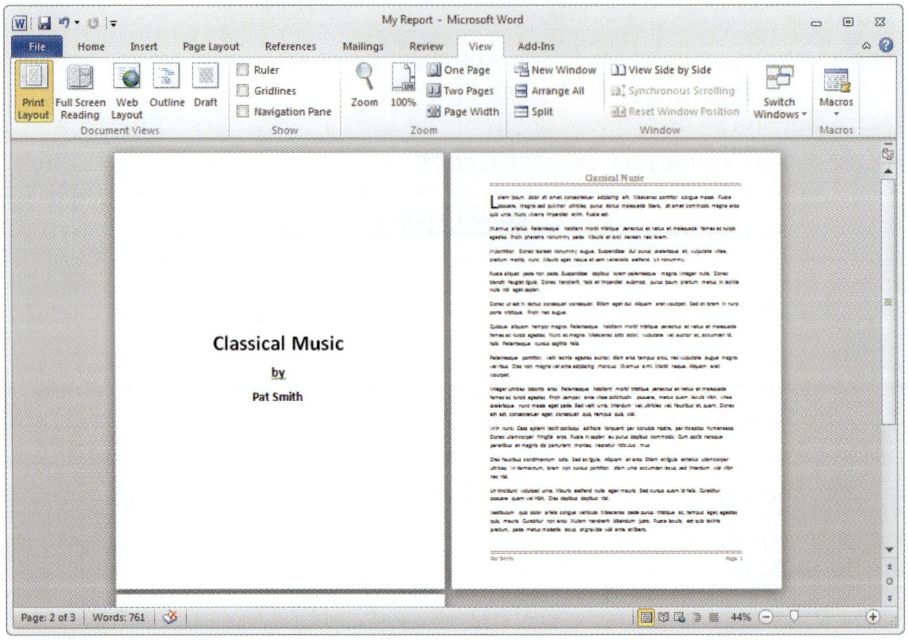

FIGURE 8-14 A report with a title page, a header, a footer, and page numbers.

In this section, you'll learn how to add different types of graphics for fun and creativity.

Clip Art

Clip art is a type of pre-made image. Microsoft makes a large selection of clip art images—drawings, cartoons, and photos—available in Word and on the Office.com website. Many other websites offer free or low-cost clip art as well.

To add clip art to your document, click the Insert tab and then click Clip Art. The Clip Art pane opens on your screen's right side, as shown in FIGURE 8-15. Type a keyword or phrase, such as "flower" or "classical music," and then browse the results. You can choose

WARNING

Be careful if you use photos or clip art from the Internet in your documents. Most are subject to copyright laws. Be sure to obtain the correct permissions before using any items that you don't own, that aren't in the public domain, or that Microsoft doesn't provide through its collections.

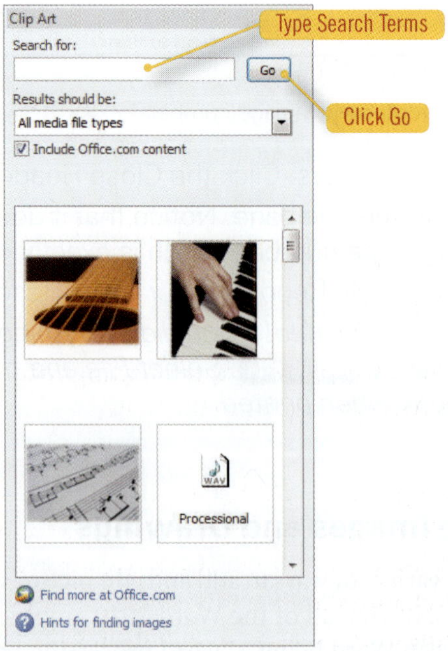

FIGURE 8-15 The Clip Art pane.

which types of images to search for by opening the Results Should Be drop-down list and checking the boxes for individual items. Your choices include illustrations, photographs, and video. You can even search for audio files.

When you find an image you want to use, hover the mouse over the image. A vertical bar with an arrow appears to the right. Click the arrow and then select Insert from the menu that appears. The image shows up in your document. Resize the image by dragging one of the resizing handles on the corners.

TIP

Resize images to a specific size using tools on the Ribbon. Click your picture to select it, and then click the Picture Tools tab. (The Picture Tools tab appears when you select a picture.) Enter the dimensions you want. The image resizes to your specifications.

WordArt

If you want to add excitement to a title or other text in your Word document, use WordArt. **WordArt** applies text effects, such as skewing, shadowing, rotating, and stretching, in a variety of shapes and colors. You can even include three-dimensional (3-D) effects.

To insert WordArt, follow these steps:

1. On the Insert tab, click WordArt in the Text group.
2. Click the style you want. The Edit WordArt Text dialog box appears. Type the text you want to create in WordArt.
3. Click OK.

The WordArt appears in your document. To change the look of the WordArt, double-click it and then select the WordArt Tools Format tab. Open the WordArt Styles gallery as shown in FIGURE 8-16. Hover your mouse pointer over items in the gallery to get a preview. Once you see the effect you like, click to accept.

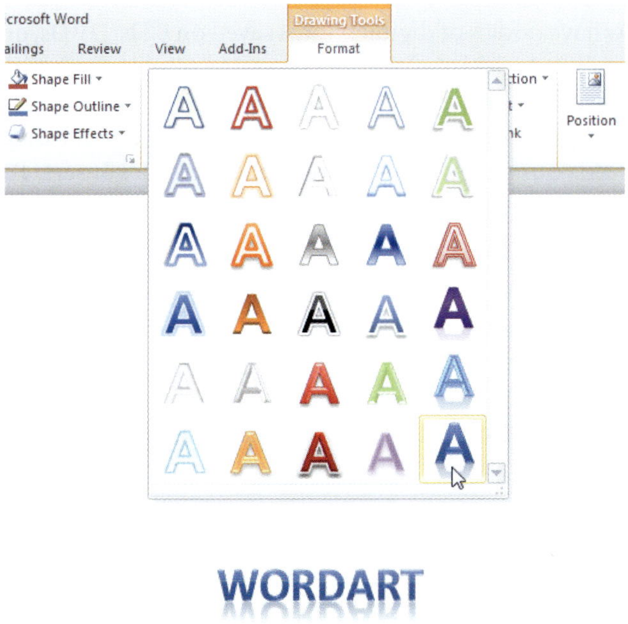

FIGURE 8-16 The WordArt Styles gallery.

Spend some time on your own experimenting with the many choices and options available with WordArt—and have fun doing it!

Shapes

Word contains ready-made shapes that you can add to your documents. To add a shape to a document, click the Insert tab. In the Illustrations group, click the **Shapes** button, as shown in FIGURE 8-17. Then click the shape you want. Click and drag the mouse in the Word document to change the size of the shape.

You can use some of the shapes as callouts in your documents. A **callout** is a visual device for associating annotations with an image. You see them all the time in cartoons. Artists use callouts to imply what their characters are thinking or saying.

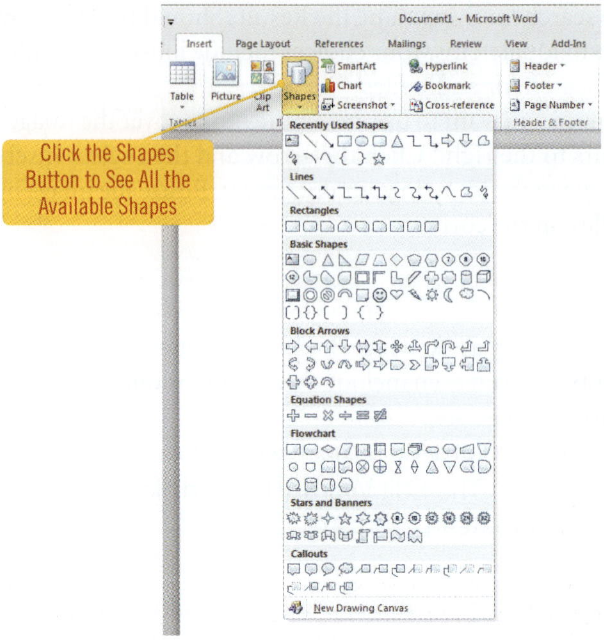

FIGURE 8-17 Available shapes.

Pictures

Many people now have oodles of digital photos saved on CDs/DVDs, on their computer hard disk, and on mobile devices. Word lets you add photos to your document, much like any other type of artwork.

To insert a photo, click the Insert tab and then click Picture. Navigate to the folder that holds the photo you want, select the photo, and then click Insert. The photo appears in your document, and you can resize it as you do other images.

Screen Shots

A screen shot, as you may recall from Chapter 6, is a snapshot of whatever is on the screen. In other words, whatever you see on the screen will become an image you can insert into a document. Word 2010 includes a Screenshot tool that allows you to easily capture any screen on your computer.

> **Note**
>
> You learned about the Windows 7 Snipping Tool in Chapter 6, which also captures screen shots.

With the Screenshot tool, you have two options: You can take a screen shot of an entire screen, or you can take a screen shot of any portion of the screen. The methods are a little different.

To take a screen shot of an entire screen, click the Insert tab and select Screenshot. A gallery appears, as shown in **FIGURE 8-18** with small previews of the screens available to capture. Just click one and the image will be inserted into your document.

Sometimes you want to capture only a selected portion of a screen. You can do that with the Screenshot tool, too. This procedure is a little trickier. If you want to capture a portion of your Word screen, click the Insert tab and click Screenshot. Click Screen Clipping at the bottom of the gallery. The screen will dim and your mouse pointer will change to look like a plus sign (+). Click and drag to select the area of the screen you want to capture.

To capture a portion of a screen outside of Word, click the open window you want to clip from before you click Screen Clipping. Word will then switch to the other window before the screen dims. Just click and drag to select the area of the screen you want to capture.

Inserting and Formatting Text Boxes

You can insert a text box into many different types of documents, especially Office 2010

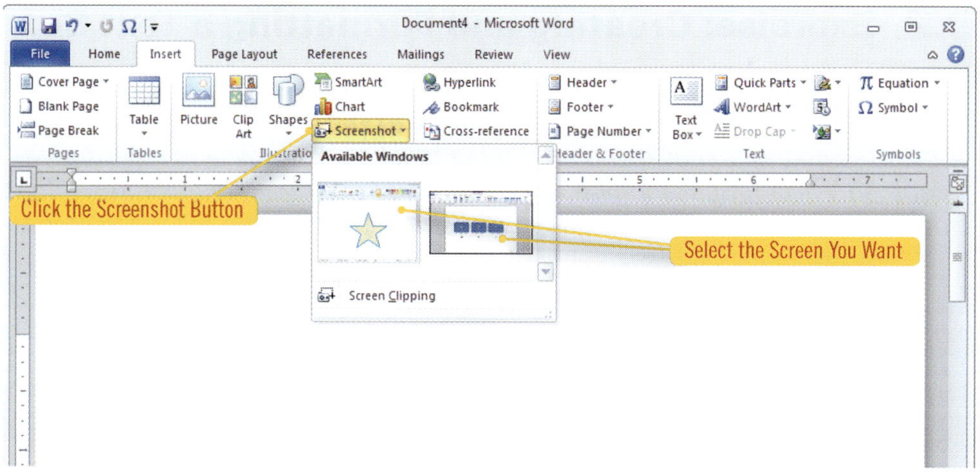

FIGURE 8-18 The Screenshot gallery.

applications. If Word is a word processor and deals with text anyway, why would you want to insert a text box into a Word document? One use is to call attention to text in the box. Newspapers use this technique to quote someone in an article, referred to as a "pull quote." Text boxes also make it easier to manage and control clip art, drawings, pictures, and other objects in a document. Many objects even automatically resize to the size of the text box.

To create a text box, click the Insert tab and then click Text Box. A drop-down menu appears. Select a predesigned text box or click Draw Text Box, as shown in **FIGURE 8-19**. Once you click Draw Text Box, just click and drag on your document to create the text box.

With the text box in your document, you can enter text or paste objects into it. You can also format the text box so that text wraps around the box. If you don't want the box border to appear, or you want to change the way the border looks, click the text box. The Text Box Tools Format tab appears on the Ribbon. Click the tab, and then click the Shape Outline button. Click No Outline to hide the border, or use any of the tools to change the border's color, width, or other attributes.

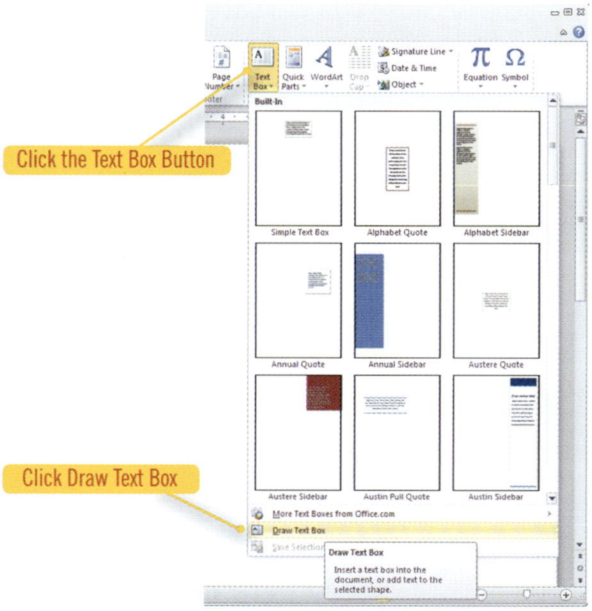

FIGURE 8-19 Text Box drop-down menu.

8.2 Exercise: Creating and Formatting a Text Box

This exercise will teach you how to insert a text box into a document, insert a picture into the text box, and format the text box. You will type a short paragraph on William Shakespeare, and place a text box with his picture within the text. To create a document with a text box, perform the following steps:

1. Type the following paragraph about William Shakespeare. Apply formatting to the text if you wish:

   Shakespeare (1564-1616): Who was he?
   Though William Shakespeare is recognized as one of literature's greatest influences, very little is actually known about him. What we do know about his life comes from registrar records, court records, wills, marriage certificates, and his tombstone. Anecdotes and criticisms by his rivals also speak of the famous playwright and suggest that he was indeed a playwright, poet, and an actor.

2. Click the Insert tab, click Text Box, and then click Draw Text Box at the bottom of the drop-down menu. Click and drag the mouse on top of the text you typed. It doesn't matter where you create the text box, but for now, create it on the upper-right of the text.
3. Paste a picture of William Shakespeare into the box. You can find a picture of him on the Internet by searching for **shakespeare creative commons**. The image on Wikimedia Commons is in the public domain, which means it's not copyrighted. When you locate the picture, right-click it and select Save Picture As or Save Image As, depending on your Web browser. Then paste the picture into the text box.
4. Right-click the outer border of the text box, not the image border. The Drawing Tools Format tab appears. It provides many tools for working with drawings. (Word considers a text box a type of drawing.) Click the Shape Outline box and select No Outline, as shown in FIGURE 8-20. This will make the text box invisible because you will have removed its border.

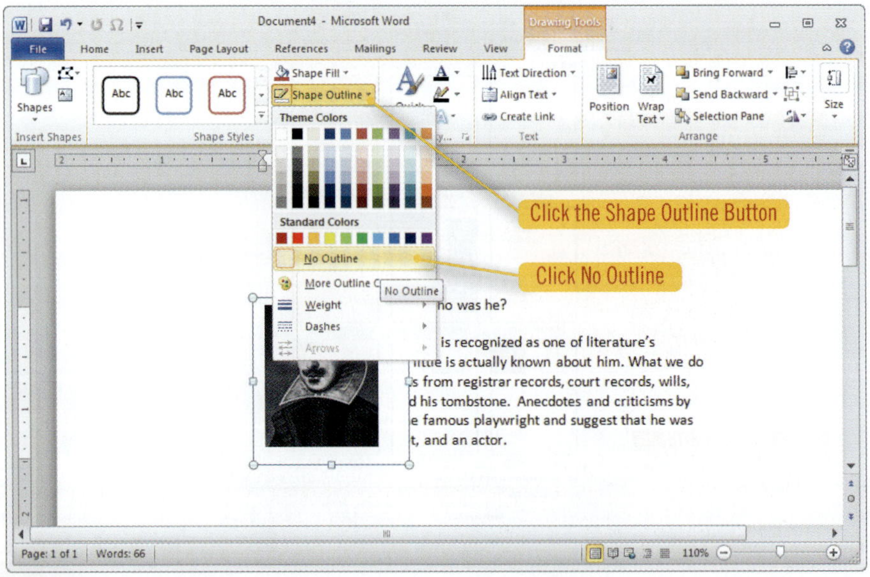

FIGURE 8-20 The No Outline option.

5. Click the Position button and select Position In Top Left With Square Text Wrapping. Then click the Wrap Text button and select Tight, as shown in FIGURE 8-21. This instructs Word to wrap the text tightly around the text box.

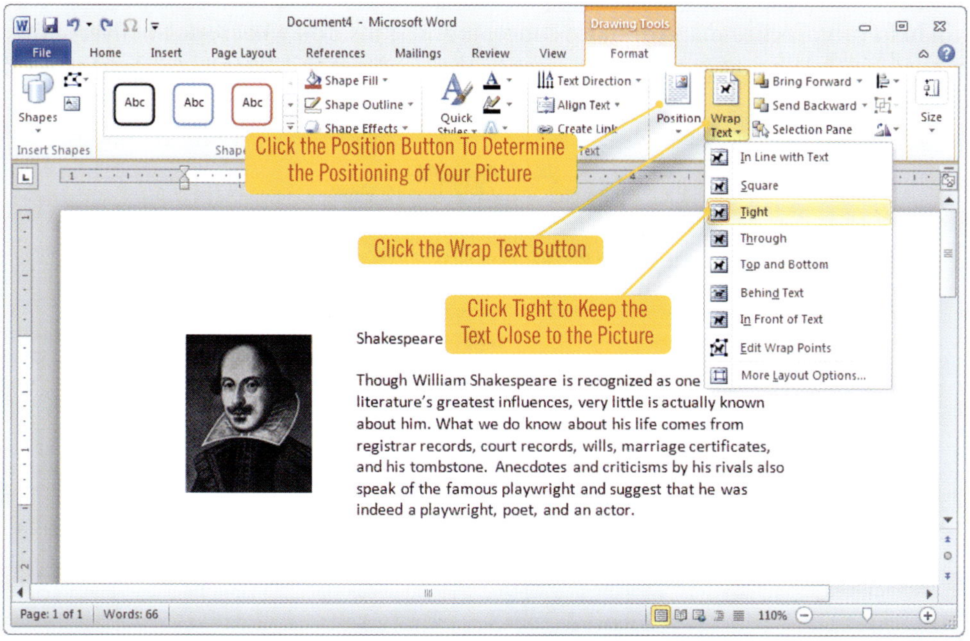

FIGURE 8-21 Positioning the image and specifying a text wrap.

6. Format the text as you like.

If you did everything correctly, your document should look similar to FIGURE 8-22*. Take some time to experiment with moving the text box around and aligning the text box to different areas of the text. Try experimenting with the way the text wraps around the image.*

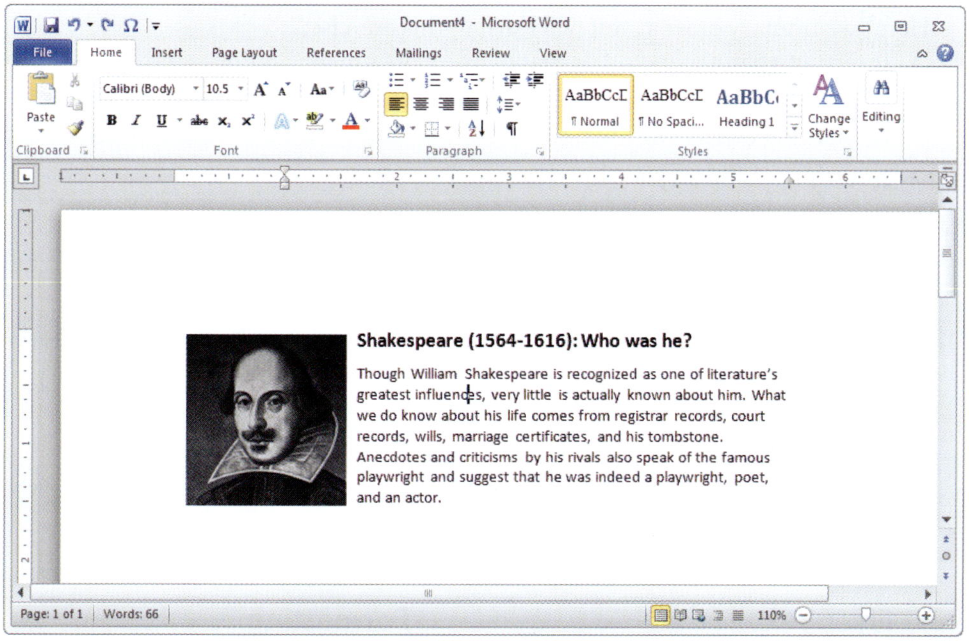

FIGURE 8-22 Completed example document.

8.3 Exercise: Creating a Flyer

You have learned quite a bit in this chapter so far, and it's a lot to remember! This exercise will help you practice many of those concepts and skills. You will create the flyer shown in FIGURE 8-23. Whenever necessary, refer to the image of this flyer as you perform the steps in the exercise.

FIGURE 8-23 Example flyer.

When you create your flyer, it doesn't have to look exactly the same as Figure 8-23. You don't have to spend time trying to find the same pictures or clip art, for example. Just follow the steps in the exercise to practice Word skills and make your flyer look similar to what's shown.

Here's a summary of what you will learn in this exercise:

- Inserting a banner and other shapes into a document, adding text to shapes, and formatting the shapes
- Formatting text as WordArt
- Inserting text boxes and clip art
- Formatting text boxes

To begin creating a flyer in Word 2010, follow these steps:

1. Open a new blank document. Save it as Flyer.docx.
2. To add a banner to your document, click the Insert tab. In the Illustrations group, click the Shapes button to view the shapes. In the Stars and Banners section, click the Up Ribbon shape, which is the first image on the second row. At the top of the flyer page, click and drag the mouse to create a banner that is approximately 6.5 inches wide and 2.5 inches tall.
3. Add text to the banner and format it, as follows:

Flyer Text	Formatting
Bake Sale	Arial Black, 36 pt
Main Building Lobby	Calibri, 24 pt

4. Format the banner by right-clicking any edge of the banner (not inside it). On the menu that appears, select Format Shape. In the Fill section, change the inside banner color to green, as shown in FIGURE 8-24.

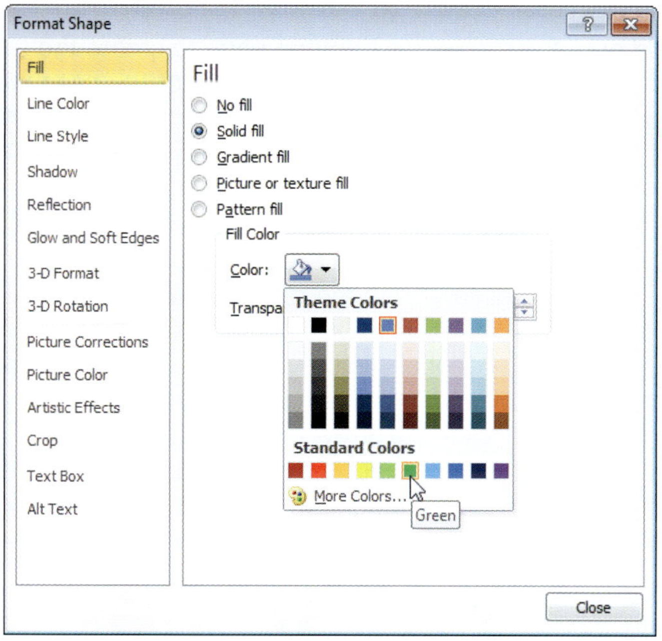

FIGURE 8-24 Formatting the banner.

5. Click Line Color and change the border line of the banner to light green (the color square to the left of green). Click Line Style and click the up arrow next to Width to increase the thickness of the border line of the banner to 4 pt. The finished banner should look like FIGURE 8-25.

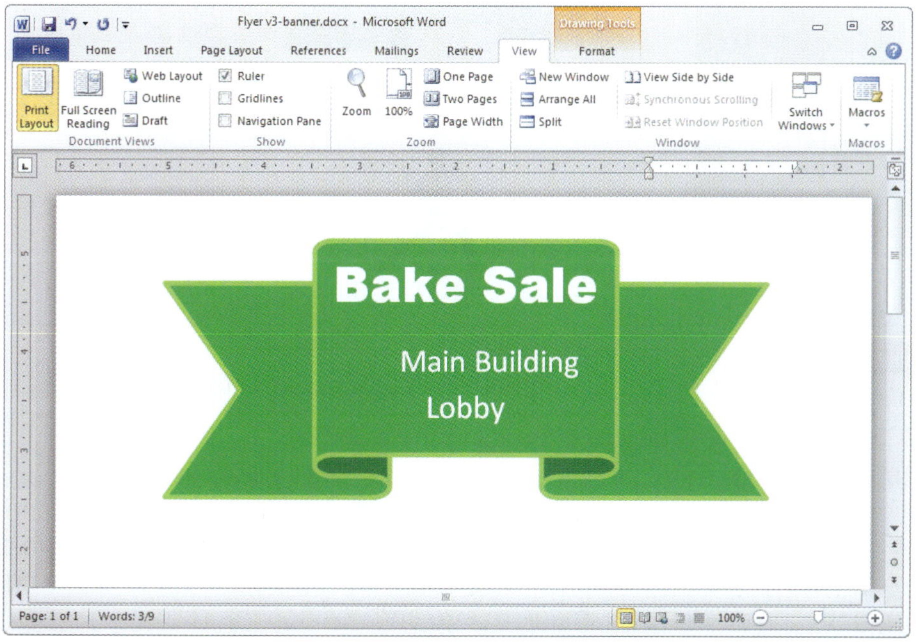

FIGURE 8-25 The finished banner.

An important part of this flyer is that the bake sale is a benefit for a youth sports league. Let's add that image first and then the callout for the image.

TIP

You can add text to a shape immediately after creating it—just start typing. To add text to a shape later, click the shape and start typing.

You will add this and other images into text boxes so you can easily resize and rearrange them as needed. Follow these steps:

6. To insert a text box for your first image, click the Insert tab, click Text Box, and then click Draw Text Box from the drop-down menu.
7. Click and drag the mouse on the flyer page to create the text box. The size of the text box should be about the size of the baseball player image shown in Figure 8-23. You can resize the text box at any time by clicking its border and dragging one of the handles, which are the small circles on the border.
8. Insert your own image of a baseball player into the text box, or use the Clip Art gallery to locate an image related to youth sports for your flyer. To use the Clip Art gallery, with the text box still selected, click the Insert tab and then click Clip Art. The Clip Art pane appears on the right side of your screen. Enter "baseball" in the search box at the top of the pane and press Enter. Hover your mouse pointer over the image you want to include in your flyer, click the arrow on the right, and select Insert. The image is inserted into your text box, as shown in FIGURE 8-26. Don't worry about the thin black border around the image—you will remove it later in the exercise.

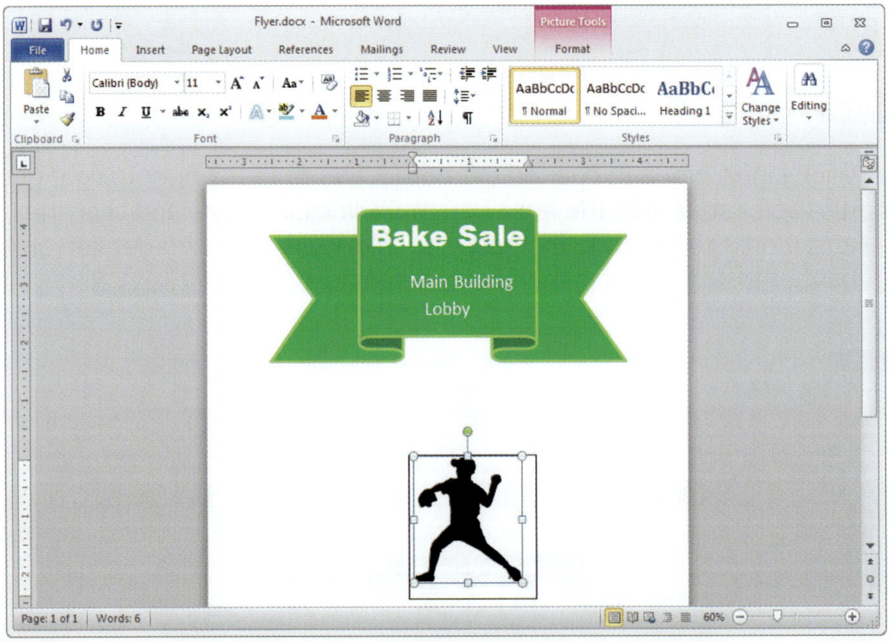

FIGURE 8-26 Inserting an image into a text box.

9. Save your work before continuing the exercise.
10. Insert a star callout to accompany the baseball player image. In your flyer, click the Insert tab and then click Shapes. In the Stars and Banners section, click the 12-point Star callout, which shows a number 12 in the middle of the star. Click and drag the mouse just above and to the right of the baseball player image to size and position the callout.
11. To format the border of the callout, click the callout to select it. On the Drawing Tools Format tab, click Shape Outline. Select the Orange color square in the Standard Colors section. Click Shape Outline again, click Weight, and then select 4½ pt. This creates a thick, orange border.
12. To add text to the callout, click inside the callout and type **Benefits**

TIP

If an image you insert into a text box in your flyer has a background you don't want, click the picture to select it. On the Picture Tools Format tab, in the Adjust group, click Remove Background. On the Background Removal tab that appears, click Mark Areas to Keep, click anywhere on the image background, and then click Keep Changes. The background should disappear, leaving only the foreground image.

Youth Sports. Highlight the text and format it as 24 pt bold centered. To apply WordArt effects, with the text still highlighted, click the Drawing Tools Format tab. Open the Quick Styles gallery, and select Fill – Red, Accent 2, Warm Matte Bevel, as shown in FIGURE 8-27.

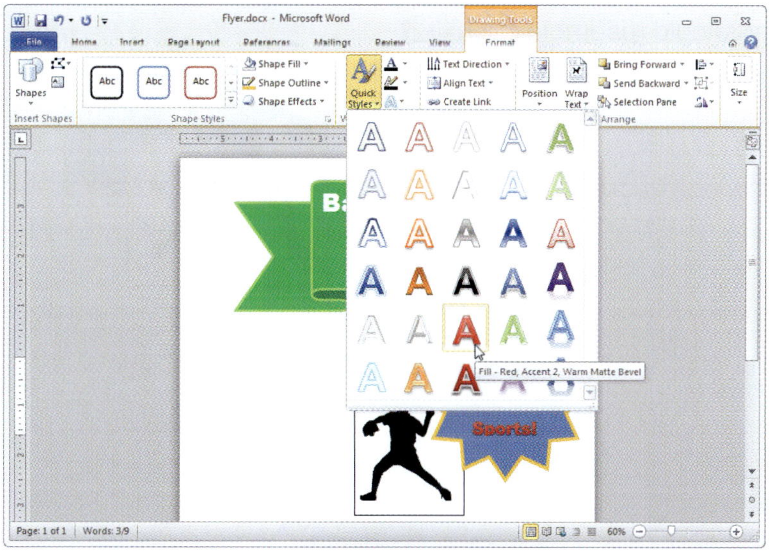

FIGURE 8-27 Formatting callout text as WordArt.

13. Again, with the text still highlighted, select Text Effects, select Transform, and then select Inflate, as shown in FIGURE 8-28.

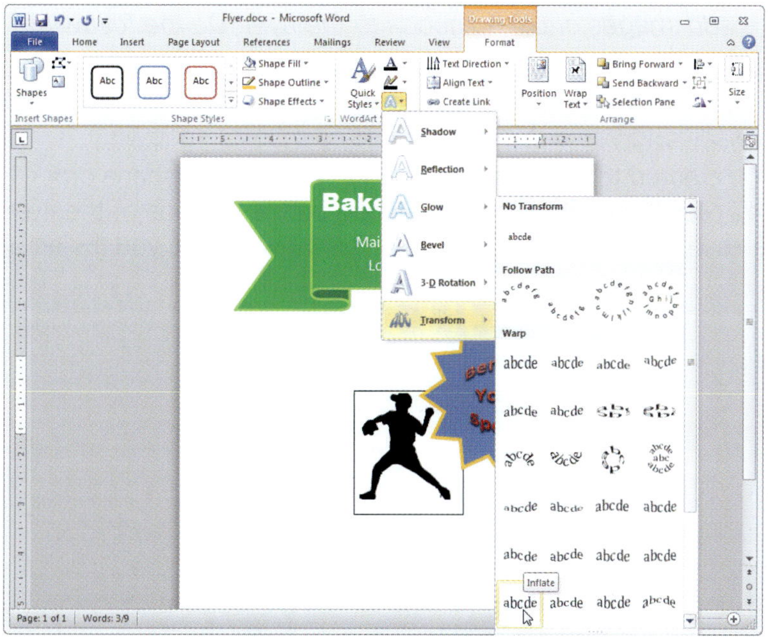

FIGURE 8-28 Adding additional WordArt effects has a more dramatic effect.

14. Save your work before continuing the exercise.

You're about halfway through the flyer! Now let's add another callout—this time the star callout in the lower-left corner that displays the date and time of the bake sale. Follow these steps:

15. To insert a star shape, click the Insert tab, click Shapes, and then click the 32-point Star in the Stars and Banners section. Click and drag to create the star in the lower-left corner of the flyer. Add two lines of text: **Friday, April 7** and **Noon to 3**.
16. Format the text as Calibri 32 pt bold centered. The lower portion of the flyer should resemble **FIGURE 8-29**.

FIGURE 8-29 Adding a different star callout.

Now let's add images of baked goods to the flyer. Do the following:

17. Repeat Steps 6 through 8, adding images of your choice. Use the completed flyer in Figure 8-23 as your guide. Your text boxes don't have to be exact, and you don't have to add as many as shown.
18. If you created text boxes that overlap, you can set shape order. In fact, if you click the white space anywhere on the left side of the flyer, you'll see an image similar to **FIGURE 8-30**. This view shows you the actual sizes

FIGURE 8-30 Viewing actual sizes of text boxes and shapes.

of the text boxes and shapes. Notice how some of the elements overlap. To ensure that an image is "on top" of any others that overlap it, use the Bring to Front command. For example, let's say you want the star callout in the lower-left corner to show fully, even if another image overlaps it. Right-click the star callout and select Bring to Front > Bring to Front.

19. Finally, remove the black borders from the text boxes. Just right-click a text box, click the Drawing Tools Format tab, select Shape Outline, and then click No Outline. Repeat for every image that has a black border.
20. Save your work.

Congratulations—you have created a flyer! Refer to the original image to see how your flyer matches up. Practice with different kinds of graphics, text, and a variety of effects to learn more about what each tool can do.

TIP

You can move an image forward or backward. Think of it as rearranging a deck of cards: You can move an image to the front one step at a time, or you can bring it all the way to the front. The same is true for moving an image backward. You can also choose to put an image on top of text, or vice versa.

Creating Tables

A **table** is a grid that usually consists of **columns** and **rows**. In Word, you access the tools to create tables on the Insert tab. Once you create a table, you can format it many different ways: Make a header or title row, apply Table Styles to add pizzazz to the table, and more.

An especially easy method to create a table is to select the Insert tab and click Table. A menu appears that allows you to click and drag the mouse to create the table, as shown in FIGURE 8-31.

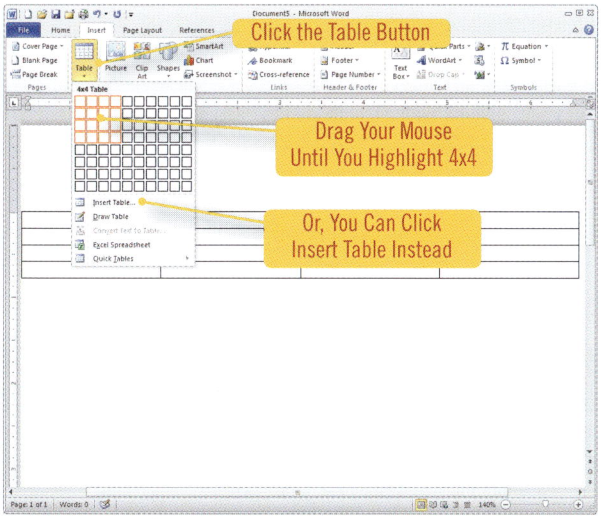

FIGURE 8-31 Using the click-and-drag method to create a table.

Another method of creating a table is to click Table, and then click Insert Table. The Insert Table dialog box appears, as shown in FIGURE 8-32. Enter the number of columns and rows you want in your table, and click OK.

Use whichever method works for you; they both do the same thing. The next exercise walks you through table creation, adding text, and formatting.

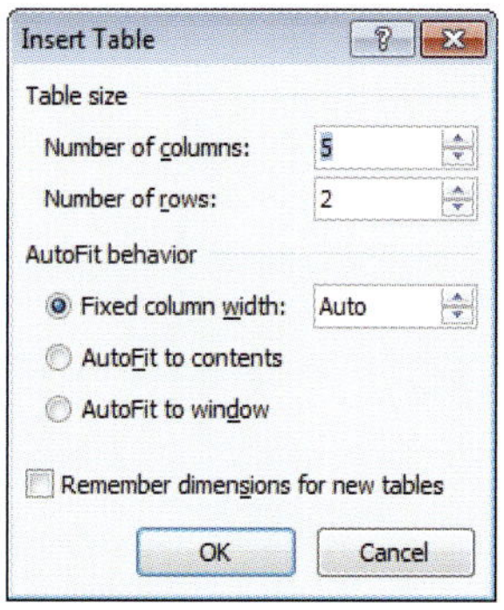

FIGURE 8-32 Using the Insert Table dialog box to create a table.

8.4 Exercise: Creating a Table

In this exercise, you will create a simple table, add text to it, and format it. As you already know, a table consists of columns and rows. The intersection of columns and rows creates a grid of individual parts called cells. You move from cell to cell by clicking each one with your mouse, or by pressing the tab key on the keyboard. In this exercise you will:

- Create a 4 by 4 table (4 columns and 4 rows).
- Bold and center the top row (title or header row).
- Type text into the table.
- Select a table style to format the table.

To create a practice table of your own, perform the following steps:

1. Create a 4 by 4 table. On the Insert tab, click Table, highlight a 4 by 4 grid, and then click. This will create a table with 4 columns and 4 rows. The image in FIGURE 8-33 depicts a 4 by 4 table.

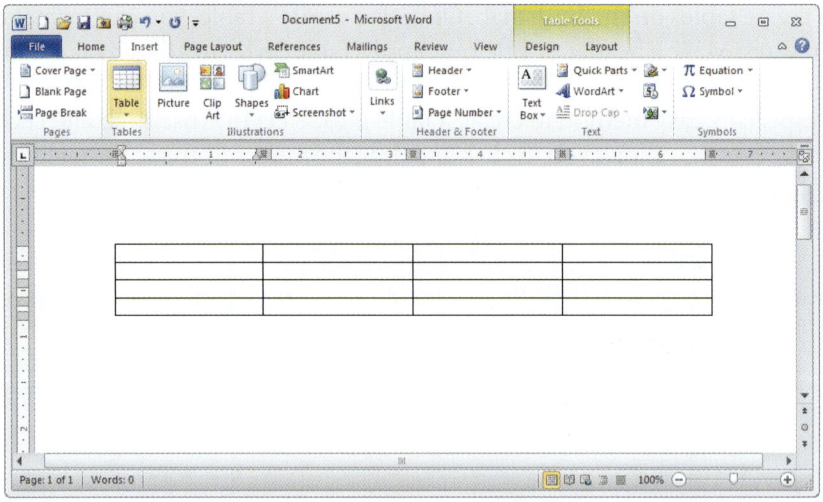

FIGURE 8-33 A 4 by 4 table.

2. Type text into your table as shown in FIGURE 8-34. Then highlight the first row of your table and apply bold and centering. This is the header row.

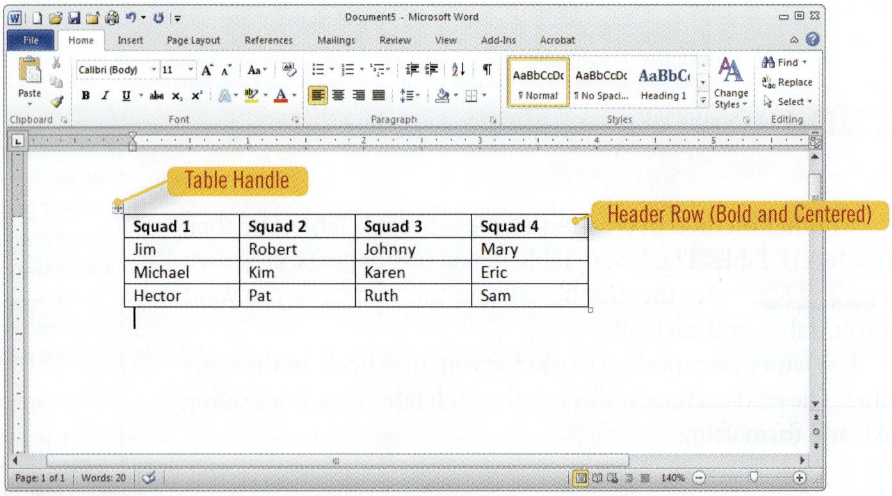

FIGURE 8-34 A table with a bold, centered header row.

3. To apply additional formatting, hover the mouse pointer near the table's upper-left corner. You will see a small table handle that allows you to select the entire table. Click the handle. The Table Tools tab appears at the top of your screen near the document title. Click Table Tools. On the Design tab is a Table Styles live gallery that lets you preview your table, as you've been able to do with the other live galleries in this book. Hover your mouse over gallery elements and watch your table change accordingly. Click the style you like to set those options for your table.

If you did everything correctly, your table should look something like the one in **FIGURE 8-35***. It will not look exactly the same because you may have chosen a different table style, font, and other attributes.*

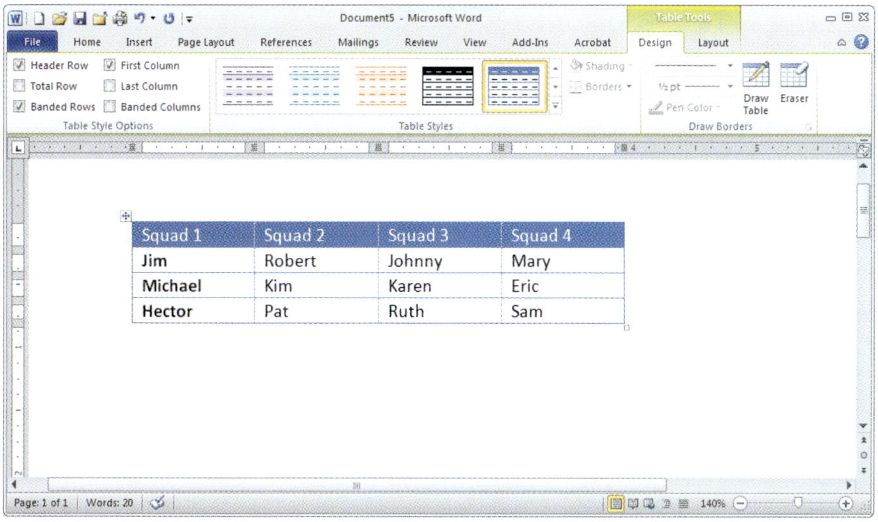

FIGURE 8-35 A formatted table.

Adding Columns

Columns are a long-standing feature of Word. The Columns feature lets you format text into columns, the way newspapers, magazines, and many newsletters lay out their copy. To create columns, click the Page Layout tab and then click Columns, as shown in **FIGURE 8-36**.

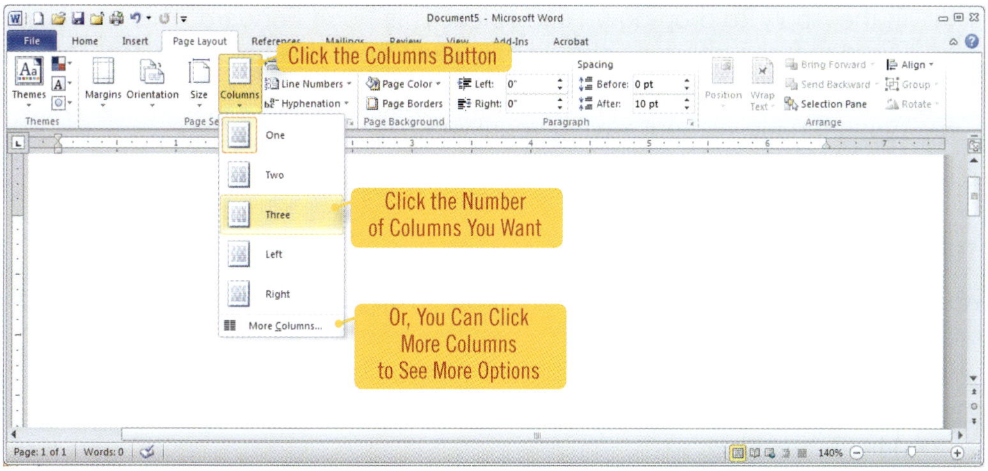

FIGURE 8-36 Column options.

Select one, two, or three columns. To fine-tune column settings, click the More Columns command at the bottom of the drop-down list. The Columns dialog box appears. Notice the Apply To drop-down box. This option allows you to select Whole Document or This Point Forward, which determines how much of your text is formatted into columns. If you highlighted text in your document before selecting More Columns, your two choices are Whole Document and Selected Text. Choosing Selected Text will apply column formatting only to specific text.

At times you may want to begin typing in the next column before you finish the first column. To do this, insert a column break. On the Page Layout tab, click Breaks and then Column. Your insertion point moves to the top of the next column.

Breaks

In this chapter, you've learned about two types of breaks: section breaks and column breaks. A section break allows you to format portions of your document independently of other sections. For example, you could use a section break to make one chapter in a book look different by changing the margins, or even changing the page orientation. You use column breaks to enter information into multiple columns.

Another more common type of break is the page break. Word automatically adds a new page when it runs out of room. But what if you don't like the balance of the text? You can use a page break to control where the text ends on each page. You have two ways to insert a page break:

- On the Insert tab, click Page Break.
- Press Ctrl+Enter on your keyboard.

8.5 Exercise: Using Columns

Perform the following steps to learn how to create columns in a document:

1. Open the report document, named My Report, that you created in Exercise 8.1.
2. Place the insertion point at the beginning of the second page, to the left of the drop cap.
3. On the Page Layout tab, click Columns and then select More Columns.
4. In the Columns dialog box, click Two to create two columns.
5. In the Apply To drop-down list, select This Point Forward. This instructs Word that the columns should only exist from this point onward—not the whole document.
6. Close the file without saving your work.

Inserting Symbols

Word lets you insert many **symbols** not available on the keyboard. For example, you may want to insert one of these symbols:

- Copyright, ©
- Em dash, —
- Plus or minus, ±
- The Spanish n, ñ

To insert symbols, click the Insert tab and then click the arrow at the bottom of the Symbol button. Select the More Symbols command. The Symbol dialog box appears, as shown in FIGURE 8-37. Just scroll through the list of available symbols and click the one you want.

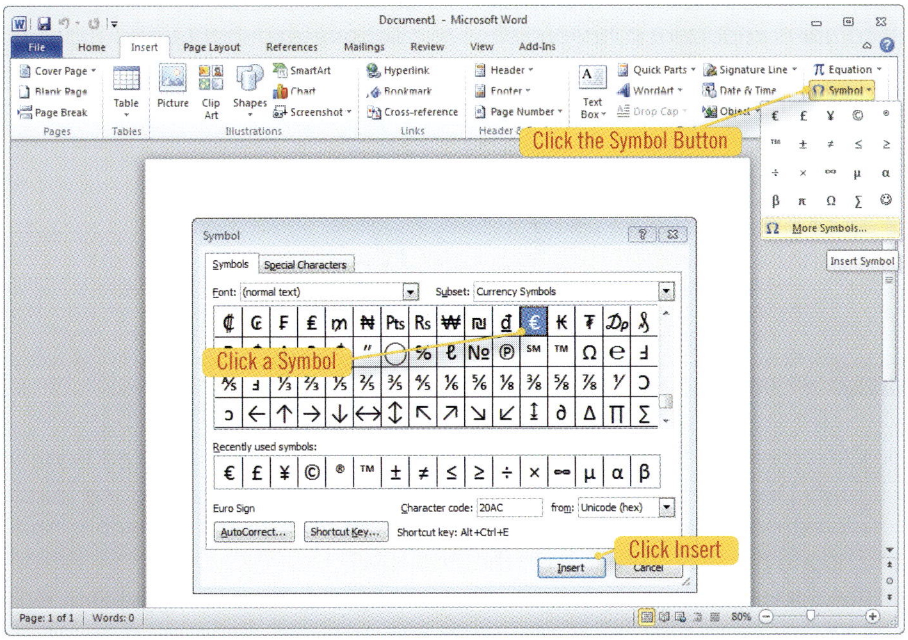

FIGURE 8-37 Symbols dialog box.

You can also assign a shortcut key to your favorite, most often-used symbols. Here's how it's done:

1. In the Symbols dialog box, select the symbol you want to assign a shortcut key to, and then click Shortcut Key.
2. The Customize Keyboard dialog box appears; it allows you to enter the shortcut key combination. Hold down the Alt key and press the letter you wish to assign.
3. Click Assign, and then click Close.

Creating Equations with Microsoft Equation

Microsoft Office Word 2010 includes built-in support for writing and changing equations. When you wish to include equations in a document, **Microsoft Equation** can be very useful. It does take a little time and practice to learn, so be patient. One thing to note—if you wrote an equation in a previous version of Word, you need to use Equation 3.0 to change that equation.

To insert an equation, click Equation on the Insert tab. You will see an equation box for typing the equation. Just as important, when you click the Equation Tools Design tab, the Ribbon will change to display the important tools and icons you will need to type fancy equations, as shown in FIGURE 8-38.

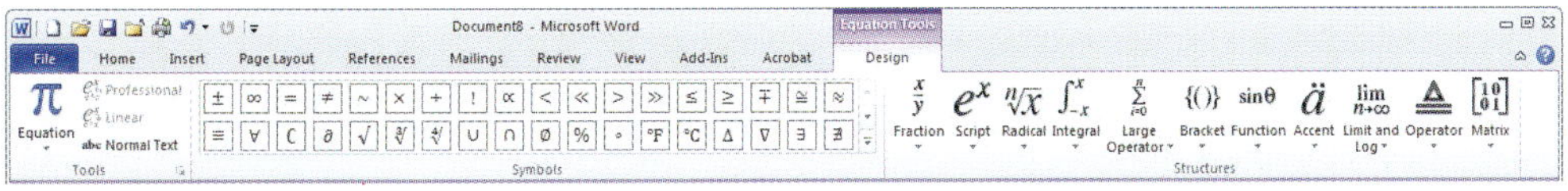

FIGURE 8-38 Equation tools.

8.6 Exercise: Using Microsoft Equation

Follow the steps below to create an equation—the one shown in FIGURE 8-39—that contains important concepts, such as fractions, exponents, and subscripts:

$$P_T = \frac{V_T^2}{R_T}$$

FIGURE 8-39 An equation.

1. Click the Insert tab, and then click Equation. A new tab called Equation Tools Design appears. Its ribbon displays many tools and icons for creating equations. Click the Script button, and then select Subscript (the second box from the left on the first row).
2. Type **P** and then **T** into the two squares in the equation box. Use the right arrow key on the keyboard to move the cursor away from the subscript. Type an equal sign. You should see the cursor blinking to the right of the equal sign.
3. Click the Fraction button and select Stacked Fraction (the first box on the top row). Then type the numerator and the denominator of the fraction into the equation.
4. Use the arrow keys on the keyboard to place the insertion point on the numerator. Click the Scripts button, and select Subscript-Superscript (third box from the left on the top row).
5. Using the arrow keys to navigate to the numerator, type the letter **V**. Use the right arrow on the keyboard to place the insertion point on the superscript. Type the number **2**. Use the down arrow to place the insertion point on the subscript. Type the letter **T**.
6. Use the down arrow key to place the insertion point on the denominator. Click the Scripts button and then select Subscript, as shown in FIGURE 8-40.

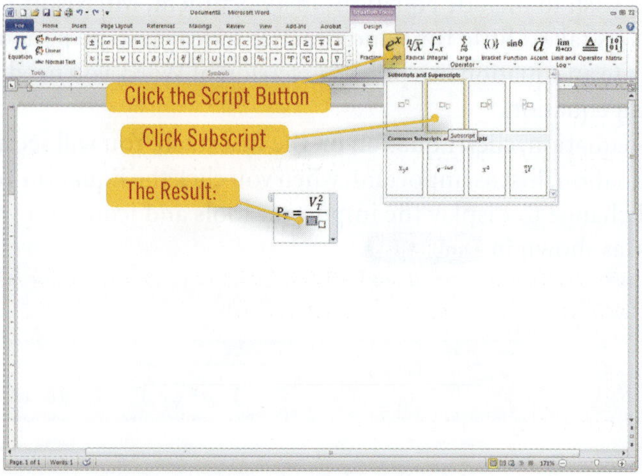

FIGURE 8-40 The insertion point on the denominator.

7. Use the arrow keys on the keyboard to place the insertion point in the desired area of the denominator, type the letter **R**, and the letter **T**. When you finish, click outside the equation box to see the final result, as shown in **FIGURE 8-41**.

$$P_T = \frac{V_T^2}{R_T}$$

FIGURE 8-41 Final equation.

By practicing, you will become more familiar with the equation tools as well as how to navigate the actual equation using the arrow keys on the keyboard.

Test Yourself

The questions in this section are meant to test your knowledge of what you read. Make sure you answer them. The page number where the answer can be found appears after each question.

1. What does it mean to "split" a document in Word? (176)
2. At least how many documents must be opened to view them side by side? (176)
   A. One
   B. Two
   C. Three
   D. None
3. What is meant by "synchronous" when comparing documents in Word 2010? (176)
   A. The two parts of the document no longer scroll.
   B. Two documents scroll together.
   C. Two documents that do not scroll together
   D. The two parts of the document scroll together.
4. On which tab do you find the options to create headers and footers? (178, 179)
   A. The Insert tab
   B. The Page Layout tab
   C. The Review tab
   D. The File tab
5. Once you create page numbers, you cannot change them. (182)
   A. True
   B. False
6. When you want to insert an image into a document, it's acceptable to use graphics wherever you find them on the Internet. (184)
   A. True
   B. False
7. What is a screen shot? (186)
   A. A picture of a camera
   B. A collection of free clip art

C. An image of a television
D. A snapshot of whatever is on your screen

8. What is WordArt? (185)
   A. A collection of free images
   B. Special effects you can apply to text
   C. A second set of fonts
   D. A list of words in a fancy font
9. In which tab do you find Shapes? (185)
   A. The File tab
   B. The Page Layout tab
   C. The Review tab
   D. The Insert tab
10. What kinds of graphics can you insert into a Word document? (184–188)
11. Why would you need to insert a symbol into a document? (198)
12. Why would you want to insert a text box into a document? (187)
    A. To have the freedom to move a portion of text anywhere in the document
    B. To give the page a highlighted look
    C. To easily search for text in a document
    D. To keep from using spell check
13. You can enter text into a text box, but you cannot paste objects into it. (187)
    A. True
    B. False
14. What is a callout? (185)
15. Which of the following can you apply to tables? (196–197)
    A. Table style
    B. Bold
    C. Border color
    D. All the above
16. What is a header row on a table? (196)
    A. The text at the very top of the page
    B. The text at the very bottom of the page
    C. The text in the first row of a table
    D. The text in the last row of a table
17. You can only create columns that span your entire document. (198)
    A. True
    B. False
18. What is a drop cap? (181)
    A. When you forget to capitalize a letter
    B. When one word runs over to the next page
    C. The same as subscript
    D. A large capital letter that drops two or more lines below the first line of a paragraph
19. What does Microsoft Equation let you do? (199)
    A. Create spreadsheets.
    B. Type equations in the proper format.
    C. Make complex calculations.
    D. Keep your household budget.

20. When you have an equation that contains fractions, subscripts, and superscripts, how do you move the insertion point to the different areas of the equation? (200)

A. By right-clicking your mouse
B. By pressing the arrow keys on your keyboard
C. By double-clicking your mouse
D. By pressing the A, S, D, and F keys on your keyboard

End-of-Chapter Project

Add additional formatting to the research document you've been working on in the projects in this book by following these steps:

1. Open the PC Basics Research.docx you created in the Chapter 7 project.
2. Add a title page.
3. Add a header, but not to the title page.
4. Add a footer, but not to the title page.
5. Add page numbers, but not to the title page.
6. Save your work, and close Word.

PART

V

Essentials of Spreadsheets

CHAPTER

9

Excel 2010 Basics

- Microsoft Excel is a spreadsheet program, designed to work mainly with numbers and calculations. In business, a spreadsheet is an invaluable tool. However, Excel is so popular and easy to use that it has become important at home for personal use. Using a spreadsheet, you can organize numbers and enter formulas. You can create charts and graphs, such as pie charts and bar graphs. You can sort data, select which data to view, and search for data.
- A typical worksheet (Excel's name for a spreadsheet) has values and formulas that calculate results based on those values. If the values change, the formulas reflect the changed results automatically. This lets you perform what-if analyses on the data and try different scenarios for which you may have to make different choices. For example, what would happen to your mortgage payment if your interest rate changed? How much product would your company need to sell per month to make $1,000 in profit by a certain date? Excel can tell you.
- This book covers Excel in two chapters. In this chapter, you will learn how to enter data into an Excel worksheet and how to arrange and format it. Chapter 10 will focus on creating formulas, functions, and charts.

CHAPTER TOPICS

This chapter covers the following topics and concepts:

- How to get started with Excel
- How to move around an Excel worksheet
- How to enter and edit data
- How to save and open Excel files
- How to select cell ranges
- How to insert and delete rows, columns, or cells
- How to change column width and row height
- How to move cells
- How to copy and fill cells
- How to format cells
- How to sort data in a worksheet
- How to print a worksheet

KEY WORDS

Active cell	Clear	Formulas	Range
Ascending	Column header	Functions	Row header
AutoFit Selection	Contextual tab	Labels	Sorting
Cell address	Descending	Name box	Values
Cell cursor	Fill handle	Number format	Workbook
Cells	Filling	Points	Worksheet

Getting Started with Excel

Because Excel is part of the Microsoft Office suite of applications, it shares certain features with the other programs. The main user interface consists of a tabbed Ribbon. Each tab displays a set of icons, arranged in groups. Each group's name appears at the bottom of its section. Some groups also have a dialog box launcher. This is a little square in the lower-right corner of the group; clicking it opens a dialog box. Certain tabs appear only when you are performing certain actions; these are called **contextual tabs.** FIGURE 9-1 shows the Ribbon with the primary parts labeled. Notice the Home tab, which is new to Excel 2010 and has some commands in common with the Home tab you worked with in Microsoft Word 2010.

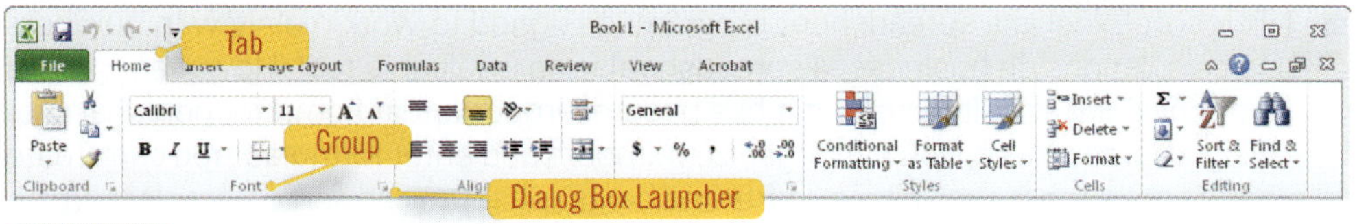

FIGURE 9-1 Parts of the Ribbon.

The Ribbon changes depending on the size of the Excel window. Remember that, as you read in Chapter 4, you can resize windows. When you change the size of any Office 2010 window, the Ribbon collapses or expands. Some groups and options become compressed when you make the Excel window smaller. You might notice those changes in some of the figures in this chapter.

9.1 Exercise: Comparing the Word and Excel Ribbons

In this exercise, you will become familiar with the Excel Ribbon. Because it's similar to the Word 2010 Ribbon, you will compare the two ribbons by exploring some of the tabs and buttons. Follow these steps:

1. Open Word and Excel:
   - **Word:** Click the Start button, and then select All Programs > Microsoft Office > Microsoft Word 2010.
   - **Excel:** Click the Start button, and then select All Programs > Microsoft Office > Microsoft Excel 2010.
2. Arrange their windows so that both Ribbons are visible.
3. Compare the buttons on the Home tab. Which buttons are the same? Make a list.

4. For the buttons that are unique to Excel, hover the mouse over each one to determine what it is.
5. In both programs, click the Insert tab. Compare the buttons on those tabs. Which buttons are the same? Which are different? For the different buttons, hover the mouse over each one to find out what it is.
6. Repeat this process for the Page Layout, Review, and View tabs. Then close Word.
7. Examine the remaining tabs in Excel (Formulas and Data). Hover the mouse over each button to find out what it is.

TIP

Wherever this chapter refers to the "mouse," the information applies to a laptop touchpad as well.

In Excel, a data file is called a **workbook**. Each workbook can have one or more tabbed sheets called **worksheets**. The tabs appear at the bottom; you can switch between worksheets by clicking a tab.

Each worksheet consists of a grid of rows and columns. At the intersection of each row and column is a box into which you can type; each of those is a **cell**. Each row is uniquely numbered, with its number appearing in the **row header** at the far left, and each column is uniquely lettered, with its letter appearing in the **column header** at the top. Each **cell address**, or name, comes from a combination of the column letter and the row number, like this: A1.

Only one cell is active at a time; whatever you type appears in the **active cell**. The active cell has a thick black border around it called the **cell cursor**. You can move the cell cursor with the arrow keys or by clicking the cell you want. The active cell's address appears in the **Name box**. FIGURE 9-2 shows the parts of the Excel screen.

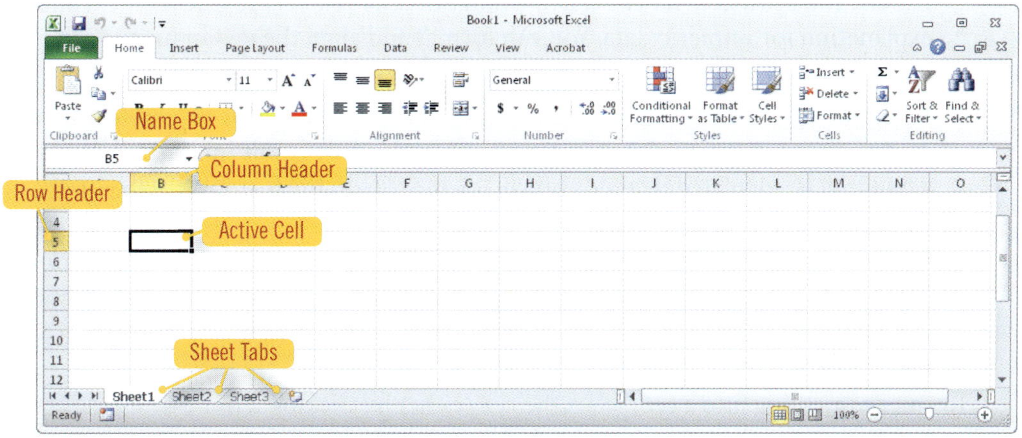

FIGURE 9-2 Parts of the Excel screen.

Note

You are not likely to run out of cells on a sheet because each worksheet has 1,048,576 rows and 16,384 columns. That's approximately 17 billion cells on each worksheet! Because there are only 26 characters in the alphabet, the letters start doubling up after the 26th column: AA, AB, AC, and so on.

Getting Help

The Help system in Excel works very much like the equivalent systems in Word and in Windows. To open the Help system, press F1 or click the Help icon in the upper-right corner of the Excel window. (It's the question mark with the blue circle background.)

Once in the Help system, you can browse or search for the topic you are interested in learning about. Chapters 4 and 7 covered the Help system in Windows and Word 2010, respectively. Refer to those chapters if you need more guidance.

Moving Around a Worksheet

You can move around in a worksheet in two different ways: You can move the cell cursor, or you can scroll the display. It's important to understand the difference because scrolling the display does not move the cell cursor automatically. When you move the cell cursor, the display scrolls to show the active cell, but the reverse is not true; you can view a part of the worksheet that is nowhere near the active cell.

To move the cell cursor:

- **With the mouse:** You can click on any cell using the mouse to place the cell cursor there. Whichever cell you click will become the active cell.
- **With the Name box:** Type the desired cell address in the Name box and press Enter. The cell cursor jumps to that cell.
- **With the keyboard:** You can use the keyboard arrow keys to move the cell cursor up, down, left, or right on a worksheet. There are also keyboard shortcuts that quickly move the cell cursor. For example, Ctrl+Home moves back to cell A1 from any other location, and Home moves to the cell in column A in the current row.

> **TIP**
>
> A full list of the keyboard shortcuts is available in the Help system. Press F1 and then type **keyboard shortcuts** and press Enter.

To scroll the display without moving the cell cursor:

- **With the mouse:** Turn the wheel on your mouse (if your mouse has one) to scroll up or down, or use the scroll bars.
- **With the keyboard:** Use the Page Up and/or Page Down keys to scroll up or down. Alt+Page Up scrolls to the left one screen, and Alt+Page Down scrolls to the right.

Entering and Editing Data

There are four types of data you can enter in an Excel worksheet. They are:

- **Labels:** You use text to **label** a cell or a range of cells. A label provides context and explanation for numeric data. You can format and align the text in many ways.
- **Values:** A **value** is a number you enter, and it changes only if you modify it.
- **Formulas:** A **formula** makes Excel a powerful tool. When you enter a formula into a cell, it automatically calculates and displays the result in that cell. What actually gets calculated depends on what you write in the formula itself. For example, =A1+B1 is a formula.
- **Functions:** A **function** is a pre-designed formula that performs specific combinations of math operations more easily than using a plain math formula. For example, =AVERAGE(A1:E1) is easier to write than =(A1+B1+C1+D1+E1)/5. Excel provides more than 200 different functions.

To enter something into a cell, select the cell (either by clicking it or by using the arrow keys to move the cell cursor to it) and then just start typing. A formula or a function always begins with an equal sign (=). When you are finished entering data into the cell, press Enter or press one of the arrow keys to move to a different cell. If you decide not to enter data into the cell after all, press Esc to cancel the entry.

When you place a formula or function in a cell, the cell itself displays the result of that calculation. When the cell is selected, the original formula or function you entered appears in the formula bar above the worksheet grid, as shown in FIGURE 9-3.

Editing Data

When you type anything in a cell, you might make a mistake. If you catch the mistake before you press the Enter key, you can make the correction right away. If you catch the mistake later, you have two choices:

- You can delete the contents and re-type the information. This is best if you're dealing with a small amount of information. To delete the contents, select the cell and press Delete, or select the cell and type a new entry; the new entry replaces the old one.

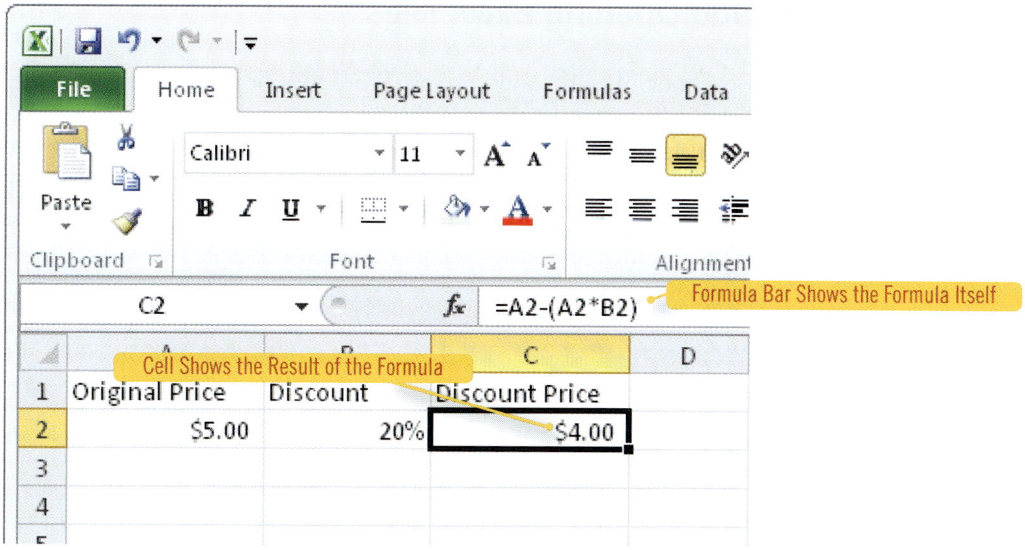

FIGURE 9-3 A formula or function shows its result in the cell.

- When there's a lot of information, such as a long formula or a long line of text, you can highlight the cell that contains the information, click in the formula bar, and correct the individual mistake without re-typing the entire cell contents.

Clearing Cell Contents

To **clear** a cell, select the cell and press Delete. (You are not really deleting the cell; you are just clearing its contents. You don't have a Clear key on your keyboard, though, so the Delete key has to suffice in this case.) Pressing the Delete key clears a cell's contents, but not any formatting that has been applied to the cell.

If you want to clear everything from the cell, including the formatting, click the Home tab and then click the Clear button in the Editing group. On the menu that appears, select Clear All, as shown in **FIGURE 9-4**. Notice in Figure 9-4 that you can also use this menu to clear only the formatting, leaving the contents.

> **Note**
>
> Some people select a cell and press the spacebar to replace the current contents with a blank space, but this is not quite the same thing. The cell is not really empty; it contains an invisible character (a space). It's better to press Delete to clear a cell.

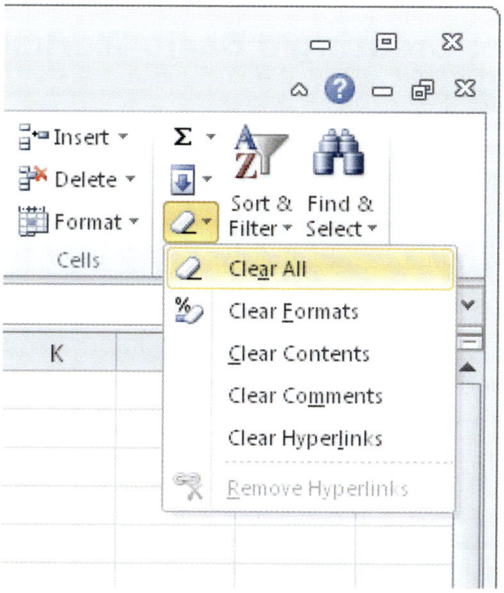

FIGURE 9-4 Use the Clear button's menu to clear everything from a cell, including its contents and its formatting.

Saving and Opening Excel Files

You save a workbook the same way you save Word files, or most other Office files. Select File > Save or click the Save icon on the Quick Access toolbar. If this is the first time you are saving this file, you are prompted for a name and location in the Save As dialog box, as shown in FIGURE 9-5. Excel won't prompt you to Save As again whenever you subsequently save the file. Instead, the program will use the settings you specified earlier. If you want to specify a different name, type, or location on a subsequent save, use the File > Save As command instead.

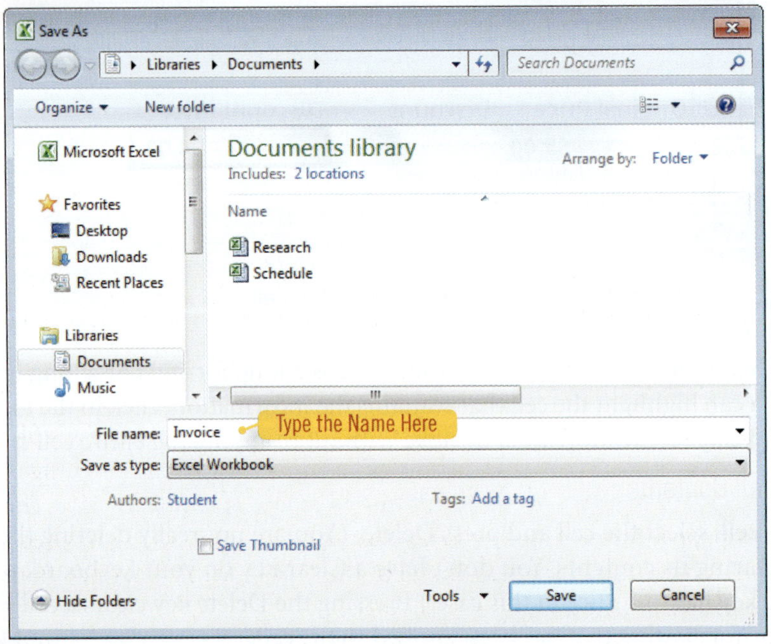

FIGURE 9-5 Use the Save As dialog box to save a file.

To open a workbook, open the File menu, click Recent, and click the file name from the list of recently opened files. If it's not there, open the File menu, click Open, and select the file from the Open dialog box.

9.2 Exercise: Creating a Basic Worksheet

In this exercise, you will create a simple worksheet. Follow these steps:

1. Click cell A1 and type **Q1**. Press Enter. The cell cursor moves to cell A2.
2. Type **$250.00** and press Enter. The cell cursor moves to cell A3.
3. Use the arrow keys to move the cell cursor to cell B1.
4. Type **Q2**. Press Enter. The cell cursor moves to cell B2.
5. Type **$300.00** and press Enter. The cell cursor moves to cell B3.
6. Click cell C1, and type **Total**. Press Enter. The cell cursor moves to cell C2.
7. Type **=A2+B2** and press Enter.
8. Click cell C2. Notice that $550.00 appears in C2, but the original formula you entered in Step 7 appears on the formula bar above the worksheet, as shown in FIGURE 9-6.
9. Save the file as **09Practice** in the default save location, or in another folder that your teacher instructs you to use.

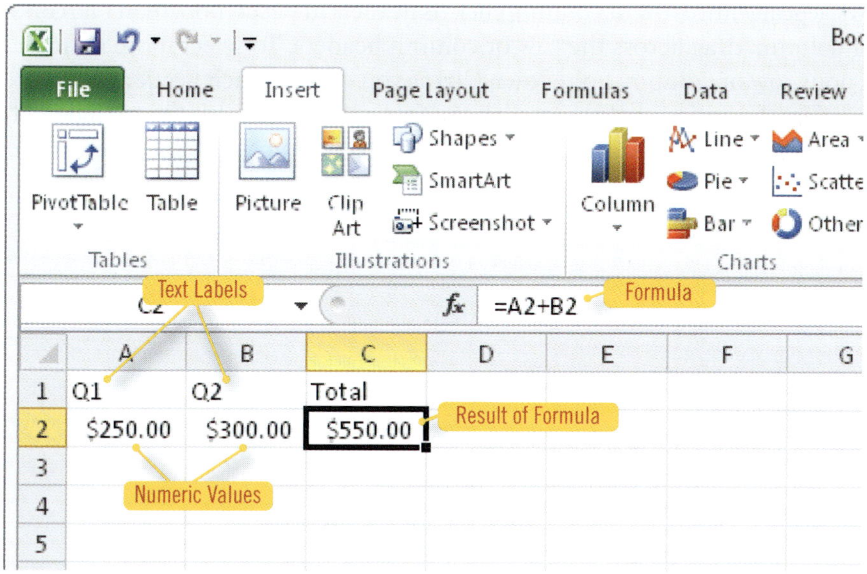

FIGURE 9-6 A simple Excel worksheet, including two labels, two values, and a formula.

Selecting Cell Ranges

A **range** of cells is one or more cells that are selected. (Usually when people refer to a range, they mean more than one cell, but technically a single cell can be a range.) Selecting a range enables you to apply the same command to multiple cells at once. For example, if you want to apply formatting to an entire row of text labels, you can select the entire row and then change the formatting for all of the cells in the row at once. You can select a range with either the mouse or the keyboard.

To select a rectangular block as a range, first select the cell that should be in one corner of the range, and then:

- **With the mouse:** Hold down the left mouse button and drag the mouse to the cell in the opposite corner of the desired range.
- **With the keyboard:** Hold down the Shift key and use the keyboard arrow keys to expand the selection.

FIGURE 9-7 shows the range E5:G8 selected. That's how Excel names a range, with the cells in the upper-left and lower-right corners separated by a colon (:). Notice that the Name box shows only the cell containing the cell cursor (E5 in Figure 9-7), not the entire range.

TIP

Ranges are usually "contiguous" rectangular blocks. Contiguous means "touching" or in contact. However, you can select non-contiguous cells as part of a single range when needed. To do so, hold down the Ctrl key as you select the cells to include. Release the Ctrl key when you are finished selecting.

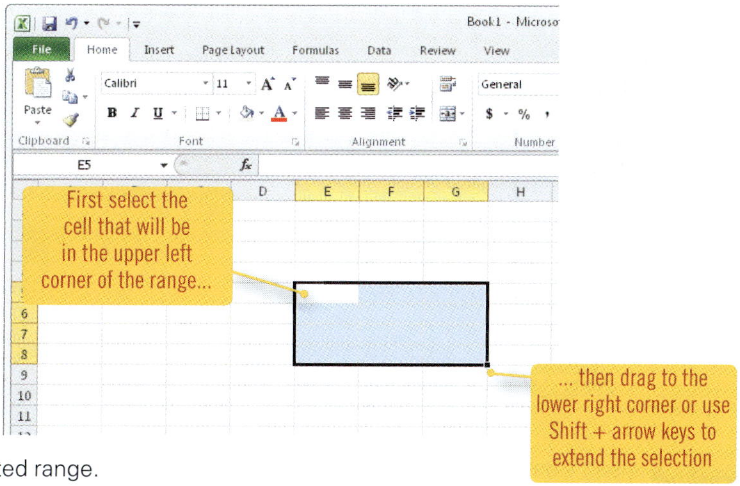

FIGURE 9-7 A selected range.

To select an entire row or column, click its header. To select more than one contiguous row or column, drag across the row or column headers. To select more than one non-contiguous row or column, hold down Ctrl as you click on each header.

To select the entire worksheet, click the Select All button. It's the triangle button in the upper-left corner, where the row numbers and column letters intersect, as shown in FIGURE 9-8.

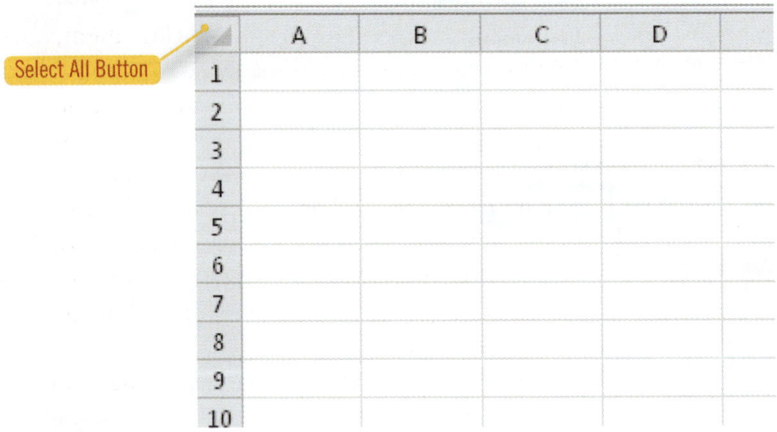

FIGURE 9-8 The Select All button selects the whole worksheet.

Inserting and Deleting Rows, Columns, or Cells

Often you may have to insert a row or column between two existing ones that already contain data. To do so, first select the row or column that is below (for a row) or to the right of (for a column) the place where you want the insertion. Then on the Home tab in the Cells group, click Insert. See FIGURE 9-9. If you select multiple rows or columns before clicking Insert, Excel inserts multiple rows or columns, matching the number that you selected.

Deleting a row or column is similar. Select the row(s) or column(s) to delete, and then on the Home tab in the Cells group, click Delete.

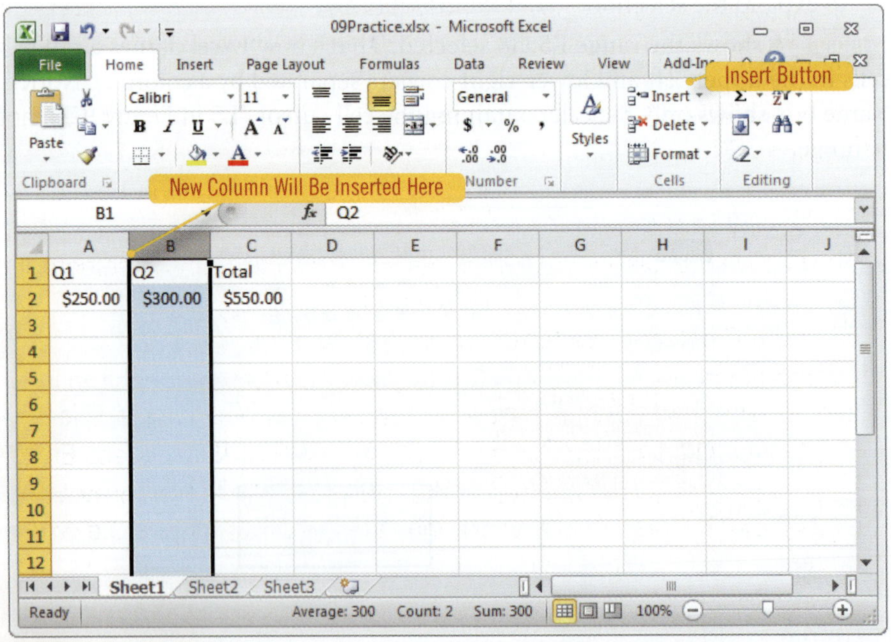

FIGURE 9-9 Insert a new row or column.

You can also insert or delete individual cells, or ranges of cells. This, however, is a little trickier because it throws off the positioning of the content in adjacent cells to the right of, or below, the cells being inserted or deleted.

Think of a worksheet as a stack of cardboard boxes, one box for each cell. When you delete a cell, you pull a box out of the stack, and gravity makes the remaining boxes in the stack fall to fill in the space. However, in a worksheet, gravity operates backward: cells fall *up*, or to the *left*, rather than falling down.

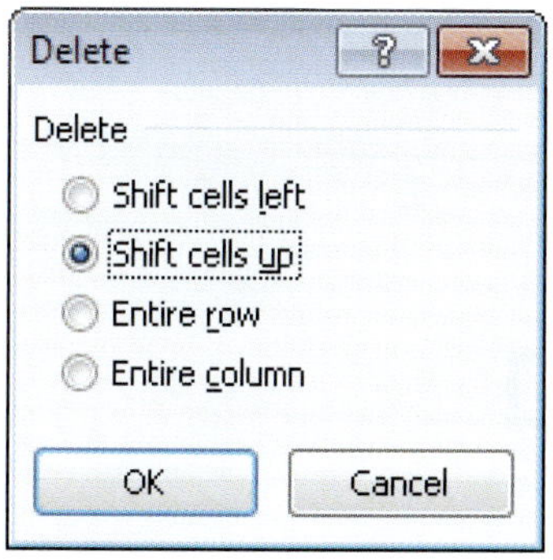

FIGURE 9-10 When deleting cells, choose where remaining cells should shift.

To delete one or more cells, select them, click Home, and then click Delete. Excel guesses which direction you want the remaining cells to shift. If it guesses incorrectly, press Ctrl+Z to undo the action, and then try this method: On the Home tab, click the down arrow to the right of the Delete button, and then click Delete Cells. The Delete Cells dialog box appears, as shown in **FIGURE 9-10**. It asks which direction you want the remaining cells to shift. Select a direction and click OK.

Excel's guess on which way to shift the content is not random; it's based on a rule. If there is no content beneath the cell(s), it shifts to the left. Otherwise it shifts up.

> **Note**
>
> Earlier in this chapter you learned that clearing a cell is not the same as deleting it. Clearing a cell leaves the cell itself intact. If you just want to erase the *contents* of a cell, clear it with the Delete key; don't delete the cell as described here.

9.3 Exercise: Selecting Ranges and Inserting a Column

In this exercise, you will practice what you just learned—selecting ranges of cells and inserting a column. Follow these steps:

1. In the 09Practice.xlsx workbook you created earlier in this chapter, click cell A1.
2. Holding the mouse left button down, drag to cell C2. Then release the mouse button. The range A1:C2 is selected. Click any cell to cancel the selection.
3. Click the Select All button. This selects the entire worksheet. Click away to cancel the selection.
4. Click the row 1 header to select that row. Then drag down to the row 4 header. All four rows are selected.
5. Hold down the Ctrl key and click cell F8. It is added to the selected range. Click away to cancel the selection.
6. Click the C column header to select that column.
7. On the Home tab in the Cells group, click Insert. A new column is inserted. The new column is now C, and the previous column C is now D.
8. In C1, type **Q3** and press Enter. In C2, type **$740.00** and press Enter.
9. Click cell D2 to select it. Then in the formula bar, edit the formula to: **=A2+B2+C2**. Press Enter when finished. **FIGURE 9-11** shows the worksheet.
10. Save your work.

> **Note**
>
> Canceling a selection by clicking any other cell is also called "clicking away."

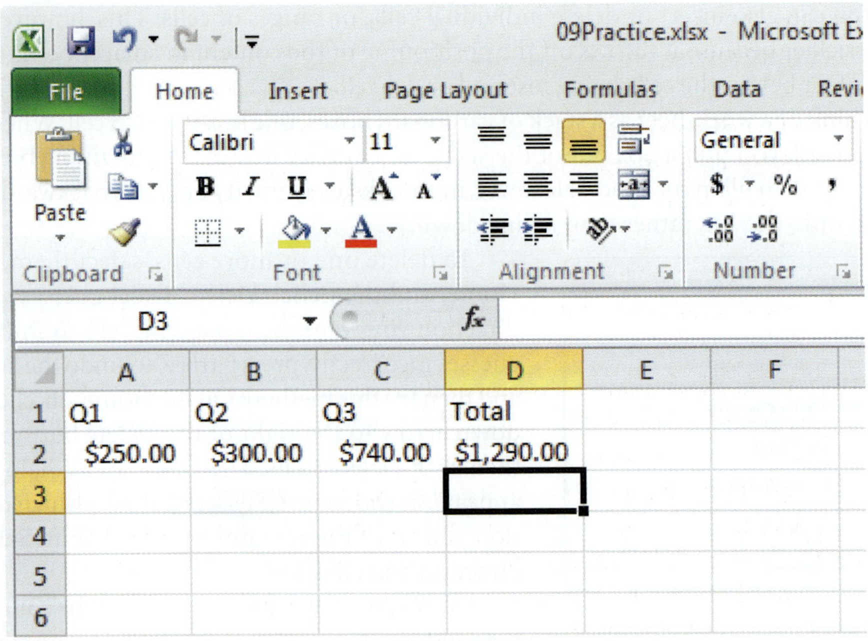

FIGURE 9-11 The practice worksheet after adding a column and more data.

Changing Column Width and Row Height

All columns start out the same width, but you can widen or narrow them as needed, from 0 to 255 characters in width. A column with a width of 0 is hidden from view.

If a cell's contents are too long to fit in the cell, one of several things happens. If there is an empty cell to its right, the contents look as if they overflow into that cell's area. If the cell to the right has content in it, the first cell's contents are truncated (cut short) or wrap to the next line, depending on how the cell is formatted. (You will learn about formatting later in this chapter.) If it's a number that won't fit, a series of pound signs (#) appears instead of the number. The number is actually still there, but you see ######. See FIGURE 9-12.

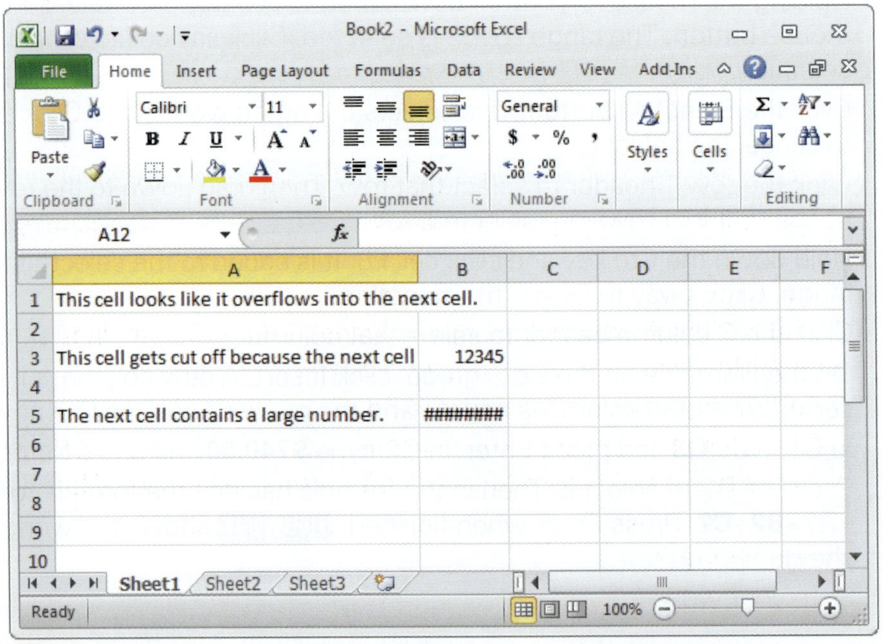

FIGURE 9-12 Examples of cells that need to have the column width adjusted.

Here are some ways to change a column's width:

- Place the mouse pointer between the column headers (the letters) and double-click. The column on the left resizes to fit the longest entry in that column. This is called **AutoFit Selection.**
- Click the column header to select the column, and then on the Home tab in the Cells group, click Format, and then click AutoFit Column.
- Place the mouse pointer between the column headers and click and drag to resize the column on the left.
- Right-click the header for the column you want to resize and select Column Width. In the dialog box that appears, type the desired value (in characters) and click OK.

You can also adjust multiple columns at the same time. For example, if you want to adjust the width of four columns, select all four columns and then use any of the above methods to resize all the columns at once.

Row heights work similarly to column widths. You can specify a row height of 0 (zero) to 409. This value represents the height measurement in **points**. (One point is equal to approximately 1/72 inch). If the row height is set to 0, the row is hidden. Row height does not usually need to be adjusted because the row height automatically changes to match the largest font (type) size used in that row.

Here are some ways to change a row's height:

- Place the mouse pointer between the row headers (the numbers) and double-click. The row on the top resizes to fit the tallest entry in that column. The only time you need to do this is if the row has been manually resized—Excel auto-sizes row height by default.
- Click the row header to select the row, and then on the Home tab in the Cells group, click Format, and then click AutoFit Row.
- Place the mouse pointer between the row headers and drag up or down. The height of the row above changes.
- Right-click the header for the row to resize and select Row Height. In the dialog box that appears, type the desired value (in points) and click OK. Allow at least three points of extra height in addition to the size of the largest font you need to accommodate.

Note

If you want the text to wrap to multiple lines within the cell, go to the Home tab in the Alignment group and click the Wrap Text button. This automatically wraps the text to multiple lines as needed, and increases the row height automatically as much as is needed for all the text to fit.

9.4 Exercise: Resizing Columns

Now let's practice resizing a column's width. Follow these steps:

1. In Excel, press Ctrl+N to start a new workbook. Save it as **09Sample.xlsx**.
2. In cell A1, type **Days** and press Enter.
3. Right-click the A column header and select Column Width. In the Column Width dialog box, type **18** and click OK.
4. In cell B1, type **Revenue** and press Enter.
5. Double-click the divider between columns B and C headers. Column B is auto-sized to fit the word *Revenue*. The worksheet should look like FIGURE 9-13 at this point.
6. Save your work.

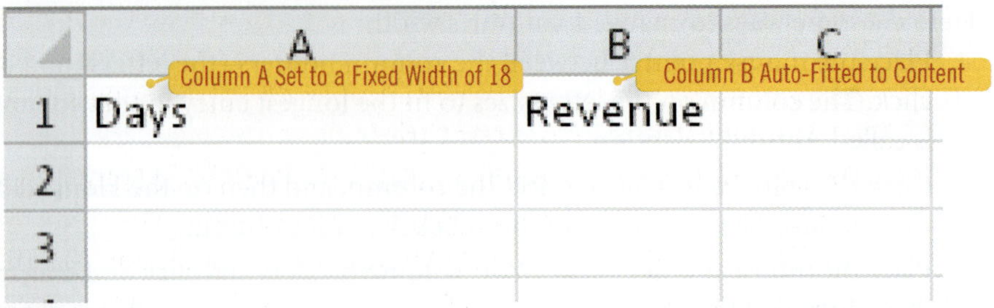

FIGURE 9-13 Setting the column widths.

TIP

When dragging a range, make sure you *do not* point at the lower-right corner of the range (the small black square). That is the fill handle and it has a special function, which you will learn about in the next section.

Moving Cells

You can move the contents of a cell or range in either of two ways:

- **Drag and drop:** Select a cell or range of cells. Hover the mouse pointer on the border of the selected cell or range until the mouse pointer turns into a four-headed arrow, as shown in FIGURE 9-14. Then click and drag to a new location.

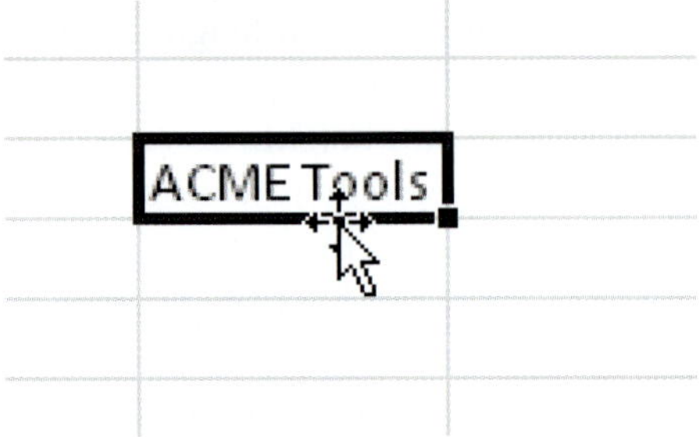

FIGURE 9-14 The four-headed arrow.

- **Cut and paste:** After selecting a cell or range, click the Home tab, and then click Cut in the Clipboard group or press Ctrl+X. A marquee (blinking dashes) appears around the cell or block of cells you selected, indicating that a Clipboard operation is in progress. Then click in the cell that should be the upper-left corner of the new location and click Home and then Paste, or press Ctrl+V.

Copying and Filling Cells

The techniques for copying are similar to the ones for moving that you just learned:

- **Drag and drop:** Select a cell or range of cells. Hover the mouse pointer on the border of the selected cell or range until the mouse pointer turns into a four-headed arrow, as shown in Figure 9-14. Hold down the Ctrl key. A plus sign appears on the mouse pointer, indicating you are about to copy (not move). See FIGURE 9-15. Click and drag to a new location.

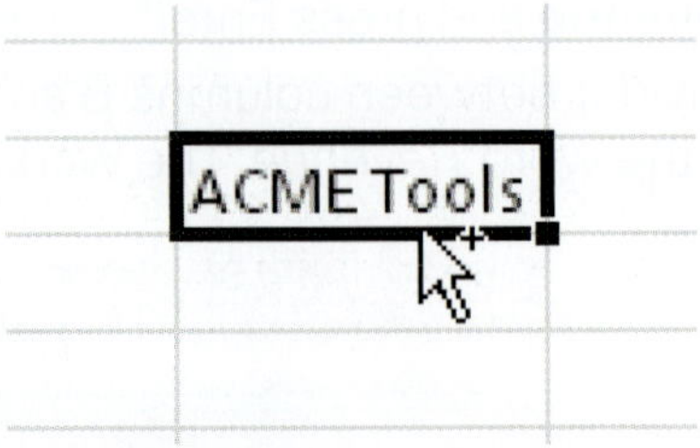

FIGURE 9-15 The plus sign indicates the cell will be copied.

- **Cut and paste:** After selecting a cell or range, choose Home and then Cut, or press Ctrl+C. A marquee (blinking dashes) appears around the cell or block of cells you selected. Click in the cell that should be the upper-left corner of the new location and choose Home and Paste, or press Ctrl+V.

Filling is like copying but more versatile and powerful. One type of fill copies a single value into multiple other cells. For example, you could place a name like "New York" in cell A1 and then fill that same name into A2:A99 with a single operation. Another type of fill inserts different values in the destination cells according to a pattern. For example, you could enter "Monday" in A2 and fill the rest of the days of the week in A3:A8. To use Excel's Auto Fill feature, select the cell (or cells) that contains the value you want to fill, or that represents the pattern you want to create, and then click and drag the **fill handle** in the direction you want to fill, across as many cells as you want to fill. (The fill handle is the small black square in the lower-left corner of the cell cursor.) See FIGURE 9-16.

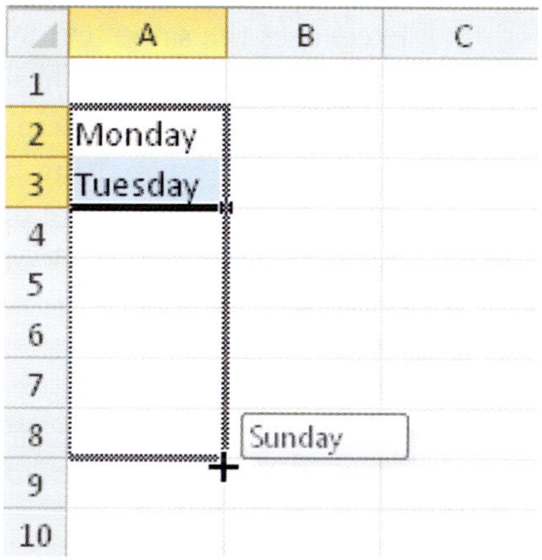

FIGURE 9-16 Using the fill handle to quickly fill a lot of cells.

9.5 Exercise: Filling Data

It's hard to understand how Auto Fill works without trying it, so let's get some practice:

1. Use the 09Sample.xlsx file you created in a previous exercise. In cell A2, type **Monday** and press Enter.
2. Select cell A2, and point the mouse pointer at the fill handle (the black square) in its lower-right corner. The mouse pointer becomes a black plus sign.
3. Click and drag the fill handle to cell A6, and then release the mouse. The rest of the weekday names are filled in (Tuesday through Friday).
4. In cell B2, type **100** and press Enter. In cell B3, type **150** and press Enter.
5. Select cells B2 and B3.
6. Click and drag the fill handle for the range down to cell B6, and then release the mouse. The pattern you began in the first two cells continues: 200, 250, and 300. The worksheet should look similar to FIGURE 9-17 at this point.
7. Save your work.

	A	B	C
1	Days	Revenue	
2	Monday	100	
3	Tuesday	150	
4	Wednesday	200	
5	Thursday	250	
6	Friday	300	
7			

FIGURE 9-17 Filling the weekdays and the numbers using Auto Fill.

Formatting Cells

As you might already know, formatting is important when you want to make your work "stand out" or look professional. Excel uses the same text formatting tools that Word does. The main difference is that Excel formatting applies to selected cells rather than to sentences and paragraphs. Excel also includes tools for placing borders around cells and ranges, and filling cells with background color. Formatting can also include specifying how numbers should appear. For example, you can enter a plain number, such as 1.23, and then format it as Currency to make it appear as $1.23, or format it as a percentage to make it appear as 123.00%.

Text Formatting

To format the text in a cell, select the cell (or select a range) and then use the buttons in the Font group on the Home tab, just as in Word. **FIGURE 9-18** describes the formatting tools in the Font group.

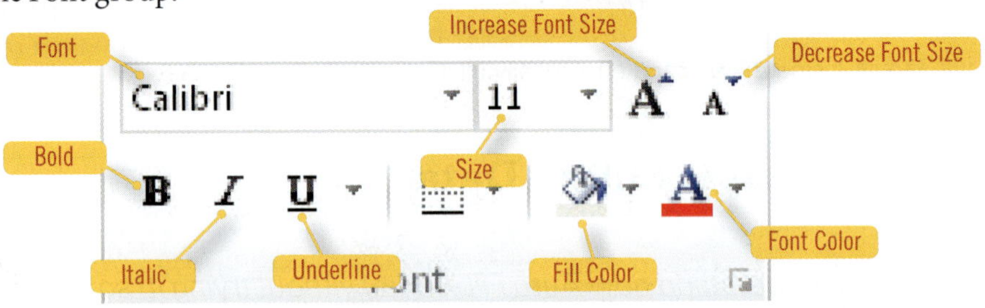

FIGURE 9-18 Use the Font group's buttons to apply text formatting.

Cell Formatting

Cell formatting includes aligning text within cells, adding borders to cells, and filling cells with color. You can apply cell formatting to individual cells or to ranges.

A cell's border and fill color are controlled from the Font group. Click the arrow on the Border button to open a drop-down list, as shown in **FIGURE 9-19**, and click the side(s) you want to add a border to. Click the Fill Color button to open a palette of colors from which to choose.

The Alignment group, also on the Home tab, contains more formatting options for cells. You can specify vertical and horizontal alignments for cell content with the buttons there, and also choose whether or not to wrap text to multiple lines in a cell if the text is too long for the cell's width. See **FIGURE 9-20**.

Number Formatting

Number formatting determines how a number appears in the cell. The default **number format** is called General; it shows the digits all by themselves, with no special symbols. Other number formats include Percent, Currency, Date, and Scientific. **TABLE 9-1** summarizes the number formats and shows some examples, using 12345.6789 as the base

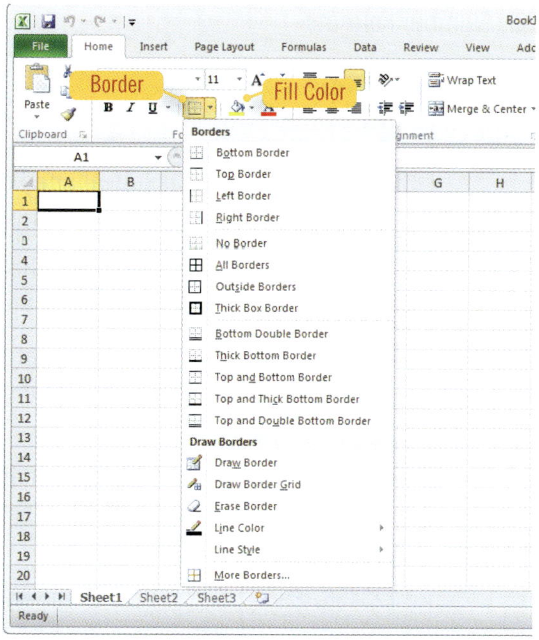

FIGURE 9-19 You can apply cell borders and fill color from the Font group.

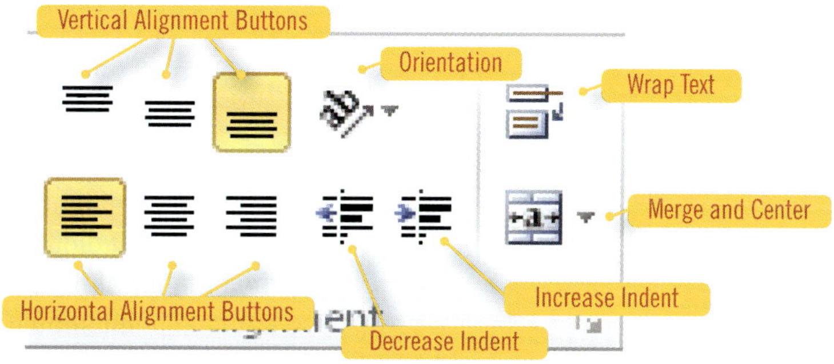

FIGURE 9-20 Use the Alignment group's buttons to control content placement within cells.

number. To apply a number format, select the cell(s) and then click a format option from the drop-down list in the Number group on the Home tab.

Table 9-1 Number Formats

Format	Example	Notes
General	12345.6789	Rounds off decimal places as needed if the cell is too narrow to show the complete number. Number is right-aligned.
Number	12345.68	Rounds off to two decimal places automatically unless you specify a different number of decimal places. Number is right-aligned.
Currency	$12,345.68	Adds the $ sign and rounds to two decimal places. Adds a comma as a thousands separator. Dollar sign is flush against the first digit. The entire number is right-aligned.

Table 9-1 (continued) Number Formats

Format	Example	Notes
Accounting	$ 12,345.68	Same as Currency, except the dollar sign is left-aligned in the cell. The rest of the number is right-aligned.
Short Date	10/18/1933	Shows the date that is the specified number of days since January 1, 1900.
Long Date	Wednesday, October 18, 1933	Same as Short Date except the date is written out in a longer form.
Time	4:17:37 PM	Shows the time that is the specified number of hours since Midnight (0:00:00).
Percentage	1234567.89%	Shows the number as a percentage, with a % sign. Because 1.0 equals 100%, the decimal point is moved two places to the right.
Fraction	12345 2/3	Rounds the number to the nearest one-digit fraction.
Scientific	1.23E+04	Shows the number in scientific notation. The decimal point appears after the first digit. The +04 refers to the number of places to the right the decimal point should be moved to translate to a general number.

You can adjust the number of decimal places used with the buttons in the Number group, as shown in FIGURE 9-21. Also in the Number group are shortcuts for applying the Accounting, Percentage, and Comma Style formats. (The Comma Style format is actually the Accounting format minus the currency symbol.)

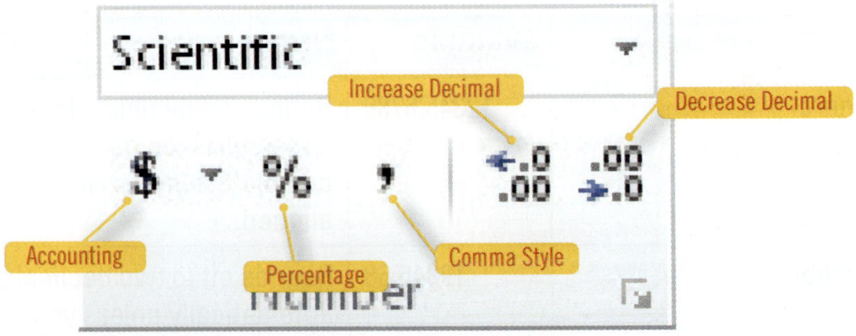

FIGURE 9-21 The Number group's buttons let you fine-tune the number format.

If none of these provides the format you want, click the dialog box launcher for the Number group to open the Number tab of the Format Cells dialog box. From there you can control the details for each number format.

9.6 Exercise: Formatting Cells

Now let's try formatting some cells. Follow these steps:

1. In the 09Sample.xlsx file you worked with earlier, select A1:B1. Click the Bold button on the Home tab in the Font group to make the text bold.
2. On the Home tab, open the Font Color drop-down list and click the bright red square in the Standard Colors area of the palette.
3. Hold down the Ctrl key and drag across cells A7:B7 to include those cells in the selection.
4. On the Home tab, open the Fill Color drop-down list and click the lightest gray square. Click away from the selection to deselect it when you are finished.
5. Select B2:B7 and apply the Currency number format to those cells. Click the Decrease Decimal button twice to show only whole dollar amounts.
6. Edit the text in B1 to read Daily Revenue. Then set that cell to Wrap Text.
7. Horizontally center the text in A1:B1 and widen the B column to 12 characters.
8. Select A6:B6 and apply a bottom border to those two cells. The worksheet should look similar to FIGURE 9-22 when you are finished.
9. Save your work.

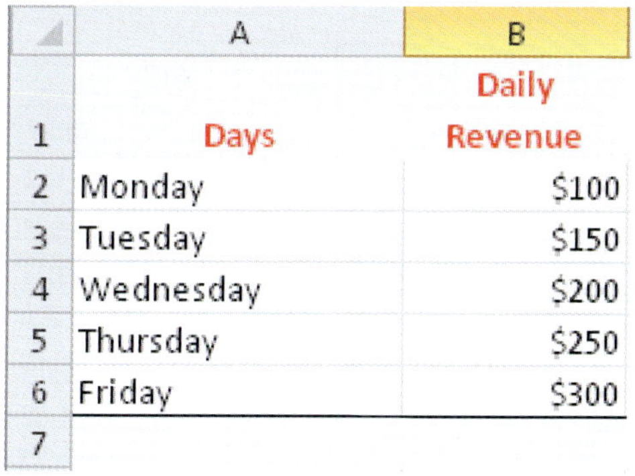

	A	B
1	Days	Daily Revenue
2	Monday	$100
3	Tuesday	$150
4	Wednesday	$200
5	Thursday	$250
6	Friday	$300
7		

FIGURE 9-22 The worksheet after following the steps in the formatting exercise.

Sorting Data

Sorting means to arrange in **ascending** (A to Z) or **descending** (Z to A) order. In ascending order, numbers come first (0 to 9), followed by letters. In descending order, letters come first. Sorting comes in handy when you use an Excel sheet as a simple database file, storing one record per row as shown in FIGURE 9-23. Figure 9-23 shows a list sorted by Enrollment Date, but it could easily be sorted by any column.

The simplest way to sort is to click in a column (any cell that contains data) and then on the Data tab, click the Sort Ascending or Sort Descending button, as shown in FIGURE 9-24. That column is sorted, and any data that was in adjacent columns comes along for the ride, too. That's a good thing if you are storing database records in the sheet, as in Figure 9-23, and each row contains information about a specific person or item.

If you need to sort by multiple columns, so that in the event of a "tie" between two records, another field will be used as a tiebreaker, you can use the Sort dialog box. On

> **TIP**
>
> What if you don't want the adjacent columns to be included when you sort? If that's the case, select the entire column before sorting. A dialog box will open asking whether you want the entire list to be sorted or just that column.

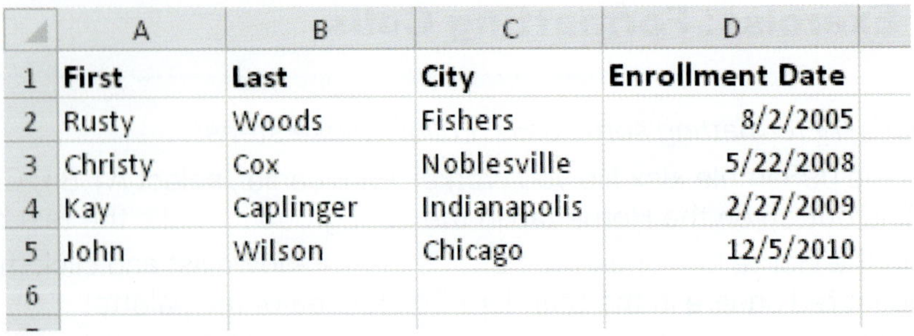

	A	B	C	D
1	First	Last	City	Enrollment Date
2	Rusty	Woods	Fishers	8/2/2005
3	Christy	Cox	Noblesville	5/22/2008
4	Kay	Caplinger	Indianapolis	2/27/2009
5	John	Wilson	Chicago	12/5/2010
6				

FIGURE 9-23 Sorted data records in a worksheet.

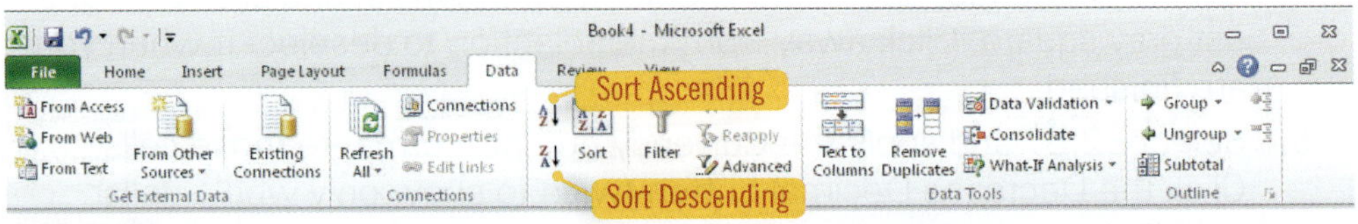

FIGURE 9-24 Click in a column and then click one of the Sort buttons on the Data tab.

the Data tab, click the Sort button. Then in the Sort dialog box, select the fields you want to use. Choose the first one, and then click Add Level to add more fields to sort by, as shown in FIGURE 9-25.

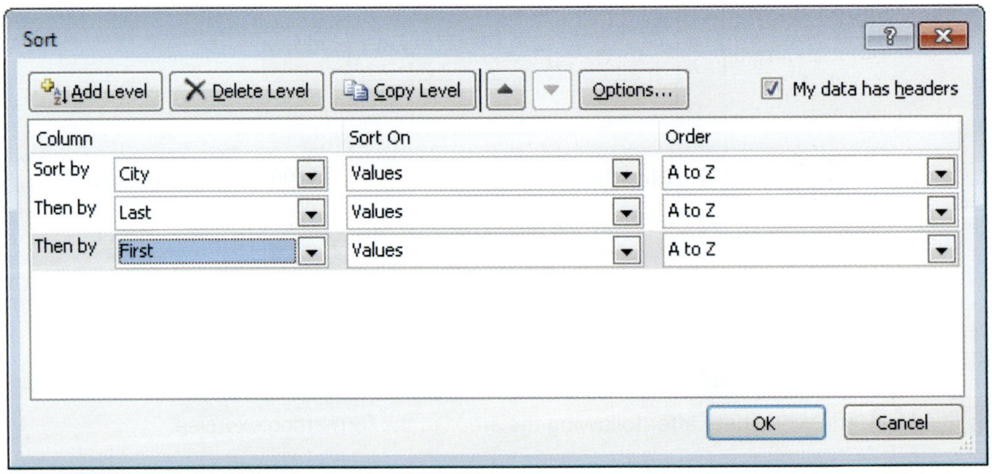

FIGURE 9-25 Sorting by multiple fields.

Printing a Worksheet

To print your work in Excel, open the File menu and click Print, the same as you do in Word. Change any of the settings as needed, and then click the Print button.

If you want to print only a certain range of the worksheet, select it first before issuing the Print command. Then in the Settings area of the print options window, click the Print Active Sheets button and select Print Selection from the drop-down list, as shown in FIGURE 9-26.

You've done a lot of work in this chapter—congratulations on how far you've come! Be sure to take the quiz and complete the project to help you learn even more about Excel basics. In Chapter 10, you will dive into formulas, functions, and chart creation. It sounds challenging, but the exercises will help you learn everything one step at a time.

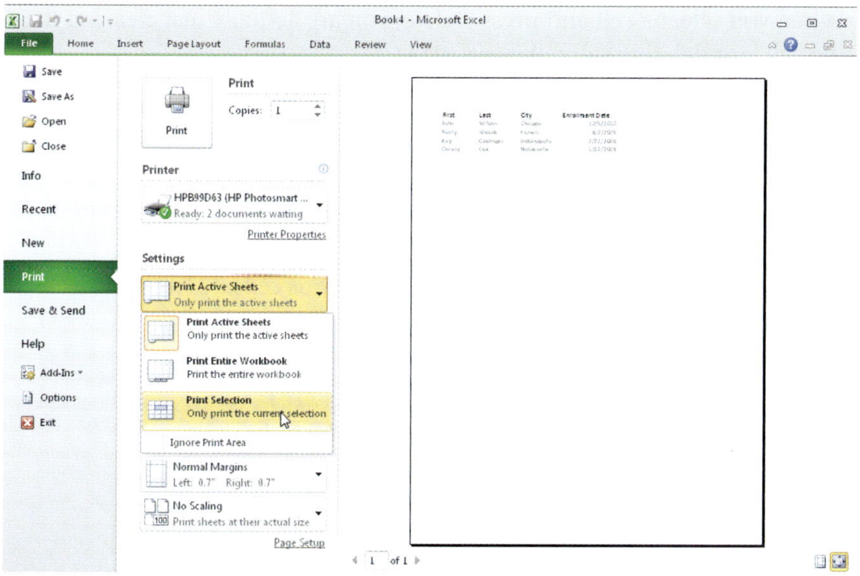

FIGURE 9-26 Adjust any printer settings as needed, and then click Print.

Test Yourself

The questions in this section are meant to test your knowledge of what you read. Make sure you answer them. The page number where the answer can be found appears after each question.

1. The main user interface for Excel consists of a tabbed ______. (208)
2. What is a data file in Excel called? (209)
   A. Worksheet
   B. Macro
   C. Template
   D. Workbook
3. The intersection of a row and a column is called a ________. (209)
4. Which of these is a valid cell address? (209)
   A. 2A
   B. A2
   C. AA
   D. 2265
5. What is a cell cursor? (209)
   A. The black border around the active cell
   B. The mouse pointer when it is over a worksheet
   C. The mouse pointer when it is over the active cell
   D. The black border around a range of two or more cells
6. The arrow keys on the keyboard can be used to move the cell cursor. (209)
   A. True
   B. False
7. Which of these is an example of a function? (210)
   A. =A1+A2
   B. =AVERAGE(A1:A2)
   C. A1+A2*3
   D. All of the above
8. The result of a formula appears in the formula bar, and the formula itself appears in the cell. (210)
   A. True
   B. False

9. When you select a cell and press Delete, you are actually just clearing the data in the cell, not deleting the cell itself. (211)
   A. True
   B. False
10. A _________ is a group of one or more selected cells. (213)
11. To select contiguous cells with the keyboard, hold down the ____ key and use the arrow keys to expand the selection. (213)
12. A range must be a rectangular area of contiguous cells. (213, 214)
   A. True
   B. False
13. What does it mean if ##### appears in a cell? (216)
   A. The cell has numeric content that is too long to fit in the cell.
   B. The cell has text content that is too long to fit in the cell.
   C. There is an error in the cell's formula.
   D. Any of the above
14. How do you auto-fit a column's width to its content? (217)
   A. Double-click the column header divider between that column and the one to its left.
   B. Double-click the column header divider between that column and the one to its right.
   C. Double-click the column letter.
   D. Triple-click the column letter.
15. How is row height measured? (217)
   A. In characters
   B. In inches
   C. In centimeters
   D. In points
16. The small black square in the lower-right corner of a selected range is the ____. (219)
17. 1.42E+08 is an example of which type of number formatting? (222)
   A. Currency
   B. General
   C. Date
   D. Scientific
18. Which of these lists is sorted in descending order? (223)
   A. 8, 200, Cow, Dog
   B. Dog, Cow, 200, 8
   C. 200, 8, Dog, Cow
   D. Cow, Dog, 8, 200
19. After selecting cells, if you want to cancel the selection you can click away. (215)
   A. True
   B. False
20. To copy a range of cells by dragging, hold down the _____ key as you drag. (218)

End-of-Chapter Project

In this exercise, you will practice some of the skills you learned in this chapter. You will create a worksheet that lists the laptops, printers, and Internet service provider research you gathered in past projects. Follow these steps:

1. Start Excel. A new workbook opens automatically with three worksheets (indicated by the tabs along the bottom of the window—Sheet1, Sheet2, Sheet3).
2. Enter the text shown in **FIGURE 9-27**, replacing the manufacturers in column A with the manufacturers of the laptops you researched.

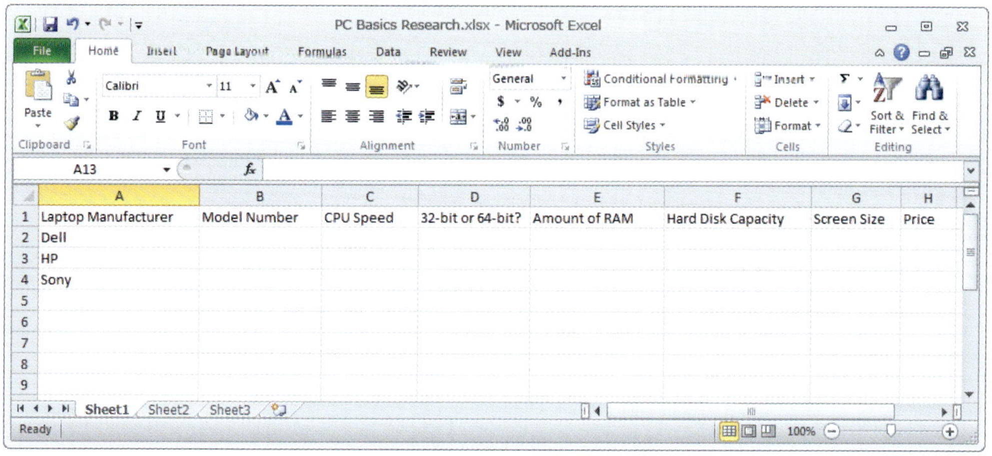

FIGURE 9-27 Start by entering this text.

3. Auto-fit the column width for columns A through H.
4. Save the file as PC Basics Research in your Class Research folder, but leave the file open and continue working.
5. Enter the rest of your data in the cells in columns B through H. If you don't have data for some of the cells, go back to the appropriate Internet sites and get the data. (You may also add columns for additional data, if necessary.)
6. Change the row height for rows 1 through 4 to exactly 20 points.
7. Select A1:H1 and apply a bottom border.
8. Format the text in A1:H1 as 12 point, bold, and blue.
9. Apply the Currency number format to H2:H4.
10. Auto-fit the column width for columns A through H.
11. Insert two new columns between G and H. The new columns become H and I.
12. In H1, type Warranty. In I1, type Store. Add the appropriate information to the column cells, researching the information as needed.
13. Sort the list by price, with the lowest-cost laptop first.
14. Save your file but continue working.
15. Click on Sheet2 at the bottom of the Excel window. Create a similar worksheet for the printer data. Feel free to change the column headers and reduce the number of columns as needed.
16. Click on Sheet3 at the bottom of the Excel window. Create a similar worksheet for the Internet service provider data. Feel free to change the column headers and reduce the number of columns as needed.
17. Save your work again, and close Excel.

CHAPTER

10

Excel 2010 Formulas, Functions, and Charts

- Excel is much more than a convenient grid in which to arrange text and numbers. Its real power lies in its ability to perform math calculations on the data you enter, and to update those calculations automatically when the numbers change.
- In this chapter, you will learn how to use Excel's formulas and functions to construct powerful worksheets that provide useful information for both business and home uses.

CHAPTER TOPICS

This chapter covers the following topics and concepts:

- How to create and work with simple formulas
- What functions are used for and how to create them
- How to use financial functions related to loans and payments
- When logical functions are needed
- Why some functions must be "nested"
- How to apply conditional formatting
- How to name a range and why it's helpful to do so
- How to create charts

KEY WORDS

Absolute referencing
Arguments
Chart
Conditional formatting
Financial functions
Formula
Function
Logical functions
Mixed reference
Nested function
Order of operations
Range name
Relative referencing

Creating Formulas

Formulas are the main reason people use Excel. Formulas help you perform math operations on data, and automatically update the results when the numbers on which they are based change.

Here are some examples of formulas:

=1+2
=B5/12
=A1+A2+A3+A4
=A1*(C2-C3)

As you might have guessed from the above examples, a formula must start with an equal sign (=). It can contain a combination of numbers, cell references, and math operators. You type formulas into cells just as you do regular text and numbers.

10.1 Exercise: Create a Formula

Let's give formulas a try. You already created a few simple formulas in Chapter 9, so this exercise should be a snap. Follow these steps:

1. Type the text and data shown in FIGURE 10-1 into a blank worksheet.

	A	B	C	D
1		Week1	Week2	Total
2	Thomas	34	33	
3	Richard	22	16	
4	Harold	15	21	
5	Alice	41	38	
6	Total			

FIGURE 10-1 Type this data as a starting point for the exercise.

2. In cell B6, type **=B2+B3+B4+B5** and press Enter.
3. Click cell B6 to move the cell cursor back to it. Look in the formula bar; the formula you entered in Step 2 appears there. In the actual cell itself, the result of the formula appears, as shown in FIGURE 10-2.
4. Delete the formula in cell B6 by pressing Delete on the keyboard. (You'll re-create it a different way.)

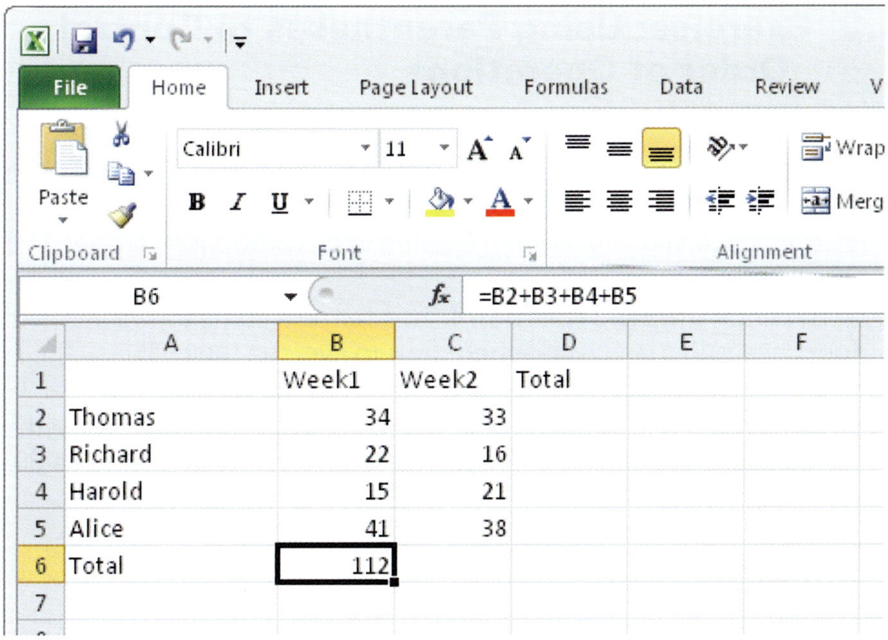

FIGURE 10-2 The cell shows the result; the formula bar shows the formula.

5. In cell B6, type **=**. Click cell B2. Its name is filled into the formula.
6. Type **+** and then click B3.
7. Repeat this process, typing **+** and clicking the next cell until the complete formula is re-created (=B2+B3+B4+B5). Press Enter.
8. Click in cell B2, type **28** (replacing the current value), and press Enter. Notice how the formula result in B6 changes to reflect the new total.
9. Click in cell B4 and enter **None**, replacing the number with text. Notice that B6 now shows an error. That's because you can't reference a cell that contains text in a math calculation.
10. Click in B4 and enter **0**, removing that day's value. Now the formula in B6 works again.
11. Save the file as **10Practice**. You'll use it again later in this chapter.

Understanding Order of Operations

Some formulas can get fairly complex, with multiple math operations in them. When there is more than one math symbol, Excel uses the following **order of operations** to decide what to do:

- **First:** Anything in parentheses
- **Second:** Exponentiation (^)
- **Third:** Multiplication (*) and division (/)
- **Fourth:** Addition (+) and subtraction (–)

That first one is significant—anything that you want to happen first, you place in parentheses.

For example, in the formula =5+2*3, Excel will first do the multiplication, and then the addition, for a result of 11 (5 plus 6). If you wanted the addition done first, you would write it like this: =(5+2)*3. The result would be 21 (7 times 3).

10.2 Exercise: Using Parentheses to Control Order of Operations

The order of operations takes some practice! Let's walk through an easy example in this exercise:

1. In 10Practice.xlsx (the file you created in the previous exercise), in cell A7, enter **Average**.
2. In B7, enter **=(B2+B3+B4+B5)/4**. This formula sums the values in the four cells, and then divides them by 4 to average their values. The result in B7 should show as 22.75.
3. Click B7, and then in the formula bar, edit the formula to remove the parentheses, and then press Enter. The result in B7 now shows as 60.25 (which is not the correct average).
4. Press Ctrl+Z to reverse the last edit, restoring the parentheses.
5. Save the file.

Copying Formulas

In the last exercise there was only one formula. That's not the case most of the time. A typical business worksheet contains many formulas. Often these formulas are the same as one another except for the cells they reference. For example, in FIGURE 10-3, the formulas in row 7 are the same in columns B, C, and D except for the letters.

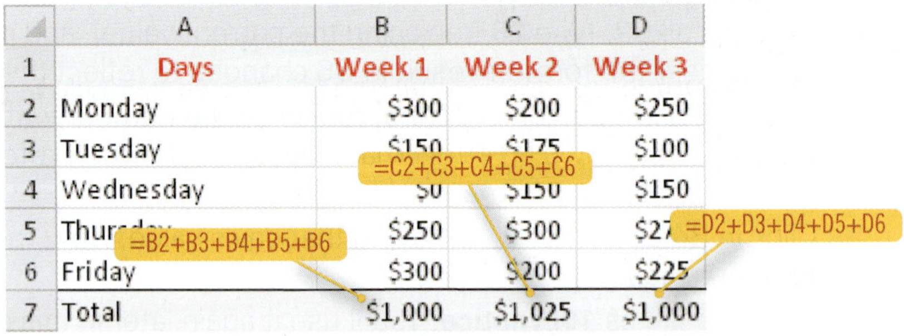
A
B
C
D
Days
Week 1
Week 2
Week 3
Monday $300 $200 $250
Tuesday $100
Wednesday $150
$250 $300
Friday $300 $200 $225
Total $1,000 $1,025 $1,000
=B2+B3+B4+B5+B6
=C2+C3+C4+C5+C6
=D2+D3+D4+D5+D6

FIGURE 10-3 Often the formulas in a worksheet are the same except for the cells they reference.

If you were to copy the formula from B7 to C7:D7, the column letters would change automatically in the new location. This is called **relative referencing**. Relative referencing is the default in Excel. Most of the time when you copy a formula, you want it to be relatively referenced.

The alternative is **absolute referencing**, in which the cell references do *not* change when you copy them to a different cell. Absolute referencing is appropriate when copying a formula in which the cell reference should remain the same regardless of where you copy the formula to. You create absolute referencing by placing dollar signs ($) before the column letter and the row number, like this: $A$1.

For example, in FIGURE 10-4, each formula calculates a discount price by multiplying the original price by a fixed value in cell B1. Therefore, B1 appears as $B$1 in the formula, to lock its reference. That way when the formula is copied to the other cells in that column, $B$1 doesn't change. The other cell references in the formula do change, however, which is correct.

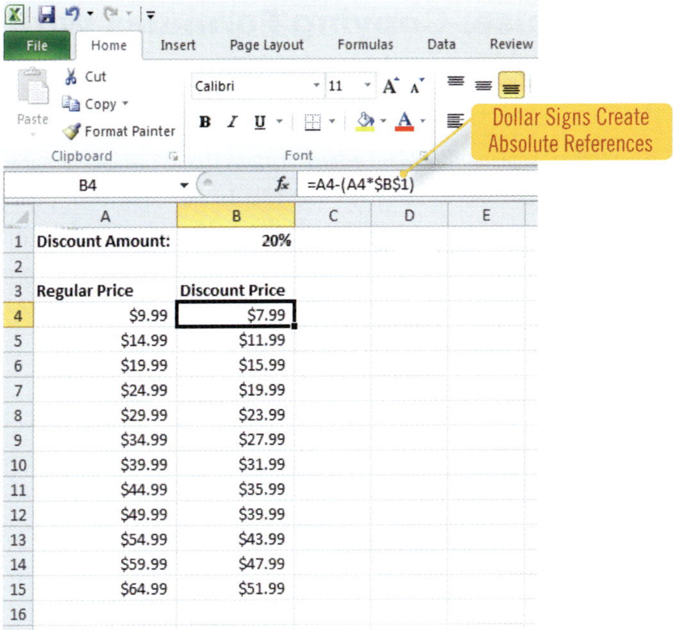

FIGURE 10-4 An example of absolute referencing.

10.3 Exercise: Copying Formulas with Relative Referencing

In this exercise, you will copy a formula with a relative reference to see how it changes in a new location. Follow these steps:

1. In the 10Practice.xlsx file that you created earlier, select B6:B7.
2. Drag the fill handle to C7. The formulas in B6 and B7 are copied to C6 and C7, respectively.
3. Click in cell C6 to look at the pasted copy. In the formula bar, notice that the formula refers to cells in column C.
4. Click in C7. Notice that the formula refers to cells in column C.
5. In D2, enter **=B2+C2**.
6. Select D2, and drag the fill handle down to D7. The formula is copied into D3:D7, with the row numbers automatically updated. **FIGURE 10-5** shows the worksheet at this point.
7. Save your work.

	A	B	C	D
1		Week1	Week2	Total
2	Thomas	28	33	61
3	Richard	22	16	38
4	Harold	0	21	21
5	Alice	41	38	79
6	Total	91	108	199
7	Average	22.75	27	49.75
8				

FIGURE 10-5 The worksheet after the relative-reference formulas have been copied.

> **Note**
>
> You can also have a **mixed reference**, which is an address in which either the row or the column (but not both) is absolute. For example, in $B1, only the column is fixed; in B$1, only the row is fixed. Mixed references are not common.

10.4 Exercise: Copying Formulas with Absolute Referencing

In this exercise, you will copy a formula with an absolute reference. You will see how it "remembers" the reference to the original data, even when the formula appears in a new location. Follow these steps:

1. Insert two new rows at the top of 10Practice.xlsx. To do so, select rows 1 and 2 and click Home, Insert (in the Cells group).
2. In A1, enter **Quota**. In A2, enter **50**.
3. In E3, enter **Performance**. In E4, enter **=D4–$B$1**.
4. Click E4, and then press Ctrl+C to copy the formula.
5. Select E5:E9 and press Ctrl+V to paste. Press Esc to turn off the dotted outline around E4.
6. Click E8 and examine the formula in the formula bar. Notice that the first reference in the formula changed as you copied it, but the reference to B1 did not. The worksheet looks like FIGURE 10-6 at this point.
7. Save your work.

TIP

Figure 10-6 contains some negative numbers. If you like, you can change the number formatting for that column so that negative numbers appear in red. To do so, select column E and then, on the Home tab, click the dialog box launcher for the Number group. The Format Cells dialog box opens. Choose Number as the number format, and then click one of the samples that shows negative numbers in red. Click OK to close the dialog box.

	A	B	C	D	E	F
1	Quota	50				
2						
3		Week1	Week2	Total	Performance	
4	Thomas	28	33	61	11	
5	Richard	22	16	38	-12	
6	Harold	0	21	21	-29	
7	Alice	41	38	79	29	
8	Total	91	108	199	149	
9	Average	22.75	27	49.75	-0.25	
10						

FIGURE 10-6 The worksheet after the absolute-reference formulas have been copied

Introducing Functions

A **function** is a named math operation, such as SUM, AVERAGE, or COUNT. Each function performs a specific calculation on the contents of one or more cells, and displays a result.

Functions have **arguments**, which are variables you specify. The arguments appear after the function's name in parentheses. The most common argument is a range of cells. For example, =SUM(A1:A10) sums the values in cells A1 through A10. A1:A10 is the argument.

Some functions have more than one argument. When there are multiple arguments, they are separated by commas. For example, in the ROUNDUP function, there are two arguments. The first argument is the range to act on, and the second argument is the number of decimal places that the result should include. For example, =ROUNDUP(A1,0) would display the value from cell A1 rounded up to 0 decimal places (that is, to a whole number). If A1 contained 44.2214, the result would be 45. If you specified 2 for the second argument, as in =ROUNDUP(A1,2), the result would be 44.23.

There are several advantages to using functions. One is that you can act on ranges of cells, rather than having to enter cell addresses individually. For example, instead of

=B2+B3+B4+B5+B6+B7, you could use =SUM(B2:B7). Another advantage is that often a function can do easily what it would take a very complex math formula to accomplish. For example, with the PMT (payment) function, you can calculate the payment amount on a loan by providing the initial amount borrowed, the interest rate, and the number of payments to be made.

You can type functions directly into cells, just as you do formulas, but you might not always know what function you want or what arguments it requires. Therefore, beginners often find it easier to use the Insert Function command to create their functions. When you click the Insert Function button (to the left of the formula bar), a dialog box opens in which you can choose a function and fill the arguments into text boxes.

Using the SUM and AVERAGE Functions

The first two functions you'll learn about are SUM and AVERAGE. The SUM function adds up the numbers in a range of cells, ignoring blank cells or text-filled cells. The AVERAGE function adds up the numbers in the range, and then counts the numbers in the range, and then divides the total by the count.

10.5 Exercise: Inserting a SUM Function

The SUM function is one of the most widely used functions in Excel. Let's see how to put it to work:

1. In 10Practice.xlsx, click B8 and press Delete to clear the formula.
2. With B8 still selected, click the Insert Function button on the formula bar. The button has fx on it. The Insert Function dialog box opens.
3. In the Select a Function list, click SUM if it is not already selected. See FIGURE 10-7.

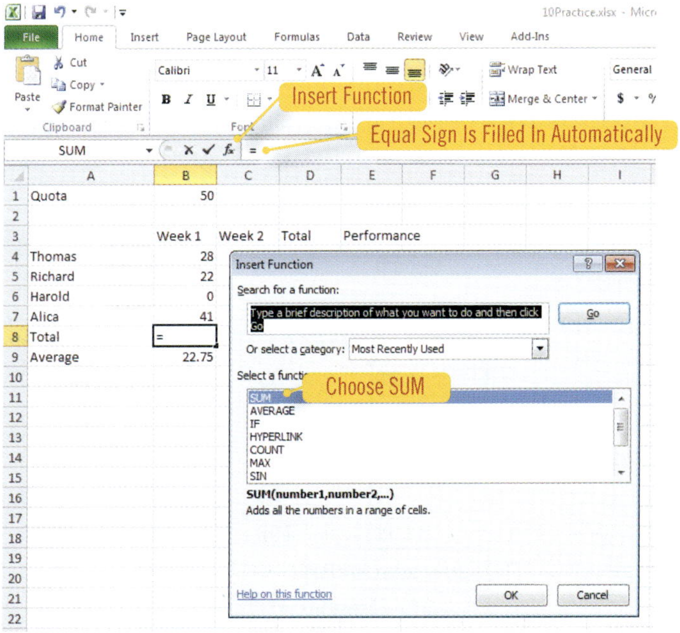

FIGURE 10-7 Inserting the SUM function.

4. Click OK. The Function Arguments dialog box opens.
5. In the Number1 box, B4:B7 is already entered. Excel guessed correctly what you want to sum.

6. Click OK. The function =SUM(B4:B7) now appears in cell B8.
7. Click in C8 and press Delete, removing the formula.
8. On the Home tab in the Editing group, click the AutoSum button, as shown in FIGURE 10-8. This button is a shortcut for the SUM function.

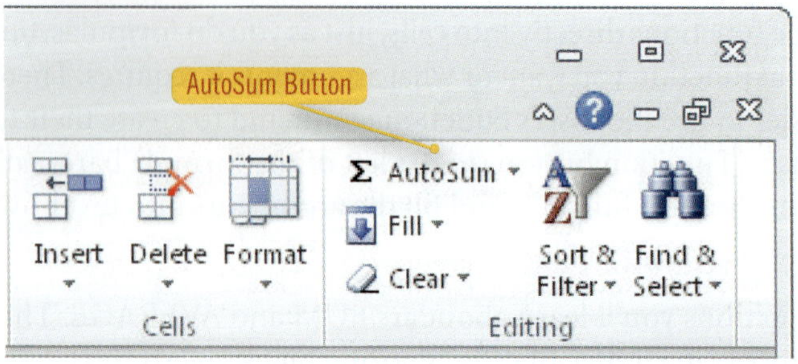

FIGURE 10-8 The AutoSum button.

> **TIP**
>
> The AutoSum button has an arrow to its right. Click the arrow for a list of other common functions you can quickly insert.

9. The range C4:C7 becomes selected automatically. (Excel guesses correctly at the range you want to sum.) Press Enter to accept it.
10. Click in cell C8. Drag the fill handle from C8 to D8, copying the function there.
11. Save your work.

10.6 Exercise: Inserting an AVERAGE Function

Now it's your turn to use the AVERAGE function. Follow these steps:

1. In 10Practice.xlsx, click B9 and press Delete to clear the formula.
2. Type **=AVERAGE(** but don't press Enter. A ScreenTip prompt reminds you which arguments this function uses.
3. Drag across B4:B7 to select those cells. The range B4:B7 is automatically filled into the function argument, as shown in FIGURE 10-9.

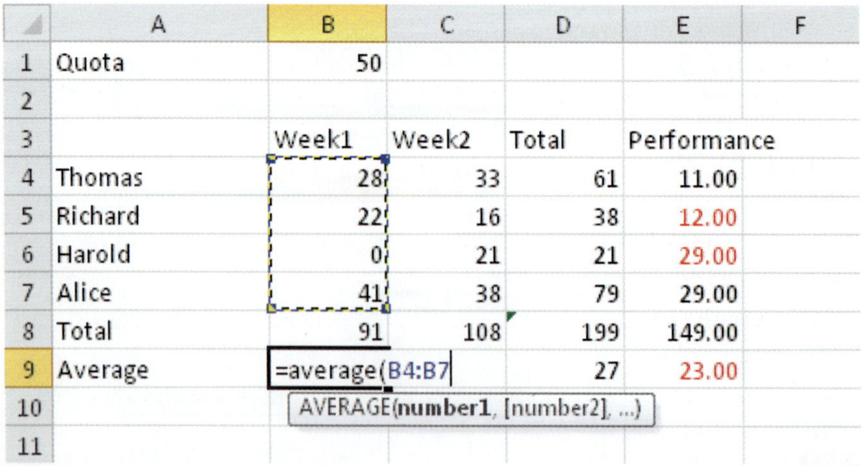

	A	B	C	D	E	F
1	Quota	50				
2						
3		Week1	Week2	Total	Performance	
4	Thomas	28	33	61	11.00	
5	Richard	22	16	38	12.00	
6	Harold	0	21	21	29.00	
7	Alice	41	38	79	29.00	
8	Total	91	108	199	149.00	
9	Average	=average(B4:B7		27	23.00	
10		AVERAGE(number1, [number2], ...)				
11						

FIGURE 10-9 The AVERAGE function and its argument.

4. Press Enter. Excel adds the closing parenthesis for you, and saves the function.

5. Click C9, and click the arrow to the right of the AutoSum button. A menu opens.
6. Choose Average from the menu. The AVERAGE function is filled into C9 and a suggested range of C4:C8 is entered.
7. You don't want C8 to be a part of the range, so Shift+click (press and hold the Shift key while you click) cell C7. That changes the range to C4:C7. Press Enter.
8. Click C9, and drag the fill handle to D9, copying the function there.

Other Common One-Argument Functions

The SUM and AVERAGE functions are very simple. Each takes a single argument: the range to be operated on. There are several other common functions in Excel that also take a single argument:

- **MIN:** Determines the minimum value in a range. Example: =MIN(A1:A3).
- **MAX:** Determines the maximum value in a range. Example: =MAX(A1:A3).
- **COUNT:** Counts the number of numeric values in a range. Example: =COUNT(A1:A3).
- **COUNTA:** Counts the number of cells that are not empty in the range. They can contain text, numbers, or another formula or function. Example: =COUNTA(A1:A3).
- **ABS:** Shows the absolute value of another cell. If the other cell's value is positive, it just repeats it. If it's negative, it converts the number to positive. Example: ABS(A1).
- **TODAY:** Shows today's date. This function's parentheses are left empty, so technically it is a zero-argument function. Example: TODAY( ).
- **NOW:** Shows the current date and time. Example: NOW( ).

Using Financial Functions

Excel includes many functions for calculating financial values, such as the interest you will earn on a savings account or the payments you will make on an installment loan. In this section, you will learn about a set of four interrelated **financial functions**. There are four values involved in an installment loan, and each of these functions, given the other three, finds the fourth value:

- **PMT:** Given the number of periods (payments), the interest rate, and the present value (amount owed) of a loan, calculates the payment amount.
- **NPER:** Given the interest rate, present value, and payment amount, calculates the number of periods.
- **RATE:** Given the present value, payment amount, and number of periods, calculates the interest rate.
- **PV:** Given the payment amount, number of periods, and interest rate, calculates the present value.

Each of these functions has three required arguments. For example, the PMT function's required arguments are:

=PMT(rate, nper, pv)

Let's say that you want to calculate the monthly payment on a $15,000, 60-month auto loan where the interest rate is 6% a year. You could use the PMT function as follows:

=PMT(.06/12, 60, 15000)

The number .06 is the 6%. You divide it by 12 because 6% is the yearly rate, and you want the monthly rate. The number 60 is the number of periods (months), and 15000 is the amount borrowed. If you place this function in a worksheet cell, you find that the payment amount is $289.99. It shows up as a negative number because it's the amount you have to pay (outgoing) rather than income (incoming). You can format the payment amount to display as ordinary currency if you want.

Now suppose you want to run some scenarios, such as changing the interest rate, the number of payments, or the amount borrowed, to see what the different payments would be. Rather than using a function with fixed numbers in it, as we did above, it would be better to place those variables in worksheet cells and refer to the cells in the function instead. FIGURE 10-10 shows the PMT function being used that way.

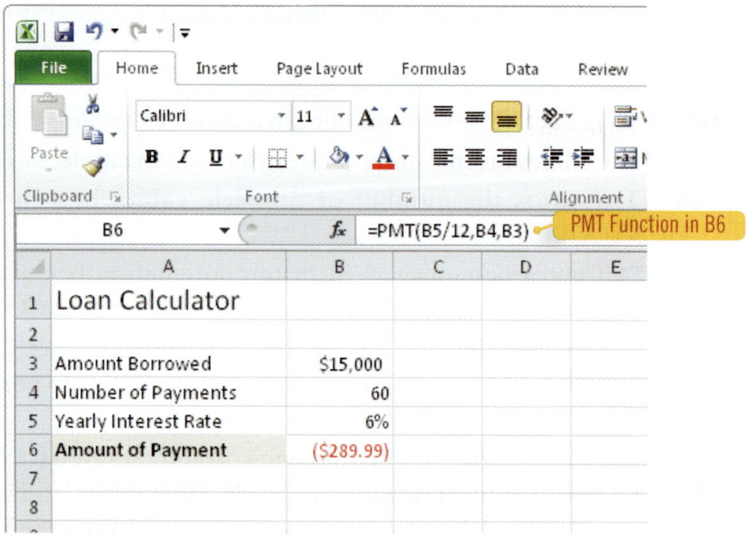

FIGURE 10-10 Set up a worksheet that calculates loan payments.

10.7 Exercise: Using a Financial Function

In this exercise, you will get some practice using the PV function. Follow these steps:

1. In 10Practice.xlsx, click the Sheet2 tab to move to a blank sheet.
2. Type the text and values shown in FIGURE 10-11. When entering the payment amount, just enter **–300** to indicate the negative value.
3. In B7, enter **=PV(B4/12,B3,B5)**.
4. The result in B7 shows as $15,151. Format the cell for zero decimal places, if needed.
5. In B3, change the number of payments to 45. The result in B7 shows as $11,843.
6. In B4, change the interest rate to 3%. The result in B7 shows as $12,753.
7. In B5, change the payment amount to –250. The result in B7 shows as $10,628.
8. Save your work.

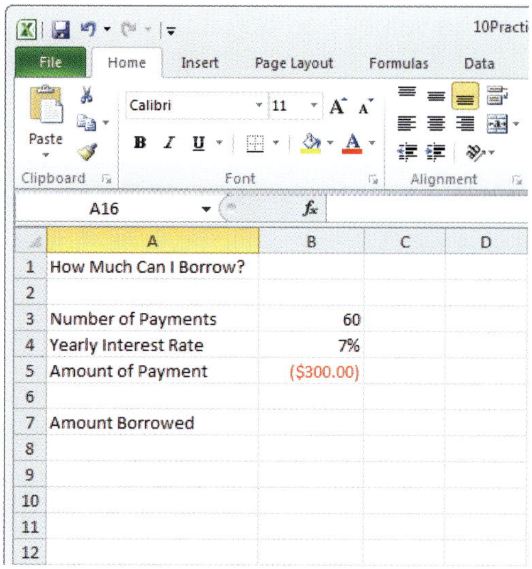

FIGURE 10-11 Type this text and these values to prepare for the exercise.

Using Logical Functions

Logical functions are those that use criteria (that is, conditions) to determine the outcome. You use logical conditions all the time in daily life, perhaps without realizing it.

> *"If I get home before 11:00 p.m., I will watch TV; otherwise I will go straight to bed."*
>
> *"If more than five members are present at the meeting, we will vote on the bylaws amendment; otherwise we won't."*

The IF function in Excel helps you set up logical conditions in your worksheets. The arguments for it are as follows:

=IF(condition,if_true,if_false)

So, for example, suppose that a worksheet has several columns of numbers. If the value in cell D7 is greater than 20, you want the word "Yes" to appear in cell E7; otherwise you want the word "No" to appear there. In E7, you would enter:

=IF(D7>20,"Yes","No")

You can also perform math operations based on the condition. For example, suppose that if D7 is greater than 20, you want the value of D7 to be multiplied by 1.2 and the result placed in D8. Otherwise D8 should show the original value from D7. In D8, you would enter:

=IF(D7>20,D7*1.2,D7)

WARNING

If you ever copy and paste a function that has quotation marks from a source that uses curly quotes rather than straight quotes, you'll need to delete and re-enter the quote marks in Excel. Excel doesn't recognize curly quotes.

10.8 Exercise: Using IF Functions

In this exercise, you will practice using the IF function by creating a worksheet that calculates bonuses for salespeople who achieve a certain level of sales performance. Follow these steps:

1. Click the Sheet3 tab in the 10Practice.xlsx workbook to get a blank worksheet.

2. Type and format the values and text shown in FIGURE 10-12.

	A	B	C	D
1	**Sales Performance**			
2	Target:	500		
3				
4	**Salesperson**	**Sales**	**Bonus**	
5	John Smith	450		
6	Harriet Jones	500		
7	Janet Black	510		
8				

FIGURE 10-12 Type this text and these values to prepare for the exercise.

3. In C5, enter **=IF(B5>=$B$2,B5*0.18, "None")**
4. Select C5 and use the fill handle to copy its function to C6:C7.
5. Format B5:C7 with the Currency number format.
6. Set the range B5:C7's horizontal alignment to Right. FIGURE 10-13 shows the finished worksheet.

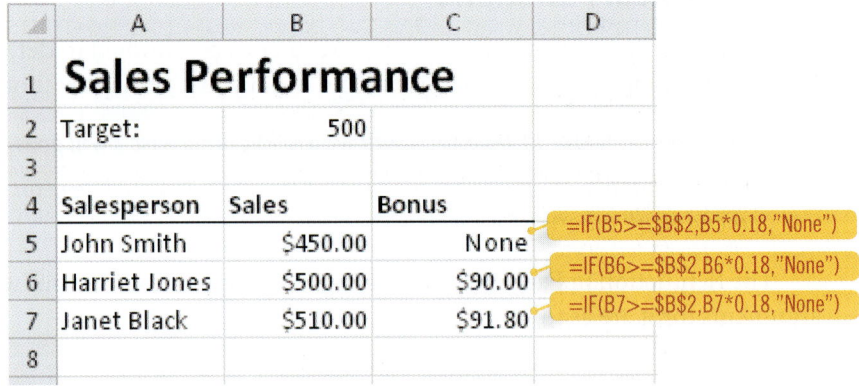

	A	B	C	D
1	**Sales Performance**			
2	Target:	500		
3				
4	**Salesperson**	**Sales**	**Bonus**	
5	John Smith	$450.00	None	
6	Harriet Jones	$500.00	$90.00	
7	Janet Black	$510.00	$91.80	
8				

=IF(B5>=$B$2,B5*0.18,"None")
=IF(B6>=$B$2,B6*0.18,"None")
=IF(B7>=$B$2,B7*0.18,"None")

FIGURE 10-13 The worksheet after completing the exercise.

Nesting Functions

Sometimes you might need to place one function inside another. For example, suppose you want to sum the range A1:A50, and then you want the absolute value of that result. You would nest the SUM function inside the ABS function, like this:

=ABS(SUM(A1:A50))

There's no trick to nesting functions, other than making sure you keep the parentheses straight. Notice, for example, that the above function ends in two parentheses. You do not need the equal sign before the **nested function**; the equal sign appears only once, at the beginning of the formula or function.

Conditional Formatting

Excel enables you to apply different formatting to a cell depending on what it contains. This is called **conditional formatting.** The Conditional Formatting feature in Excel is very robust, with many options; in this chapter you'll learn how to do a very basic conditional format.

To get started with conditional formatting, select a range of cells you want to apply it to, and then on the Home tab, click Conditional Formatting in the Styles group. A menu of conditional formatting types appears. Point the mouse at each of the items on this menu, and notice the formatting previews shown in the highlighted range as you move through the menu items. You can apply one of these presets if you like, and then customize what values it uses, or you can create your own conditions.

10.9 Exercise: Applying Conditional Formatting

In this exercise, you will gain practice applying conditional formatting using Excel's Conditional Formatting tools. Use Sheet3 of 10Practice.xlsx and follow these steps:

1. In rows 8 and 9, enter these additional salespeople:

   Betsy Wakeland 610
   Brooke Allan 501

2. Copy the function from C7 into C8:C9.
3. Select C5:C9, and on the Home tab, click Conditional Formatting.
4. On the menu that appears, point to Icon Sets, and then click the three flags. A green flag is applied to the highest value, and red flags are applied to the other values. No flag is applied to the cell that contains text. Widen column C, if needed, to display the content in all cells.
5. Click Conditional Formatting, Manage Rules. The Conditional Formatting Rules Manager dialog box opens.
6. Double-click the rule to open it in the Edit Formatting Rule dialog box.
7. In the Edit the Rule Description area, on the row with the green flag, open the Type drop-down list and select Number. Then in the Value text box for that row, type **100**.
8. On the line for the yellow flag, open the Type drop-down list and select Number. Leave the Value text box's default entry of 0. See FIGURE 10-14 to check your work so far.

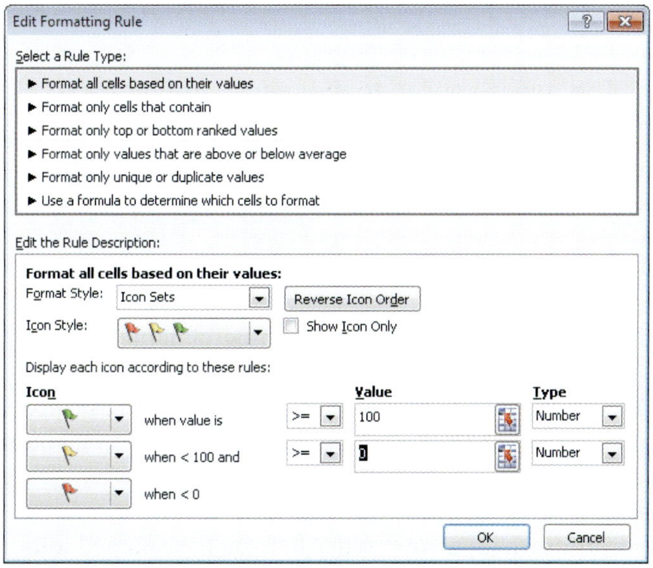

FIGURE 10-14 Specifying what each flag means.

9. Click OK to close the Edit Formatting Rule dialog box.
10. Click OK to close the Conditional Formatting Rules Manager dialog box. Cells C6, C7, and C9 all have yellow flags, and C8 has a green flag.
11. With C5:C9 still selected, on the Home tab, select Conditional Formatting, New Rule. The New Formatting Rule dialog box opens.
12. In the Select a Rule Type list, click Format Only Cells That Contain.
13. In the Edit the Rule Description area, open the second drop-down list (which shows "between") and click Equal To.
14. In the text box on the right, type **None**.
15. Click the Format button. The Format Cells dialog box opens.
16. On the Font tab, open the Color drop-down list to display the color palette. Click a bright red square, and then click OK. The New Formatting Rule dialog box should look like FIGURE 10-15 at this point.

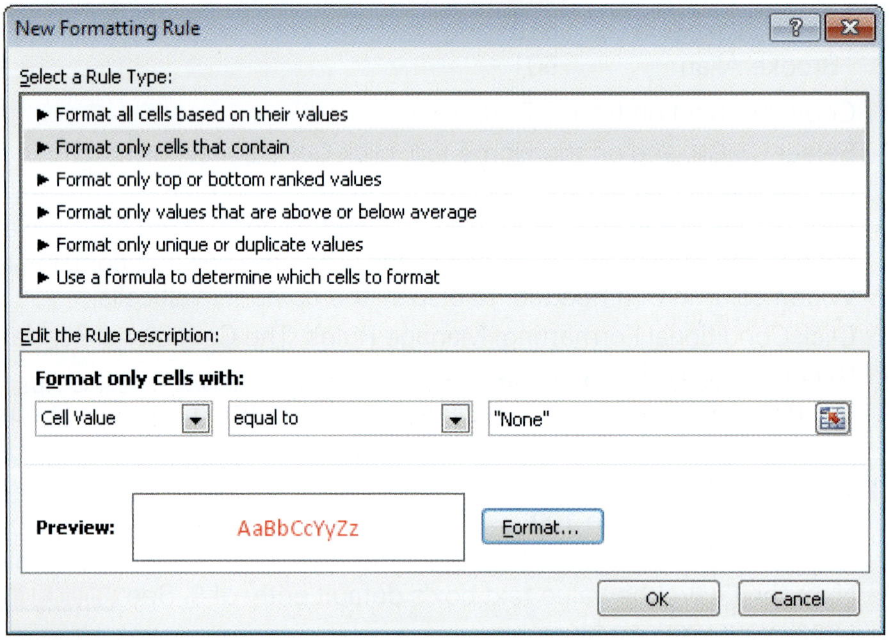

FIGURE 10-15 Create this new rule that makes the cell entry appear in red font when it is "None."

17. Click OK. The rule is applied to the range, and the word "None" in C5 appears in red.
18. Save your work.

Naming a Range

Naming a range enables you to use a more meaningful name in a formula or function than the bare-bones cell addresses. For example, in Figure 10-15, you could name the range B5:B9 Sales, and the range C5:C9 Bonus. You could then use those names anytime you would normally use the ranges. Instead of getting a sum of all bonuses paid using =SUM(C5:C9), you could use =SUM(Bonus).

You can also use **range names** to quickly jump to a certain range. Notice that the Name box has a drop-down list arrow on it. After you have named some ranges, clicking the arrow opens a menu of named ranges in the current workbook, and you can click one of the names there to jump to that range.

To name a range, select the range and then type the name in the Name box, replacing the cell address that appears there, as shown in FIGURE 10-16. Another way to name a range is to right-click the selected range, select Define Name, and then provide a name in the dialog box that appears.

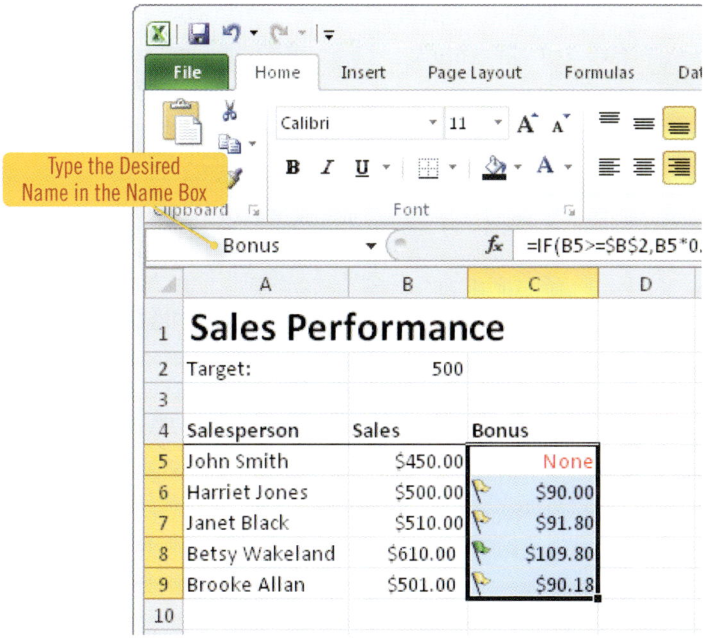

FIGURE 10-16 Range names appear in the Name box instead of a cell address.

To manage the names you create (edit, delete, and other commands), on the Formulas tab, click the Name Manager button and work in the Name Manager dialog box.

Creating Charts

A **chart** is a visual representation of data. Using charts, you can see what the data means and identify trends in it. For example, suppose you have a large worksheet that lists thousands of orders that customers have placed. You could create a pie chart that shows what percentage of total sales are made up from each product sold, and thereby determine your best-selling product and stock more of that item. Further, you could create a bar chart that showed the number of orders on each day of the week, to find out what your busiest sales day typically is, so you could have extra employees working on that day.

To create a chart, enter the data in the worksheet, and select the range you want to chart. Include any text labels that should be part of the chart, too. Then, on the Insert tab, click the button that best represents the type of chart you would like. A menu opens, as shown in FIGURE 10-17. Click the sub-type that matches best—3-D Clustered Column, in this example—and the chart appears. It's as easy as that!

Parts of a Chart

Familiarize yourself with the parts of the chart shown in FIGURE 10-18. It's useful to know the proper names for the parts of the chart because Excel refers to those names in the dialog boxes used to customize the chart. Not all of the parts shown in Figure 10-18 are shown on every default chart—this chart was formatted for presentation purposes. In the next section, you'll learn how to display and hide the optional components, such as the chart title, data labels, and data table.

The main parts of a chart are:

- **Chart area:** The entire chart, including all the parts listed in Figure 8-18.
- **Plot area:** The background directly behind the bars, lines, or other data markers

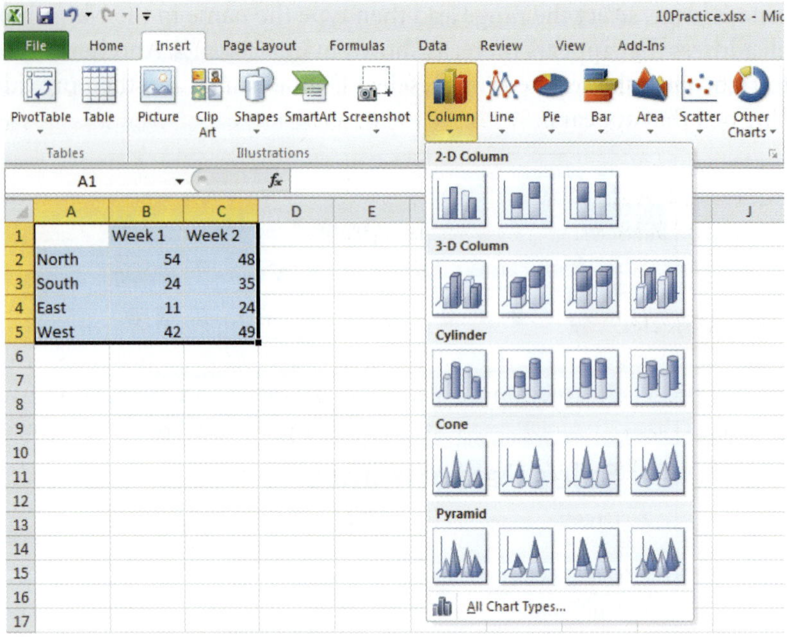

FIGURE 10-17 Choosing a chart type to create from the selected data.

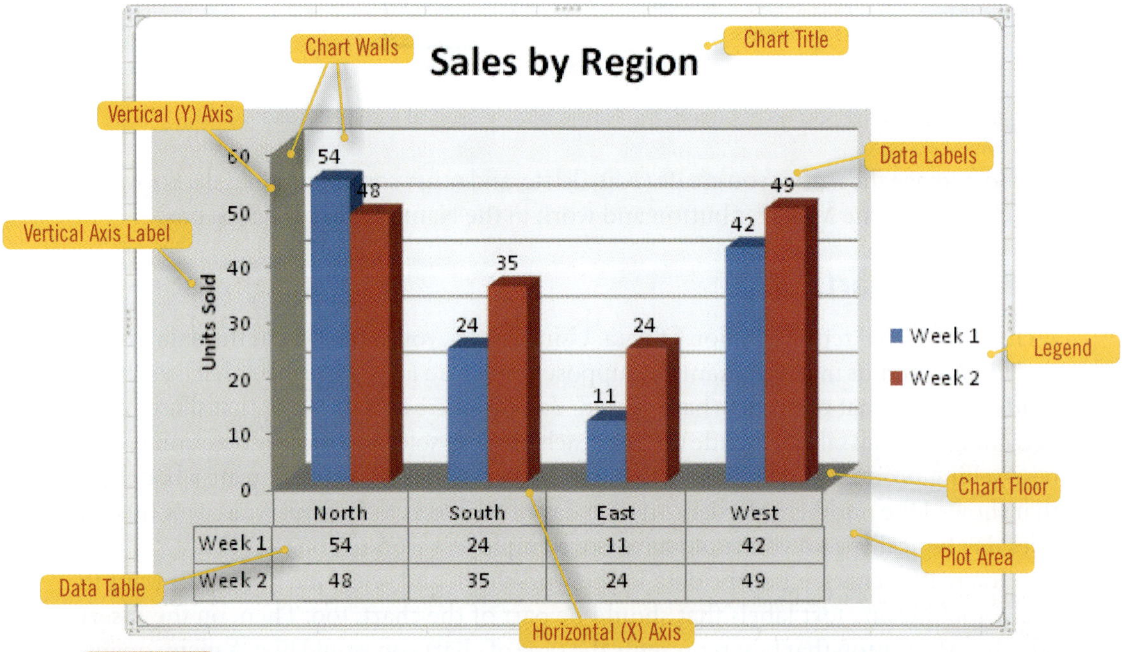

FIGURE 10-18 The parts of a chart.

in the chart, and behind the data table if present. In Figure 10-18, it is shaded for your benefit, but it is usually transparent, so it blends right into the background of the chart area.

- **Chart title:** An optional text label that appears above the chart.
- **Vertical and horizontal axes:** The axes on which the data is plotted.
- **Axis label:** A label that describes the unit of measurement of one of the axes.
- **Legend:** A color-coded key that tells what each bar color represents in a chart that contains multiple data series.
- **Data table:** An optional grid that appears below the chart, containing the original data on which the chart was constructed.

- **Data labels:** Optional labels that appear on each data point, providing the exact number being plotted.
- **Data series:** All the bars of a single color (in a multi-series chart). In Figure 10-18, there are two series. A pie chart can have only a single data series; most other chart types can have multiple series.
- **Data point:** A single bar, point, or pie slice, representing a single numeric value. In Figure 10-18, each data point is represented by a bar.

Showing and Hiding Optional Parts of a Chart

When a chart is selected, the Layout tab becomes available. On the Layout tab is a series of buttons that open drop-down lists for the optional parts of the chart. **FIGURE 10-19** shows the options for the legend, for example. Click one of these buttons and then choose an option that turns that part on or off. For most parts you can also click a More command at the bottom of the menu that opens a dialog box where you can fine-tune its settings.

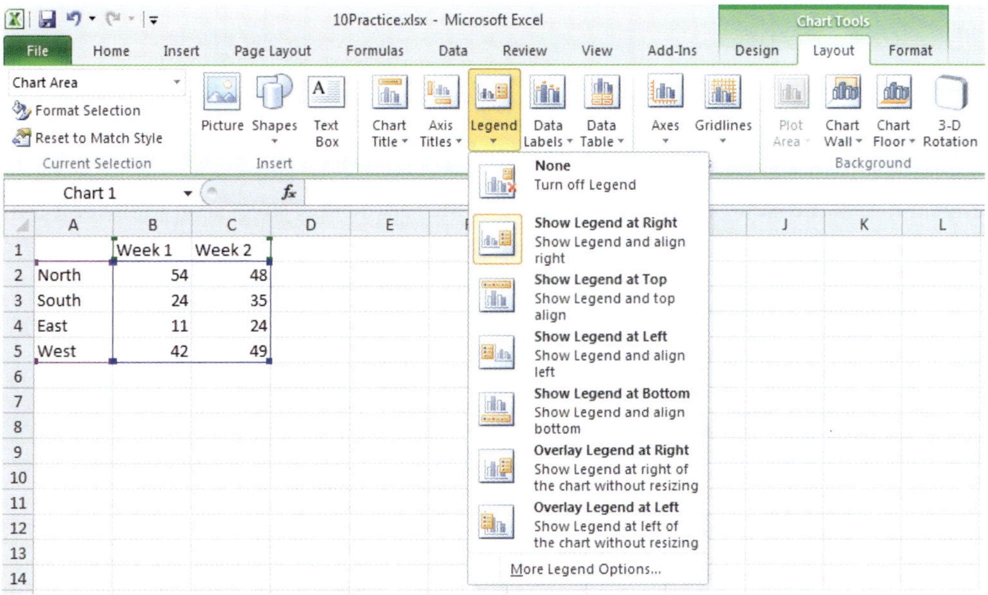

FIGURE 10-19 Show or hide parts of a chart from the Layout tab.

Formatting Parts of a Chart

Nearly every part of a chart can be customized. You can apply different fill and outline colors to it; you can place it in different locations; and, if it contains text, you can adjust the font, size, and color of that text.

To customize a part of a chart, right-click that part and select the Format command from the bottom of the shortcut menu. The exact name of the command depends on what you right-clicked. For example, if you right-clicked the plot area, it's Format Plot Area. Then, in the dialog box that appears, apply any formatting you like. In **FIGURE 10-20**, for example, the screen shot shows how you'd change the color of the plot area.

Moving and Resizing a Chart

By default a chart is a floating object on the same sheet as the data it is constructed from. You can drag the chart around by its border, and resize it by dragging one of the border edges.

You can also place a chart on its own separate tab in the workbook. To do so, right-click the chart's frame border and select Move Chart. In the Move Chart dialog box that

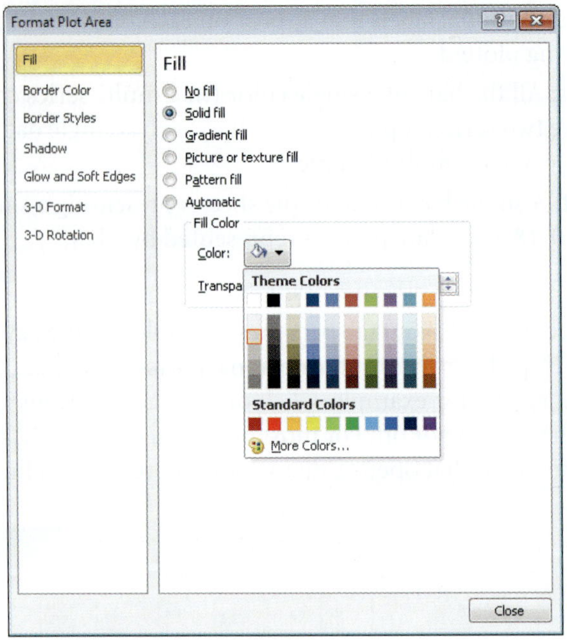

FIGURE 10-20 Format specific pieces of a chart by right-clicking them and choosing Format.

appears, click the New Sheet option. Type a name for the new sheet's tab in the adjacent text box, as shown in FIGURE 10-21. Click OK.

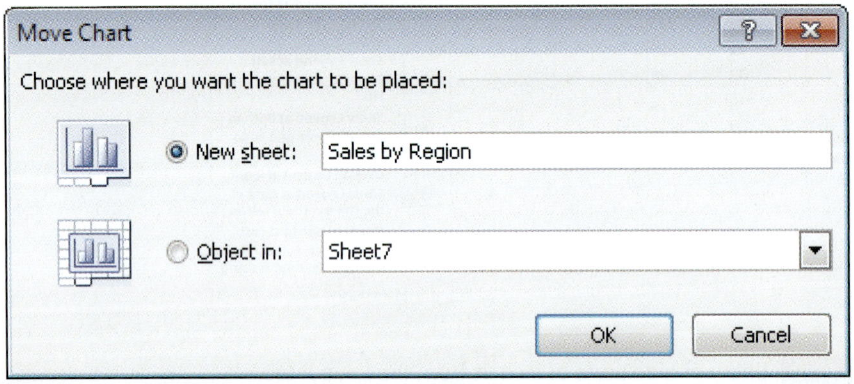

FIGURE 10-21 You can move a chart to its own sheet if you like.

10.10 Exercise: Creating and Formatting a Chart

Now let's practice creating and formatting a chart. Start on Sheet3 of 10Practice.xlsx, which you created earlier in the chapter. It's the worksheet that shows the sales performance of five salespeople, shown in FIGURE 10-22. Re-create this worksheet if you need to. Then complete the following steps:

1. Select A4:B9.
2. On the Insert tab, click the Pie button, and click the first sample in the 3-D Pie section. A pie chart appears on the worksheet.
3. Right-click the border of the pie chart and click Move Chart. Click New Sheet, and type Pie Chart for the sheet name. Click OK. A new sheet appears that contains the pie chart.
4. Click back to Sheet3, and select A4:B9 if it's not still selected.

	A	B	C
1	**Sales Performance**		
2	Target:	500	
3			
4	Salesperson	Sales	Bonus
5	John Smith	$450.00	None
6	Harriet Jones	$500.00	$90.00
7	Janet Black	$510.00	$91.80
8	Betsy Wakeland	$610.00	$109.80
9	Brooke Allan	$501.00	$90.18
10			

FIGURE 10-22 Start with this worksheet, from the previous exercise.

5. On the Insert tab, click Column, and then click the first sample in the Cylinder section. A bar chart appears on the worksheet, with cylindrical bars.
6. On the Chart Tools Layout tab, click Legend, and click None. (You do not need a legend because the chart consists of a single data series.)
7. Click Data Labels, and click Show.
8. Click Axis Titles, Primary Vertical Axis Title, Rotated Title.
9. Triple-click in the placeholder that appears on the vertical axis, to select all the text in it. Type **Gross Sales**.
10. Click any of the cylinders. All the cylinders become selected.
11. Right-click a cylinder and choose Format Data Series.
12. Click Shape, and then click the Box option.
13. Click Fill, and then click Solid Fill. Open the color palette and choose any color you like.
14. Click Close to close the dialog box.
15. Click the border of the chart frame. On the Chart Tools Design tab, click Change Chart Type. A dialog box opens.
16. Click the first sample in the Area section and click OK.
17. Save your work and close 10Practice.xlsx.

That's it for Excel, at least in this book. There is much more to learn about formulas, functions, and charts though, so spend some time practicing on your own or taking more advanced courses if you need to expand your skills. The next chapter focuses on Microsoft Office PowerPoint 2010. Before you move on, test your knowledge of Excel by going through the questions in the Test Yourself section, and be sure to complete the End-of-Chapter Project.

Test Yourself

The questions in this section are meant to test your knowledge of what you read. Make sure you answer them. The page number where the answer can be found appears after each question.

1. Which of these is an example of a correctly written formula? (230)
   - **A.** B10=B11
   - **B.** =B10+B11

C. B10+B11=
D. =B10:B11

2. Which of these is an example of a correctly written function? (234)
   A. =SUM(B10:B11)
   B. SUM(B10)(B11)
   C. =SUM( )
   D. SUM=B10+B11
3. What would be the result of this formula: =3+2*6/(1+1)? (231)
   A. 21
   B. 15
   C. 7.5
   D. 9
4. When you copy a formula and the cell references in it change, that's an example of _____ referencing. (232)
5. What symbol do you place before the column letter and row number in a formula to create an absolute reference? _______ (232)
6. What is a mixed reference? (233)
   A. A range that consists of more than one cell
   B. A cell reference where the row is absolute and the column is relative, or vice versa
   C. A function that references non-contiguous cells
   D. A cell reference where the row number comes before the column letter, like this: 1A
7. Function ____ are placed in parentheses after the function name. (234)
8. If a function has more than one argument, how are they separated? (234)
   A. Periods
   B. Semicolons
   C. Commas
   D. Exclamation points
9. What does the COUNTA function do? (237)
   A. Counts the number of numeric values in a range
   B. Counts the number of cells that are not empty in the range
   C. Counts the number of cells containing text in the range
   D. Counts the number of cells in the range, regardless of content
10. What does the PV function calculate? (237)
    A. Number of periods in a loan
    B. Starting amount owed on a loan
    C. Interest rate
    D. Monthly payment
11. If you wanted to determine how many months it would take to pay off a loan, which function would you use? (237)
    A. RATE
    B. PMT
    C. NPER
    D. PV
12. In the IF function =IF(B6=0, "Yes", "No"), what will the result be if the value in B6 is 2? (239)
    A. Yes
    B. No
    C. Error message
    D. Nothing (empty cell)

13. Which of these is an example of a nested function? (240)
A. =IF(A1=2,25,6)
B. =IF(A1=2,SUM(B2:B6),0)
C. ABS(B5)
D. =COUNT(B5:B12)

14. When a cell's text appears in a different color when its value is within a certain range, that's an example of ____. (240–242)

15. One benefit of naming a range is being able to jump to that range quickly by selecting it from the Name box's drop-down list. (242)
A. True
B. False

16. How do you access the dialog box where you can change the color of a bar or column on a chart? (247)
A. Right-click the bar or column and click Format Data Series.
B. On the Layout tab, click Color.
C. Right-click the bar and click Select Data.
D. On the Shape tab, click Fill.

17. A ____ is a color-coded key that tells what each bar color represents in a chart that contains multiple data series. (244)

18. A chart can be on its own separate tab in a workbook. (245)
A. True
B. False

19. A ____ is an optional grid that appears below a chart, showing the original data on which the chart was based. (244)

20. From which tab would you access the Name Manager, for managing range names? (243)
A. Formulas
B. Insert
C. Edit
D. View

End-of-Chapter Project

Using the workbook you created in the Chapter 9 project, named PC Basics Research.xlsx, determine the average cost of the laptops you researched. Do the same for the printers and Internet service provider plans. Create a column chart for the actual costs of the laptops. Create two additional column charts for the costs of the printers and Internet service providers.

Challenge Project

This project is optional but is provided if you want additional practice with Excel 2010. In this project you will set up a worksheet that calculates home loan payments based on different criteria. Perform the following steps:

1. Open Excel and create the worksheet shown in **FIGURE 10-23**. Apply shading to B6:D6 and B10:D11. Those are the cells where you will be creating formulas and functions.
2. In B6, enter a formula that calculates the down payment amount (B2 times B5). Don't forget to use an absolute reference to B2 so you can copy the formula.
3. Copy the formula from B6 to C6:D6.
4. In B10, enter a formula that sums the values in B6 and B7.

	A	B	C	D
1	Loan Comparison			
2	Purchase Price	$200,000		
3				
4		Loan 1	Loan 2	Loan 3
5	Down Payment %	5%	10%	7%
6	Down Payment Amount			
7	Closing Costs	$2,000	$1,000	$2,000
8	Interest Rate	5.25%	6.00%	6.00%
9	Loan Term (in Years)	30	30	15
10	Total Due at Closing			
11	Monthly Payment			

FIGURE 10-23 Start with this worksheet.

5. Copy the formula to C10:D10.
6. In B11, use the PMT function to determine the monthly payment for the loan. Some tips:
   - Use an absolute reference whenever referring to cell B2.
   - Divide the yearly interest rate by 12 because you are dealing with monthly payments.
   - Multiply the loan term by 12 for the same reason.
   - For the present value (PV) argument, subtract the down payment amount from the loan amount.
   - Hint: Here's the formula to use: =PMT(B8/12,B9*12,$B$2–B6)
7. Copy the formula to C11:D11.
8. Save your work as 10Exercise, and close Excel.

PART

VI

Essentials of PowerPoint Presentations

CHAPTER

11

Microsoft PowerPoint 2010

- Multimedia software allows you to create sophisticated presentations that help an audience understand information easily. This chapter explains how to use Microsoft PowerPoint 2010, a presentation software program that lets you easily combine text, charts, animations, video, and photos. Here are some basic things you should know about PowerPoint 2010:
  - It is part of the Microsoft Office 2010 suite and runs on Microsoft Windows operating systems. A separate edition is available for Mac OS X.
  - It helps you communicate more effectively through the use of pictures or graphics alongside text. This combination is more memorable and persuasive than text alone. PowerPoint 2010 offers a variety of built-in clip art, photos, tables, charts, and graphs to help you develop your information in a visual format.
  - You create a presentation by creating individual slides that zero in on important points. A slide can stand alone, focusing on a single topic, or you can discuss a topic across many slides in a presentation.
  - Once you have completed these slides, you can present them as a slide show in person, over the Internet, or via e-mail for your audience to view at their own pace.
- In this chapter, you will explore the basics of PowerPoint 2010. You will learn how to open, create, save, and print files, how to work with the Ribbon, how to apply graphics and animations, and how to work with Microsoft's themes and color schemes.

CHAPTER TOPICS

This chapter covers the following topics and concepts:

- What PowerPoint is
- How to open the program
- How to use the PowerPoint Ribbon, menus, and toolbars
- How to change PowerPoint views
- How to create a presentation
- How to add text to a slide
- How to add photos and clip art to a slide
- How to use shapes in presentation slides
- How to save a PowerPoint file
- How to apply themes
- How to use color schemes
- Why transitions are valuable to presentations and how to add them
- How to open a file
- How to print a file
- How to create a master slide

KEY WORDS

- Background
- Backstage view
- Color scheme
- File tab
- Layout
- Notes Page view
- Presentation theme
- Reading view
- Slide
- Slide master
- Slide Navigator pane
- Slide pane
- Slide Sorter view
- Transitions

TIP

PowerPoint 2010 files can easily be opened in versions of PowerPoint prior to PowerPoint 2010.

What Is PowerPoint 2010?

PowerPoint 2010 is the latest presentation software from Microsoft. It has been improved and updated from previous versions to make it as easy as possible for you to build presentations and communicate quickly and easily with others. It is part of the Office 2010 suite. PowerPoint 2010 is the presentation program you are learning in this book.

When you work in PowerPoint, you are working on a **slide**. Each slide lets you include photos, text, clip art, charts, graphs, and/or video. You can format the slide in any way you like. Graphics can be animated to add movement to each slide, and you can create transitions between slides to help your audience move easily from topic to topic.

If you've used previous versions of PowerPoint, there are a variety of new features in PowerPoint 2010. Perhaps the most important is the inclusion of a new tab: the **File tab**. This tab replaces the Microsoft Office Button, which previously housed commands such as Save, Open, and Exit. The File tab, shown in FIGURE 11-1, now houses those and similar commands. This tab is also referred to as the **Backstage view**.

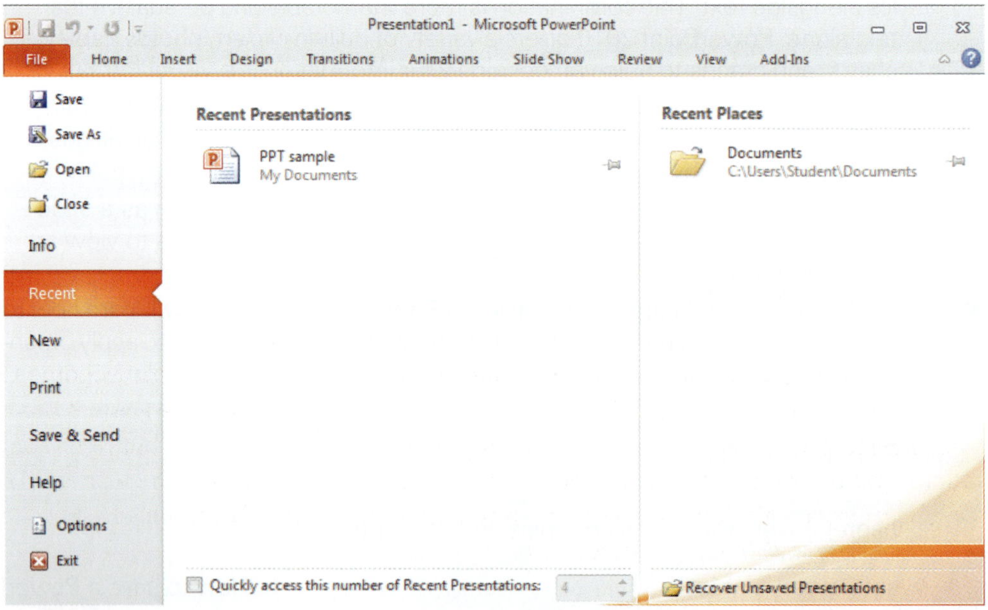

FIGURE 11-1 The File tab, also known as the Backstage view.

When you click the File tab, it opens automatically to information about your presentation, including permissions and properties. Just select a different option—Save, for example—to move to a different command and perform another function. This tab gives you a centralized, organized place to manage all your presentation tasks.

Additional new features in PowerPoint 2010 include:

- The ability to embed and edit video
- New features for cropping photos
- Sophisticated artistic effects that can be applied to photos
- A broadcast capability so you can present your presentation on the Web in real time
- Additional SmartArt layouts
- Easier management and organization of slides
- More dynamic slide transitions and animation effects
- Completely separate windows for each open presentation

Opening Microsoft PowerPoint

You can open Microsoft PowerPoint 2010 much like any other Office 2010 program. Just click the Start button, and then select All Programs > Microsoft Office > Microsoft PowerPoint 2010. The main window appears, as shown in FIGURE 11-2.

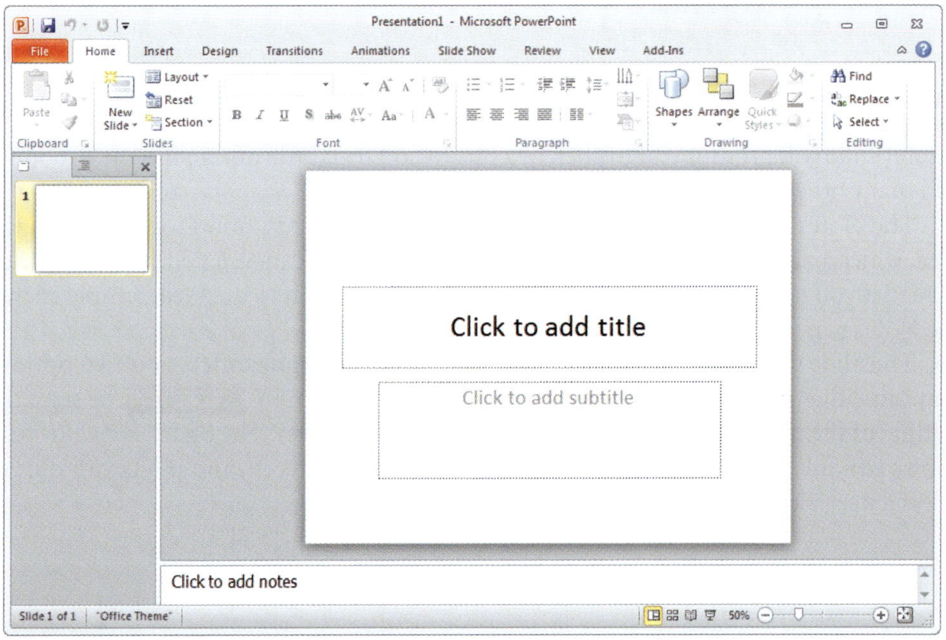

FIGURE 11-2 The main PowerPoint window.

If you plan to use PowerPoint 2010 often, you can pin it to the top portion of your Start menu for one-click access. Simply perform the initial steps for opening PowerPoint—click the Start button, and then select All Programs > Microsoft Office—but right-click Microsoft PowerPoint 2010 and select Pin to Start Menu. After you use the software for a while, any presentations you worked on will appear in a jump list when you point to Microsoft Office 2010 on the Start menu.

The PowerPoint Window

When PowerPoint starts, it automatically opens to a blank presentation window. In this window are three key areas: the Slide pane, the Notes pane, and the Slides tab or Slide Navigator pane. See FIGURE 11-3.

The **Slide pane** is where you will perform most of your work on a presentation. It's the largest part of the window and contains the actual slide that you are working on. The

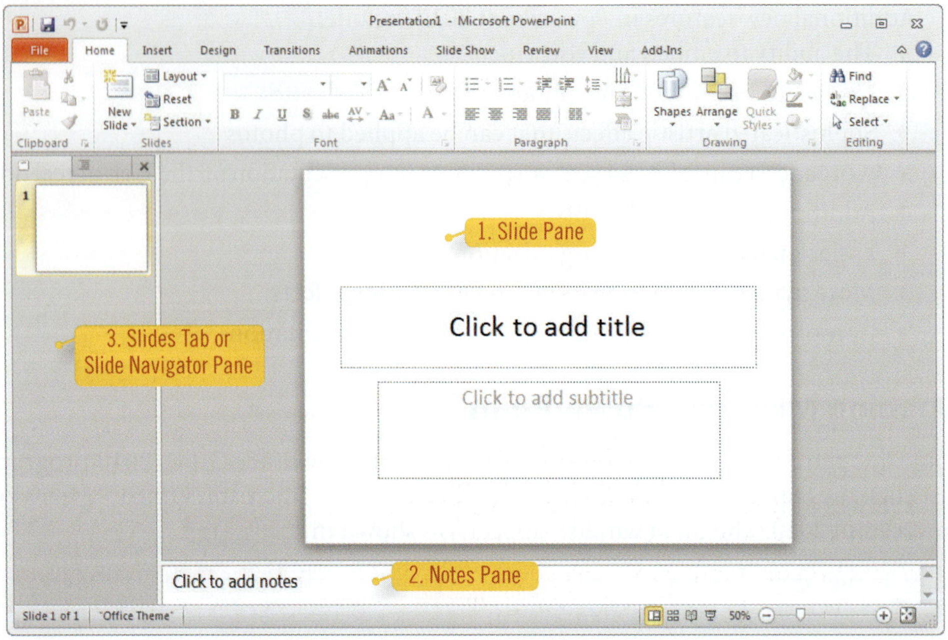

FIGURE 11-3 The (1) Slide pane, (2) Notes pane, and (3) Slides tab or Slide Navigator pane.

default slide will prompt you to click in a box to add text, but you can use the Ribbon to add many other types of content.

The Notes pane is directly below the Slide pane. You add notes to yourself in this area, which help you deliver a presentation in person. You can also add notes for others to read if you distribute the presentation via e-mail or post it to the Web. Simply click in the Notes pane and start typing to add comments.

The Slide tab, also referred to as the **Slide Navigator pane**, offers you two options: You can either see multiple slides at once (Slides), as shown in FIGURE 11-4, or see a text outline of the presentation, as shown in FIGURE 11-5 (Outline). The Slide Navigator pane shows you the flow of how your presentation will be delivered, and it lets you quickly select a new slide to work on.

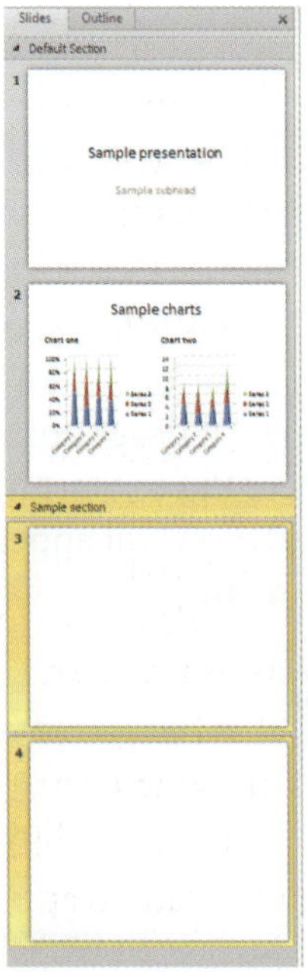

FIGURE 11-4 The Slide Navigator pane, Slides view.

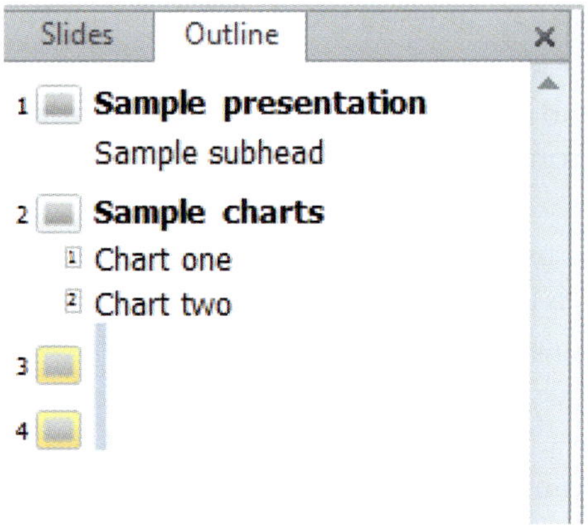

FIGURE 11-5 The Slide Navigator pane, Outline view.

You can easily resize the pane by grabbing and pulling the right border. A new organizational feature in PowerPoint 2010 is the ability to split this pane into sections, such as Introduction or Summary, when using Slides view. This feature can help you find and manage your slides more effectively. You will learn about creating sections a bit later in the chapter.

The Ribbon

The tabbed navigational structure across the top of the window is the Ribbon, shown in **FIGURE 11-6**. It is very similar to the Ribbon in other Office 2010 programs. You can easily access tools and commands—they're displayed in the order in which most people typically perform tasks.

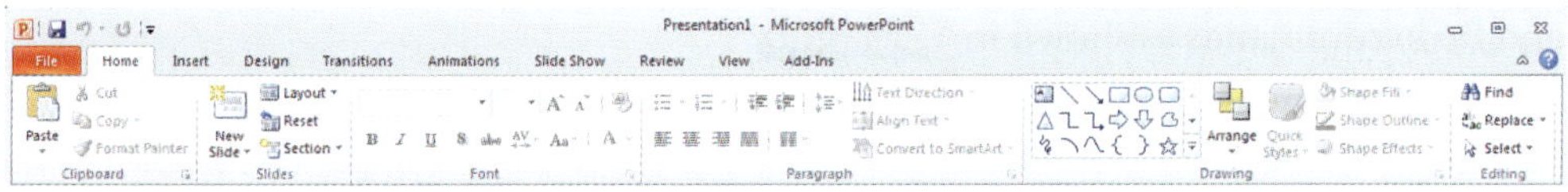

FIGURE 11-6 The PowerPoint Ribbon.

Each tab within the Ribbon is a group that holds the commands you need. The Home tab, for example, contains six command groups: Clipboard, Slides, Font, Paragraph, Drawing, and Editing. Inside each command group are various commands you can select.

As mentioned in previous chapters, command groups are contextual: They are displayed only within the context of the work you are doing within the presentation itself. That means if you're working on text and have a text box selected, the Font group shows commands available to work on a text box. If, however, you have not selected a text box and try to access a command in the Font group, PowerPoint will not allow access.

Tabs

There are 10 primary tabs to know on the Ribbon:

- The File tab holds file management tools and options.
- The Home tab includes tools for drawing shapes and editing, cutting, copying, or pasting your text and graphics. It also includes font and paragraph tools to help you design text and add bullets or numbers.
- The Insert tab lets you add tables, images, and illustrations to your slide. You can also use this tab to add symbols, video, audio, hyperlinks, text boxes, WordArt, date and time, slide numbers, and other objects.
- The Design tab is used when you want to apply a theme or a background to your presentation. You can also adjust page setups using this tab.
- The Transitions tab allows you to create customized transitions between your slides.

> **TIP**
>
> Sometimes you will see additional tabs on the Ribbon. These tabs open when certain items are selected on a slide. For example, if you select a photo, the Picture Tools Format tab appears. These tabs are designed to provide you with additional editing and design tools. However, because you require those tools only when you're working with certain items, PowerPoint hides them until you need them.

- The Animations tab includes all the tools you need to make objects on your slides move, including a gallery of entrance, emphasis, exit, and motion path effects.
- The Slide Show tab lets you see and rehearse your slide show. You can also broadcast your show from here, create a custom slide show, or use the Presenter View from this tab.
- The Review tab is used when you need to perform proofing tasks, such as checking spelling. This is also where you can add comments to a presentation, translate text, and set language preferences.
- The View tab allows you to see several different views of your presentation, along with master views. You can also show the ruler, gridlines and guides from here, zoom in and out on your slide, change the color of your presentation to grayscale or black and white, and arrange your windows.
- The Add-Ins tab appears only when you have added a plug-in to PowerPoint 2010. Plug-ins are separate programs that work directly within PowerPoint to provide added tools and features.

The Quick Access Toolbar

FIGURE 11-7 The Quick Access toolbar.

Above the Ribbon is a small toolbar called the Quick Access toolbar. This toolbar holds commands that you use often. You can customize it to include a variety of commands depending on your needs. For example, if you frequently check spelling in your slides, you can add the Spelling command to this toolbar. Then, instead of going into the Ribbon to find the spell-check command, you simply click the Spelling command on the Quick Access toolbar. By default, the toolbar includes the Save, Undo and Redo commands as shown in FIGURE 11-7.

> **TIP**
>
> To remove a command from the Quick Access toolbar, right-click the command, and then select Remove From Quick Access Toolbar.

Adding commands to the Quick Access toolbar is easy. Follow these steps to add the Spelling command:

1. Click the down arrow on the Quick Access toolbar.
2. Select Spelling from the menu that appears, as shown in FIGURE 11-8.

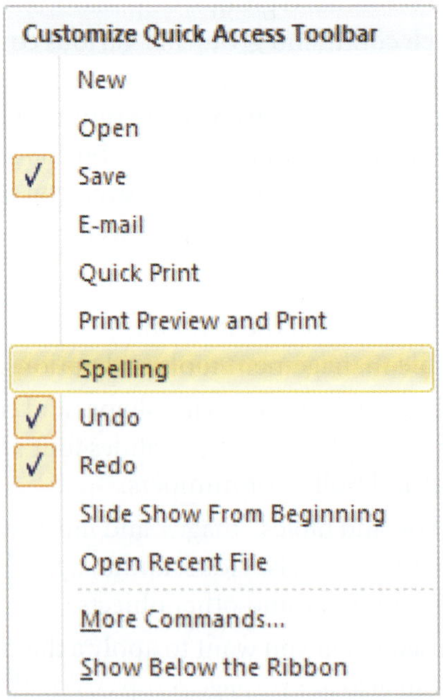

FIGURE 11-8 Quick Access toolbar menu.

The Spelling command now appears in the Quick Access toolbar (see FIGURE 11-9). To use the Spelling command, just click its button.

FIGURE 11-9 Spelling command added to Quick Access toolbar.

The Mini Toolbar

There's a second toolbar designed to help you find commands quickly and easily: the Mini toolbar. It's a modified, small version of the Home tab that appears when you double-click on text in your presentation. As you double-click, it will first appear faintly in the background. Move your mouse pointer over it, however, and it becomes a clear, bright toolbar near the selected text, as shown in FIGURE 11-10. To use the toolbar, just select the tool that you want to apply.

> **TIP**
>
> To apply multiple formatting features to your text using the Mini toolbar, you need to reselect the text each time before choosing a different tool.

FIGURE 11-10 The Mini toolbar.

Getting Help

The Help features in PowerPoint 2010 are fairly extensive. You can find Help by clicking the blue question mark in the upper-right corner of the PowerPoint window or by pressing F1 on your keyboard. Either will open PowerPoint Help and How-to, shown in FIGURE 11-11.

Click on a topic to open more Help topics or use the search box at the top of the window if you don't see exactly what you're looking for.

FIGURE 11-11 The Help feature in PowerPoint 2010.

Changing Presentation Views

Up to this point, we have been using the Normal presentation view to show you how things work in PowerPoint 2010. That's the default view that appears when you open any new presentation. There are three other views you can use, as shown in FIGURE 11-12. Let's take a quick look at each one.

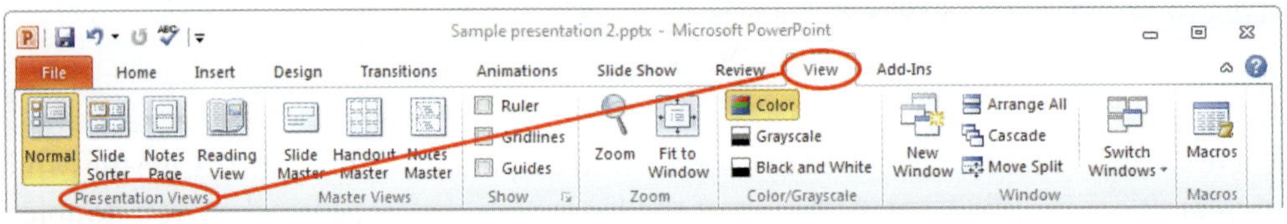

FIGURE 11-12 Presentation views.

- The **Normal view** allows you to work on a slide using the Slide pane, the Slide Navigator pane, and the Notes pane discussed earlier in this chapter.
- In the **Slide Sorter view**, your slides are shown as mini-slides within the PowerPoint window. You can use this view to see whether slides are in the right places; if not, you can grab and move slides to where you want them. You can also add sections to your presentation using this view.
- The **Notes Page view** lets you add notes to your slides. Each notes page includes a thumbnail of the slide, along with notes you enter. Notes pages can also be printed as handouts; each slide prints its own notes page.
- The **Reading view** is typically used when you are delivering your presentation to someone who is viewing the slides on his or her own computer. This view lets you see your presentation in a window with simple controls.

TIP

In Slide Sorter view, you might have to scroll down to see all your slides if you have quite a few. You can also use the Zoom slider bar at the bottom right of your window to zoom in and out. Notice that next to the Zoom toolbar is a tiny toolbar that allows you to click quickly through the available views, too.

You can change presentation views by following these steps:

1. Click the View tab.
2. In the Presentation Views group, click Slide Sorter.
3. In the Presentation Views group, click Notes Page.
4. In the Presentation Views group, click Reading View.
5. Click on the screen until it says End of Slide Show, and then click again to exit.

Creating a New Presentation

Earlier in this chapter, you learned how to open PowerPoint 2010. You also learned that when you open the program, it automatically opens to a new presentation. If you are already working on one presentation, however, you might want to create another new presentation. To do that, follow these steps:

1. Click the File tab.
2. In the menu on the left, click New.
3. Click Blank Presentation as shown in FIGURE 11-13.
4. In the pane on the right, click Create.

Selecting a Layout

One thing you'll do often is select a layout for your slides. A **layout** is the way the items on your slide are arranged, such as the text, photo, or a chart. Click Home, Layout to open the Layout gallery. There are nine options, as shown in FIGURE 11-14.

The layout you choose will depend on the information you're sharing: You might need a title slide to open your presentation, a slide where you can compare details side

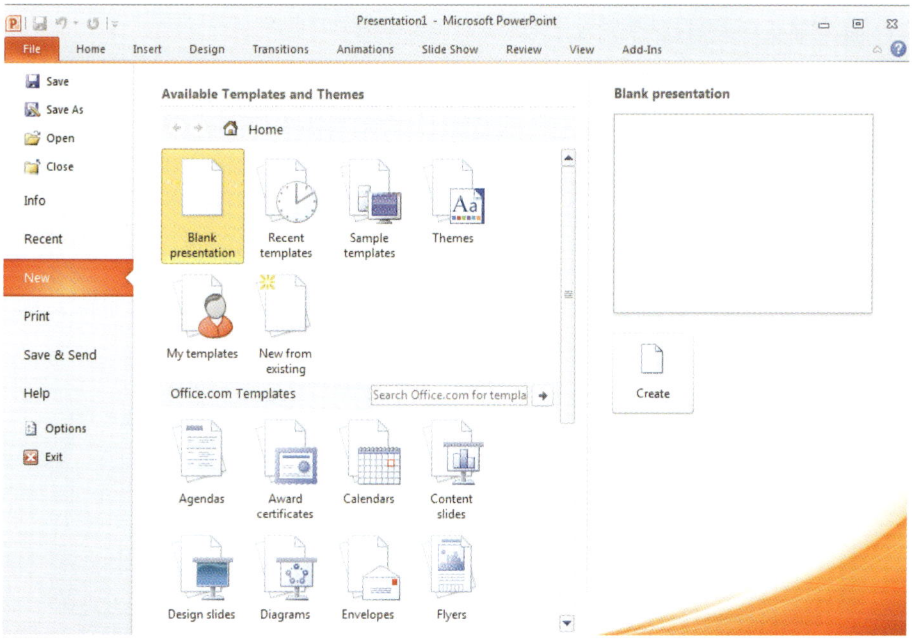

FIGURE 11-13 Creating a new presentation.

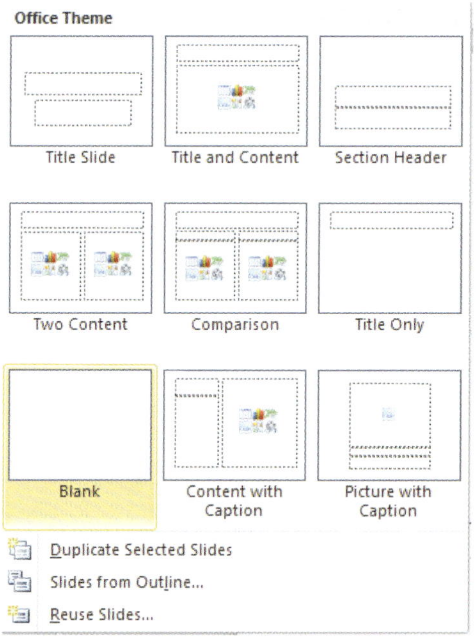

FIGURE 11-14 The Layout gallery.

by side, or perhaps just a blank slide to design in any way you want. **FIGURE 11-15** shows a slide created based on the Comparison layout.

There are three ways you can choose a layout. You can create your own, you can select a layout when you first insert a slide into the presentation, or you can change the current layout of a slide to a new layout.

Inserting Additional Slides

Most finished presentations include multiple slides. Inserting additional slides into your presentation is very simple. Follow these steps to insert a new blank slide:

1. Click the Home tab on the Ribbon.
2. In the Slides group, click New Slide.

TIP

In the center pane, under Available Templates and Themes, you have the option of creating a new presentation from a blank slate, templates, themes, or an existing presentation. A template is essentially a prebuilt presentation to which you add your own content. A theme provides a consistent look and feel across an entire presentation, even one that's already created. You'll learn about themes later in the chapter.

TIP

Just because you use a predefined layout doesn't mean you can't change it. It's often easier to start with one of PowerPoint's layout options and move things around to suit your needs than it is to start from scratch building your own layout.

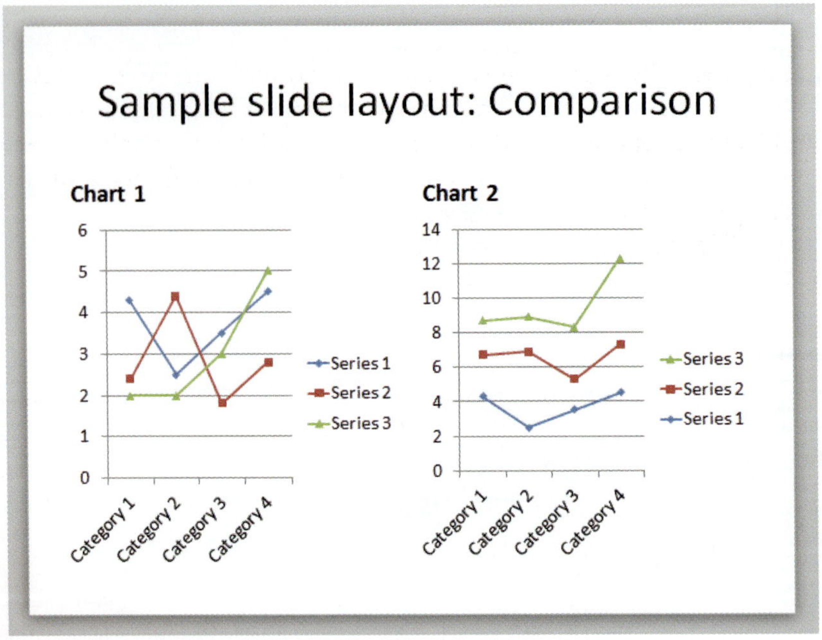

FIGURE 11-15 A sample slide layout: Comparison.

3. In the gallery, click Blank.

PowerPoint inserts the new blank slide and displays it in the Slide Navigator pane.

Creating Sections for Slides

Sections are a new feature in PowerPoint 2010. If you have many slides in a presentation and want to group the slides by major topic, for example, you can use sections to organize the slides.

Follow these steps to create a section:

1. In the Slide Navigator pane, right-click the blank slide.
2. Click Add Section in the menu. An Untitled Section bar appears above the slide in the Slide Navigator pane.
3. Right-click Untitled Section, and then click Rename Section as shown in **FIGURE 11-16**.

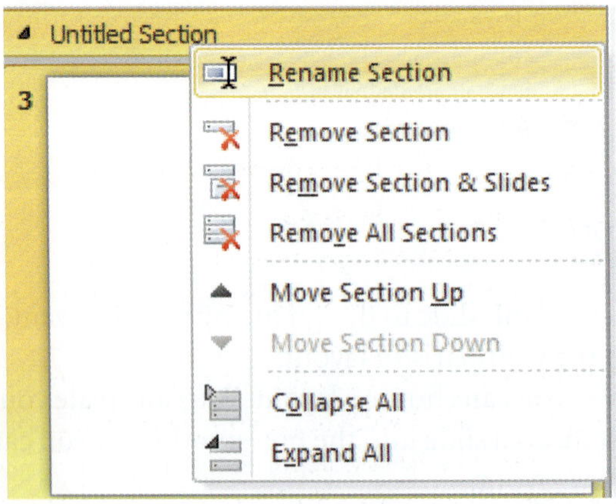

FIGURE 11-16 Rename section.

4. In the Rename Section dialog box, under Section Name, type a name for the section, such as **Sample Section**.
5. Click Rename.

Entering Text on a Slide

Now we'll begin actually adding information to the PowerPoint slides. Text is generally added into text boxes, which you can format and move around. Text boxes enable you to control the placement of your text. Most default PowerPoint slide templates that you saw in the Layout gallery have text boxes set up for you. The blank slide does not.

To add a text box to a slide, follow these steps:

1. On the Ribbon, click the Insert tab.
2. In the Text group, click Text Box as shown in FIGURE 11-17.

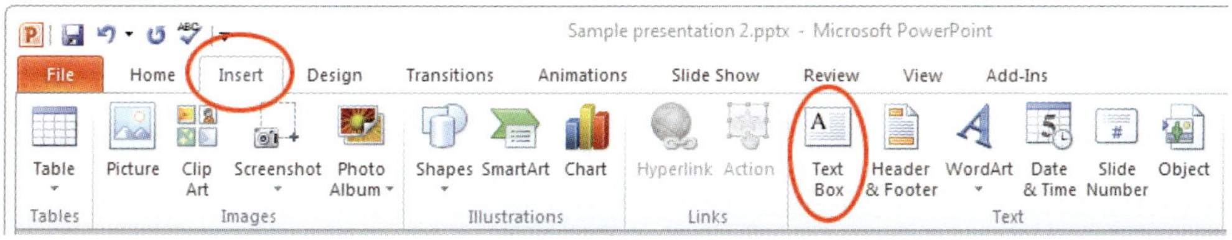

FIGURE 11-17 Adding a text box to your slide.

3. Move your mouse pointer to the location on the slide where you want to create the text box. Click and drag to draw a small box.
4. Begin typing inside the box, such as **My Sample Text**.
5. Click outside the text box anywhere on the slide or within PowerPoint. Your text box will now be set on the slide.

There are no specific rules for how text should be formatted in a slide. However, consider that your audience at a live presentation might be in a large room. Small text, even magnified on a projector, will be difficult to read for people in the back of the room. The following are guidelines for creating most text-based slides in PowerPoint:

- Headings = 40 point
- Primary text = 32 point
- Secondary text = 28 point
- Contrasting font color/background color, such as black text on a white background, dark blue on white, white on dark blue, and white on burgundy
- A "clean" font, such as Arial, Calibri, Georgia, Helvetica, and Times New Roman—avoid overuse of fancy fonts

TIP

To move a text box, click the text and move your mouse pointer to the outside line of the text box. The pointer will change to a four-headed arrow. When it does, you can grab the text box and pull it to any location on the slide. When the mouse pointer is a doubled-headed arrow, you can resize the text box by pulling the circles or squares on the edges of the text box.

Adding Pictures and Clip Art

Photos and clip art are often a big part of a presentation. You can use photos saved on your computer, as long as they are your own photos and you have rights to them. Microsoft also offers photos through its clip art collection, which is a large collection of artwork easily accessed through PowerPoint. This collection includes animations, cartoons, photos, and even short videos.

While some of the collection is provided through PowerPoint, some of it is accessible only through Office.com, a Microsoft website. If you want to use those pieces, you'll need to be connected to the Internet. When you search for clip art in PowerPoint, a new pane, called the Clip Art pane, opens inside the window to the right of your slide.

The Clip Art pane, shown in FIGURE 11-18, lets you find art using a simple search function. In this figure, a search was made for a nature graphic of any kind. You can designate the types of files you want to see (Illustrations, Photographs, Video, or Audio) and tell PowerPoint whether to search Office.com, too. As the search is conducted, results will display inside the pane.

TIP

Be careful if you use photos or clip art from the Internet in your presentations. Most are subject to copyright laws. Be sure to obtain the correct permissions before using any items that aren't yours or that aren't provided through Microsoft's collections.

FIGURE 11-18 The Clip Art pane.

At the bottom of the pane are options to search Office.com directly for what you want along with hints to help you find more images.

The Images group on the Insert tab is where you find the commands to insert photos and clip art. To insert a photo, click the Insert tab and then click the Picture command. Follow the prompts to locate the photo on your computer or network. You can move the picture and resize it as needed.

Adding Clip Art to a Slide

To add clip art to a slide, click anywhere on the slide and then follow these steps:

1. On the Ribbon, click the Insert tab.
2. In the Images group, click Clip Art (FIGURE 11-19).

FIGURE 11-19 The Clip Art command button.

3. The Clip Art pane appears on the right side of the PowerPoint window.
4. In the Search box, type a search term, such as **dog**. In the Results Should Be drop-down list, select whatever media file types you want included. If you want to see images from Office.com, leave the check mark next to Include Office.com Content.
5. Click Go.

6. In the results section, click one of the pieces of art.
7. The art will automatically drop onto the center of your slide. To move or resize it, click the edges and grab it or pull it when the mouse pointer turns into a four-headed arrow.

Using Shapes

Shapes are a fun way to add a graphic element to your presentation, and they can also be used to build unique graphics to draw focus to a topic. The PowerPoint 2010 Shapes gallery has dozens of predefined shapes to choose from, as shown in **FIGURE 11-20**.

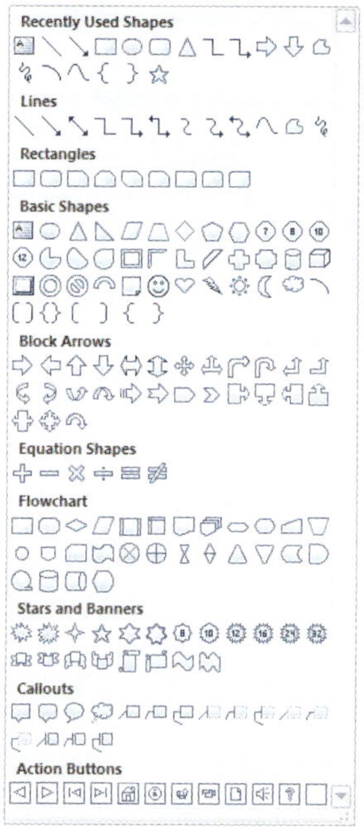

FIGURE 11-20 The Shapes gallery.

To find a shape, check the section most likely to fit your needs: Lines, Rectangles, Basic Shapes, Block Arrows, Equation Shapes, Flowchart, Stars and Banners, Callouts, or Action Buttons. As you begin using various shapes, another section appears at the top of the gallery: Recently Used Shapes. This section lets you quickly locate shapes you have used previously in presentations.

Adding Shapes to a Presentation

To add a shape to a slide, click anywhere on the slide you're working on and then follow these steps:

1. On the Ribbon, click the Home tab.
2. In the Drawing group (shown in **FIGURE 11-21**), click Shapes.

FIGURE 11-21 The Drawing group.

3. In the gallery, click the shape you want to add. For example, select the heart in the Basic Shapes section.

TIP

If you don't like the default color that PowerPoint uses for your shape, select the shape and use the Quick Styles command in the Drawing group of the Home tab to quickly apply a new look to the shape. You can also right-click the border of the shape, select Format Picture, and change the shape's border, fill, and other attributes.

4. Move your mouse pointer back to the slide. The mouse pointer is now in the shape of a plus sign.
5. Click and drag the mouse to the approximate size you want for the heart, as shown in FIGURE 11-22.

FIGURE 11-22 Drawing a heart shape.

6. Release the mouse.
7. The heart appears on your slide. Use the sizing handles to adjust it to the exact size and look you want.

Saving a File

It's a good idea to save your work early—and often! You don't want to put a lot of work into your presentation only to have some sort of computer failure erase it all. You can find the Save and Save As commands in the File tab. Use any filing system that works for you, and that makes it easy for you to find and open your presentation later on.

There are many different ways to save a presentation. The most common—and the one that is usually easiest for others to open—is a .pptx file. If you know that all your viewers are using older versions of PowerPoint (97-2003), however, save your presentation as a PowerPoint 97-2003 Presentation (*.ppt).

11.1 Exercise: Creating a Simple Presentation

A lot of elements have been covered in this chapter so far. Let's apply some of them and build a simple presentation that you can continue to work with throughout this chapter. Follow these steps:

1. In PowerPoint, open a new presentation.
2. Click in the title text box (where it says "Click to add title") on the title slide, and type **Caring for Your Pets During the Dog Days of Summer**, as shown in FIGURE 11-23.

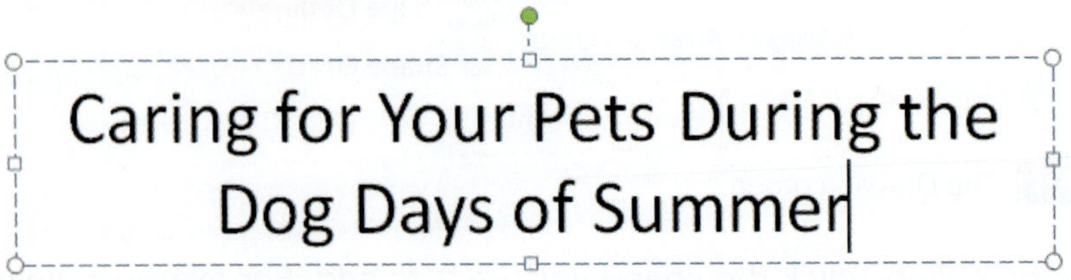

FIGURE 11-23 Adding text to a text box.

3. Click the sides of the subtitle text box, making sure that your mouse pointer turns into a four-headed arrow.
4. Press Delete on your keyboard.
5. On the Home tab, click New Slide in the Slides group.
6. Click Comparison in the Slides gallery.
7. Using the Slide Navigator in the left pane, select the first slide again.
8. Click the Insert tab.
9. Click Clip Art in the Images group as shown in FIGURE 11-24.

FIGURE 11-24 Selecting the Clip Art command.

10. In the Clip Art pane on the right, open the Results Should Be drop-down list and uncheck all options except Photographs. Leave Include Office.com Content checked. Type **dog** in the search box and click Go.
11. Click any of the pictures of dogs that appear.
12. The picture should appear on your slide. Click it and drag it down so that your text is not covered.
13. Close the Clip Art pane.
14. In the Slide Navigator, select the second slide.
15. On the Home tab, click Layout in the Slides group as shown in FIGURE 11-25.

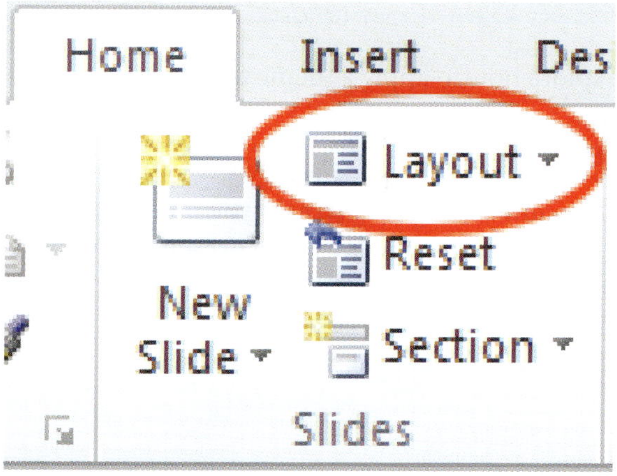

FIGURE 11-25 Opening the Layout gallery.

16. In the Layout gallery, click Blank.
17. Add a text box and type:

    Don't leave dogs in the car
    Provide plenty of fresh water
    Limit outdoor exercise to early morning or late evening

18. Use the Mini toolbar to format the text as 32-point Georgia bold. Insert a blank space between each line.

To save your presentation, follow these steps:

19. Click the File tab on the Ribbon.
20. Click Save as shown in FIGURE 11-26.

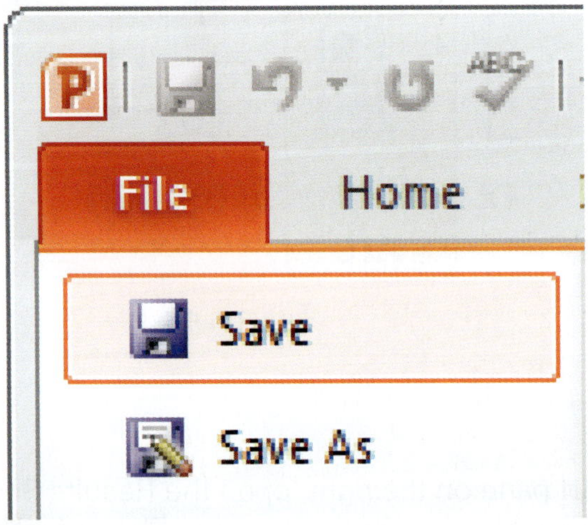

FIGURE 11-26 The Save command.

21. In the Save As window that opens, use the left pane to navigate to the place on your computer or network where you want the file saved.
22. In the right pane, select the folder you want to save the presentation to.
23. In the File Name box, type **My Presentation**.
24. In the Save As Type box, use the drop-down arrow to select PowerPoint Presentation (*.pptx).
25. Click Save.

> **TIP**
> You can see a live preview of a theme before you apply it to your presentation. Just hover your mouse pointer over the different options in the Themes gallery and watch as your slide changes to match the theme.

Next, you will explore how to apply a theme to presentations.

Applying a Theme

PowerPoint offers a few different options to help you quickly apply a consistent look and feel to your presentations. One method is to use a **presentation theme**, which offers slide layouts in coordinating colors, fonts, backgrounds, and effects. With a theme, you build your own presentation and apply a theme to it to give it a professionally designed look. Themes are provided in a Design tab gallery.

11.2 Exercise: Changing the Presentation Theme

In your My Presentation.pptx presentation, select the second slide using the Slide Navigator pane. Then follow these steps to change the presentation theme:

1. Click the Design tab.
2. In the Themes group, click the down arrow to the right of the themes gallery thumbnails, as shown in FIGURE 11-27.

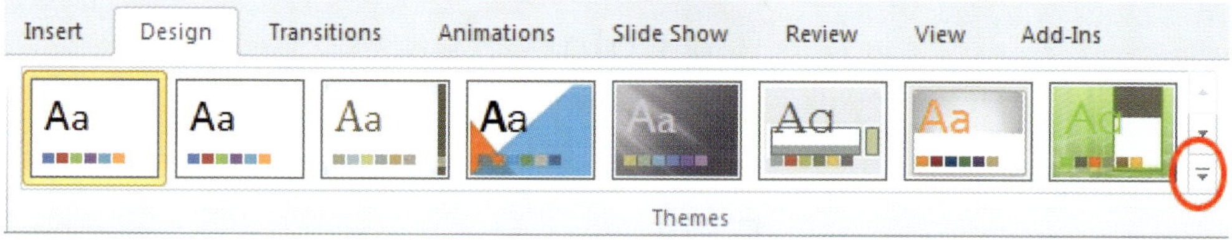

FIGURE 11-27 Opening the Themes gallery.

3. When the gallery opens, click the Civic theme as shown in FIGURE 11-28.

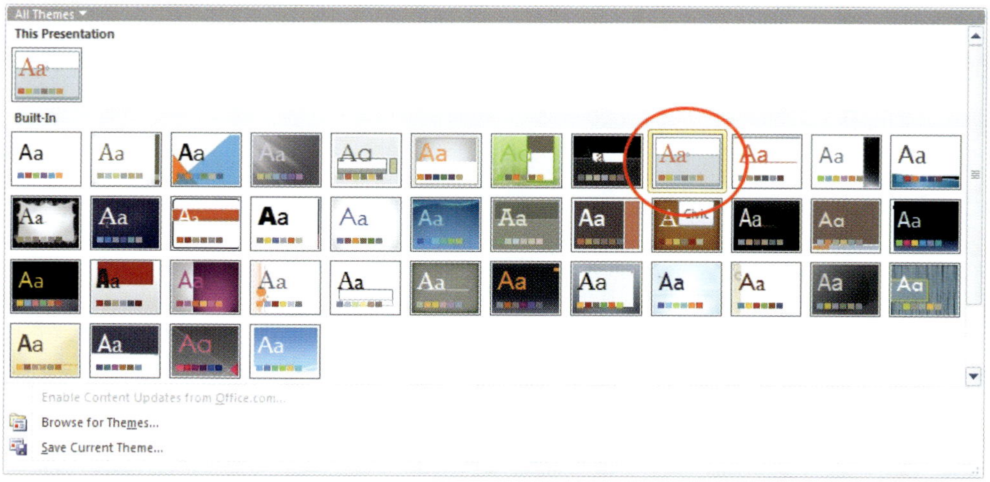

FIGURE 11-28 The Civic theme in the Themes gallery

The background should be in shades of gray. Look in the Slide Navigator pane, too, to see how the theme was applied to your first slide as well.

Using Color Schemes

One of the great things about PowerPoint themes is that you can easily modify them to meet your specific needs. One way to do that is to change the **color scheme** of the theme. Color schemes are prebuilt matching palettes of color that PowerPoint supplies.

It doesn't matter where you are in your presentation; once you change a color scheme it will be applied throughout your presentation—just as the theme was.

You can also change colors in specific shapes throughout your presentation using the Home tab or the Drawing Tools Format tab. Just click the shape you want to change, and look for the Shape Fill command on either of those tabs. On the Drawing Tools Format tab, it's located in the Shape Styles group. On the Home tab, it's located in the Drawing group.

TIP

You can build your own color scheme, too. At the bottom of the color scheme menu, choose Create New Theme Colors. PowerPoint will prompt you to select specific colors based on text, hyperlink, and accent decisions. Once you've chosen all your colors, just name the new color scheme and click Save. PowerPoint will save the new color scheme for you to use in the current and future presentations.

11.3 Exercise: Changing the Color Scheme

In your presentation, select the first slide with the dogs and text using the Slide Navigator pane. Then follow these steps to change the color scheme:

1. Go to the Design tab.
2. In the Themes group, click Colors as shown in FIGURE 11-29.

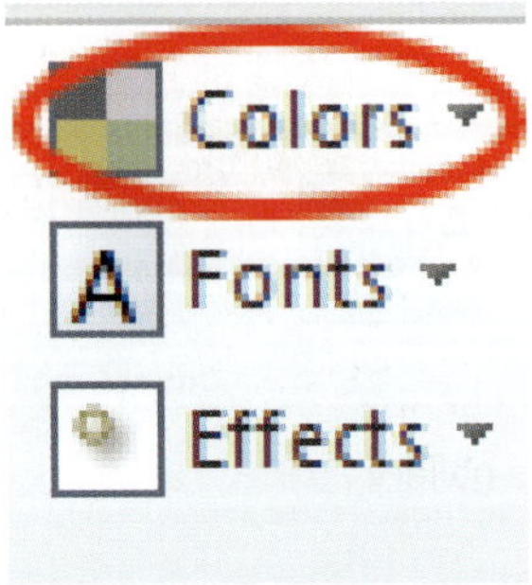

FIGURE 11-29 The Colors command.

3. When the gallery opens, click the Adjacency color theme as shown in FIGURE 11-30.

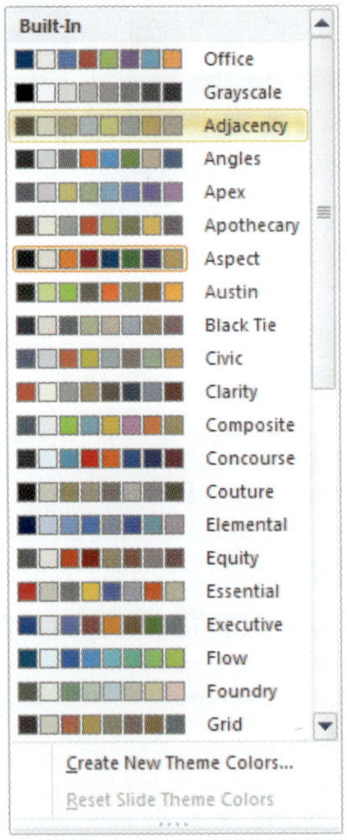

FIGURE 11-30 The Adjacency theme in the Color Scheme gallery.

4. Your slides will now reflect the new color scheme, and should look similar to FIGURE 11-31.
5. Save your work.

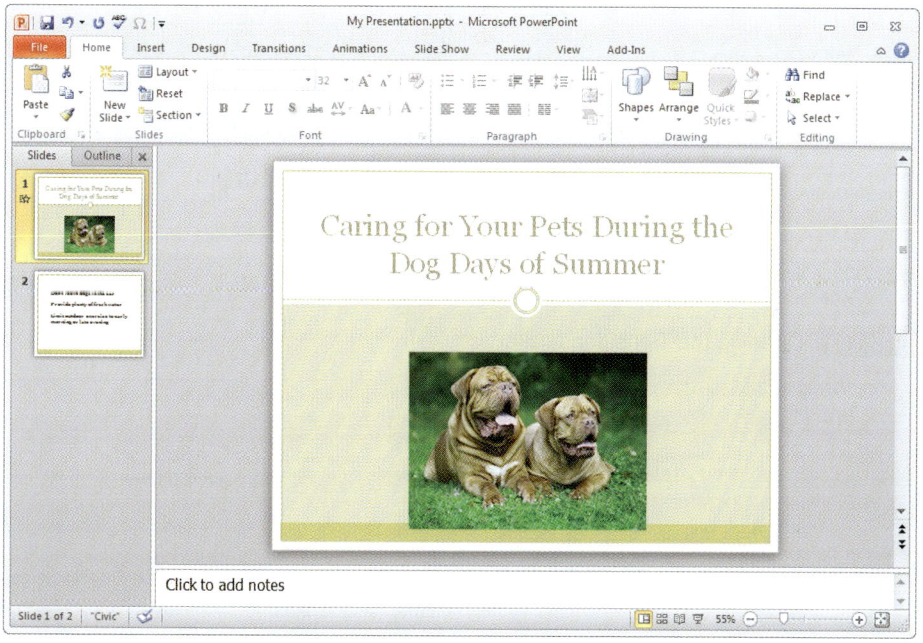

FIGURE 11-31 The modified presentation.

Adding Transitions

To help your audience make a smooth move between concepts or topics, it's a good idea to add transitions to some or all of your slides. **Transitions** are motion effects that appear between slides when you present your slide show to an audience.

You can control several aspects of transitions: speed, sound, length, and the actual effect itself. In PowerPoint 2010, a separate Transitions tab has been added to the Ribbon as shown in FIGURE 11-32.

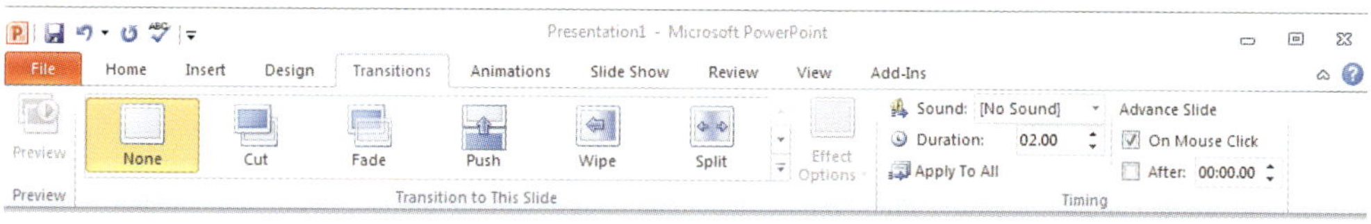

FIGURE 11-32 The Transitions tab.

As you look at this tab, you'll see that there are just three groups: Preview, Transition to This Slide, and Timing.

The Preview command lets you see how the transition will look and how long it will last. The Timing group allows you to add sound, determine how long the transition will last, and when the transition should occur (on a mouse click or after a certain amount of time has elapsed between slides).

To find and apply a transition, use the Transition to This Slide group. Click the down arrow to the right of the mini gallery (see FIGURE 11-33) to open the full gallery of transitions.

When the gallery opens as shown in FIGURE 11-34, you'll see there are three sections: Subtle, Exciting, and Dynamic Content.

Within each section are transition options. Click one—Honeycomb, for example—in the Exciting section, to see how it appears on your screen.

TIP

If you want to apply the same transition to all the slides in your presentation, click Apply to All in the Timing group on the Transitions tab.

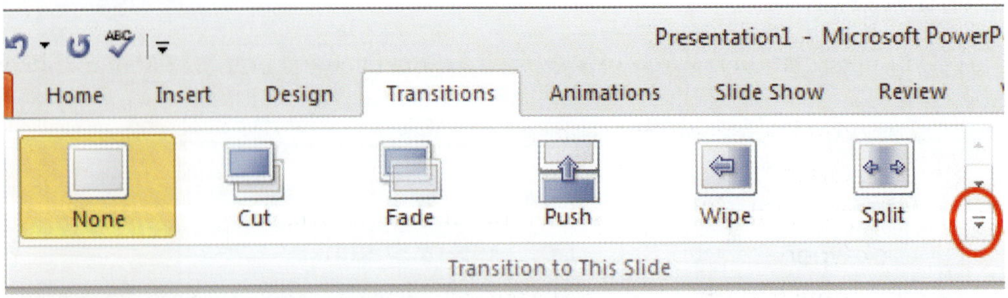

FIGURE 11-33 Opening the Transitions gallery.

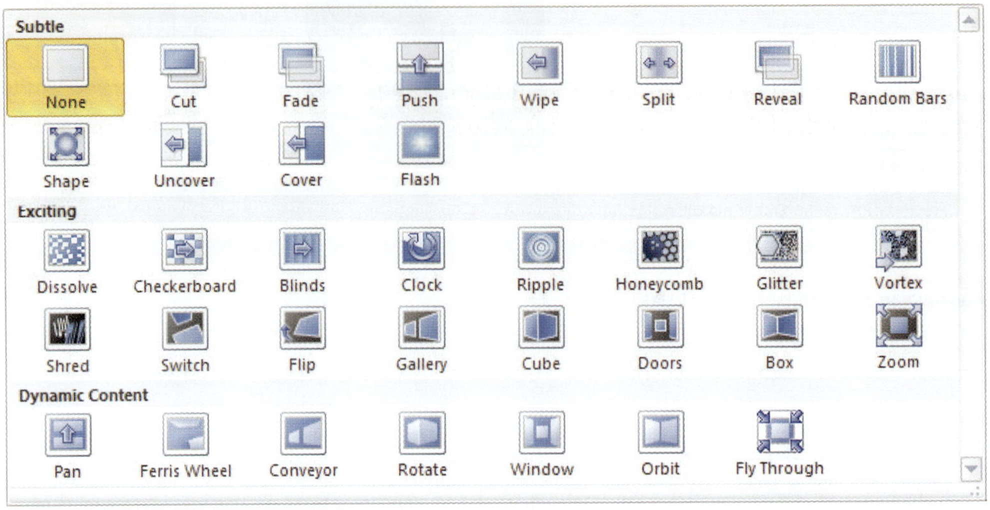

FIGURE 11-34 The Transitions gallery.

11.4 Exercise: Adding Transitions Between Slides

To add a transition to the first slide in your My Presentation.pptx presentation, follow these steps:

1. Click the first slide in the Slide Navigator pane.
2. On the Ribbon, click the Transitions tab.
3. In the Transition to This Slide group, click the down arrow to open the Transitions gallery.
4. Click Ferris Wheel in the Dynamic Content section as shown in FIGURE 11-35.

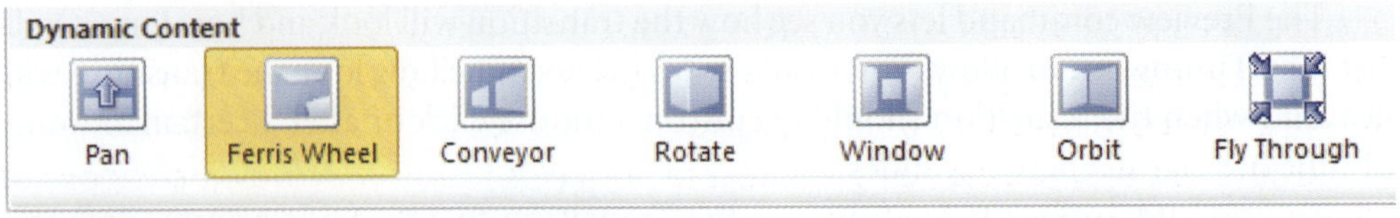

FIGURE 11-35 The Ferris Wheel transition.

5. Save your work, and close the PowerPoint file.

Opening a File

To open a presentation that you've been working on, open PowerPoint and then follow these steps:

1. Click the File tab on the Ribbon.
2. Click Open.
3. Navigate to the file on your computer or network.
4. Click Open.

A quicker method is to click the File tab, click Recent, and then select a file you recently worked on in the file list.

Printing a File

There are several different Print options that you should know about. To access the print options, click the File tab, and then click Print. The Print window appears, as shown in FIGURE 11-36.

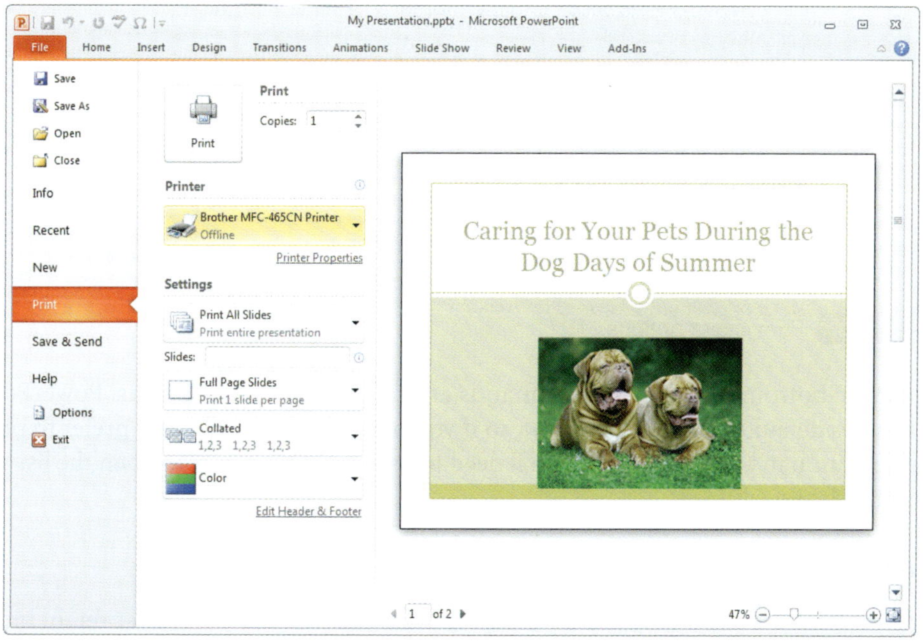

FIGURE 11-36 Print window.

First, you can select how many copies of the presentation you want to print. Under Print > Copies, use the arrows to choose a number or double-click on the number already in the box and change it to a number you prefer.

Next, under Printer, you can select the printer to send the presentation to for printing. If you don't like the selection that PowerPoint has defaulted to, click the arrow to open a list of other printers on your computer or network. If you don't see the printer you want, you might need to install it on your system.

Under Settings, you can select whether to print all slides in your presentation or just certain ones. When you click the arrow next to the default (Print All Slides), a list appears with the following options:

- Print All Slides
- Print Selection
- Print Current Slide
- Custom Range

If you choose Custom Range, you'll be prompted to enter the specific slides (for example, 1,2,5) or the specific range of slides (6-9) that you want printed.

Under Settings, you can also tell PowerPoint how many slides to print on each page of paper such as one slide per page or six slides on the page in a vertical format, for handouts. The default is to print one slide per page. Click the down arrow in that option to open a larger list of options as shown in FIGURE 11-37. Simply click the option you prefer.

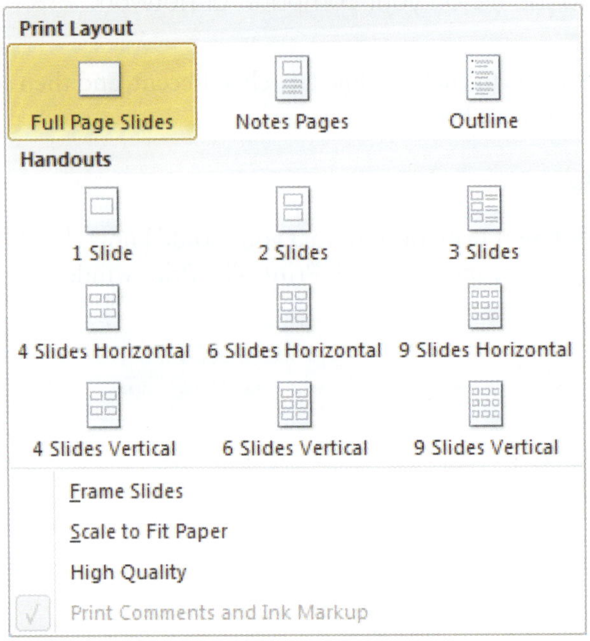

FIGURE 11-37 Print layout options.

At the bottom of the Print commands are collate and color options. PowerPoint will always default to printing in color, so if you have a color printer and prefer to print a presentation in black and white you'll need to use the down arrow to open the list and select black and white.

Working with a Slide Master

Slide masters are extremely useful in presentations. These are slides that retain information about the theme and slide layouts in your presentation. What's nice about slide masters is that you can make a change to the master, and it is applied universally throughout your presentation. Each slide master also typically has several supporting layouts associated with it as shown in FIGURE 11-38.

A slide master consists of several prebuilt elements. In FIGURE 11-39, for example, five text boxes have already been created for the master: a master title text box, a master text box with bulleted levels, a date box, a footer box, and a page number box.

If you want to include a footer that shows the title of the presentation on every slide, you would make that footer on the slide master. Every slide in the presentation will then show that information. You can get far more detailed in creating slide masters and its supporting slide layouts than this, but this chapter will focus on basic elements to help you get started.

To change a footer in a slide master, follow these steps:

1. Click the View tab on the Ribbon.
2. Click Slide Master in the Master Views group.
3. In the Slide Navigator, click the slide master or title master you want changed.

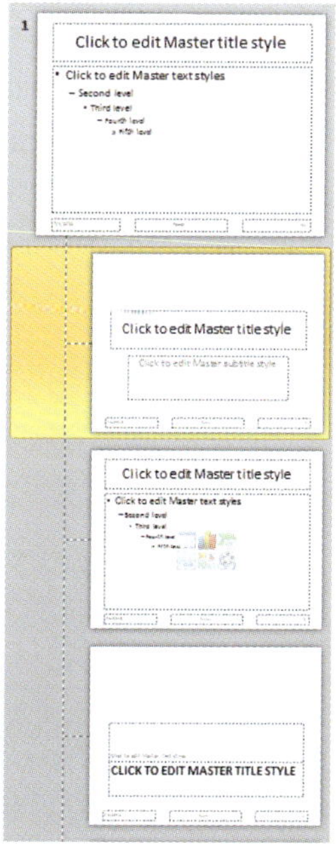

FIGURE 11-38 A slide master and supporting layouts.

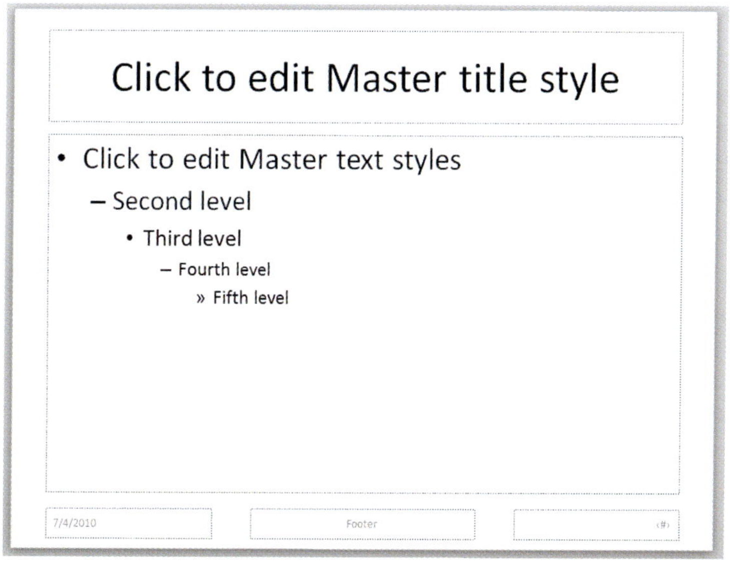

FIGURE 11-39 A slide master.

4. On the slide itself, click the Footer box.
5. In the Footer box, type some footer text, such as **My Presentation Rocks!**, as shown in **FIGURE 11-40**.

FIGURE 11-40 Changing text in a master slide footer.

6. In the Slide Master tab, click Close Master View in the Close group.

The change will apply to all presentations associated with the slide master.

Test Yourself

The questions in this section are meant to test your knowledge of what you read. Make sure you answer them. The page number where the answer can be found appears after each question.

1. When you work in PowerPoint, you are working on what? (254)
   A. A page
   B. A slide
   C. A notebook
   D. The Internet
2. The File tab is also known as what? (254)
   A. The Backstage view
   B. The Control Panel
   C. A taskbar
   D. A transition
3. The PowerPoint window consists of three main sections. Which of the following is not one of those sections? (255)
   A. The Slide Master
   B. The Slide pane
   C. The Slide Navigator pane
   D. The Notes pane
4. Which of the following presentation views shows your slides as mini-slides in the PowerPoint window? (260)
   A. The Slide Sorter view
   B. The Notes Page view
   C. The Normal view
   D. The Reading view
5. Which command lets you add a new slide to your presentation? (261)
   A. Home tab > Layout
   B. Insert tab > Text Box
   C. Home tab > New Slide
   D. Home tab > Reset
6. Which tab do you use to add pictures and clip art to your presentation? (264)
   A. Design tab
   B. Animations tab
   C. Insert tab
   D. Transitions tab
7. When you add a shape to your presentation, it will appear at the top of the Shapes gallery under Recently Used Shapes. (265)
   A. True
   B. False
8. A presentation theme lets you change slide layouts in which of the following ways? (268)
   A. With coordinating colors
   B. With coordinating backgrounds
   C. With coordinating fonts
   D. All of the above
   E. A and B only
9. A color scheme is a prebuilt matching palette of color. (269)
   A. True
   B. False

10. You can change colors in specific shapes throughout your presentation using the Home tab or the Drawing Tools Format tab. (269)
    A. True
    B. False
11. Which of the following aspects can you control when creating transitions for your slides? (271)
    A. Speed
    B. Sound
    C. Effect
    D. All of the above
12. Which tab do you use to find the Save command? (254)
    A. The Home tab
    B. The Review tab
    C. The File tab
    D. The View tab
13. Where is the Print command located? (273)
    A. The Home tab
    B. The Transitions tab
    C. The File tab
    D. The Slide Show tab
14. A ___________ is a slide that retains information about the theme and slide layouts in your presentation. (274).
15. You can apply a transition to all slides using which of the following commands? (271)
    A. Apply to All Graphics
    B. Apply to All Objects
    C. Apply to All
    D. Apply to All Presentations
16. The ____________ lets you find art on Office.com using a simple search function. (263)
17. The ___________ of a slide, which shows how items are arranged, depends on the information you're sharing. (260)
18. Which tab includes all the tools you need to make objects on your slides move? (258)
    A. The Design tab
    B. The Insert tab
    C. The Animations tab
    D. The Home tab
19. What is the pane called that lets you see either multiple slides at once or a text outline of your presentation? (256)
20. Which tab would you use to see and rehearse your slide show? (258)

End-of-Chapter Project

The projects in this book have built on the scenario that you are interested in buying a new laptop computer and printer, and need to sign up for Internet access through a service provider. You researched specifications, plans, and costs. You entered them into Word, and then entered the data into an Excel workbook, ran average cost calculations, and created charts. Now it's time to make your final selections.

In this project, you will create a presentation that highlights the laptop computer, printer, and Internet service provider you chose. Follow these steps:

1. Open PowerPoint 2010 to a new presentation.
2. Click in the Title text box and type: **Research Selections**.
3. Click in the Subtitle text box and type your name. On the next line type the name of your course, type a comma, and type the semester and year. Format the text to make it fit, if necessary.
4. Click the Home tab on the Ribbon.
5. In the Slides group, open the New Slide gallery.
6. In the gallery, click Title and Content.
7. In the Title text box, type **My Selections**.
8. In the text box, type **My laptop computer is a** [insert manufacturer, brand, and model number]. Press Enter. The entry becomes a bulleted list item.
9. On the next line, type **My printer is a** [insert manufacturer, brand, and model number]. Press Enter.
10. On the next line, type **My Internet service provider is** [insert your provider].
11. Click the Design tab and select a theme of your choice.
12. Click the File tab.
13. Click Save As.
14. Navigate to the location on your computer where you save your files, for example, the Class Research folder.
15. Type Research Selections in the File Name box.
16. Click Save, and close PowerPoint.

Glossary

Absolute reference In Excel, a cell reference that does not change when you copy it to a different cell.

Active cell The "current" cell in Excel. There can be only one active cell at a time.

Address bar The area near the top of Windows Explorer or a Web browser that displays the path to the currently displayed location.

Aero A type of 3D theme that is the default in Windows 7.

Aero Peek In Windows 7, the feature that makes open windows transparent so you can see what's on the desktop behind them.

Aero Shake In Windows 7, the feature that enables you to quickly minimize all open windows except the active one by "shaking" any open window.

Alignment buttons In Microsoft Office applications, the buttons on the Ribbon that align text. You can left-align, right-align, center, and justify text.

Application See *program*.

Argument A variable in a function.

Ascending A sorting arrangement, such as from A to Z.

Aspect ratio The ratio between the horizontal and vertical values of an image.

Attachment A file that an e-mail recipient receives that's attached to the e-mail message.

AutoFit Selection In Excel, a method of quickly resizing a column to fit the longest entry.

Backbone A high-speed communications line that carries vast amounts of information. Provides a foundation for the Internet.

Background In Windows 7, refers to a program that runs without an active window open, such as antivirus software. Can also refer to the image or solid color that appears throughout the Windows 7 desktop or as a backdrop to a PowerPoint presentation.

Backstage view In Microsoft Office 2010 applications, the screen that appears when you click the File tab. On this screen you can use commands such as Save, Open, and Exit.

Backup and Restore A Windows 7 feature that lets you back up your data files and restore them if necessary.

BIOS Short for Basic Input/Output System, a combination of chips and software that contains hardware and system settings, and that loads the operating system.

Blog Short for Web log, a journal meant for the general public, usually representing the views or ideas of the person or company who creates it.

Bluetooth A type of wireless connection that creates short-range networks commonly called personal arca networks (PANs). You can use Bluetooth to connect a smartphone to a wireless headset, for example, as long as both devices are Bluetooth-enabled.

Bold A formatting feature that applies boldface to characters.

Broadband A kind of high-speed connection. Cable and digital subscriber line (DSL) customers use broadband connections to access the Internet.

Browser A client program that accesses files from a Web server.

Bulleted list A list that uses bullet symbols at the beginning of each entry.

Callout A visual device for associating annotations with an image. You see them all the time in cartoons. Artists use callouts to imply what their characters are thinking or saying.

CD Short for compact disc, a type of optical media that stores approximately 650 to 700 megabytes (MB) of data.

Cell The box at the intersection of each row and column in Excel. You can type cell addresses, labels, formulas, and more in a cell.

Cell address The name of a cell in Excel. The cell address is a combination of the column letter and the row number, such as A1.

Cell cursor The black border around the active cell in Excel.

Central processing unit (CPU) The "brain" of the computer that controls the operations. The processor interprets and executes all the instructions that are processed on the computer.

Chart A visual representation of data.

Checkbox Similar to an option button in that clicking a checkbox enables or disables the feature associated with it. However, you can select multiple checkboxes in a group at once. When you've selected a checkbox, it contains a check mark; deselected checkboxes are empty.

Clear To remove the contents of a cell in Excel.

Client A computer that connects to a server.

Clip art A type of pre-made image, such as a drawing, cartoon, or photo.

Clipboard In Windows 7, the area in memory that holds anything you copy.

Close button The button in the upper-right corner of most Windows 7 programs and windows that lets you close the window. The Close button has an X on it.

Color scheme Prebuilt matching palettes of color in PowerPoint.

Column A grouping of cells that runs from the top to the bottom of a worksheet in Excel. Word tables also have columns.

Column header The letter that appears at the top of a column in Excel.

Command bar A bar that displays near the top of Windows Explorer and other applications that contains commands.

Command button A button that opens another dialog box, or that applies or cancels the settings you have made.

Computer A machine that runs software and lets you perform computing tasks. Computers have basic components that make them work—a central processing unit (CPU), hard disk, and memory, for example.

Computer ports The points where external devices—peripherals—connect to a computer.

Conditional formatting In Excel, the ability to apply different formatting to a cell depending on what it contains.

Contextual tab In the Ribbon, a tab that appears only when you're performing certain actions.

Controller An interface circuit that connects an I/O device to the CPU of a computer.

Cursor The position indicator on a computer display where a user can enter text.

Descending A sorting arrangement, such as from Z to A.

Desktop The main screen in Windows 7 that you see when your computer boots up. When you open programs, they display in windows overlaid on top of the desktop.

Desktop computer A common type of computer that sits on top of a desk with the monitor placed on top of it.

Destination The file, folder, or program that receives a copied item from the Clipboard.

Details pane In Windows Explorer, the pane that lets you view information about a selected file. The details that display differ depending on what type of file you select.

Dialog box A window that appears when a program needs more information from you to process a command. Dialog boxes let you specify options, such as the number of copies to print or the measurements to use for document margins.

Digital camera A camera that encodes images digitally and can store them.

Domain name The part of a URL that indicates the domain of a website.

Domain Name System (DNS) A system that converts text names to Internet Protocol (IP) addresses automatically.

Downloading Copying files from the Internet or another network to your computer.

Drag and drop A method of moving an object, such as a file, folder, or picture, to another location in Windows 7 or in an application.

Drop-down list box An element in a dialog box that has a down arrow on the far right side. You change the setting in a drop-down list box by clicking the down arrow and selecting the desired setting from the list that appears. Also called a "drop-down list."

DVD Short for digital versatile disc or digital video disc, a type of optical media that stores 4.7 gigabytes (GB) or more of data.

E-mail Short for electronic mail, a service on the Web that allows you to send messages (usually text messages but not limited to text) to anyone else who has an e-mail address, in seconds, anywhere in the world.

Embed To insert an object, such as a comment.

E-reader A device that lets you read electronic books or e-books.

File A collection of data stored in one unit, under a single name. This can be a document, a picture, an audio or video file, a library, a program, or other collection of data.

File extension The part of a file name that follows the period and indicates what type of file it is. For example, the default Word 2010 file extension is .docx.

File list A part of Windows Explorer that lists subfolders and files in a selected folder.

File path The route to a specific folder. In Windows Explorer, an example of a file path in the Address bar is Libraries > Documents > My Documents > Book Project. The same file path in the Properties dialog box may look like C:\Users\Pat\Documents\My Documents\Book Project.

File tab The tab in Microsoft Office 2010 applications that replaces the Microsoft Office Button, which previously housed commands, such as Save, Open, and Exit.

Fill handle The small black square in the lower-right corner of a cell or range in Excel.

Filling Quickly populating cells in Excel. Similar to copying but more versatile and powerful. One type of fill copies a single value into multiple other cells.

Financial function In Excel, a function for calculating financial values. Excel includes many different financial functions.

Find A feature in Microsoft Office that enables you to search for text.

Flash drive A small, lightweight, removable, and rewritable data storage device that uses flash memory.

Flash memory Functions like RAM and a hard disk combined. Flash memory stores bits of electronic data in memory cells like RAM. However, like a hard disk, the data is nonvolatile, which means it isn't erased when you turn the computer or device off.

Flip 3D A feature in Windows 7 that lets you display open programs in a 3D stack on your screen. You press the Windows logo key+Tab to use Flip 3D. It is available only when you are using an Aero theme.

Folder A location on your hard disk, flash drive, or other media where files are stored.

Font A style of type.

Footer Text that appears at the bottom of every page in a document.

Formatting To apply fonts, font sizes, margin settings, and more to make a document look the way you want.

Formula An equation in Excel that performs mathematical operations on data, and automatically updates the results when the numbers on which it is based change. A formula must start with an equal sign (=). It can contain a combination of numbers, cell references, and math operators.

Function In Excel, a named math operation, such as SUM, AVERAGE, or COUNT. Each function performs a specific calculation on the contents of one or more cells, and displays a result.

Graphical user interface (GUI) A user interface based on graphics rather than just text. With a GUI, you can click icons with a mouse or touchpad to execute commands. Windows 7 has a GUI.

Hard disk drive A computer's primary storage device for data, programs, and more.

Header Text that appears at the top of every page in a document.

Hibernate In Windows 7, copies the contents of RAM to a hidden area of the hard disk for safekeeping, and then shuts the computer's power off, so that it uses no electricity at all. When you resume from Hibernate, the previous content of RAM is recopied back into RAM, and the computer starts up with everything just as you left it.

Home page The first page you see on most websites.

Homegroup A feature in Windows 7 that lets you set up a small serverless network, such as in a home or very small business.

Icon A visual symbol of a computer resource. In Windows, icons are small pictures that represent programs, folders, files, drives, and any other computer resource.

Indentation Determines the distance of a paragraph from the left or right margin.

Insertion point In Windows 7 and other programs, a blinking vertical bar that indicates your cursor.

Instant messaging A form of communication that allows users to exchange text messages in real time.

Internet A global collection of networks with more than 1 billion users.

Internet Explorer The Web browser created by Microsoft.

Internet Protocol (IP) address A unique identifying number each device has when connected to the Internet.

Internet router A computer that determines the path that data on the Internet takes from one point to another. An Internet router's basic job is to make sure that information makes it to the intended destination.

Internet service provider (ISP) A company with advanced equipment and the facility to connect to other computers and provide Internet access to customers.

iPad A portable tablet-like computer with a touchscreen, manufactured by Apple.

Italic A formatting feature that applies italics to characters.

Jump list A menu that appears in Windows 7 when you point to an open program on the taskbar, enabling you to quickly open a recently used file of the same type. Jump lists also appear on the Start menu by program listed there.

Keyboard A common input device for computers.

Label In Excel, text assigned to a cell or range of cells that provides context and explanation for numeric data.

Laptop computer A portable computer that offers most of the same features and capabilities as a desktop computer.

Layout In PowerPoint, the way the items on your slide are arranged, such as the text, photo, or a chart.

Library In Windows 7, a virtual folder that displays content from different locations on your computer. A library looks like an ordinary folder, but actually just points to locations.

Library pane One of the panes in the Windows Explorer window. Options in the library pane let you specify how items in the file list should be sorted. Options include by folder, author, date, type, and name.

Link A word, phrase, or some type of image on a webpage that when clicked brings you to another webpage.

Linux An operating system that looks and operates much as Windows and Mac OS operating systems do, but it's free.

Lock A command on the Windows 7 Shut Down menu. Returns the user to the logon screen without logging off. The logged-on user account cannot be accessed until you type its password (if it has one).

Log Off A menu item on the Shut Down menu in Windows 7 that logs off the current user, shutting down any open programs and files, but leaves Windows running.

Logical function In Excel, a function that uses criteria (that is, conditions) to determine the outcome. An IF function is an example of a logical function.

Mac OS An operating system for the Apple Macintosh line of computers.

Macintosh A family of computers manufactured by Apple.

Margins The blank space around the edges of a page.

Maximize button In Windows Explorer and other Windows programs, expands the current window to its maximum size (entire screen).

Menu bar A bar near the top of Windows Explorer and other Windows programs that lists commands. When you click a command on the menu bar, a menu appears with other commands you can select.

Metadata Information about a file's contents.

Microsoft Equation A feature in Word for creating complex equations.

Microsoft Hotmail A popular online e-mail service provided by Microsoft.

Microsoft Outlook A popular e-mail client installed on a computer. It's part of the Microsoft Office suite.

Mini toolbar In Microsoft Office applications, the feature that displays automatically when you select text. The Mini toolbar remains transparent yet visible until you move the mouse pointer away from it. It provides the most frequently used formatting options, such as font formatting and alignment.

Minimize button In Windows Explorer and other Windows programs, collapses (shrinks) the current window to a small button on the taskbar. These buttons glow when the mouse hovers over them.

Mixed reference In Excel, an address in which either the row or the column (but not both) is absolute.

Modem A device that enables you to connect to the Internet and other remote networks.

Monitor The device attached to a computer that displays what you enter and how the computer responds to commands.

Motherboard The largest board inside the system unit of a computer. The motherboard lies flat against the case, and many of the internal components in the computer plug into the motherboard. Some of those components are the central processing unit, memory, and graphics card.

Mouse A common input device for computers that allows you to point and click at objects on the screen.

Multitasking The ability to open and work on multiple programs at the same time.

Music player A small portable device that allows you to play and listen to songs and other audio files.

Name box The area near the top of an Excel worksheet where the active cell's address appears.

Navigation pane In Windows Explorer, provides shortcuts to several Windows 7 features, such as Libraries, Homegroup, and Favorites.

Nested function A function placed inside another function, using parentheses to separate them.

Netbook computer A "micro" size laptop computer with limited capabilities. Netbooks are used mainly to browse the Internet and check e-mail.

Notes Page view A view in PowerPoint that shows any presenter notes displayed below each slide.

Notification area The far-right part of the Windows 7 taskbar that contains icons that provide notifications (important messages) about your computer. Icons commonly found in the notification area include the Action Center flag, connectivity, volume control, and on laptops, a battery indicator.

Number format Determines how a number appears in a cell in Excel. Number formats include Currency, Date, and Percentage.

Numbered list A list that uses a number at the beginning of each entry.

Object An entity that you can manipulate using commands in a program. An object can be a shape, text box, image, or similar element. Also refers to a specific area in an image.

Operating system The essential software on a computer. The operating system is the first program installed on a computer, and you cannot use a computer without an operating system installed. Popular operating systems include Microsoft Windows, Mac OS, and Linux.

Option button An element in a dialog box that is usually a round circle. Clicking an option button enables or disables the feature associated with it. You can select only one option button in a group.

Order of operations The order in which Excel performs mathematical operations in complex formulas.

Paint A drawing program built into Windows 7.

Parent folder A folder that contains subfolders.

Path The full instruction or route that uniquely points to a location, starting with the drive letter—like this: C:\Books\Chapter1\Ch01.txt.

PC Short for personal computer, an ordinary computer used by business and home users.

Peeking Clicking the Show Desktop button on the Windows 7 taskbar shows a preview of the desktop, referred to as peeking.

Phishing The act of tricking someone into giving confidential information. It often comes in the form of an e-mail message.

Pin To make shortcuts appear on the Start menu or taskbar in Windows 7 until you remove them.

Pixel A tiny dot. Certain kinds of images are made up of tiny dots that, together, create the image you see. A single image can contain hundreds to millions of pixels. A pixel is also a standard unit of measurement used for images.

Point A unit of measurement. One point is equal to approximately 1/72 inch.

Power supply The device in a computer that provides electricity. It contains the electronic circuits that provide the power that the computer requires to operate properly.

Presentation theme In PowerPoint, a set of slide layouts in coordinating colors, fonts, backgrounds, and effects. With a theme, you build your own presentation and apply a theme to it to give it a professionally designed look.

Preview pane In Windows Explorer and some Microsoft Office applications, a pane that displays the content of a file.

Printer An output device that provides a hard copy of your documents and images. The two main types of printers are laser and inkjet.

Program Computer software designed to help a user perform a task. Also called an "application."

Program window A window in which a program is running.

Properties Attributes associated with files, folders, drives, and other items.

Quick Access toolbar In Microsoft Office applications, the small toolbar in the upper-left corner of the window. It has icons for the most often-used tasks, such as Save, Undo, and Repeat/Redo. You can customize the Quick Access toolbar to contain any command you want.

Random access memory (RAM) The memory in a computer. RAM comes on small printed circuit boards that are installed on the system motherboard. These little memory boards are commonly called sticks, modules, or DIMMs (short for dual inline memory module). Also called "system memory" or "primary memory."

Range In Excel, one or more cells that are selected.

Range name The name of a block of cells in Excel.

Reading view In PowerPoint, a view that lets you see your presentation in a window with simple controls. You use Reading view when delivering a presentation to someone who is viewing the slides on his or her own computer.

Recycle Bin The feature in Windows 7 in which deleted files are temporarily stored until you permanently delete them.

Relative reference In Excel, a cell reference that changes to reflect its new location when you copy it to a different cell.

Replace A feature in Microsoft Office that enables you to search for and replace text.

Restart To reboot a computer while it is running.

Restore button Restores a window to its previous size. The Restore icon displays only when you have maximized a window. While the window is maximized, the Restore icon replaces the Maximize icon.

Ribbon A tabbed toolbar that contains graphical buttons that are shortcuts for issuing different commands. Some Windows programs include the Ribbon in lieu of traditional pull-down menus and toolbars. The Ribbon displays groups of related buttons and options in tabs.

Rip To copy music from a disc or other media to a computer.

Row A grouping of cells that runs from the left to the right side of a worksheet in Excel. Word tables also have rows.

Row header The number that appears to the left of a row in Excel.

Scanner A device that scans a document or an image from paper and converts it to a computer file.

Screen shot A snapshot of whatever is displayed on your computer screen.

Scroll bar A vertical and/or horizontal bar that appears in a program window if your file is too large to view in its entirety in the work area. You move the scroll bar to view parts of the file not currently on screen.

Scroll box When the content of a window, such as a document, is too large to view in its entirety, a scroll bar appears. The box within the scroll bar acts like a handle, enabling you to drag it up or down and see the part of the document that's not in view.

Search box A text box in which you type a string of characters you want the program to find. In Windows Explorer, for example, as you type each letter, the list of files that match your search displays immediately.

Search engine A program designed to find information on the Internet.

Server A computer that provides services to other computers, mainly clients.

Shapes A feature in many Microsoft Office applications that lets you add a variety of shapes to your document or presentation.

Shortcut A link or pointer provided for quick access to the original file, folder, or program.

Shut Down A command in Windows 7 that logs off the current user, closes Windows, and turns the computer off.

Sleep In Windows 7, places the computer in a low-power state that is very close to being entirely off. Only enough electricity is used to keep the RAM powered. When you resume from Sleep, the computer starts up almost immediately, and all the programs and files that were previously open are still open, just as you left them.

Slide In PowerPoint, the basic "page" on which you include photos, text, clip art, charts, graphs, and/or video.

Slide master A slide that retains information about the theme and slide layouts within a PowerPoint presentation. When you make a change to a slide master, the change is applied universally throughout the presentation.

Slide Navigator pane The area along the left side of the PowerPoint 2010 window that shows you the flow of how your presentation will be delivered. It also lets you quickly select a new slide to work on.

Slide pane In PowerPoint, the area where you perform most of your work on a presentation.

Slide Sorter view A view in which slides are shown as mini-slides within the PowerPoint window. You can use this view to see whether slides are in the right places; if not, you can move slides to where you want them.

Smartphone A cell phone with advanced features and capabilities. A smartphone usually has personal data assistant (PDA) capabilities, such as the ability to store contact information for friends, family, and business associates. It also includes the ability to surf the Internet and access e-mail.

Snap A Windows 7 feature that lets you quickly arrange windows on the desktop.

Snip See *screen shot.*

Social media Web-based technologies used to promote social interaction among people using the Internet. Social media describes social applications, including forums, message boards, blogs, wikis, and podcasts. Social media applications include Google, Facebook, and YouTube.

Sorting To arrange data in ascending or descending order.

Sound card A small circuit board in a computer that processes audio, such as music, speech, and sound effects.

Source The file, folder, or program that you send to the Clipboard when you copy it.

Spam Unwanted and unsolicited e-mail.

Spell check A feature in Microsoft Office applications that enables you to check the spelling of words and correct misspellings.

Spyware Software that gathers information about an Internet user, without his or her knowledge.

Start button The orb in the lower-left corner of the Windows 7 interface that opens the Start menu.

Start menu The primary menu in Windows 7 that displays icons that represent programs, folders, and services.

Subfolder A folder within a parent folder.

Switch User A feature in Windows 7 that lets you quickly switch from one logged on user account to another.

Symbol A letter or icon that stands for something, such as the © symbol for copyright.

System unit A computer case and the components it houses.

Tab Can refer to the main categories listed in boxes across the top of the Microsoft Office Ribbon. Also refers to the key you press to move a certain amount of space in a Word document, or the key that moves you from cell to cell in Excel.

Tab stop A predetermined setting that allows you to quickly move the insertion point to the right, and to indent only the first line of a paragraph. Every time you press the Tab key, the insertion point moves to the right by one-half inch.

Table A grid that usually consists of rows and columns.

Taskbar The bar at the bottom of the Windows desktop. The taskbar contains the Start button, the notification area, and the clock. It also displays button icons of any opened programs.

Text box A box you insert in a Word document that contains text.

Theme A collection of coordinated colors, fonts, and so on. A theme provides a consistent look and feel across an entire document or presentation.

Title bar The topmost area of any window. The title bar displays the name of the program or file being used in that window.

Title page In Word, contains the title of a report or other type of document as well as other related information. A title page differs from the rest of the document in that it usually doesn't have a header, footer, or page number.

Toolbar A set of tools grouped together on a bar in Windows Explorer or an application.

Tooltip A small window that appears and displays a descriptive message when you hover your mouse pointer over a command or feature.

Touchpad A flat-surface device that's the equivalent of a mouse on a laptop or netbook computer.

Tower computer A computer similar to a desktop computer but built to be upright.

Transitions In PowerPoint, motion effects that appear between slides when you present your slide show to an audience.

Underline A formatting feature that applies underlining to characters.

Undo A Microsoft Office feature that undoes the last action.

Uniform resource locator (URL) A website's address, such as *http://www.yahoo.com.*

Universal serial bus (USB) port One of the most common types of ports in a computer. It connects many different devices to your computer. All new motherboards come with USB ports.

Uploading Sending a file from one computer to another, usually via the Internet. The opposite of downloading.

Value In Excel, a number you enter. A value changes only if you modify it.

Video card Also called a graphics card, is where you plug the monitor into the system unit. The video card is responsible for displaying text, pictures, and video—and anything you do on the computer—on the monitor.

Views button In Windows Explorer, opens a menu of viewing options that control how large the icons appear and in what layout.

Virus A program designed to interrupt or harm your computer programs and your work.

Web 2.0 Today's Web, which incorporates lots of graphics, linking, social networking activities, and more.

Website A collection of webpages that share the same domain name. A website can contain text, images, videos, and links to other websites. Generally, a Web server hosts a website.

Wi-Fi A trademarked term indicating the Wi-Fi Alliance but commonly used to indicate a wireless network.

Windows The most common operating system in the world, created by Microsoft. Also refers to the windows that open on the desktop.

Windows Media Player A program that lets you enjoy music, photos, and videos on your computer.

WordArt A feature in many Microsoft Office applications that applies text effects, such as skewing, shadowing, rotating, and stretching in a variety of shapes and colors.

WordPad A word processing program built into Windows 7.

Work area In a program, the area in which files open, allowing you to work on them.

Workbook An Excel data file.

Worksheet A spreadsheet in an Excel workbook.

World Wide Web (WWW) The system of hyperlinked webpages that are accessed on the Internet. The World Wide Web is basically the information available on the Internet.

Answer Key

CHAPTER 1

1. E
2. B
3. Windows, Mac OS, and Linux
4. A
5. B
6. B, C, and D
7. A
8. C and D
9. A
10. Bluetooth
11. B
12. Subwoofer
13. A
14. A, B, and C
15. A
16. DVD
17. B
18. B
19. A
20. Hotmail

CHAPTER 2

1. B
2. Heat
3. If you exceed the power rating of your power supply, the computer will not work properly or may not work at all.
4. B
5. Central processing unit (CPU)
6. B and D
7. D
8. A
9. "Booting up" means turning your computer on when it's powered off. "Rebooting" means to restart your computer while it is running.
10. Sticks or DIMMs
11. B
12. B
13. E
14. A
15. A, B, and C
16. A
17. D
18. B
19. A
20. A

CHAPTER 3

1. A
2. World Wide Web
3. B
4. A
5. C
6. A
7. A
8. D
9. A search engine is a program designed to find information on the Internet.
10. B
11. A
12. B
13. An attachment is simply a file that the recipient can receive at the same time with the text message.
14. B
15. B and D
16. An MP3 file

17. A
18. Answers may include research, collaboration, learning, and others.
19. C
20. Spyware is software that gathers information about an Internet user without his or her knowledge.

CHAPTER 4

1. D
2. A and C
3. Theme
4. A
5. B
6. C
7. B
8. B
9. Folder
10. B
11. B
12. C
13. A
14. Shortcut
15. Desktop
16. Aero
17. Taskbar
18. Notification area
19. Title bar
20. Tab

CHAPTER 5

1. B
2. A
3. D
4. C
5. B
6. A
7. B
8. B
9. A
10. A and D
11. B
12. B

13. C
14. The Windows Clipboard is an area of memory (RAM) where Windows stores data temporarily.
15. B
16. The drag-and-drop method is considered risky.
17. D
18. A
19. A
20. B

CHAPTER 6

1. D
2. A
3. B
4. A
5. B
6. B
7. D
8. B
9. A
10. Print Preview
11. A
12. C
13. A
14. Paint
15. An object
16. A
17. B
18. D
19. A
20. Ripping

CHAPTER 7

1. You can hover your mouse pointer over a gallery element to temporarily apply whatever you've selected.
2. C
3. B
4. A
5. D
6. A
7. C

8. D
9. A
10. B
11. A
12. B
13. C
14. Left, Right, Center, Justify
15. C
16. D
17. C
18. B
19. B
20. E

CHAPTER 8

1. Splitting a document allows you to see two parts of the same document at once. You can split the screen in two, and see one part of the document on the top half and another part of it on the bottom half.
2. B
3. B
4. A
5. B
6. B
7. D
8. B
9. D
10. You can insert clip art, pictures, shapes, WordArt, screen shots, and more.
11. Some characters are not available on the keyboard.
12. A
13. B
14. A shape often used in comics to convey a character's speech or thoughts
15. D
16. C
17. B
18. D
19. B
20. B

CHAPTER 9

1. Ribbon
2. D

3. Cell
4. B
5. A
6. A
7. B
8. B
9. A
10. Range
11. Shift or Ctrl
12. B
13. A
14. B
15. D
16. Fill handle
17. D
18. B
19. A
20. Ctrl

CHAPTER 10

1. B
2. A
3. D
4. Relative
5. $
6. B
7. Arguments
8. C
9. B
10. B
11. C
12. B
13. B
14. Conditional formatting
15. A
16. A
17. Legend
18. A
19. Data table
20. A

CHAPTER 11

1. B
2. A
3. A
4. A
5. C
6. C
7. A
8. D
9. A
10. A
11. D
12. C
13. C
14. Slide master
15. C
16. Clip Art pane
17. Layout
18. C
19. The Slide Navigator pane
20. The Slide Show tab

Index

Figures are indicated by "f" following the page numbers.

A
ABS (absolute value) function, 237
Absolute referencing, 232, 234, 233*f*, 234*f*
Academic user websites, 56–57
Accounting cell format, 222
Active cell, 209
Actuators, 37
Adding text, 130, 130*f*
Add-Ins tab
 in PowerPoint, 258
 in Word, 156
Address bar, 83, 96, 99, 99*f*
Address book, 60, 63
Advanced Micro Devices (AMD), 29
Advanced search engine options, 55
Advanced Technology Attachment (ATA) standards, 35
Advanced Technology Extended (ATX) form factors, 28
Aero Glass, 75
Aero Peek, 76, 79, 81
Aero Shake, 79
Aero themes, 75
Air cards, 50
Airline tickets online, 67
Aligning cells, 220
Aligning text
 in Word, 159–160, 160*f*
 in WordPad, 130–131, 130*f*
Alignment button, 131, 131*f*, 276, 276*f*
All-in-one printers, 13, 13*f*
All Programs menu, 77
AMD (Advanced Micro Devices), 29
Android operating system, 19
Animations tab, 258
Antivirus software, 68
Apple computers, 5–6
Apple iPhone, 19
Apple iTunes store, 18
Application programs, 6, 74, 117
Arguments, 238–239
ARPANET, 46
Arranging windows, 78–80
Artistic effects, 152, 153*f*
Ascending (A to Z) data sorting, 223, 224*f*

Aspect ratio, 134
ATA (Advanced Technology Attachment) Standards, 35
Athlon II processors, 29
Attachments, e-mail, 60, 61–62, 62*f*
ATX (Advanced Technology Extended) form factors, 28
AutoFit Selection, 217
Automatic backup, 142–143, 143*f*
Automatic time and date updates, 160
Automations tab, 240
AutoSum, 236, 236*f*
AVERAGE function, 235–237, 236*f*
Axes of charts, 244
Axis label, 244

B

Backbones, 48
Background
  of desktop screen, 85–86, 86*f*
  of PowerPoint slides, 263
  running programs in, 76
Backing up and restoring files, 142–145, 143–145*f*
Backstage view window
  in PowerPoint, 254, 254*f*
  in Word, 152, 152*f*
Backward-compatibility, 17
Bandwidth, 7
Barcode scanners, 13–14, 13*f*
Batteries, laptop, 5
Berners-Lee, Tim, 47
Bibliography information, 155
Bing, 53, 53*f*
BIOS (basic input/output system), 30
BlackBerries, 19
Blank documents, 153
Blogs, 58, 66
Bluetooth, 9, 9*f*
Bold format, 158, 158*f*
Bookmarking sites, 60
Booting up, 30
Bootstrap loader, 30
Borders, 187, 220, 221*f*
Breaks, 218
Broadband Internet connection, 7, 50
Browsers, 50–52, 51–52*f*
Brushes tool, 133, 133*f*
Bulleted lists in Word, 164–165, 164*f*
Burning CDs, 140

C

Cable modem Internet access, 7
Cable printers, 12
Calendar
  in Outlook, 65, 65*f*
  in Windows, 86–87, 86*f*
Callouts, 185
Capacity. *See also* Storage capacity
  CPU, 29
  IP addresses, 49
Carbonite, 142
Cascade windows, 79, 79*f*
CD drives, 16
C drive, 39, 95
CDs (compact discs), 16, 16*f*, 140
Cell address, 209, 209*f*
Cell cursor, 209
Cell phones, 9, 19, 32, 50, 58
Cells
  borders of, 220, 221*f*
  clearing contents of, 211, 211*f*
  copying and filling, 218–220, 218–220*f*
  decimal places in, 222
  defined, 209
  entering and editing data in, 210–211, 211*f*
  fill colors, 220, 221*f*
  formatting, 220–223, 220–223*f*
  inserting and deleting, 214–216, 214–216*f*
  moving, 218, 218*f*
  moving between, 210
  resizing, 216–218, 216–218*f*
  selecting ranges, 213–214, 213–214*f*
Centering text, 130–131, 130*f*, 159–160, 159–160*f*
Central processing units (CPUs), 6–7, 28–29

CF (compact flash) memory cards, 15
Change Your View button, 101, 102*f*
Changing colors in PowerPoint, 269–270, 270*f*
Changing column width and row height, 216–218, 216–218*f*
Changing fonts, 130
Changing presentation views, 260, 260*f*
Chart area, 243
Charts, 243–247, 244–247*f*
Chart title, 244
Chat rooms, 66
Chatting, 65–66
Checkboxes, 84, 122
Chip sets, 29–30
Citations, 155
Classmates.com, 58
Clearing cells, 211, 211*f*, 215
Clicking away, 215
Clicking the mouse, 74
Clients, server, 48
Clip art, 184–185, 184*f*, 263–265, 264*f*
Clipboard, 108, 136
Clock, 76, 86–87, 86*f*
Closing files or programs, 125–126, 125–126*f*
CMOS (complimentary metal-oxide semiconductor), 30
Collating printed copies, 127
Coloring fonts, 159
Coloring fonts in Word, 159*f*
Color schemes, 240, 269–270
Color schemes in PowerPoint, 270*f*
Column breaks, 218
Column header, 209, 209*f*
Columns
  in Excel, 214–218, 214–218*f*
  in Word, 155, 217–218, 217*f*
COM1 and COM 2 ports, 33
Command bar, 83, 96
Command button, 84, 122
Comma Style cell format, 222
Comments
  in PowerPoint, 256, 258
  in Word, 156
Communication devices and connections, 7–9, 8–9*f*
Compact discs. *See* CDs
Compact flash (CF) memory cards, 15
Composing e-mail messages
  in Hotmail, 61–62, 62*f*
  in Outlook, 64, 64*f*
Compressing files, 67
Computer basics, 3–24. *See also* E-mail; Internet
  Bluetooth, 9, 9*f*
  cable modem Internet access, 7
  CDs as storage devices, 16, 16*f*
  communication devices and connections, 7–9, 8–9*f*
  computers, defined, 4
  desktop computers, 4–5, 4*f*
  digital cameras, 14–15, 15*f*
  DSL Internet access, 7
  DVDs as storage devices, 16–17, 16*f*
  e-readers, 19
  external storage devices, 15–18, 16–18*f*
  flash drives, 17–18, 17*f*
  input devices, 10–11, 10*f*
  iPads, 19
  keyboards, 10–11, 10*f*
  laptops, 4*f*, 5, 6, 10
  Macs, 5
  mobile broadband, 9
  modems, 7
  monitors, 9–10, 9*f*
  mouse and touchpad, 10, 10*f*
  music players, 18, 18*f*
  netbooks, 4*f*, 5
  operating systems, 5–6
  output devices, 9–10, 9*f*, 11–14, 11*f*, 13–14*f*
  PCs, 5
  peripheral devices, 9–11, 9–11*f*
  printers, 11–13, 11*f*, 14
  satellite broadband Internet access, 7–8, 8*f*

scanners, 13–14, 13*f*
Smartphones, 19, 19*f*
speakers, 11, 11*f*
tips for buying, 6–7
touchpads, 10
tower computers, 4–5, 4*f*, 6, 26*f*
types of, 4–5, 4*f*
USB devices, 18, 18*f*
wireless routers (Wi-Fi), 8, 8*f*, 13
Computer command, 82–83, 83*f*
Computer hardware. *See* Hardware
Computer ports, 32–34, 33*f*
Conditional Formatting, 240–242, 241–242*f*
Connecting to Internet, 7–9, 49–50
Consecutive items, selecting, 105–106, 105*f*
Consolidating e-mail accounts in Outlook, 65, 66*f*
Contacts, Outlook, 63
Content view, 101
Contextual tabs, 208
Contiguous ranges of cells, 213
Controllers, 34–35, 38
Control panel, 84–86, 85*f*
Cooling fans, 27–28
Copiers, 14
Copying
formulas, 233–234, 233–234*f*
music from CDs, 140
and pasting files and folders, 104, 107–109, 108–109*f*
text and objects, 136–138, 136–138*f*
Copyrighted photos and clip art, 184–185
Core i7 processors, 29
Cores, 29
COUNTA function, 237
COUNT function, 237
CPUs (central processing units), 6–7, 28–29
Creating and formatting documents, 157–160, 158–160*f*
Creating files, 123, 123*f*
Creating folders, 102–104, 104*f*
Creative Labs, 36
Cropping objects, 134
Curly quotes in Excel, 239
Currency cell format, 221
Cursor, 122
Cut and paste
in Excel, 218–219
folders, 109
in Paint, 136–137, 136–137*f*

D

Data labels, 245
Data point, 245
Data series, 245
Data table, 244
Date and time
in Windows 7, 86–87, 86*f*
in Word, 160, 161*f*
DDR SDRAM (double data rate SDRAM), 31
Debian, 6
Decimal places in cells, 222
Decimal point alignment, 166
Decimal tab, 166–167
Default folders, 94
Default number format, 220
Deleted items folder, 60
Deleting files and folders, 75, 111–112
Deleting rows, columns, or cells, 214–216, 214–216*f*
delicious, 60
Descending (Z to A) data sorting, 223, 224*f*
Deselecting items, 107
Deselecting text, 130
Design tab, 257
Desktop computers, 4–5, 4*f*
Desktop screen
changing background of, 85–86, 85–86*f*
defined, 74, 74*f*
Destination cell, 219, 219*f*
Destination folder, 104, 108–111, 109–110*f*
Details pane, 96
Details view, 100

Dialog boxes, 83–84, 84*f*, 121–122, 122*f*
Dial-up Internet connection, 7, 50
Different First Page, 182, 184*f*
Digital cameras, 14–15, 15*f*, 18
Digital storage cards, 15
Digital subscriber line (DSL), 7
Digital visual interface (DVI) connectors, 35
Digital zoom, 15
Dining information online, 67
Disk buffers, 38
Disk caches, 38
Disk vs. disc spelling, 16
Displaying multiple pages or documents, 156
Distributions of Linux, 6
Documents library, 94
Document views, 176–177, 176–177*f*
Domain names, 49
Domain Name System (DNS), 49
Dot leader, 167, 167*f*
Double-clicking through folders, 96–97, 97*f*
Double data rate SDRAM (DDR SDRAM), 31
Double-sided single layer DVDs, 17
Downloading, 55, 55*f*, 146
Drag and drop, 109–110, 110*f*, 218, 218*f*
Drawing tools
  in Paint, 132–133, 133*f*
  in PowerPoint, 265–266
Drop-down list box, 122
DSL (Digital Subscriber Line), 7
Dual core CPUs, 29
Dual-sided dual layer DVDs, 17
DVDs as storage devices, 16–17, 16*f*
DVI (digital visual interface) connectors, 35

E

EBSCOhost Electronic Journal Service (EJS), 57
Editing text
  in PowerPoint, 257–258
  in WordPad, 130
Electronic book readers (e-readers), 19
E-mail
  quick-start guide to, 19–22, 20–22*f*
  using Hotmail, 60–62, 61–62*f*
  using Outlook, 62–64, 63–64*f*
E-mail servers, 48
Embedding text and objects, 136–138, 136–138*f*
Emptying Recycle Bin, 112
Encyclopedia.com, 57
Entering and editing data in Excel, 210–211, 211*f*
Entertainment on Internet, 67–68
Envelopes and labels, 155
Equations, 219–220, 219–220*f*
Eraser tool, 133, 133*f*
E-readers, 19
eSATA ports, 35
Ethernet network port, 33
Excel 2010, 207–250
  AVERAGE function, 236–237, 236*f*, 237*f*
  charts, 243–247, 244–247*f*
  Conditional Formatting, 240–242, 241–242*f*
  copying and filling cells, 218–220, 218–220*f*
  copying formulas, 233–234, 233–234*f*
  deleting rows, columns, or cells, 214–216, 214–216*f*
  entering and editing data, 210–211, 211*f*
  financial functions, 237–239, 238–239*f*
  formatting cells, 220–223, 220–223*f*
  formulas, 230–234, 230–234*f*
  functions, 234–240, 235–236*f*, 238–240*f*
  getting started, 208–209*f*
  help and support, 209
  IF functions, 239–240, 240*f*
  inserting rows, columns, or cells, 214–216, 214–216*f*

logical functions, 239–240, 240*f*
moving cells, 218, 218*f*
nesting functions, 240
number formatting, 220–223, 221–222*f*
one-argument functions, 237
order of operations, 231–232
printing worksheets, 224–225, 225*f*
range names, 246–247, 247*f*
resizing columns and cells, 216–218, 216–218*f*
the Ribbon, 208–209, 208*f*
saving and opening files, 212–213, 212–213*f*
selecting cell ranges, 213–214, 213–214*f*
sorting data, 223–224, 224*f*
SUM function, 235–236, 235–236*f*
text formatting, 220, 220*f*
worksheets, 210, 246–247, 247*f*
Exiting files or programs, 125–126, 125–126*f*
Explorer. *See* Internet Explorer 8; Windows Explorer
External hard drives, 38, 38*f*
External monitors for laptops, 10
External storage devices, 15–18, 16–18*f*
External USB drives, 18, 18*f*

F

Facebook, 7, 58
Fans, 27–28
Favorites, 83
Faxes, 14
Fedora, 6
File backup, 142–145, 143–145*f*
File extensions, 107
File list, 96
File manager. *See* Windows Explorer
File path, 99
Files and folders, 93–116
copying and pasting, 104, 107–109, 108–109*f*
creating folders, 102–104, 104*f*
customizing, 100–102, 101–102*f*
defined, 82
deleting and restoring, 111–112
double-clicking through folders, 96–97, 97*f*
drag and drop, 109–110, 110*f*
emptying Recycle Bin, 111–112
managing, 104–112, 105–110*f*
moving, 109
naming, 106–107
navigating, 95–99*f*, 95–100
properties of, 94–95, 94–95*f*
renaming, 106–107
searching for, 112–113, 113*f*
selecting, 105–106, 105–107*f*
File tab
in PowerPoint, 254, 254*f*
in Windows 7, 121
in Word, 155
File Transfer Protocol (FTP), 47
Fill handle, 218–219, 219*f*
Filling cells, 219, 220*f*
Fill With Color tool, 133, 133*f*
Financial functions, 237–239, 238–239*f*
Find and replace, 170–171, 171*f*
Finding lost files or folders, 112
Firewalls, 68
FireWire/IEEE 1394 ports, 33, 34*f*, 35
First-level domain names, 49
Flash cards, 18
Flash drives, 17–18, 17*f*, 32
Flash memory, 32
Flatbed scanners, 13, 13*f*
Flat monitors, 9–10, 9*f*
Flip 3D, 80, 81*f*
Floppy disks, 16
Folders. *See* Files and folders
Font face and size, 158–159, 158–159*f*, 158*f*, 163–164
Fonts, 130, 163*f*
Footers, 155, 177–179, 178–179*f*
Footnotes, 155
Formatting
cells, 220–223, 220–223*f*

charts, 245, 246*f*
disks, 38–39
documents, 157–160, 158–160*f*
numbers, 220–223, 221–222*f*
text, 220, 220*f*
Form factors, 28
Formula bar, 210, 211*f*
Formulas, 210, 230–234, 230–234*f*
Four-headed arrow, 218, 218*f*, 245
Fraction cell format, 222
Free-form Snip, 139
Free-form tool, 133–134
Free online file backup, 142
FTP (File Transfer Protocol), 47
FTP servers, 48
Full-screen Snip, 139
Functions, 210, 234–240, 234–240*f*, 238–240*f*, 238–244

G
Galleries, 154
General cell format, 220–221
Glowy Edges, 152
Google, 53
Google Chrome, 52
Grammar check, 156, 169–170, 170*f*
Graphical user interface (GUI), 10, 74
Graphic effects
in Paint, 132–138, 133–138*f*
in PowerPoint, 263–265, 264*f*
in Word, 152, 153*f*, 175–178, 176–178*f*
Graphics cards, 35–36
Graphics software, 6
GUI (graphical user interface), 74
GUI systems, 10

H
Handheld scanners, 13–14, 13*f*
Hands-free headsets, 9, 9*f*
Hard disk drives, 6–7, 37–40, 37–40*f*
Hardware, 25–41
BIOS, 30
chip sets, 29–30
controllers, 34–35
CPUs, 29
flash memory, 32
graphics cards, 35–36
hard disk drives, 37–40, 37–40*f*
IDE (integrated drive technology), 35
memory banks, 31–32, 32*f*
motherboards, 28–29, 28*f*, 31, 32*f*, 34*f*
ports, 32–34, 33*f*
RAM, 30–31, 30*f*
SATA, 35
SCSI, 35
sound cards, 36–37, 37*f*
speakers, 36–37
system unit and internal components, 26–28*f*, 26–30
USB ports, 33, 34
video cards, 35–36
HDMI (High-Definition Multimedia Interface) video ports, 33–34
Headers and footers, 177–179, 178–179*f*
Headsets, 9, 9*f*
Help and support
Excel 2010, 209
PowerPoint, 259, 259*f*
Windows 7, 87–88, 87*f*
Word 2010, 157, 157*f*
Hibernate mode, 88
Hidden icons, 76
Hiding chart parts, 245, 245*f*
High-Definition Multimedia Interface (HDMI) video port, 33–34
Highlighting. *See* Selecting
High-speed Internet access, 7
History of Internet, 46–47, 46*f*
Homegroups, 83
Home pages, 52
Home tab
in PowerPoint, 257
in Word, 155
Horizontal alignment of cells, 220
Horizontal axis, 244
Hotmail, 20–22, 20–22*f*, 60–62, 61–62*f*

Hotmail connector, 65
Hotspots, 8, 50
Hot-swapability, 35
HTML (Hypertext Markup Language), 49
HTTP (Hypertext Transfer Protocol), 49
Hypertext, 56

I
Icons
  in Windows 7, 75, 76*f*, 85–86, 85–86*f*
  in Windows Explorer, 100, 101*f*
Icon size, 85–86, 85–86*f*
IDE (integrated drive technology), 35, 38
IEEE 1394 ports, 33, 34*f*, 35
IF functions, 239–240, 240*f*
i.Link ports, 33, 35
Illegal characters in file and folder names, 106–107
Illustrations group, 155
Images and drawings, 183–186, 184–186*f*
Inbox folder, 60
Increasing Internet search speed, 55
Indenting text, 131, 131*f*, 155, 160, 160*f*
Index insertion, 155
Ink cartridges, 11
Inkjet printers, 11–12, 11*f*
InPrivate Browsing, 50–51
Input devices, 10–11, 10*f*
Inserting pictures
  in PowerPoint, 263–265, 264*f*
  in Word, 160–161, 161*f*
Inserting rows, columns, or cells, 214–216, 214–216*f*
Inserting slides, 261–262
Insertion point, 122
Insert tab
  in PowerPoint, 257
  in Word, 155
Installing new programs, 145–146
Instant messaging, 65–66
Integrated drive electronics (IDE), 35
Intel Corporation, 29
Interactive games, 67–68
Internal components, 26–28*f*, 26–30
Internal hard drives, 38
Internet, 45–70
  blogs, 66
  bookmarking sites, 60
  browsers, 50–52, 51–52*f*
  chatting, 65–66
  Classmates.com, 58
  connecting to, 7–9, 49–50
  delicious, 60
  downloading, 55, 55*f*
  e-mail, 60–64, 61–64*f*
  entertainment, 67–68
  Facebook, 58
  history of, 46–47, 46*f*
  Hotmail, 60–62, 61–62*f*
  how it works, 47–49
  IP addresses, 48–49
  ISP accounts, 50
  LinkedIn, 59–60, 59*f*
  MySpace, 58
  Outlook 2010 e-mail, 60, 62–65, 63–65*f*
  Outlook calendar, 65, 65*f*
  quick-start guide to, 19–22, 20–22*f*
  search engines, 53–54*f*, 53–55
  security issues, 68
  social media, 57–60
  Stumbleupon, 60
  Twitter, 58, 59*f*
  uploading, 55–56, 56*f*
  URLs and domains, 49, 49*f*
  Web 2.0, 57–60
  websites, 52–57
Internet Explorer 8, 51–52, 51–52*f*
Internet relay chat (IRC), 66
Internet routers, 48
Internet search speed, 55
IP addresses, 48–49
iPads, 19
iPhone, 19
ipl2 (Internet Public Library), 57
iPods, 18

IPv4 (Internet Protocol version 4) format, 48
ISO (International Standards Organization) ratings on film, 14
ISPs (Internet service providers), 47, 47*f*, 50, 51
Italic format, 158, 158*f*
iTunes store, 18

J
JPEG files, 15
Jump lists, 76, 76*f*
Junk e-mail, 68
Justifying text
  in Word, 159–160, 159–160*f*
  in WordPad, 130–131, 130*f*

K
Key (Product ID), 146
Keyboards, 10–11, 10*f*
Keyboard shortcuts, 210
Keypads, 10, 10*f*
Kindle, 19

L
Labels, 155, 210
Landscape orientation, 155
Laptop computers, 4*f*, 5–10, 13, 16, 16*f*, 27, 29, 33, 50
Laser printers, 11–12, 11*f*
Launching programs, 118–120, 118–120*f*
Layout gallery, 260–261, 261*f*
Layouts for slides, 260–262, 261–262*f*
LCD camera screens, 15, 15*f*
LCD flat monitors, 9–10, 9*f*
Left-align text
  in Word, 159–160, 159–160*f*
  in WordPad, 130–131, 130*f*
Left-clicking the mouse, 74
Legend, chart, 244
Libraries, 83, 94
Library pane, 96
Line tool, 133
LinkedIn, 59–60, 59*f*
Links, 52–55
Linux operating system, 6
Liquid crystal display (LCD) flat monitors, 9–10, 9*f*
Listening to music in Windows Media Player, 139–140, 140*f*
Lists with bullets and numbers, 164, 164*f*
List view, 100
Live previews, 154, 154*f*
Lock user account, 89
Logical functions, 239–240, 240*f*
Log Off, 88
Long Date cell format, 222
Lost files or folders, 112

M
MAC OS, 5
Macs (Macintosh computers), 5
Mailings tab, 155
Malicious, defined, 51
Managing files and folders, 104–112, 105–110*f*
Mandriva Linux, 6
Manual file backup, 143–144, 144*f*
Margins, 165*f*
MAX (maximum value) function, 237
Maximize button, 78
Megapixels, 14
Memory, 6–7
Memory banks, 31–32, 32*f*
Memory cards, 15
Memory sticks, 15
Menu bar
  in Outlook, 60
  in Windows 7, 81–82, 82*f*
Metadata, 112
Mice. *See* Mouse
Microblogging, 58
Microdrives, 15
Microsoft Equation, 219–220, 219–220*f*
Microsoft Excel 2010. *See* Excel 2010
Microsoft Internet Explorer 8. *See* Internet Explorer 8

Microsoft Outlook 2010. *See* Outlook 2010
Microsoft Paint, 132–138, 133–138*f*
Microsoft PowerPoint 2010. *See* PowerPoint 2010
Microsoft Windows Explorer. *See* Windows Explorer
Microsoft Windows 7. *See* Windows 7
Microsoft Word 2010. *See* Word 2010
Microsoft WordPad, 129–132, 130–132*f*
MIDI (Musical Instrument Digital Interface), 36
MIN (minimum value) function, 237
Minimize button, 78
Mini toolbar
  in PowerPoint, 259, 259*f*
  in Word, 156, 156*f*
Mixed reference, 237
Mixed references, 233
Mobile broadband, 9
Mobile broadband modems, 50
Modem ports, 34
Modems, 7, 49–50
Monitors, 9–10, 9*f*
Moonbase Alpha, 67
Motherboards, 28–29, 28*f*, 30–37, 32*f*–34*f*
Mouse, 10, 10*f*, 74
Movie tickets online, 67
Moving
  cells, 218, 218*f*
  charts, 245–246, 246*f*
  files and folders, 109
  text and objects, 136–138, 136–138*f*
Mozilla Foxfire, 52
Mozy Home, 142
MP3 files, 67
MP3 flash drives, 17
MP3 players, 18, 18*f*
Multimedia, 36
Multiple CPUs, 29
Multiple programs running, 120, 120*f*
Multitasking, 80, 80*f*
Music
  on Internet, 67
  portable music players, 18, 18*f*
  Windows Media Player, 139–140, 140*f*
Musical Instrument Digital Interface (MIDI), 36
Music files, 139–140, 140*f*
Music library, 94–95
MySpace, 58

N

Name box, 209, 209*f*
Naming a range, 242–243, 243*f*
Naming files and folders, 106–107
NAPs (network access points), 48, 48*f*
Navigating
  files and folders, 95–99*f*
  in Microsoft Windows 7, 82–83, 83*f*
  program windows, 120–121, 121*f*
  in Windows Explorer, 95–99*f*
Navigation pane, 83, 96, 97–99, 98*f*
Negative numbers, 234, 238
Nesting functions, 240
Netbooks, 4*f*, 5
Network cards, 50
New folders, 102–104, 104*f*
New PowerPoint presentations, 260–262
New presentations, 261–262*f*, 266–268, 266–268*f*
New program installation, 145–146
Next button, 140
Non-consecutive items, selecting, 106, 107*f*
Non-contiguous cells, 213
Nonvolatility, 37
Nook e-book readers, 19
Normal presentation view, 260
Notepad, 76, 76*f*
Notes Page view, 260
Notes pane, 255–256, 256*f*

Notification area, 76
NOW (current date and time) function, 237
NPER (number of periods) function, 237
Number cell formatting, 220–223, 221–222*f*
Numbered lists in Word, 164–165, 164*f*
Numbering pages, 179–180, 179*f*
Number of copies to print, 127

O

Objects, 135. *See also* Pictures
On-board items, 36
One-argument functions, 237
Online file backup, 142
Online resumes, 59
Opening files
  in PowerPoint, 273
  in Windows Explorer, 97–99, 97*f*
  in WordPad, 126–127, 127*f*
Opening programs, 118–120, 118–120*f*
Opera, 52
Operating systems, 5–6. *See also* Windows 7
Optical media, 16, 16*f*
Optical zoom, 14–15
Optional chart parts, 245, 245*f*
Option button, 122
Order of operations, 231–232
Organizing folders, 100–102, 101–102*f*
Outlook 2010
  calendar, 65, 65*f*
  Contacts, 63
  e-mail, 60, 62–65, 63–65*f*
Outlook Calendar, 65, 65*f*
Output devices, 9–10, 9*f*, 11–14, 11*f*, 13–14*f*
Oval tool, 133
Overheating, 27–28

P

Page breaks, 218
Page Layout tab, 155
Page numbers, 155, 179–180, 179*f*
Page range to print, 127
Page setup, 165–166, 165*f*
Paint, 132–138, 133–138*f*
PANs (Personal area networks), 9
Parallel ports, 33
Parent folders, 95, 95*f*
Pasting. *See* Copying; Cut and paste
PATA (parallel ATA) connections, 35, 38
Path, 83
PCs (personal computers), 5
Peeking at the desktop, 79
Pencil tool, 133, 133*f*
Percentage cell format, 222
Peripheral devices, 9–11, 9–11*f*
Personal area networks (PANs), 9
Personal computers (PCs), 5
Personal data assistants (PDAs), 19
Personalizing Microsoft Windows 7, 84–86*f*, 85*f*
Pervious button, 140
Phenom II processors, 29
Phishing, 68
Photos in Windows Media Player, 141, 141*f*
Pictures
  in PowerPoint, 263–265, 264*f*
  in Word, 160–161, 161*f*, 186, 187*f*
Pictures library, 95
Picture Tools Format tab, 240
Pinned items, 77
Pinned shortcuts, 76
Pin to Start Menu, 77
Pin to Taskbar, 119
Pixels, 14, 134
Platters, 37
Plot area, 243–244
Plug and Play (PnP), 12
Plug-ins, 240
PMT (payment) function, 237–238, 238*f*
PnP (Plug and Play), 12
Points (row height), 217
POP (point of presence), 48, 48*f*
Pop-up Blocker, 51

Portability, 5, 17
Portable music players, 18, 18*f*
Portable routers, 50
Portrait orientation, 155
Ports, 32–34, 33*f*
POST (Power-on Self-Test), 30
PowerPoint 2010, 253–278
  changing presentation views, 260, 260*f*
  clip art, 263–265, 264*f*
  color schemes and changing colors, 269–270, 270*f*
  creating new presentation, 260–262, 261*f*, 266–268, 266–268*f*
  entering text on slides, 263, 263*f*
  Graphic effects in, 263–265, 264*f*
  Help and support, 259, 259*f*
  inserting slides, 261–262
  layouts for slides, 260–262, 261–262*f*
  Mini toolbar, 259, 259*f*
  opening, 255*f*
  opening files, 273
  overview, 254–255, 255*f*
  pictures, 263–265, 264*f*
  presentation window, 255–256
  printing files, 273–274, 273–274*f*
  Quick Access toolbar, 258–259, 258–259*f*
  The Ribbon in, 257, 257*f*
  saving files, 266
  shapes, 265–266, 265–266*f*
  slide masters, 274–275, 275*f*
  slide sections, 262, 262*f*
  themes, 268–269, 269*f*
  transitions, 271–272, 271–272*f*
Power supply, 27–28, 28*f*
Presentation themes, 268–269, 269*f*
Previewing fonts, 163–164, 163*f*
Preview pane, 83, 96
Primary memory, 30
Printer resolution, 12
Printers, 11–13, 11*f*, 14
Printing
  in Excel, 224–225, 225*f*
  in PowerPoint, 273–274, 273–274*f*
  in Word, 172, 172*f*
  in WordPad, 127–129, 128–129*f*
Print Preview, 128–129, 129*f*
Print Screen, 139
Processors. *See* CPUs
Product ID, 146
Programs
  closing, 125–126, 125–126*f*
  defined, 121
  exiting, 125–126, 125–126*f*
  installing new, 145–146
  launching, 118–120, 118–120*f*
  opening, 118–120, 118–120*f*
  recently opened, 77
  running, 80–81
  running in background, 76
  running multiple, 120, 120*f*
  starting, 118–120, 118–120*f*
Program windows, 81–82, 82*f*
Properties of files and folders, 94–95, 94*f*
PS/2 ports, 32–33
Publishing websites, 55–56, 56*f*
PV (present value) function, 237

Q

Quad core CPUs, 29
Quick Access toolbar
  in Excel, 212, 212*f*
  in PowerPoint, 258–259, 258–259*f*
  in Word, 156, 156*f*
  in WordPad, 121, 121*f*, 131
Quick Styles command, 266
Quote marks in Excel, 239

R

RAM (random access memory), 6, 30–31, 30*f*
Range names, 242–243, 243*f*
Range of cells, 213–214, 213–214*f*
RATE function, 237
RCA jacks, 33
Reading e-mail messages
  in Hotmail, 60–61, 61*f*
  in Outlook, 62, 63*f*
Reading view, 260

Read/write heads, 37–38
Rebooting, 30
Recently opened programs, 77
Recently Used Shapes, 265
Rectangle tool, 133–134
Rectangular Snip, 139
Recycle Bin, 75, 111–112
Red Hat Linux, 6
Redo, 156
RefDesk.com, 57
References tab, 155
Relative referencing, 232–233, 233*f*
Renaming files and folders, 106–107
Repeat button, 140, 156
Replace, 170–171, 170*f*, 171*f*
Replace All, 171
Resize and Skew dialog box, 134, 134*f*
Resizing
  charts, 245–246, 246*f*
  columns and rows, 216–218, 216–218*f*
  images, 134–135, 134*f*, 161, 161*f*
Resolution, printer, 12
Restore button, 79
Restoring backed-up files, 145, 145*f*
Restoring files and folders from Recycle Bin, 111–112
Review tab, 156, 258
Rewritable CDs/DVDs, 16
The Ribbon
  defined, 82, 82*f*, 121
  in Excel, 208–209, 208*f*
  in Paint, 132–133, 133*f*
  in PowerPoint, 257, 257*f*
  in Word, 153, 154–155, 154–155*f*
Rich text format (RTF), 118
Right-aligning text, 130–131
Right-align text, 130*f*, 159–160, 159–160*f*
Right-clicking the mouse, 74
Ripping music from CDs, 140
Rotating images, 134–135, 134*f*
Routers, 48, 50
Row header, 209, 209*f*
Rows
  in Excel, 214–218, 214–218*f*
  in Word, 215–217, 215–217*f*
RTF (rich text format), 118
Ruler, 166, 166*f*
Running multiple programs, 120, 120*f*
Running programs, 80–81, 81–82*f*

S
Safely Remove Hardware, 17
Sampler circuits, 36
SATA (serial advanced technology attachment), 35, 38
Satellite Internet connections, 7–8, 8*f*, 50
Save As
  in Excel, 212, 212*f*
  in PowerPoint, 266
  in WordPad, 124, 124*f*
Saving files
  in Excel, 212–213, 212–213*f*
  in PowerPoint, 266, 268*f*
  in Word, 156, 161–162
  in WordPad, 123–124, 124*f*
Scanners, 13–14, 13*f*
Scientific cell format, 222
Screen Clipping, 186
Screen shots
  in Word, 186, 187*f*
  in WordPad and Paint, 138–139, 138*f*
Scroll bars, 82
Scroll box, 82, 121
SCSI (small computer system interface), 35
SD (secure digital) memory cards, 15
SDRAM (synchronous dynamic RAM), 31
Search box, 83, 96, 112–113, 113*f*
Search engines, 53–54*f*, 53–55
Search function in Windows 7, 77
Searching for files and folders, 112–113, 113*f*
Second-level domain names, 49
Section breaks, 218
Secure digital (SD) memory cards, 15

Security
of flash drives, 17
Internet, 68
Select all, 106, 133–134
Selecting
cell ranges, 213–214, 213–214*f*
files and folders, 105–106, 105–107*f*
printer, 127
text, 130, 157, 159, 159*f*
Sensitivity settings on digital cameras, 14
Sent items folder, 60
Serial advanced technology attachment (SATA), 35
Serial ports, 33–34, 35
Servers, 48
Setting margins, 165–166, 165*f*
Setting tab stops, 166–169, 166–169*f*
Setup configuration program, 30
Shapes
in Paint, 133, 133*f*
in PowerPoint, 265–266, 265–266*f*
in Word, 186, 187*f*
Shapes gallery, 265, 265*f*
Sheet-fed scanners, 13, 13*f*
Shortcuts, 75, 78, 103, 210
Short Date cell format, 222
Show Desktop button, 79
Show optional chart parts, 245, 245*f*
Show times, 67
Show windows side by side, 79
Show windows stacked, 79
Shuffle button, 140
Shutting down, 88–89, 88*f*
Side-by-side display, 176, 177*f*
Single-sided dual layer DVDs, 17
Single-sided single layer DVDs, 17
64-bit processors, 29
Sizing and arranging windows, 78–80, 79*f*
Sleep mode, 88
Slide layouts, 260–262, 261–262*f*
Slide masters, 274–275, 275*f*
Slide Navigator pane, 256–257, 256–257*f*
Slide pane, 255–256, 256*f*
Slides. *See also* PowerPoint 2010
adding pictures and clip art to, 263–265, 264*f*
entering text in, 263, 263*f*
overview, 254
selecting layouts for, 260–262, 261–262*f*
using shapes in, 265–266, 265–266*f*
Slide sections, 262, 262*f*
Slide Show tab, 258
Slide Sorter view, 260
Slide tab, 238–239, 238–239*f*
Small computer system interface (SCSI), 35
Smartphones, 9, 14, 19, 19*f*
SmartScreen Filter, 50–51
Snap, 79
Snipping tool, 138–139, 138*f*
Social media, 7, 57–60
Solid-state disk (SSD) flash hard drives, 38
Sony memory sticks, 15
Sorting data in Excel, 223–224, 224*f*
Sound-blaster compatible, 36
Sound cards, 36–37, 37*f*
Source folder, 107, 108–109*f*
Spacing text, 132, 132*f*
Spam, 68
S/PDIF sound port, 33
Speakers, 11, 11*f*, 36–37
Special function keys, 11
Speed
CPU, 7, 28–29
Internet connection, 7–9
printer, 11–12
Speeding up Internet search, 55
Spelling and grammar check
in PowerPoint, 258–259, 259*f*
in Word, 156, 169–170, 170*f*
Spin button, 122
Splitting documents, 176, 177*f*
Spyware, 68
SSD (solid-state disk) flash hard drives, 38

Start button, 76
Starting programs, 118–120, 118–120*f*
Start menu, 77–78, 77*f*, 82, 87, 113, 113*f*, 118–119, 118–119*f*
Stop button, 140
Storage capacity
  CDs, 16
  digital storage cards, 15
  DVDs, 16–17
  hard drives, 6–7, 37, 39
Storage formats for cameras, 15
Store and Display Recently Opened Programs, 77
Straight quotes in Excel, 239
Stumbleupon, 60
Subfolders, 95, 95*f*, 102–104, 104*f*
Subwoofers, 11, 36
SUM function, 235–236, 235–236*f*
Support. *See* Help and support
Surround sound, 36
Switching programs, 80–81, 81–82*f*
Switch users, 88
Symbols, 218–219, 219*f*
Synchronous Dynamic RAM (SDRAM), 31
Synchronous scrolling, 176
System memory, 30
System unit and internal components, 26–28, 26–30*f*

T

Tabbed browsing, 51, 51*f*
Table of contents, 155
Tables, 215–217, 215–217*f*
Tablet computers, 19
Tabs
  in dialog boxes, 84
  in Excel, 209, 209*f*
  in Word, 155–156, 166–169, 166–169*f*
  in WordPad, 122
Tab stops, 166–169, 166–169*f*
Taskbar, 75–76, 75*f*
TCP/IP (Transmission Control Protocol/Internet Protocol), 46
Telnet, 47
Text alignment
  in Word, 159–160, 160*f*
  in WordPad, 130–131, 130*f*
Text boxes
  defined, 84
  in PowerPoint, 266–267, 266*f*
  in Word, 155, 186–189, 187*f*
  in WordPad, 122
Text formatting, 220, 220*f*
Text Highlight Color, 159, 159*f*
Text indentation, 131, 131*f*
Text spacing, 132, 132*f*
Text tool, 133, 133*f*
Themes
  in PowerPoint, 268–269, 269*f*
  in Windows 7, 75
Thesaurus, 156
32-bit processors, 29
Thumbnail, defined, 83
TIFF files, 15
Tiles view, 101
Tile windows horizontally or vertically, 79
Time, 86–87, 86*f*
Time and date insertion, 160, 161*f*
Time cell format, 222
Time zones, 87
Title bar, 78–79, 79*f*, 121–123, 121*f*
Title pages, 180, 180*f*
TODAY function, 237
T1 lines, 48
Toner, 11
Toolbar, 60, 81–82. *See also* Mini toolbar; Quick Access toolbar
Tooltips, 155, 155*f*
Top-level domain names, 49
Touchpads, 10, 10*f*
Tower computers, 4–5, 4*f*, 6, 26*f*
Transitions, 271–272, 271–272*f*
Transitions tab, 257
Transmission Control Protocol/Internet Protocol (TCP/IP), 46
Travel arrangements online, 67
T2 lines, 48

Tweets, 58
Twitter, 7, 58, 59*f*

U
Ubuntu, 6
Ultimate Memory Guide, 32
Underlined text, 158, 158*f*
Undo, 156
Uninstall, 146
Updating time and date, 160
Uploading, 55–56, 56*f*
URLs (uniform resource locators), 49, 49*f*
USB devices, 18, 18*f*
USB ports, 33, 34
USB thumb drives, 32

V
Vacation and travel arrangements, 67
Values, 210
Vertical alignment of cells, 220
Vertical axis, 244
VGA (video graphics array) connectors, 9, 33, 35
Video cards, 35–36
Video graphics array (VGA) connectors, 9, 33
Video ports, 33
Videos in Windows Media Player, 141, 141*f*
Videos library, 95
Viewing photos in Windows Media Player, 141, 141*f*
Views button, 83
View Side by Side, 176, 177*f*
View tab
  in PowerPoint, 258
  in Word, 156
Viruses, 68
Vista, 5
Volatility, 31, 37
Volume slider, 140
VRAM (video RAM), 35

W
Watching videos in Windows Media Player, 141, 141*f*
WAV (Waveform Audio Format) files, 67
Web 2.0, 57–60
Web-based chat rooms, 66
Web servers, 48
Websites, 50–51, 52–57, 53–56*f*
Web surfing, 50–51
White balance, 14
Wi-Fi, 8, 19
Window controls, 121
Windows, sizing and arranging of, 78–80, 79–80*f*
Windows Explorer, 93–116
  creating folders in, 102–104, 104*f*
  customizing, 100–102, 101–102*f*
  managing files and folders in, 104–112, 105–110*f*
  navigating in, 95–99*f*, 95–100
  overview, 82–83, 83*f*
Windows Live Web, 20
Windows Media Player, 139–141, 140–141*f*
Windows menu button, 120
Window Snip, 139
Windows 7, 73–148. *See also* Windows 7 programs
  changing date and time, 86–87, 86*f*
  changing desktop background and icon size, 85–86, 85–86*f*
  described, 5–6, 74–75
  dialog boxes, 83–84, 84*f*
  entry points to, 82
  help and support, 87–88, 87*f*
  Hotmail and, 20–22, 20–22*f*
  navigating in, 82–83, 83*f*
  personalizing, 84–86*f*, 85*f*
  printers and, 12–13
  program windows, 81–82, 81–82*f*
  running programs, 80–81, 81–82*f*
  Safely Remove Hardware, 17
  sizing and arranging windows, 78–80, 79*f*
  start menu, 77–78, 77*f*
  switching programs, 80–81, 81–82*f*

taskbar, 75–76, 75*f*
turning computer off, 88, 88*f*
Windows 7 files and folders. *See* Files and folders
Windows 7 programs, 117–148
backing up files, 142–145, 143–145*f*
closing files or programs, 125–126, 125–126*f*
copying, moving, and embedding text and objects, 136–138, 136–138*f*
creating files, 123, 123*f*
dialog boxes, 121–122, 122*f*
installing new programs, 145–146
navigating program windows, 120–121, 121*f*
opening files, 126–127, 127*f*
opening programs, 118–120, 118–120*f*
Paint, 132–138, 133–138*f*
printing files, 127–129, 128–129*f*
restoring backed-up files, 145, 145*f*
saving files, 123–124, 124*f*
screen shots, 138–139, 138*f*
Windows Media Player, 139–141, 140–141*f*
WordPad, 129–132, 130–132*f*
Windows Vista, 5
Windows XP, 6
Wired printers, 12
Wireless cards, 9
Wireless Internet connections, 50
Wireless printers, 12
Wireless routers (Wi-Fi), 8, 8*f*, 13
Word 2010, 151–204
aligning text, 159–160, 160*f*
bold, italic, and underline formats, 158, 158*f*
breaks, 218
bullets and numbering, 164–165, 164*f*
clip art, 184–185, 184*f*
coloring fonts, 159, 159*f*
column breaks, 218
columns, 217–218, 217*f*
creating and formatting documents, 157–160, 158–160*f*
date and time insertion, 160, 161*f*
document views, 176–177, 176–177*f*
equations, 219–220, 219–220*f*
fonts, 158, 158*f*, 163–164, 163*f*
graphic effects, 153*f*, 183–186, 184–186*f*
headers and footers, 177–179, 177–179*f*
help and support, 157, 157*f*
highlighting text, 159, 159*f*
images and drawings, 183–186, 184–186*f*
indenting text, 160, 160*f*
margins, 165–166, 165*f*
Microsoft Equation, 187–188, 187–188*f*
Mini toolbar, 156, 156*f*
new features of, 152–153*f*
opening, 152–154, 154*f*
page breaks, 218
page numbers, 179–180, 179*f*
picture insertion, 160–161, 161*f*
printing, 172, 172*f*
Quick Access toolbar, 156, 156*f*
the Ribbon, 153, 154–155, 154–155*f*
rows, 215–217, 215–217*f*
saving files, 161–162
section breaks, 218
shapes, 186, 187*f*
spelling and grammar check, 156, 169–170, 170*f*
splitting documents, 176, 177*f*
symbols, 218–219, 219*f*
tables, 215–217, 215–217*f*
tabs, 155–156, 166–167, 166–167*f*
text boxes, 155, 186–189, 187*f*
WordArt, 185, 185*f*
WordArt, 155, 185, 185*f*
Word count, 156
WordPad, 129–132, 130–132*f*

Word processing. *See* Word 2010; WordPad
Work area, 82
Workbooks, 209, 209*f*
Worksheets, 209, 209*f*, 210, 224, 246–247, 247*f*
World Wide Web, 47. *See also* Internet
Wrap Text, 187

Y
Yahoo, 53

Z
Zoom controls
  in PowerPoint, 260
  in Word, 156
  in WordPad, 121, 122*f*, 128
Zune Marketplace, 18

Credits

Chapter 1

1-1 (top left) © Lucian Coman/Dreamstime.com; **1-1 (top right)** © Gleb Semenov/Dreamstime.com; **1-1 (bottom left)** © Jacques Rousseau/Dreamstime.com; **1-1 (bottom right)** © Ivan Kmit/Dreamstime.com; **1-2** © Madmaxer/Dreamstime.com; **1-3** © Natalia Siverina/ShutterStock, Inc.; **1-4** © Iurii konoval/Dreamstime.com; **1-5** © Ljupco Smokovski/Dreamstime.com; **1-6** © Claudio Fichera/Dreamstime.com; **1-7** © Insago/ShutterStock, Inc.; **1-8** © Ivaschenko Roman/ShutterStock, Inc.; **1-9** © Nagy Jozsef - Attila/ShutterStock, Inc.; **1-10** © Yuriy Chaban/ShutterStock, Inc.; **1-11** © Lepas/ShutterStock, Inc.; **1-12** © Petar Neychev/Dreamstime.com; **1-13** © prism68/ShutterStock, Inc.; **1-14** © patrimonio designs limited/ShutterStock, Inc.; **1-15** © Murat Baysan/ShutterStock, Inc.; **1-16** © Cgidesigner/Dreamstime.com; **1-17** © Elnur/ShutterStock, Inc.; **1-18** © Anthony Aneese Totah Jr/Dreamstime.com; **1-19** © BrandonHot/ShutterStock, Inc.; **1-20** © Grecu Alin Mihail/Dreamstime.com; **1-21** © Fernando Blanco Calzada/ShutterStock, Inc.; **1-22** © Moreno Soppelsa/ShutterStock, Inc.

Chapter 2

2-1 (monitor) © Ljupco Smokovski/Dreamstime.com; **2-1 (keyboard)** © Ivaschenko Roman/ShutterStock, Inc.; **2-1 (mouse)** © Claudio Fichera/Dreamstime.com; **2-1 (tower)** © Bora Ucak/Dreamstime.com; **2-1 (hard drive)** © Franz Pfluegl/Dreamstime.com; **2-1 (power supply)** © robootb/ShutterStock, Inc.; **2-1 (CPU)** © Péter Gudella/Dreamstime.com; **2-1 (RAM sticks)** © S1001/ShutterStock, Inc.; **2-2** © Bora Ucak/Dreamstime.com; **2-3** © Jiri Pavlik/ShutterStock, Inc.; **2-4** © robootb/ShutterStock, Inc.; **2-5** © Péter Gudella/Dreamstime.com; **2-6** © S1001/ShutterStock, Inc.; **2-8** © Gyukil Gyula/ShutterStock, Inc.; **2-9** © Shcherbakov Sergii/ShutterStock, Inc.; **2-10** © Alexey Stiop/Dreamstime.com; **2-11** © Stephen Bonk/Dreamstime.com; **2-12** © Franz Pfluegl/Dreamstime.com; **2-13** © Norman Chan/Dreamstime.com

Chapter 3

3-5 © Google; **3-12** © Linkedin® Corporation; **3-13** © Twitter

Chapter 5

5-4 Inset photo on hard drive used with permission of Kate Shoup; **5-9 (leaves)** © javarman/ShutterStock, Inc.; **5-9 (chrysanthemum)** © Crisit Matei/ShutterStock, Inc.; **5-9 (creek)** © Ishbukar Yallifatar/ShutterStock, Inc.; **5-9 (desert landscape)** © Katrina Brown/ShutterStock, Inc.; **5-9 (desert)** © Photodisc; **5-9 (dock)** © Filip Fuxa/ShutterStock, Inc.; **5-9 (flowers)** © Ingvar Bjork/ShutterStock, Inc.; **5-9 (forest)** © Aleksander Bolbot/ShutterStock, Inc.; **5-11, 5-12, 5-13** Inset photos on hard drive used with permission of Kate Shoup.

Chapter 6

6-35, 6-36 Inset photo on hard drive used with permission of Kate Shoup.

Chapter 7

7-4 (photo) © LiquidLibrary; **7-18 (photo)** © Andy Z/ShutterStock, Inc.

Chapter 8

8-15 (guitar) © AbleStock; **8-15 (piano)** © AbleStock; **8-15 (music)** © Gautier Willaume/ShutterStock, Inc.; **8-20, 8-21, 8-22 (photo)** © National Library of Medicine; **8-23 (cake)** © lenoardo255/ShutterStock, Inc.; **8-23 (pie)** © pichayasri/ShutterStock, Inc.; **8-23 (baseball player)** © Terry Underwood Evans/ShutterStock, Inc.; **8-23 (cookies)** © Paul Maguire/ShutterStock, Inc.; **8-23 (cupcakes)** © Sander Crombeen/ShutterStock, Inc.; **8-26, 8-27, 8-28, 8-29 (baseball player)** © Terry Underwood Evans/ShutterStock, Inc.; **8-30 (cake)** © lenoardo255/ShutterStock, Inc.; **8-30 (pie)** © pichayasri/ShutterStock, Inc.; **8-30 (baseball player)** © Terry Underwood Evans/ShutterStock, Inc.; **8-30 (cookies)** © Paul Maguire/ShutterStock, Inc.; **8-30 (cupcakes)** © Sander Crombeen/ShutterStock, Inc.

Chapter 11

11-18 (photo) © deedl/ShutterStock, Inc.; **8-31, 8-36 (photo)** © Ksoloits/Dreamstime.com